BRIDGES TO BAGHDAD

The U.S. Navy Seabees in the Iraq War

RADM Charles R. Kubic, CEC, USN (Ret.)
and
James P. Rife

Copyright © 2009 Charles R. Kubic and James P. Rife

Printed and bound in the United States of America

Published by Thomas Publications
P.O. Box 3031
Gettysburg, Pa. 17325

All rights reserved. No part of this book may be used or reproduced or transmitted in any form or by any means, electronic or mechanical, including photocopying, recording or by any information storage and retrieval system, without written permission from the authors, except for the inclusion of brief quotations embodied in critical essays and reviews.

Library of Congress Cataloging-in-Publication Data

Kubic, Charles R., 1950-

Bridges to Baghdad: The U.S. Navy Seabees in the Iraq War / Charles R. Kubic and James P. Rife

p. cm.

Includes bibliographical references and index.

ISBN-978-0-9819929-5-2

1. Afghan War, 2001—Campaigns. 2. Iraq War, 2003—Campaigns. 3. United States. Navy—History—21st century. 4. Global War on Terrorism. I. Title.

Library of Congress Control Number: 2009927844

Cover photographs courtesy U.S. Navy. Cover photographs by Photographer's Mate 2nd Class Eric Powell.

The Seabee Memorial at Arlington National Cemetery. Sculpted by former Seabee Felix de Weldon (who also sculpted of the more famous USMC Iwo Jima monument), the memorial depicts scenes of Seabees at work in various construction trades in both peace and war. A bare-chested, muscular Seabee, with rifle slung over one shoulder and offering a helping hand to a small child, is the focal point of the monument, which was dedicated on May 27, 1974. (Photograph by James P. Rife)

**WITH WILLING HEARTS AND SKILLFUL HANDS,
THE DIFFICULT WE DO AT ONCE,
THE IMPOSSIBLE TAKES A BIT LONGER
WITH COMPASSION FOR OTHERS
WE BUILD - WE FIGHT
FOR PEACE WITH FREEDOM
CAN DO!**

U.S. Navy Seabees attend a memorial service honoring the seven members of NMCB 14 who were killed by Iraqi insurgents during the attacks of April 30 and May 2, 2004 in Al Anbar Province.

(U.S. Navy Photo by Photographer's Mate 2nd Class Eric Powell)

Bridges to Baghdad is dedicated to all Seabees who have served our Nation in war or peace since our founding in the early days of World War II, especially those who have been gravely injured and those who have made the ultimate sacrifice by giving their lives building and fighting for Peace with Freedom.

Seabees killed in Operation Iraqi Freedom
& Operation Enduring Freedom:

BU2 Michael C. Anderson, 36
May 2, 2004   NMCB 14
Daytona Beach, Fla.

SW3 Eric L. Knott, 21
Sept. 4, 2004   NMCB 4
Grand Island, Neb.

BUC Joel E. Baldwin, 37
Dec. 21, 2004   NMCB 7
Arlington, Va.

CE2 Charles V. Komppa, 35
Oct. 28, 2006   NMCB 18
Belgrade, Montana

BU3 Doyle Bollinger, 21*
June 6, 2003   NMCB 133
Poteau, Ok.

BU1 Alec Mazur, 35*
March 9, 2005   UCT 1
Vernon, New York

CS1 Regina Clark, 43
June 23, 2005   NMCB 18
Centralia, Wash.

BU3 Fabricio Moreno, 26*
October 14, 2005   NMCB 3
Brooklyn, New York

EO3 Christopher M. Dickerson, 33
April 30, 2004   NMCB 14
Eastman, Ga.

CM3 Scott R. McHugh, 33
May 2, 2004   NMCB 14
Boca Raton, Fla.

EO2 Trace W. Dossett, 37
May 2, 2004   NMCB 14
Orlando, Fla.

EO1 Gary T. Rovinski, 44
June 5, 2005   NMCB 25
Roseville, Ill.

SW2 Jason B. Dwelley, 31
April 30, 2004   NMCB 14
Apopka, Fla.

BU1 Jerry A. Tharp, 44
July 12, 2006   NMCB 25
Aledo, Ohio

SW3 Ronald A. Ginther, 37
May 2, 2004   NMCB 14
Auburndale, Fla.

LTJG Francis L. Toner, IV, 26
March 27, 2009   CSTC-A
Narragansett, RI

HM2 Jamie S. Jaenke, 29
June 5, 2006   NMCB 25
Bay City, Wis.

SW3 Emory J. Turpin, 23*
Nov. 20, 2005   NMCB 74
Dahlonega, Ga.

BU2 Robert B. Jenkins, 35
May 2, 2004   NMCB 14
Stuart, Fla.

CDR Duane G. Wolfe, CEC
May 25, 2009   NFELC
Los Osos, Ca.

non-hostile action

Contents

Preface ix
Chapter 1   Can Do! 1
Chapter 2   New Doctrines for a New Era 11
Chapter 3   War Plans 29
Chapter 4   The Road to War 43
Chapter 5   Bridging Issues 61
Chapter 6   Learning Curves 81
Chapter 7   Concept of Operations 120
Chapter 8   "Hitting Pads" 143
Chapter 9   Into Iraq 158
Chapter 10   Across the Tigris 200
Chapter 11   Babylon Falls 222
Chapter 12   Stabilization and Civil Military Operations 244
Chapter 13   Homeward Bound 288
Chapter 14   Aftermath-OIF Continues 297
Closing Thoughts 319
Appendix I   A History of the Civil Engineer Corps and the U.S. Navy Seabees, 1799-1991 329
Appendix II   Acronyms 364
Endnotes 370
Bibliography 393
Index 403

Preface

The United States Navy Seabees are perhaps the most well-known military engineering and construction force in the world. Made famous by John Wayne in the film *The Fighting Seabees* at the height of World War II, the Seabees have since gained a global "Can Do!" reputation for building and fighting while serving in the Nation's later conflicts, civil works and humanitarian relief efforts, and peacekeeping missions.

In the early spring of 2003, the Seabees once again ventured into harm's way when they marched deep into the heart of Iraq alongside the U.S. Marines to help overthrow the corrupt, brutal regime of dictator Saddam Hussein. Their primary mission during the campaign, now called Operation IRAQI FREEDOM I (OIF I), was to support the Marines' critical supply lines by improving roads and building semi-permanent Mabey & Johnson steel military bridges and other expeditionary culvert bridges over a number of river and canal crossing sites during the overland drive to Baghdad. Following the collapse of Saddam's regime, the Seabees' mission changed to Civil Military Operations that involved the building of new cultural and economic bridges between the Iraqis and the U.S.-led Coalition. Hence, the title *Bridges to Baghdad*.

To carry out their mission during Operation IRAQI FREEDOM I, the Seabees had to re-organize into regimental-sized, task-oriented formations, something that they had not really done since World War II. A wholly new division-level organization, the First Marine Expeditionary Force (I MEF) Engineer Group (i.e. I MEG), was created to manage the joint Seabee/Marine expeditionary engineering operations. Originally conceptualized by I MEF commander Lieutenant General Anthony C. Zinni in the 1990s for a potential conflict on the Korean peninsula, the "MEG" revolutionized joint expeditionary military engineering in the 21st century battlespace.

The new MEG doctrine, written mostly on the fly in late 2002 and early 2003, called upon the Seabees to become much "lighter" and more versatile, and to operate not from a fixed location, but alongside the Marines as they advanced deep into Iraq. This was very different from what they had been used to doing in recent conflicts past, and the change took some by surprise. But, as Baghdad fell after just over three weeks of combat, most stood in awe at what they had accomplished. Chief Steelworker and DESERT STORM veteran Manuel Manipon of Naval Mobile Construction Battalion (NMCB) 4 told an embedded reporter that "This is the first time I saw Seabees go in with the first wave of troops. Back then [in DESERT STORM], we stayed back until things were normal. The enemy was in Kuwait and we were in Saudi Arabia. Now, we are right in their territory." Commodore William L. Rudich, who commanded the 30th Naval Construction Regiment and the MEG's Task Force Mike, was more succinct: "Wherever we ended up at the end of the day, we unrolled our sleeping bags and that's where we slept...it was a whole new way of doing things."

Consequently, the MEG generated a significant amount of confusion, consternation, and controversy among more conservative elements within the U.S. Navy and Marine Corps, who questioned the concept's practicality and necessity. This despite the opinion of battle-hardened Seabees like Chief Steelworker Gerald Wheeler of NMCB 4, who had little doubt that they had "saved over a thousand of Marine lives" by building and fighting as they did.[1]

In his book *Basrah, Baghdad, and Beyond*, published by the U.S. Naval Institute Press in 2005, the U.S. Marine Corps' Officer in Charge of Field History Colonel Nicholas E. Reynolds wrote that the MEG "was a concept that was unfamiliar to many Marines" and that its point was "for the MEF to be able to do "one-stop" shopping for its engineering needs, especially in major deployments." This gross understatement reveals that the MEG remains poorly understood even though it is now a combat-proven concept. Consequently, this book aims to fill the gap in Colonel Reynolds' otherwise excellent history of the Marines' OIF I operations, and to supplement that narrative with a full discussion of the MEG, while also telling the story of the Seabees in Iraq in 2003 and 2004.

Much of the research for this book was performed by History Associates Incorporated, based in Rockville, Maryland, under Public Contract N62604-04-P-0263 with the 1st Naval Construction Division, in coordination with the Contemporary History Branch of the U.S. Naval History & Heritage Center. Oral histories were conducted for the record (at the unclassified level) with uniformed Seabee personnel to preserve their perspectives and memories by Captain Jim Ostrich and Commander Andrew Storch of the U.S.

Naval History & Heritage Command's Reserve Detachment 206. Work under this contract was halted following the initial research, and the Navy Expeditionary Combat Command released the transcripts of these interviews on June 12, 2008 via a Freedom of Information Act request of July 2, 2007.

The basis for this book was a rough memoir that Rear Admiral Kubic wrote during the summer of 2003 in order to preserve his memories from a command perspective, and to document the organization and operational hurdles that the MEG and the Seabees had to overcome in the months leading up to and during OIF I. In writing this book, Rear Admiral Kubic and I have also drawn heavily upon the official "war diary" submitted to I MEF by the MEG on July 4, 2003, entitled "The MEG in Operation Iraqi Freedom" by Colonel Michael C. Howard (USMC), with the assistance of Major James D. Gonsalves (USMC), Major Larry F. X. Henigan (USMC), Captain Joseph C. Swanson (USMC), and Lieutenant Junior Grade Mark V. Rossi (CEC, USN).

Commander of the 4th Combat Engineer Battalion and a historian in his own right, Colonel Howard not only served as the Operations Officer on the MEG staff during OIF I, but he also had been present at the MEG's conceptual birth when he served on Lieutenant General Zinni's staff in the 1990s. Consequently, we are most grateful to Colonel Howard for his significant contribution to the MEG's theoretical development and ultimate implementation in Iraq. We owe him an additional debt of thanks for his official OIF I history of the MEG, which the Navy Expeditionary Combat Command made available to us through our FOIA request.

We relied upon the official MEG history for operational details so that we could better tell and illustrate this story. This historical information was unclassified and was previously released via 1st Naval Construction Division's Public Affairs Office through a video presentation on the MEG in OIF I using Colonel Howard's narrative as the script. All photographic images used in this book are either from Rear Admiral Kubic's personal collection or are official U.S. Navy or USMC photographs, taken by Seabee or Marine photographers and publicly released.

To make this book more accessible to both the general public and the Seabee community, we wrote it in the third person, integrating a strong historical emphasis into the narrative based upon Colonel Howard's MEG history, the Seabee oral histories, and contemporary news stories and articles written during the Seabees' operations in Iraq. All source materials are documented in end note citations and in a select bibliography of works consulted, as appropriate. The spotlight, of course, is on the military history of the Seabees in Iraq, in which we interweave three separate but equally important stories: 1) the memoirs of Rear Admiral Kubic while serving as MEG advocate and I MEG Commander; 2) the MEG's conceptualization, development, and utilization for Operations ENDURING FREEDOM and IRAQI FREEDOM; and most importantly, 3) the achievements of the U.S. Navy Seabees, men and women - officers and enlisted, who put their lives on the line and did the vast bulk of the "grunt work" for the MEG in a very difficult, high intensity, fast moving combat environment.

While this book was intended to focus primarily upon MEG/Seabee operations from 2002 through 2003, we necessarily had to take occasional detours in the narrative to place OIF I (and then OIF II) into the appropriate political and historical context. Further, to bring it up to date and keep its information relevant in light of the subsequent violence in Iraq, we close with a chapter briefly describing the Seabees' return to Iraq in 2004 for OIF II and their operations through April 2009, when we completed the book's manuscript.

We hope that this book will fully explain the concept of the MEG within the structure of the I MEF order of battle and its OIF I operations plan, and the MEG's mission and employment during the Iraq War. We also hope this book properly highlights the significant contributions of the U.S. Navy Seabees to the ongoing Global War on Terrorism, and offers lessons learned and thoughts for the future while documenting and building upon the finest traditions of our Nation's expeditionary military engineers.

James P. Rife

CHAPTER 1

Can Do!

"Figure out how to sneak some Seabees into Kuwait!" So ordered Lieutenant General Earl B. Hailston at his Bahrain headquarters in the early spring of 2002. As the double-hatted commander of Marine Forces-Pacific (MARFORPAC) and the U.S. Marine Forces Central Command (MARCENT), Hailston was the man most responsible for planning Marine operations throughout the Pacific and in the Middle East in support of America's Global War on Terrorism (GWOT). As the commander of the 3rd Naval Construction Brigade (NCB), and the chief "Seabee" of the Pacific Fleet (PACFLT), Rear Admiral Charles R. "Chuck" Kubic was responsible for all of the Navy's construction battalion operations for both of those key military theaters. The order's implications as it related to a possible future invasion of Iraq, as well as the practical difficulties in executing it, were enormous. Some five hundred Seabees would be required to ensure sufficient bridging for a vanguard force to get across the Euphrates River alone, with hundreds or perhaps thousands more needed to help the Marines march all the way to Baghdad. Kubic knew that it would be hard to slip that many souls out of their bases and then move them quickly into the theater without attracting undue attention. He therefore replied, with some astonishment, "Sir, sneak them in? Somebody will miss them, at least their wives…"

Hailston was determined though. He was then deeply involved in helping refine the U.S. Central Command's (CENTCOM) plan for attacking and ultimately liberating Iraq from the corrupt and tyrannical regime of Saddam Hussein. The war plan, called Operations Plan (OPLAN) 1003 V, envisioned a lighter, more agile attack force than that used during Operation DESERT STORM, but it was fraught with uncertainties. Foremost among these were the critical questions of precisely when to begin an attack and what would trigger it.[1]

Complicating CENTCOM's planning further was Saddam himself. His notorious predisposition for rash and wholly irrational reactions to crises was especially worrisome. At the time, the U.S. Army maintained only a very light ground force in Kuwait to contain Saddam, with Marines afloat and on a short tether in Camp Pendleton, California to reinforce them if needed. Although Saddam's once-vaunted military had been significantly weakened during DESERT STORM and afterward by the combined effects of United Nations (U.N.) sanctions and weapons inspections, most American officials believed that he was still dangerous. His anti-aircraft units had been regularly shooting at Coalition aircrews patrolling the northern and southern "no-fly zones" in Iraq ever since 1992. Planners noted with concern that the attacks had been occurring with greater frequency through 2001 and early 2002. The law of averages dictated that the Iraqis were bound to get lucky sooner or later, and in the view of both the Bush Administration and CENTCOM, a downed Coalition aircraft would embolden Saddam to escalate the conflict further.[2]

While the specter of a "shoot down" was worrisome enough, CENTCOM's commanders harbored even darker fears. They strongly suspected that Saddam might once again "miscalculate," as he was prone to do, by instigating some sort of onerous, overt action out of petty revenge, such as attacking the Kurds or the dissident Shi'ites, flooding the southern Iraqi plains, or even destroying his own oil fields. A far worse miscalculation could even land in the form of an Iraqi chemical or biological warhead, launched either against American forces in Kuwait, or against the Israelis, who would surely retaliate with their own weapons of mass destruction. In fact, Saddam's heinous record of gassing Kurds and Iranian soldiers in the 1980s, lobbing SCUD missiles into Israel, Saudi Arabia, and Bahrain during DESERT STORM, and then torching the Kuwaiti oil fields and dumping millions of gallons of oil into the Persian Gulf, suggested to CENTCOM that he was perfectly willing to commit any atrocity to protect his regime.[3]

Further, there was the possibility that Saddam's regime might simply implode under the combined weight of American political pressure and a military build-up against Iraq. The disastrous wars with both Iran and the DESERT STORM Coalition, followed by eleven years of crippling UN sanctions, had left Iraq's economy moribund, its infrastructure ruined, and many of its citizens deeply impoverished. Saddam had maintained his grip on power by terrorizing Iraq's largely suburban population with his ruthless intelligence and security services and by funneling billions of dollars from the UN's corrupt Oil-for-Food Program into his personal coffers. This illicit money funded not only numerous fortress-like palaces scattered throughout the country but also his Republican Guard units, which he heavily relied upon to prevent any potentially ambitious officers from turning their forces inward against Baghdad.[4]

Despite his totalitarian control over Iraq, many in CENTCOM felt that he might become vulnerable to assassination or a coup d'etat once it became readily apparent to his cronies and commanders that his days really were numbered. Should Saddam's regime suddenly collapse or perhaps surrender before coalition ground forces arrived, then the inevitable power vacuum would likely instigate a wholesale breakdown of civil authority, and shatter the country along religious and ethnic lines. A humanitarian crisis of catastrophic proportions would ensue, and his WMDs would be wide open for pilfering by any Islamic terrorists who happened to stumble upon them.

All of these grim scenarios had weighed heavily upon Hailston and his CENTCOM colleagues. Sensing Kubic's unease with his order, Hailston explained that the joint Army-Marine force needed to be able to "go early and ugly," and he was turning to the United States Navy Seabees to help make that happen if an immediate invasion proved necessary. Kubic carefully considered the matter and realized that a great deal of heavy military construction would be required to support a lightning invasion of Iraq, as Hailston envisioned it, and that he would need a regimental sized element of Seabees to do the initial beddown work. Moving a large naval construction force quickly into Kuwait inconspicuously was a daunting task, but he knew it was not impossible.

The Seabees had in fact been organizing and preparing themselves for just this type of possible deployment since the late-1990s. Indeed, they were no longer a static, rear-echelon logistics force as deployed after World War II, but had evolved into an extremely mobile organization capable of maneuvering with the Marines deep in enemy territory. Moreover, their routine humanitarian missions and regular rotations to and from their forward bases in Spain, Okinawa, and Guam, as well as in Afghanistan, meant they could discreetly move across the globe without anyone taking particular notice. Therefore, after carefully considering both the order's stringent requirements and Seabee global capabilities, Kubic confidently told Hailston, "Can Do!"

This was the beginning of the Seabees' involvement in what would ultimately become Operation IRAQI FREEDOM, or as it has been called in the emerging historical literature, the Second Iraq War. The Seabees' subsequent success in helping topple Saddam Hussein's corrupt regime stands as a testament to their strength, courage, and ingenuity, and also climaxed Kubic's thirty-two year career as both an officer in the U. S. Navy's Civil Engineer Corps (CEC) and as a Seabee. It was unclear to him at this time whether Marines and Seabees would actually be called to war, but he knew that they needed to move quietly into this theater, get to work, and be ready. It was also clear that if war came, it would be the Seabees' toughest mission since World War II.

A Pretty Good Outfit

When Rear Admiral Kubic enlisted in the Navy in Pittsburgh, Pennsylvania as a Seaman Recruit on September 1, 1970 at age 19, he knew he wanted to be a Seabee. He did not know at the time that the U.S. Navy Seabees, as a military organization, were only twenty-eight years old, having been founded on March 5, 1942. When Seabees crossed the line of departure into Iraq with Marines on the attack in March 2003, they were sixty-one. He had grown up with the Seabees thinking they had been around forever and never really focused on the fact that their organization was not much older than he was.

Kubic was born in Greensburg, Pennsylvania on December 7, 1950, the 9th anniversary of the Japanese attack on Pearl Harbor. He attended twelve years of Catholic school, usually as one of fifty-plus baby boomers crowded into a small classroom with a no-nonsense nun up front running the show. He started wearing a uniform at age eight when he joined the cub scouts, and continued throughout grade school and high school in a Boy Scout troop, earning the rank of Eagle Scout at age fifteen. Trips to the 1964 Boy Scout Jamboree at Valley Forge, Pennsylvania, and to the Philmont Scout

Ranch in New Mexico in 1965 opened his mind to the "greatness of America," as he later put it. A visit to the Air Force Academy on the way to Philmont picqued Kubic's interest in joining the military, hopefully as a fighter pilot.

His dad, Bill Kubic, had been an Army Air Corps officer during World War II and was a self-made man who had earned his professional engineer's license without a college degree. His father, Louis Kubic, was born in Hungary, part of which later became Czechoslovakia, and had immigrated to America when he was seventeen. Another hard working, self-made man, Kubic's grandfather had mined coal and farmed all of his life. Kubic's father wanted him to focus first on earning an engineering degree, and to consider the military as a lower priority. Despite his son's hard-headed nature and desire to fly, the elder Kubic prevailed and talked him out of the Air Force Academy and into Lehigh University in Bethlehem, Pennsylvania, where he became a structural engineering student and an Air Force Reserve Officer Training Corps (ROTC) cadet. As the oldest of six children, Kubic considered himself as the "experimental model," but could always count on his mom, Roberta Mologne Kubic, and dad to show him the way and to set the highest standards to which a young man could aspire. "I owe both of them more than I can ever express and certainly more than I can ever repay," the younger Kubic later reflected.

During Kubic's sophomore year, his plans suddenly changed. The vision in his left eye turned up 20/25 and he drew #12 in the first draft lottery. As a result, the Air Force would not let him fly, but as he later put it, "Uncle Sam would be happy to give me one of his new M-16 rifles and send me off to Vietnam." Kubic's dad counseled him to avoid "ground pounder" service in the Air Force, but to keep tracking towards military service while protecting his ability to finish his college degree. The elder Kubic also said that he had "heard about these Navy Seabees in World War II and thought they were a pretty good outfit."

So off Kubic went in late July 1970 to the Navy Reserve Center near old Forbes Field in Pittsburgh, where Master Chief Crawford "parted the waves" to accelerate his entry into the U.S. Navy before he had to commit to a ROTC scholarship, followed by obligated ground service in the Air Force. The Air Force Colonel in charge of his ROTC unit was not happy when he showed up back at Lehigh as a Seaman Recruit. When he asked why he had turned down his scholarship, Kubic simply replied, "If you won't let me fly your jets, I'll be damned if I'll patch your runways." Little did Kubic know that "runway patching" would become a big part of his life in later years.

"Crossed Bananas"

Kubic was graduated from Lehigh University Phi Beta Kappa at the head of his class in June 1972 with a Bachelor of Science degree in Civil Engineering, and was subsequently commissioned an Ensign in the U.S. Navy's Civil Engineer Corps (CEC) in November 1972 through the Reserve Officer Candidate Program. Between graduation and commissioning, Kubic married Anne Renee Sheroda in Clarks Summit, Pennsylvania, on July 29, 1972. "I often thought the Navy only tolerated me for thirty-plus years because they got Anne as part of the deal," Kubic later said. The couple later had three children, Charlie (1976), Katie (1980) and Andy (1984) – all great kids in Kubic's estimation and each of them an accomplished scholar, athlete, and leader in his or her own right. His wife Anne carried the burden of the home for the many years of their Navy marriage and raised their children well. Charlie was born during Kubic's first Seabee deployment, and the couple named him Charles Brian or C.B. Kubic. He is now a Seabee Lieutenant Commander and, according to his father, "much more squared away than his old man ever was."

Kubic also believed that he had "married up." In fact it was Anne who made the appropriate contact, while he was completing Officer Candidate School in Newport, Rhode Island, which led to his interview and acceptance of the last quota into the Civil Engineer Corps in 1972. If not for her, Kubic would have been a "haze grey and underway" destroyer sailor with a much different story to tell. Becoming a CEC Officer was both a relief and a thrill to Kubic since he wanted to fulfill his military obligation while gaining experience towards his professional engineering license.

He learned quickly that CEC officers were a special breed within the Navy and developed immediate respect for the first ones he met, especially those Vietnam War veterans who had extended the Seabees' distinguished legacy throughout that troubled conflict. This respect and admiration would endure throughout his many years of proudly wearing the Corps' "crossed bananas" uniform device (comprised of golden oak leaves and acorns—arranged quite unintentionally to resemble bananas).

Kubic also found that Seabees had earned a special place in the hearts and minds of the American people based on their legendary exploits in World War II and their enduring battle cries of "We Build! We Fight!" and "Can Do!," made world famous by the 1944 John Wayne movie, "The Fighting Seabees." Everyone still loved the Seabees it seemed, despite the military's tarnished image near the end of America's involvement in the Vietnam War, and he was truly psyched to join that proud fraternity of "Can Do builders and fighters."

Freshly Minted

Ensign Kubic's first assignment as a freshly minted CEC officer was to the Officer in Charge of Construction (OICC)—Thailand, where he served as the Assistant Director of the Contracts Division, AROICC Bangkok, and Assistant Head of the Construction Department, coordinating military construction throughout Southeast Asia from 1973 to 1975. Following his promotion to Lieutenant (Junior Grade), he was assigned to Naval Mobile Construction Battalion (NMCB) 4 from 1975 to 1977, serving as Bravo Company Commander, Plans, Intelligence and Training Officer, and Officer in Charge (OIC) of the Battalion's Guantanamo Bay Detachment. Soon thereafter, Kubic was selected as a Chief of Naval Operations (CNO) Scholar and pursued postgraduate work at Lehigh University.

Attending graduate school as a CNO Scholar was one of the many great opportunities the CEC sent Kubic's way throughout his career. He never applied for this Zumwalt-era scholarship, and learned later that he had been mentored without knowing it by then Commander (later Rear Admiral) Dave Bottorff. Kubic earned his Masters in Civil Engineering, focusing on Structures, in nine months. Since he finished early, he had time to publish his thesis on "Two Way Flexure of Steel Deck Reinforced Slabs" in the June 1979 edition of the American Society of Civil Engineers' *Structural Journal*. "It felt great to be a part of a military organization that valued technical education and professional development so highly," he wrote later.

After earning his Master's degree, he was assigned in 1978 to the Bureau of Naval Personnel as the CEC junior officer detailer. From 1980 to 1982, he served as the Assistant Public Works Officer at the Bethesda Naval Medical Center, and was then assigned to the Officer in Charge of Construction (OICC), Mediterranean, in

Madrid, Spain, where he served as the Assistant OICC for Design and Project Management until 1985, when he was selected as a White House Fellow. For the next year, Kubic served on the White House Staff as Senior Policy Analyst for President Reagan's Domestic Policy Council, while still serving as a CEC lieutenant commander.

How Kubic became a White House Fellow was an interesting process. The program holds an annual competition for civilians and military men and women from across the country interested in serving for a year in Washington, DC at the highest levels of government. Admiral James Stockdale was the Chairman of the President's Commission on White House Fellows the year Kubic was selected. After submitting the most challenging application he had ever completed and undergoing grueling regional and national interviews, over 1,400 applicants were trimmed to fourteen fellows in the class of '85-'86. It was a truly amazing year of work, learning and growth, as far as Kubic was concerned. He became comfortable operating with very senior leaders, and also improved his understanding of executive and political decision-making processes. The Fellows experience was at once humbling and a huge confidence builder for the young CEC officer, and the opportunity to support President Reagan directly was an unforgettable and truly remarkable experience for him as well.

In 1986, Lieutenant Commander Kubic returned to naval duty and was assigned to the Naval Facilities Engineering Command (NAVFAC), where he served as Director of the Strategic Programs Office and Program Coordinator for the Strategic Homeporting and Trident military construction programs. He spent a lot of time in the Pentagon and on Capitol Hill learning even more about the inner workings of government and the proclivity of political bureaucracies to meander aimlessly, unless key individuals served as prime movers, applied intense personal energy, and just "made things happen." The lesson was not lost on him.

An Honest Broker

From October 1988 through February 1989, the newly promoted Commander Kubic was again detailed to the White House Office of Policy Development, where he served as Senior Staff Member for transition coordination between the outgoing Reagan and incoming Bush administrations. When it became apparent that President Bush would succeed President Reagan, Kubic was invited to the White House Mess one day in October 1988 by some senior staffers whom he had known years earlier. They were struggling with the question of how to migrate the President's domestic policy initiatives to the Bush team without compromising their focus or "ruffling" the new team's "feathers." In short, they were looking for an "honest broker" to lead this effort, and offered Kubic the job. He gladly accepted.

The four months Kubic served as a White House Senior Staff Member during this transition period were even more fascinating to him than his year as a Fellow. He was asked to remain longer, but he also had the chance to command a Seabee battalion. He truly enjoyed serving in the White House and felt exhilarated each morning as he entered the South West gate from the ellipse. But departing to wear Seabee green again was an easy decision for him to make. His family, on the other hand, was not anxious to uproot and leave their home in Northern Virginia. The Kubics put it to a secret family vote, and following a 3-2 split decision, they headed west to the West Coast's Construction Battalion Center in Port Hueneme, California.

At Port Hueneme, Kubic commanded NMCB 3 from August 1989 until August 1991. The battalion was deployed to Europe and North Africa when Iraq invaded Kuwait. However, the U.S. European Command (EUCOM) would not immediately release "their" Seabees for a CENTCOM mission and so NMCB 3 did not move directly into Saudi Arabia – a mission that clearly made sense given its location, readiness, and recent Sahara desert experience in Tunisia and Morocco. It was ordered instead to return to homeport, and to train for a quick re-deployment into the Saudi dessert for the assault into Kuwait, taking a round-a-bout route. However, Operation DESERT STORM's ground campaign started and ended only one hundred hours later, before the battalion had a chance to reach the Kuwaiti Theater of Operations. Instead, NMCB 3 made an operational deployment to the South Pacific, thereby missing all of the action.

From September 1991 to July 1994, Kubic served as the Production Officer at the Navy Public Works Center in Norfolk, Virginia, where he was promoted to Captain. Beginning in August 1994, he served as Vice Commander of the Naval Facilities Engineering Command's Atlantic Division, a billet that also gave him the opportunity to complete the Advanced Management Program of the University of Pennsylvania's Wharton School of Business in 1995.

In Zone

In June 1997, Captain Kubic became the Commander of the 22nd Naval Construction Regiment (NCR), based at that time at Naval Amphibious Base (NAB) at Little Creek, Virginia, near Norfolk. While serving as the Vice Commander of the Atlantic Division (LANTDIV) and later as a Seabee Regimental Commodore, Kubic traveled to Bosnia, and began to see the need for Seabees to transform both in structure and tactics to meet the demands of the emerging "millennial battlefield." He felt that as a Seabee Commodore, he could now do his part to advance and transform the Naval Construction Force during his two or three year tour, and then retire well before he was even "in zone" for possible selection to flag rank.

Much to his surprise, the Navy selected Kubic very early for promotion to Rear Admiral (Lower Half) in September 1997. The selection panel was composed of line and CEC flag officers who deliberated privately and selected new Admirals after reviewing scores of highly qualified records. When Kubic heard that he had been selected, he was "shocked, humbled and inspired all at the same time." But reality soon set in, and he realized his life would never be the same again. He also knew his wife and children would pay a price as he took on new and even weightier responsibilities. But his family was "the greatest a Seabee could ever have," he later said, and "they were more supportive during my flag officer years than I or the Navy really deserved." Kubic soon began what would become seven years of non-stop motion and global engagement in the most exciting work of his career and with the greatest people he could ever imagine.

As a new Rear Admiral (Lower Half), he became the Vice Commander of the Naval Facilities Engineering Command in Washington DC in April 1998 and served in that capacity until August 1999, when he was appointed Commander of the 3rd Naval Construction Brigade, and Commander of the Pacific Division of the Naval Facilities Engineering Command, both based in Pearl Harbor, Hawaii. This assignment gave him two significant hats to wear in the years leading up to his all-important meeting with Lieutenant General Hailston in Bahrain in 2002.

CHAPTER

2

New Doctrines for a New Era

DESERT STORM roughly coincided with the end of the Cold War between the U.S. and its North Atlantic Treaty Organization (NATO) allies and the Soviet-led Warsaw Pact. The demise of the Soviet Union in December 1991 left the U.S. as the world's sole superpower and the Department of Defense (DOD) accordingly began reevaluating and reshaping the armed forces' missions and doctrines for the post-Cold War world, particularly in light of the "lessons-learned" from DESERT SHIELD and STORM. Part of this "realignment" period involved the execution of humanitarian and peacekeeping missions in such places as Somalia, Haiti, Bosnia, and Croatia where the Seabees deployed repeatedly throughout the 1990s and drew upon their Civic Action experience to assist local populaces following natural and man-made disasters.

On the doctrinal level, the Defense Department also began placing a new emphasis upon "joint" warfare. "Jointness" in American military thought was nothing new, and had appeared as early as 1903 when the Secretaries of War and the Navy established a Joint Army-Navy Board to devise broad policies for both services and to do joint contingency planning. The initial concept spelled out the responsibilities of both services during amphibious operations, such as those later conducted during World War II.

Despite much infighting and parochialism among the services, Defense Department thinkers refined and revised the theory after defense unification in the late 1940s. By the 1980s, "jointness" meant that all of the country's armed services and civilian agencies should fight wars as a single team, with both compatible and complementary capabilities, rather than trying to fight single-handedly using only their own resources. Considering that each of the services had enjoyed relative autonomy since World War II, this was easier said than done. The 1986 Goldwater-Nichols Defense Reorganization Act went a long way though toward imposing joint doctrine throughout the military, and DESERT STORM had demonstrated joint characteristics to a certain extent. Still, a great deal of work remained to be done during the 1990s to implement joint doctrine fully within the armed forces and to forge them into a single team to fight as one in future conflicts.[1]

While the Defense Department began reviewing and reshaping doctrine at the grand level, the Navy and Marine Corps jointly developed their own strategy, christened *From the Sea*, for warfighting in the twenty-first century. First published in 1992 by the Chief of Naval Operations Admiral Frank B. Kelso and Marine Commandant General Carl E. Mundy Jr., the new strategy shifted the focus away from global, blue-water warfare against the Soviet Navy to regional theater, littoral, and expeditionary operations. *From the Sea* and its 1994 revision, *Forward...from the Sea*, clearly envisioned another war with Iraq, or more likely, with North Korea.

The Marines had also been refining their tactical doctrine since before DESERT STORM. This was based heavily on the warfighting philosophy of the 29th Commandant of the Marine Corps, General Alfred M. Gray, who had promoted a multi-dimensional blitzkrieg style of attack called *maneuver* warfare. He had first published his theory in a 1989 manual entitled *Warfighting* and had charged every officer "to read and reread its text, to understand it, and to take its message to heart." Successfully tested during DESERT STORM, it changed the way that Marines thought about warfare, and became the basis for their naval doctrine through the 1990s and into the twenty-first century.[2]

Doctrinally, Gray defined maneuver warfare as a "warfighting philosophy that seeks to shatter the enemy's cohesion through a variety of rapid, focused, and unexpected actions which create a turbulent and rapidly deteriorating situation with which the enemy cannot cope." He believed that to maximize the usefulness of maneuver, the Marines should consider it in other dimensions other than the traditional *spatial* maneuver, particularly *in time*, which entailed the generation of a faster operating tempo than the enemy to gain a temporal advantage. Through this process, he argued, an "inferior force can achieve decisive superiority at the necessary place and time."[3]

Gray also emphasized the bypassing of an enemy's defenses in order to "*penetrate* [its] system and tear it apart," rather than wearing the enemy down. The aim was to render the enemy incapable of resistance by shattering his cohesion and ability to fight as an effective, coordinated whole rather than destroying him piecemeal through "incremental attrition." Combined with concentrated firepower, speed, and surprise, this would "create a situation in which the enemy cannot function" and impose "menacing dilemmas in which events happen unexpectedly and more quickly than the enemy can keep up with them." To comply with Goldwater-Nichols requirements, Gray's doctrine was specifically tailored to be joint so that the Marines could maneuver harmoniously with the other services.[4]

Within the framework of the *Forward...From the Sea* strategy and Gray's maneuver warfare doctrine, and in accordance with joint requirements, senior Marine generals began exploring new ways in which to coordinate and manage engineers across a large "battlespace" such as the Korean peninsula. The problem as they saw it was how to command and control a division-sized joint unit of Seabee, Reserve Marine, and Army engineers who would directly support but not be a permanently integrated component, or "organic," to the 1st Marine Expeditionary Force (I MEF). A potential second Korean War would compound the dilemma since Republic of Korea (ROK) engineers would have to be included as well, making the division level organization a "combined" force.[5]

A close analysis of the DESERT STORM experience, in which Seabees and Marine engineers were in high demand but seemingly short supply, led I MEF commander Lieutenant General Anthony C. Zinni to decide in January 1995 that he needed an "engineer group" that would concentrate and embed over 12,000 U.S. and Allied non-organic engineers" within I MEF in the event of a Korea-like scenario. Declaring that "I want to be able to reach out and touch the belly button of my engineers," Zinni reached back to the original World War II Marine Engineer Regiments—the 16th, 17th, 18th, 19th, and 20th Marines—for a possible doctrinal framework. Organized late in the war, each of these had been attached to a Marine Division and comprised a Marine Combat Engineer Battalion, a Marine Pioneer (shore party) Battalion, and a Seabee Battalion. Zinni also pointed to the joint 5th Marine Amphibious Corps staff of Marine General Holland Smith, which contained a number of Army, Navy, and Marine engineer officers, as an ideal model for managing the large joint I MEF Engineer Group (MEG) that he had in mind.[6]

Although there was no formal organizational structure, no gear or equipment, and no agreed upon command and control scheme, much less a commander, the U.S./Korea Combined Forces Command integrated Zinni's MEG concept into the Korea OPLANs and began incorporating it into the annual MEF EX, Reception, Staging, Onward Movement, and Integration (RSO&I), and ULCHI FOCUS LENS exercises. Because of its homeport location in Hawaii, the 3rd Naval Construction Brigade (NCB) assumed most of the exercise burden for the MEG, which was also exported to CENTCOM's INTERNAL LOOK and LUCKY SENTINEL exercises for a possible Middle East war.[7]

The MEG underwent a number of conceptual changes based upon the various exercises' results and the research of several staff officers, including I MEF engineer Lieutenant Colonel James Harbison, Seabee representative Commander William L. Rudich, and the Marine Forces-Pacific (MARFORPAC) Engineer Office Liaison to I MEF, Lieutenant Colonel Michael C. Howard. By mining archived historical documents and operational orders pertaining to joint and combined engineer operations, these engineer officers did much to help build a nascent doctrinal foundation for the new organization.[8]

One document in particular, *Naval Construction Force Support of MAGTF Operations*, which the Marine Corps and Navy had released jointly in August 1991, gave a firm precedent. Its authors declared that "the formation of engineer groups is appropriate when a large, dedicated construction effort is required." "These temporary organizations," they continued, "are usually formed to address a specific or group of related construction projects and provide a single commander to effect their completion." They concluded that "Although organizational integrity should be maintained, Naval Construction Force units may be placed, along with Marine, naval, joint, and/or combined (military or civilian) construction forces, under the [operational control] of an engineer group commander at the direction of the MEF commander. This organizational model was reminiscent of the old World War II Seabee "task unit," which was based upon centralized engineer planning but decentralized execution, and envisioned much more authority for its Seabee commander, such as that enjoyed by Commodore Andrew G. Bisset, who commanded some 110,000 military engineers in combined joint Task Unit 99.3.5 during the final months of the Pacific War. Consequently, the MEG's early proponents moved away from the more limited Marine Engineer Regiment model and toward this broader organizational framework.[9]

Agreement on the MEG's viability and necessity was by no means unanimous. Throughout the exercises, Marine Corps logisticians repeatedly, and often heatedly, criticized the MEG concept despite the Seabees' typically strong performances and the solid backing of successive I MEF commanders. One point of contention concerned the emerging MEG Concept of Operations (CONOPs) in which a "single Engineer battlespace manager" would control and allocate all engineer resources within a given theater. To many hardened bureaucratic in-fighters within the Major Subordinate Commands and the MEF G3 and G4 (Operations and Logistics) staffs, such a change impacted their traditional roles and responsibilities as well as resource distribution within the MEF. Also, many opponents of the MEG either did not understand the principle of jointness, or did not care to embrace it for reasons of their own. But it was just this type of change and joint thinking/behavior that senior Marine Generals were trying to generate to solve very real Engineer employment issues on the modern battlefield.[10]

Unfortunately, throughout the 1990's, the Seabees lagged behind emerging Marine maneuver warfare doctrine. During DESERT STORM, the four Seabee battalions which deployed to the Kuwaiti Theater of Operations had been largely immobilized because their tools, heavy equipment, and camp gear within their Tables of Allowance (TOAs) had been too heavy to move. Consequently, they had encountered real difficulties in supporting the Marines' advance into Kuwait. Indeed, just to get the Seabees into position on the Kuwaiti border before Schwarzkopf's ground attack, senior Seabee commander Commodore Michael Johnson (of the 3rd Naval Construction Regiment) had to order NMCB 74 to leave part of its equipment behind and then scavenge all line haul trucking from the other three battalions for two days at a time until it was redeployed. He then had to repeat the same procedure with each battalion in turn. All in all, it took well over a week to move all the Seabees into their new positions before the ground war started.[11]

Subsequent Seabee and Naval Construction Force doctrinal and policy documents failed to lighten the Seabees' Tables of Allowance or address their ability to maneuver at the tactical level. A November 1997 naval warfare publication entitled *Seabee Operations in the MAGTF* and a similar August 1998 document entitled *Navy Civil Engineer Operations for Component Commanders* both described Seabees as highly skilled specialists capable of executing expeditionary, combat service support engineer projects of a more complex nature than naturally accomplished by combat engineer organizations. However, they further emphasized that the Seabees were only "defensive units," and were "not trained or equipped for combat engineer missions" or other tasks "normally associated with direct support to ground combat." The Chief of Naval Operations' OPNAV INSTRUCTION 5450.46K concerning Naval Construction Force Policy, dated May 25, 1999, reconfirmed the Seabees' traditional missions as general engineers and contingency builders. While faithful to Seabee original World War II functions, these policy statements were inconsistent with the Marines' new emphasis on maneuver warfare. In short, tactical mobility was not an issue in these documents, and Navy policymakers failed to recognize that the Seabees' usefulness in future Marine operations might be limited because we would be unable to keep up.[12]

The debate climaxed following the 2000 ULCHI FOCUS LENS exercise in August 2000. During the exercise, elements of the MEF had to conduct an amphibious assault north of a key city and then move south to link up with the rest of the MEF that was attacking north. The rugged terrain slowed the northern amphibious group significantly while the MEF's unimpeded southern wing moved quickly northward. I MEF commander Lieutenant General Michael W. Hagee needed a road to bypass the city and link up both of his wings. But he discovered that his Marine and Seabee engineers were badly positioned and were also burdened with too much equipment to move quickly to the front and build the critical by-pass. No link-up occurred and the exercise ended with dissatisfaction all around. A better command and control system for large-scale engineer management was clearly needed.[13]

Following ULCHI FOCUS LENS 2000, Hagee summoned a MEG Validation Conference in December at Camp Pendleton, California, to formalize the MEG concept and to establish a MEG command element with an overall "battlespace" engineer commander. During the conference, the various competing factions—Reserve

Marines from the 4th Force Support Services Group (FSSG), U.S. Army National Guard and Reserve engineers, and the Navy Seabees— discussed MEG command and control and other related concept of operations issues, and focused on which flag officer would command the MEG should it become operational. Despite strong claims to the command position by the Army and Marine generals, Hagee was particularly impressed by what the Seabees brought to the table.[14]

Just after the ULCHI FOCUS LENS exercise, Hagee had asked Rear Admiral Kubic, as commander of the 3rd Naval Construction Brigade and the Pacific Division's Naval Facilities Engineering Command, what could have been done differently. Kubic had been recently working on two new concepts to improve the Seabees' tempo of operations. These were lighter and more mobile Seabee regiments and Seabee Engineer Reconnaissance Teams (SERTs), and he firmly believed that they could significantly help resolve the issue.

Seabee Light Regiments

Prior to DESERT STORM, Seabee doctrine was battalion centric with the ability to deploy separately a self-sufficient eighty-nine man Air Detachment (Air Det). In April of 1990, NMCB 3 exercised with the 22nd Marine Expeditionary Unit (MEU) and Spanish Marines in an Amphibious Landing Exercise (PHIBLEX) at Sierra de Retin on the Southern Atlantic coast of Spain. Tasked to supply a company of about 125 Seabees for the PHIBLEX, they created a "heavy Air Det" augmented with extra troops and crew served weapons to meet this requirement. This formation gave a tremendous accounting of itself in a realistic combat exercise and was built upon by NMCB 3 in their preparations for DESERT STORM, and later by the entire NCF in the years that followed.

When Seabees entered Bosnia and then Kosovo, they were faced at times with a requirement for an even heavier combat construction detachment in the range of 250-300 troops with the Commanding Officer and/or Operations Officer (S-3) in command. These units almost had the combat and construction power of a full battalion, but did not have the internal sustainment capability of a full NMCB. This shortfall was met by Army troop and contract support. These large combat construction detachments (called Dets or NMCB(-) formations in Seabee parlance) once again performed extremely well in combat, and clearly demonstrated the power and agility of task tailored Seabee Dets.

When Seabee Tables of Allowance were "modularized" to load the Maritime Pre-positioning Force (MPF) ships, the modules were shaped around 250-strong units with embedded heavy air detachments of 125 Seabees. This provided a convenient way to tailor an MPF offload to any specific operation or task. It also provided a way to use one Table of Allowance to support detachments from multiple battalions. In effect, a Seabee Commodore could employ three 250-man detachments from three separate NMCBs — with the commanding officer leading each Det, and such a Det would become an NMCB(-), with the combined three Detachment unit serving as a Seabee Light Regiment.

This approach provided superb employment flexibility. For example, one NMCB(-) could move to an Air Port of Departure (APOD) with a Core Module (the fundamental building block of a Table of Allowance), a second NMCB(-) could move to a Sea Port of Departure (SPOD) with both a Core and a Basic Module, and a third NMCB(-) could move forward to provide mobility with a Core and a Heavy Module. By adding a downsized regimental command element supported by the Fly-In-echelon, one Maritime Pre-positioning Ship Squadron (MPSRON) from the U. S. Navy's Military Sealift Command could land a Seabee light regiment. Such a regiment could expand by deploying the rest of the NMCB troops and additional Table of Allowance modules. Or, following a quick victory, one battalion could send the rest of its forces forward for Civil Military Operations while the other NMCBs redeployed.

In sum, the concept of the task-organized light regiment would allow a highly capable combat construction force to move forward quickly to execute taskings such as the by-pass road that caused the unplanned tactical pause in the 2000 ULCHI FOCUS LENS exercise.

Seabee Engineer Reconnaissance Teams (SERTs)

The increasingly apparent necessity for Seabees to task organize lighter and move quicker than ever before had also driven a requirement for speedier Engineer reconnaissance, assessment, design and project planning. A Seabee Light Regiment must know how many troops, what kind of equipment, and exactly what materials to move forward – it cannot afford to drag a lot of insurance items with it.

This need for reconnaissance is not new. Seabees have always looked years ahead and sent project officers to sites to compile a backlog of planned projects. NMCBs always make pre-deployment visits a couple of months before they actually deploy to conduct reconnaissance, while Deployment for Training (DFT) Officers-in-Charge always inspect their sites a couple of weeks before their detachments arrive. But in a maneuver battlespace, the requirement for a reconnaissance and planning cycle is not measured in months or weeks, but in days or even hours. Seabees therefore needed to move very far forward on the battlefield to conduct reconnaissance if they were to move task-organized forces quickly to execute critical mobility assignments. Small, heavily armed Seabee Engineer Reconnaissance Teams (SERTs) could conceivably meet this need.

As with all new concepts there were skeptics. But fortunately there were also visionaries like Chief Warrant Officer Bill Johnson who combined his Underwater Construction Team (UCT) diver skills with undying energy and developed the initial ten-man SERT, its equipment, and its tactics, techniques, and procedures (TTPs). He led a series of exercises and made this concept operational very quickly. The team would have an Officer-In-Charge/Liaison Officer (OIC/LNO) element with an officer and two petty officers, a Recon element with an officer and three petty officers, and a Security element with a Chief Petty Officer and two Petty Officers. Each SERT element would travel in a High-Mobility Multipurpose Wheeled Vehicle (HMMWV, or Humvee to most people), mounted with either a .50-caliber M2 or M60 machine gun, and sporting a high-end high frequency (HF) voice and data communications suite. When required for water-based operations, a fourth Humvee would be added with a four-man Dive element. SERTs would be linked to regimental command elements, Navy or USMC, through their Liaison Officers, who would in turn be given "reach-back" engineering support from Division and NAVFAC engineers in the rear and/or in the U.S. Once fully developed, trained, and implemented, SERTs promised to revolutionize Seabee planning and speed of employment.

Armed with these two new concepts, Rear Admiral presented some new ideas to General Hagee as possible partial solutions to I MEF's Engineer problem during the conference. He immediately endorsed both of Kubic's ideas for inclusion into the MEG blueprint. After a very long presentation, in which all sides submitted their arguments, a majority opinion emerged that the Seabees, who were the only active duty force present with a qualified flag officer, represented the best option for building a potentially full-time MEG command and staff structure. Consequently, Hagee decided that the MEG would become an operational part of the MEF for the deliberate OPLANs and that a Seabee admiral would command it. He tapped Kubic for the job, and they then sealed the deal by jointly signing a Decision Memorandum in January 2001, which granted the Seabees a charter to plan, establish, and lead a joint MEG staff.[15]

Not surprisingly, the memorandum encountered some fierce resistance outside of the conference circle. The Marine Force Service Support Groups, which would be losing some control over their engineers and feared so many would be siphoned off into the new MEG that they would be unable to fulfill their own missions, were the chief critics of the plan. But it also drew fire from the Pacific Fleet Commander who became concerned about the increased demands on his single CEC Flag billet and the potential additional costs that could accrue to Pacific Fleet "blue dollars." The East Coast Marines also questioned the MEG's cost and dragged their feet in supporting the concept or supplying any staff or equipment. More feathers were ruffled in the spring and summer when Kubic ordered a series of exercises, in conjunction with MEF exercises, to get the MEG off the ground and to test the new "single Engineer battlespace manager" concept.

Complaints from the I MEF staff and the Force Service Support Groups soon ran up and down the command chain, and the admiral had to make some concessions to keep peace in the family. This resulted in a compromise command system in which he would act as the senior engineer officer who could give the I MEF commander the whole battlefield picture, while the I MEF Engineer and the Force Service Support Groups retained some input into how scarce engineer resources were allocated. Despite all the hew and cry, Hagee kept the interference minimized, and Kubic and his Seabee-led staff and continued designing the MEG's command and control system through the summer of 2001.

A Different War

Al Qaeda's devastating terrorist attacks on September 11, 2001 rudely interrupted MEG planning and suddenly threw the Seabees onto a war footing. Based in Afghanistan and led by the Muslim fanatic and Saudi millionaire Osama Bin Laden, Al Qaeda had been operating against the U.S. for years, beginning with the 1993 bombing of the World Trade Center. As an ardent disciple of a particularly virulent form of Islam called Wahhabism, Bin Laden's avowed goals were to drive the U.S. out of Saudi Arabia and the Middle East, overthrow the House of Saud, and spread Wahhabi Islam around the globe, by sword and fire if necessary.

Unfortunately, in what the 9/11 Commission later described as multiple failures of "imagination, policy, capabilities, and management," both the Clinton and Bush Administrations underestimated the Al Qaeda threat even though they knew that Bin Laden was dangerous. Indeed, based upon "the character and pace of their policy efforts," the Commission concluded that neither administration "fully understood just how many people Al Qaeda might kill, and how soon it might do it." Therefore, without any sense of urgency about the increasing Al Qaeda threat emanating from the U.S. government, especially in an era of "peace dividends" and military "downsizing," no national political will existed for sustained military attacks against Bin Laden's sanctuaries. The U.S. had instead offered only tepid responses to Al Qaeda's escalating series of overseas attacks, relying mostly on retaliatory cruise missile strikes, diplomacy, and law enforcement measures. These were all ineffective, and an emboldened Bin Laden began plotting to carry his *jihad* to the American homeland.[16]

With nearly 3,000 killed in the attacks, 9/11, as that day became known, belatedly opened the country's eyes to the Al Qaeda threat. President George W. Bush and Secretary of Defense Donald H. Rumsfeld decided that the attacks constituted outright war, and that America should respond by waging a ruthless campaign of annihilation against Al Qaeda and its affiliates. Shortly thereafter, Bush announced a "Global War on Terrorism" (GWOT) aimed at the complete destruction of the Al Qaeda terrorist network and punishment of those governments that supported terrorism, beginning with the Islamic fundamentalist Taliban regime in Afghanistan, which harbored Bin Laden and his organization.[17]

Seabee Bunker

Kubic's role in the U.S. military's ultimate response, which came to be known as Operations ENDURING and IRAQI FREEDOM, started when the phone rang in his room at the Hilton Hotel in Anchorage, Alaska, just before 0600 on September 11, 2001. It was Captain Charlie Khan, the Pacific Division Operations Officer. He was supposed to play golf with Kubic in the Society of American Military Engineers Regional Conference tournament. They had arrived at 0200 that morning and Kubic's wake up time was not until 0700.

Kubic's initial thought was that Captain Khan wanted to go out early, but his first words were "Admiral, turn on the TV. The World Trade Center's been hit by a plane." The first image Kubic saw was a burning tower, followed soon afterward by its collapse.

The Seabees' world changed forever that morning. The Nation was suddenly at war, and orders soon reached the U.S. military at all levels and at all locations to "Be ready!" It was time for Seabees everywhere to get ready to build and to fight.

Kubic's new aide, Lieutenant Dave McAlister, and others quickly set up a command post in the admiral's suite on the top floor of the Anchorage Hilton. They had their laptop computers with them, and the Hilton cleared them for unlimited phone service free of charge.

Kubic established communications quickly with Seabees nodes around the world and established command and control from the Hilton. Kubic and his impromptu staff were relieved when they were finally able to call Washington DC and determined that the Chief of Civil Engineers, Rear Admiral Mike Johnson, had survived the attack there, as did the other CEC flags. It seemed that many CEC officers who might otherwise have been trapped in the burning Pentagon that morning were all safely playing golf at Andrews Air Force Base. Golf clearly was the right move that day, in Kubic's view.

Kubic was facing an immediate crisis, including the need to find a way back to Pearl Harbor. The Federal Aviation Administration had shut down U.S. airways, on a scale not seen since the early days of World War II. Fortunately the Pacific Fleet Commander was able to send a Navy plane to retrieve the admiral once the airways reopened.

Back in Pearl Harbor, Kubic directed the Pacific Division and the 3rd Naval Construction Brigade to stand up a twenty-four hour/seven days a week Engineer Operations Center (EOC) to respond to a wide range of contingency missions, such as immediate infrastructure expansion on Diego Garcia to support rapidly deploying U.S. forces. The Engineer Operations Center also became the Seabee center of gravity for all future operations planning and command and control of initial operations in support in the Global War on Terrorism.

The 3rd Naval Construction Brigade/Pacific Division Engineer Operations Center soon became known as the "Seabee Bunker" since it was a small windowless conference room on the first deck of the Pacific Division's Headquarters building in the Makalapa compound. This room was outfitted with an impressive array of computers and communications equipment.

Little did Kubic know at the time that the new Seabee Bunker would operate non-stop, "full speed ahead" for almost two years. Nor did he know that a counterpart Engineer Operations Center, known by the call sign "Seabee Bridge" would stand up almost a year later, shortly after the 2nd and 3rd Naval Construction Brigades were realigned to form the 1st Naval Construction Division (NCD) at Naval Amphibious Base, Little Creek, Virginia. Nor did Kubic realize that he would be personally deployed and exercising global command and control of the new Seabee Division through a very small command cell, with call sign "Seabee BUG;" while, using his personal call sign of "Budweiser." Nor could he even imagine that he would also be exercising command and control of the I MEF Engineer Group (I MEG) from a forward deployed combat operations center (COC) with call sign "Wagon Master." And of course none of the Seabees had even the slightest idea that in eighteen months they would find themselves in the Iraqi desert, attacking north towards Baghdad. As he settled back into the Seabee Bunker, Kubic knew the world had changed forever and that the Seabees had work to do.

Afghanistan

Missions began to emerge quickly, but without defined scope or schedule, as Kubic and his team worked through the chaotic weeks immediately after 9/11. The Seabee Bunker was soon staffed with Reserve Officers and enlisted Seabees from Contingency Engineer Unit, Pacific. They began to track and execute a wide range of contingency actions in support of the Global War on Terrorism, the first phases of which were collectively dubbed Operation ENDURING FREEDOM, and together they soon set a battle rhythm that included daily "Bunker Briefs."

They began planning missions to Afghanistan, Tajikistan, and Basilan Island in the southern Philippines, where Al Qaeda and its affiliates were strongly entrenched. In response to a CENTCOM/MARCENT request, the Joint Forces Command (JFCOM) issued the 1st Naval Construction Division a "be prepared to" (BPT) mission to support the newly formed Combined Joint Task Force Consequence Management (CJTF-CM) in Doha, Kuwait. The 1st Naval Construction Division, in turn, assigned this mission on a rotating basis to Seabee Air Detachments based at the Construction Battalion Center in Gulfport, Mississippi.

An execute order finally came in November for Afghanistan. Elements of NMCB 133 that were deployed in Guam soon joined Brigadier General James N. Mattis' Joint Task Force 58, and took part in the longest helicopter insertion of troops in the history of warfare, becoming the first Seabees to strike back against Al Qaeda. The initial plan called for one hundred fifty Seabees and over forty pieces of equipment to fly in with Mattis' Marines, and then to build and maintain an airfield at an advanced base camp that was to be established in southern Afghanistan. But the sheer distance of the assault, four hundred forty-one miles inland from the amphibious assault ship, the U.S.S *Peleliu* (LHA-5), stationed in the Arabian Sea, reduced that number to the "bare bone" level of twenty-seven Seabees and fifteen pieces of equipment. Lieutenant Commander Len Cooke would serve as Officer In Charge.[18]

Called Operation SWIFT FREEDOM, Mattis' assault took place on Thanksgiving Day, November 25, 2001. His first wave of Marines from the 15th Marine Expeditionary Unit (Special Operations Capable), flying aboard six CH-53E Super Stallion heavy-lift helicopters, landed at an abandoned airstrip designated Objective Rhino, located about ninety-five miles southwest of Kandahar. There, they established their initial forward operating base, called Camp Rhino. Four plane loads of Marines landed soon afterward to beef-up force protection, while the fifth landed the next day carrying the "Kang'roos" of NMCB 133 (which descended from the Seabee 133 of Iwo Jima fame). Camp Rhino's airstrip was situated in a dry riverbed. The Seabees had to get there as quickly as possible after Mattis touched down because planners feared that it would rapidly deteriorate under the weight of the incoming C-17 and C-130 transports and cause a crash. Consequently, their transport plane carried a road grader, bulldozer, and water truck to compact and stabilize the runway immediately. Although the Marines had established a particularly strong security perimeter around Camp Rhino, and would be guarding the work site, the Seabees also brought their weapons along just in case the Taliban counterattacked.[19]

The twenty-seven Seabees who landed at Camp Rhino on November 26 and the days that followed immediately went to work on the airstrip. As predicted, the sandy riverbed was unstable and treacherous. Fortunately, a private company called Environmental

Products & Applications, Inc. had donated a large quantity of an unusual product to the Seabees called Envirotac. It had been specifically designed using pinesap to help civil engineers incorporate poor quality soils (like silty sand) into unpaved road and airfield designs. At Camp Rhino, the Seabees mixed it with water and sprayed it on top of the ground. As the water evaporated, the substance bonded with the sand and formed a crust tough enough to stabilize the ground temporarily to land airplanes or drive trucks over it. Because of the substance's viscosity, the Seabees originally called it "Gorilla Snot," but the Marines' began calling it "Rhino Snot" after their camp, and the name took hold.[20]

Because Mattis' Marines moved much faster and farther inland than emerging doctrine had postulated as possible (even for the next twenty years), most of the Seabees' equipment had to remain in Guam. As a result, they supplemented their equipment with salvaged Russian and Czech equipment found in-country and Navy Civil Engineer Support Equipment that had been prepositioned in Bahrain after DESERT STORM.

While keeping Camp Rhino's airstrip open, the Seabees also built the first detention facilities in Afghanistan to hold captured Al Qaeda and Taliban fighters. In the course of the work, Builder 1st Class Robert Tanner gave the Marines a New York City flag that had flown above the Department of Environmental Protection Police Precinct building on 9/11. The department's police chief had given it to NMCB 133 and had asked that it be flown in memory of the World Trade Center victims wherever the unit served. A couple of Marines at the camp raised it on a bamboo pole beneath the U.S. flag, where it flew before it was later moved to the new Seabee-built detention center at Kandahar. Before leaving Afghanistan, NMCB 133 Commander Douglas Morton retrieved the flag, which now bore a number of signatures, including Kubic's and those of Generals Tommy Franks and James Mattis, and took it with him to Guantanamo Bay. There, with some irony, the New York City flag flew over the new Camp X-Ray terrorist detention facility, which had just been completed by a second detachment from NMCB 133.

While the New York City DEP flag made its way from Camp Rhino to Camp X-Ray, the Seabees of NMCB 133 in Afghanistan undertook their usual camp improvement projects to make life as comfortable for themselves and the Marines as possible. This work continued until an Army sustainment force moved in and relieved the Marines and Seabees in February 2002 after the

Taliban had been driven from power. NMCB 133's success in moving quickly and deeply with a very light but highly capable force into enemy territory with the Marines, and operating there under real combat conditions made it clear to Kubic when he flew into Khandahar in January 2002 that naval expeditionary warfare had been changed forever.

Tajikistan

The Afghan winter of 2001 and 2002 was difficult as usual. Senior planners at the Defense Department and CENTCOM feared that Joint Task Force-58 would get bogged down and would not be able to capture Khandahar's airport until the spring thaw. Since the Navy's aircraft carriers could not stay on station indefinitely, CENTCOM determined that a land strip capable of handling large C-130 transport planes was necessary to keep momentum going until the weather improved. Accordingly, CENTCOM analysts chose an obscure airfield near Chulyab, Tajikistan as the best site for basing Marine strike aircraft for supporting continuing conventional ground and Special Forces operations. Seabees from NMCB 3, deployed in Rota, Spain, at the time, and elements from the 3rd Marine Aircraft Wing (MAW) were earmarked for this new mission. By late December 2001, the plan was ready and the Seabees and Marines were prepared to go. But Kandahar and its airport fell much sooner than expected, and Defense Secretary (SECDEF) Rumsfeld personally cancelled the Chulyab mission forty-eight hours before the first planes were supposed to load and launch from Rota. As a result, NMCB 3 and the 3rd Marine Aircraft Wing stood down for the time being.[21]

Kubic's future aide, Lieutenant Jeff Lengkeek, was the Officer-in-Charge for the mission, and the admiral's son, Lieutenant (Junior Grade) Charlie Kubic, was his Operations officer. Lieutenant Kubic sent his father an e-mail expressing how disappointed he and his Seabees were that the mission was cancelled. They had planned and trained hard, and many of them had cancelled Christmas leave plans to be ready to go. He wanted advice about what he should tell his troops. Admiral Kubic replied that everyone was disappointed, and that the Secretary of Defense himself had called off the mission to conserve troops and resources since the enemy had been routed and American troops would no longer need air support from Tajikistan. As for his troops, the admiral advised his son to simply say: "When the Taliban heard that Seabees from

NMCB 3 were coming, they gave up!" The U.S. had dealt a heavy counterblow to Al Qaeda, but it was clear to Kubic and the Seabees that the Global War on Terrorism was just getting started.

Basilan Island-Philippines

While the Afghan phase of Operation ENDURING FREEDOM was drawing to a successful conclusion, the U.S. launched another phase against the Abu Sayyaf terrorist group in the Philippines, which was holding U.S. hostages with no process and apparently no desire to effect their early repatriation. Even worse, the terrorists maintained links to Al Qaeda and nurtured a brutal reputation for beheading captives. The six-month combined joint operation against Abu Sayyaf began on January 15, 2002, and initially included 1,650 American troops and 150 Special Forces personnel. United States Air Force Brigadier General Donald C. Wurster, who commanded Task Force 510 and the U.S. Special Operations Command-Pacific, led the operation from his headquarters at Zambowanga.[22]

From Okinawa, NMCB 4's Air Detachment and Water Well Team joined Marines from the 9th Engineer Support Battalion, also stationed in Okinawa, and flew to Zambowanga, which was just under an hour ride by Zodiac boat from Basilan Island. There they encountered a remote jungle environment and enemy guerillas, but no existing logistics support system. Unfortunately, as Kubic later recalled, their sister services did not understand nor did they appreciate the full construction, logistics, and project management capabilities which Seabees brought to operations such as this. The on-site Marine and USAF Special Operations Force leaders were dedicated Americans doing their best to succeed in their mission. However, their failure to understand contingency construction, despite many long discussions at all levels, and their uninformed, micro-management of the Class IV procurement process produced delays and inferior materials, (e.g. four-inch clear aggregate for road construction) and led to rationalizations that their version of "expeditionary construction" (viewed as a euphemism for "low quality" by Seabees) was good enough.

Operational challenges aside, NMCB 4 built a perimeter road around the island, repaired a timber pier, cut back the jungle, and also rehabilitated a 3,000-foot runway originally built by Seabees in 1944. The Seabees also constructed Seahuts, bridges, helicopter landing zones, and installed water wells for the combined joint forces operating on the island. Midway through this deployment,

NMCB 1 relieved NMCB 4, much to the amazement of their sister service colleagues who did not understand how routine it was for Seabees to turnover projects, materials, tools, and equipment, and to rotate smoothly in and out of work sites, even under contingency conditions.[23]

The mission ultimately succeeded, but in Kubic's opinion, so much more could have been done with far better results if the Marine in command of the Engineer Task Group and his USAF Task Force 510 boss had just stood back and "let Seabees be Seabees." It was obvious to Kubic then that Seabees needed senior Seabee leadership on future operations such as this if they were to meet their own high standards of performance.

Each of these "warm up" operations brought their own measure of success and their own lessons to build upon. More importantly, they instilled confidence throughout the Naval Construction Force, and produced an even stronger bond between the 2nd and 3rd Naval Construction Brigades as the Navy moved towards a global Seabee realignment. The operations demonstrated that Seabee success was rooted not just in the skill and determination of highly motivated Seabees, but also in the superb construction management skills of their officers and chiefs and in the global Seabee logistics system. Seabee success also reflected the efforts of dedicated military and civilians who daily supported Seabee operations and logistics around the world and who, on a moment's notice, could quickly make the transition from peace to war.

So, following the fall of the Taliban in Afghanistan and while the Basilan mission was underway in the Spring of 2002, the clouds of war in Iraq were already building, and a highly compartmented planning effort was underway at Camp Pendleton. It was time to apply the full energy and experience of the Seabee "first team" and the lessons learned quickly during "spring training" to the emerging plan for the "big game." Seabees needed to be lighter, faster and more agile than ever before. Task-organized Seabee forces had delivered world class performance for decades at the platoon and company level, but it was time to think bigger, and to organize regiments for a division-level operation – unknown to Kubic at the time, but an operation ultimately to be named Operation IRAQI FREEDOM.

CHAPTER

3

War Plans

Even before Mattis' Joint Task Force 58 had landed in southern Afghanistan, the Bush Administration was eyeing Iraq as the next big front in the Global War on Terrorism. In the decade since DESERT STORM, Saddam Hussein had routinely flaunted a whole series of U.N. resolutions aimed at stripping him of his WMD stockpiles and long range missiles. Through the discredited U.N. Oil-for-Food program, launched in 1995, he had also managed to cut private deals with key U.N. leaders and friendly officials from nations such as France, Russia, and Germany to effect the erosion of crippling U. N. sanctions. Furthermore, he had continued a low-grade war over the years by ordering his antiaircraft forces to fire routinely on Coalition aircraft patrolling the "no-fly" zones that had been established after DESERT STORM to protect the northern Kurds and the southern Shi'ite Arabs. That a shoot-down had been avoided up to that point was as much a testament to good luck as it was to the pilots' flying skills.[1]

Saddam's political and military provocations aside, the U.S. State Department had long recognized Iraq as a state sponsor of terrorism. In its publication *Patterns of Global Terrorism 2001*, the Department reported that Iraq provided bases to several terrorist groups including the Mujahedin-e-Khalq (MEK), the Kurdistan Workers' Party (PKK), the Palestine Liberation Front (PLF), and the Abu Nidal organization (ANO). According to the State Department, Baghdad continued to host other Palestinian terrorist groups, including the Arab Liberation Front (ALF) and the 15 May Organization, and also provided material assistance to the three Palestinian terrorist groups that were in the forefront of the second Palestinian *intifadah*, the Popular Front for the Liberation of Palestine-General Command, Hamas, and the Palestine Islamic Jihad. Moreover, based upon public testimonials by Palestinian civilians and officials and cancelled checks captured by the Israelis in the West Bank, the Department showed that Saddam had been paying the families of Palestinian suicide bombers to encourage further such attacks against Israel.[2]

In 2002, the State Department suddenly announced that the Iraqi Intelligence Services had laid the groundwork for possible attacks in the U.S. and other Western countries, and had reportedly instructed its agents in early 2001 that their main mission was to obtain information about US and Israeli targets. The Department also noted for the first time the presence of several hundred Al Qaeda operatives fighting with the small Kurdish Islamist group Ansar al-Islam in the northeastern corner of Iraqi Kurdistan. Without citing a source for its evidence, the State Department further reported that an Iraqi agent positioned somewhere within the most senior levels of Ansar al-Islam had offered Al Qaeda a safe haven in the region as early as 2000. Additionally, small numbers of highly placed Al Qaeda militants had been seen in Baghdad and other Iraqi areas that Saddam controlled. Arguing that it was "inconceivable these groups were in Iraq without the knowledge and acquiescence of Saddam's regime," the Department claimed that Al Qaeda operatives in northern Iraq had concocted suspect chemicals under the direction of a senior Bin Laden associate named Abu Mus'ab al-Zarqawi and had tried to smuggle them into Russia, Western Europe, and the United States for terrorist operations.[3]

As a result of this murky information, the Bush Administration became convinced that a "sinister nexus between Iraq and the Al Qaeda terrorist network" had occurred, one that combined "classic terrorist organizations and modern methods of murder." This was a fearsome development, if it was in fact the case, but the idea contained a number of problems, as critics quickly pointed out. The foremost of these was the fact that Saddam's brand of secular Islam was wholly incompatible with Osama Bin Laden's radical fundamentalist faith. In response, Secretary of State Colin Powell later argued at the United Nations that "Ambition and hatred [were] enough to bring Iraq and Al Qaeda together" and that an Al Qaeda source had revealed that "Saddam and Bin Laden had reached an understanding that Al Qaeda would no longer support activities against Baghdad." Therefore, in the minds of senior U.S. policymakers, it was entirely possible that "Al Qaeda could turn to Iraq for help in acquiring expertise on weapons of mass destruction."[4]

The case for moving against Iraq was thin, as senior British officials later observed in a secret meeting at Downing Street in London. They concluded that "Saddam was not threatening his neighbors," and their excellent MI-6 intelligence service had reported that "his WMD capability was less than that of Libya, North Korea or Iran." Additionally, the Bush Administration's early assertions that the leader of the 9/11 hijackers, Mohammed Atta, met with an Iraqi intelligence agent in Prague shortly before the attacks were unsubstantiated. Indeed, the Undersecretary of Defense for Policy Douglas J. Feith, whose job entailed the development of strategy and policies for dealing with terror networks, later admitted that the claim was based upon "alternative analysis" and that Saddam had no known link to 9/11.[5]

Nevertheless, President Bush decided that Saddam was a serious threat to America and had to be dealt with sooner rather than later. On November 21, 2001, he asked Defense Secretary Rumsfeld about the current war plan for Iraq. Rumsfeld in turn asked CENTCOM commander General Thomas R. "Tommy" Franks for an update. Franks replied that the war plan, called OPLAN 1003, was outdated and was essentially DESERT STORM II, in terms of force levels, strategy, and tactics. It was built around an American force of over 500,000 soldiers, Marines, sailors and airmen, grouped into the lumbering mass formations of the Cold War military. Current troop dispositions, technology advances, and lighter force employment and tactics, as envisioned in Rumsfeld's recent military "transformation" program, were thus not reflected in the plan. To keep President Bush's options open, Rumsfeld ordered Franks to "dust it off" and start revising it for a *possible* second war against Iraq, should it become necessary.[6]

MARCENT commander Lieutenant General Earl B. Hailston, headquartered in Bahrain, and I MEF commander Lieutenant General Michael W. Hagee, at Camp Pendleton, drew the assignment for shaping the anticipated Marine operations for the revised OPLAN 1003. Since Saudi Arabia's support for a new American-led military campaign to oust Saddam was doubtful at best, they realized that the Marines would have to operate from Kuwait, whose military infrastructure was miniscule as compared to its much larger southern neighbor. They also understood that a great deal of construction would be needed to bed down and support I MEF before any attack could be launched, but it would have to be done discreetly since any talk about a new war with Iraq was politically sensitive. Further, Hagee believed that a MEG would be ideal for managing Navy and Marine engineer assets in this specific situation.

"I Think We Need a MEG"

In February 2002, the 3rd Naval Construction Brigade was the Seabee lead for all future operational engineering planning in the Pacific and Asia. At that time, the 3rd Brigade was focused on the multitude of missions underway and emerging, such as in Afghanistan and the Philippines, in support of the Global War on Terrorism. This was a natural consequence of the brigade's proximity to the U.S. Pacific Command, which served as the supporting combatant command for both OPLAN 5027 (war in Korea), and OPLAN 1003 (war in Iraq).

One potential mission was to provide Seabee support to I MEF forces that could be deployed to Southwest Asia, most probably Kuwait, in response to hostile intent or actions by the Iraqi regime. This force was known as the Continental United States (CONUS) Contingency Response Force or CCRF, and had been established in the 1990s while the United States contained Iraq's behavior.

The CCRF had been written into OPLAN 1003, and so Lieutenant General Hagee placed a call to Rear Admiral Kubic at the 3rd Naval Construction Brigade. He said that a very small planning team was being assembled to plan an attack on Iraq should such action be directed by the Commander in Chief, and he wanted Seabees on his team once more. The engineer effort would be both crucial and complex for any rapid Marine drive though the Tigris-Euphrates valleys, and to manage it, he thought it was time to put their charter to work. He therefore told the admiral, "Chuck, I think we need a MEG."

Hagee had only about a dozen of his senior planners "read into" the emerging 1003V OPLAN. At that time the planning work was highly compartmented and both TOP SECRET and SECRET access was tightly controlled by a further designation known as "Originator Controlled" or ORCON information. Written rosters dictated who could participate in the planning, and Kubic was authorized to name two planners plus himself to have access to the Top Secret ORCON information during this period. 3rd Naval Construction Brigade Future Operations planner Commander Gary Thompson (USNR), and the Commander of the 30th Naval Construction Regiment, Commodore Greg Shear, were the only Seabees besides Kubic who had access to the inner circle of I MEF ORCON planning for the next six months. In June 2002, Commodore Bill Rudich relieved Commodore Shear and was also given ORCON clearance.

The details of this planning effort must remain classified, but suffice it to say that this group had a very difficult and extremely critical job to do and that they gave shape to the war plan that was ultimately executed with speed and lethal precision. In parallel with the ORCON planning effort, I MEF set a much broader planning effort in motion at the Secret (non-ORCON) level to refine the details of the existing OPLAN 1003V as part of the annual series of MEF Command Element exercises or MEFEX's. This approach required those in the ORCON planning world to keep the details of both the real and exercise plans straight in their own minds and properly protected. Never the less, it was a very effective way to raise the situational awareness and staff teaming skills while not compromising what would become the boldest and most dangerous plan the U.S. military had undertaken since perhaps the Inchon Landing during the Korean War.

Following Kubic's phone call from Lieutenant General Hagee, the admiral flew to Bahrain for a discussion with Lieutenant General Hailston, during which he requested that the 3rd Naval Construction Brigade "sneak some Seabees into Kuwait" to start building new bed down facilities there and to provide direct support to the Marines in case they had to "go early and ugly." Kubic left the meeting with the understanding that serious construction lay ahead in extremely challenging conditions, political as well as environmental, in the coming summer, and that a MEG would manage it. However, at the time, he was not at all sure if an attack was imminent, based upon conflicting signals from the Bush Administration and the Defense Department. Regardless, the Seabees had much work to do, since up to that point, the MEG existed as an organization only in theory and without any written doctrine to support it despite the exercises of the previous years.

Kubic returned to Pearl Harbor and, along with his 3rd Naval Construction Brigade staff, began planning the mission. Time was precious though. Initial talk suggested that CENTCOM might attack Iraq as early as the end of May 2002. However, the prospect of fighting in Iraq during the summer heat led to a somewhat more reasonable estimate that September could be the earliest month at which the Marines could jump off. This too proved to be wildly over optimistic, and CENTCOM began looking at possible new attack dates between Christmas and New Year's. Even with the projected end-of-year G-Day—"G" for ground attack-—it was clear that Kubic and the Seabees did not have much time to get their act together.

With the clock now ticking, Kubic and his staff organized themselves into a command element for the new 1st Marine Expeditionary Force Engineer Group (I MEG). They then began refining their new organization and doctrine from scratch through a series of exercises and planning sessions conducted at Camp Pendleton, California, and at Pearl Harbor, Hawaii. That the MEG would be a true joint force became clear early on when the 265th Engineer Group of the U.S. Army's Georgia National Guard, under Colonel Peter Kole, came aboard for the exercises. The 265th already had a good working relationship with the 3rd Naval Construction Brigade since the Guard unit had been augmenting I MEF as part of I MEG over the past several years during the Korean exercises, and the Army therefore had no problem releasing it for service in the "real MEG" for a potential Iraqi campaign.

Despite the Army's acquiescence in releasing the 265th Engineer Group to the MEG, many mid-career officers in I MEF and the Marine logistics forces were not enthused about parting with engineers and scarce supporting resources for the MEG, even though their senior commanders had strongly endorsed it. Kubic faced particularly stiff opposition from retired Marine Lieutenant General James A. Brabham over the issue of a Seabee admiral rather than a Marine general acting as I MEFs single Engineer "battlespace" manager. Brabham, who had commanded I MEF's 1st Force Service Support Group during DESERT STORM, now used his role as an MSTP (MAGTF Staff Training Program) mentor to question and criticize the MEG throughout the 2002 MEF exercises.

Following a MEFEX in the spring of 2002, Hagee responded to advice from the senior mentors and moved the MEF Engineer from the G4 (Supply) to the G3 (Operations). Before making this move, he consulted Kubic, who strongly endorsed this idea. In effect, the force Engineer would assume a role similar to Force Fires to coordinate and synchronize the Engineer effort across the battlespace. This move also silenced the critics of the MEG assuming the role of the single Engineer battlespace manager and offered Seabees the promise of an influential advocate within operations as opposed to being buried in logistics. In the past, Seabees found that logisticians tended to filter Engineer issues and concerns related to operations if such issues clouded the logistics picture. The move of the MEF Engineer would ultimately prove to be wise, but it was not without its growing pains before and during the war. In fact, there remains a strong case that the MEG Commander should be double-hatted as the MEF Engineer with a small, joint Marine, Seabee, Army staff to support the G3, and given his seniority and experience, the MEG Commander should serve as the single Engineer battlespace manager.

Planning the MEG

Following Hagee's MEG compromise, the 3rd Naval Construction Brigade conducted a comprehensive training exercise called KEDGE HAMMER, which highlighted the dual needs for better training in the Marine Corps Planning System and for close coordination and synchronization of all of the MEG's units. The latter issue was particularly important since an accidental tactical "pause" arising from misaligned or misscheduled units could result in disaster for I MEF, such as an Iraqi chemical weapon counterattack. KEDGE HAMMER taught the MEG staff how to command and control a large, joint engineer group, something not seen since World War II, and also unveiled the enormous scope, difficulty, and complexity of what the Seabees had to do to fulfill their mission in an Iraqi war. The exercise also clarified command and control issues, the need for increased Class IV construction materials, and the requirements for semi-permanent, expeditionary, non-standard bridging.

During KEDGE HAMMER, Kubic's staff focused on tactical mobility as the MEG's prime Concept of Operations (CONOPS) since the evolving OPLAN 1003 called for speed and maneuverability. I MEF did not possess enough Armored Vehicle Launched Bridges (AVLBs), or pontoon or medium girder assault bridges to cross all of the expected waterways and gaps on the roads to Baghdad. So it became obvious that the primary joint mission of the Seabees' and the 265th Engineer Group would be to move behind the advancing Marines, and to repair existing but damaged bridges or to build semi-permanent non-standard bridges so that the Marines' assault bridges could be "leapfrogged" forward with their assault forces.

Kubic accordingly organized the MEG into three regimental-sized task forces, the 265th Army Engineer Group under combat engineer Colonel Pete Kole, the Hawaii-based 30th Naval Construction Regiment under Seabee Commodore William L. Rudich, and the Atlantic Seabees of the 22nd Naval Construction Regiment under Seabee Commodore William C. McKerall. Army and Marine Multi-Roll Bridge Companies as well as an Army Mechanized Engineer Battalion were rolled into the 265th while an Army Wheeled Engineer Battalion joined the 30th and 22nd Naval Construction Regiments. To manage Kole's Marine bridging companies, Kubic designated the 8th Engineer Support Battalion (ESB) as a command element within the 265th.

The initial task force plan called for Kole's 265th sappers and combat engineers to be on point and to provide direct support to the 1st Marine Division (MARDIV) during a theoretical advance up the Tigris and Euphrates valleys. This only made sense because Kole's troops could put up a hardened defense with their armored personnel carriers and big guns. In the meantime, the more lightly armed 30th and 22nd Naval Construction Regiments would then follow closely behind in echelon to undertake non-standard bridging, road repairs and maintenance, and other types of contingency construction behind the immediate danger area.

The DESERT SHIELD and DESERT STORM experiences, in which the Seabees and their heavy equipment were principally arrayed in static base camps around the Marines' main bed down area at Jalibah, had demonstrated the difficulties they had encountered in moving forward to support the Marines. In short, they had been too heavy. Only one full Seabee unit, NMCB 74, had moved north fully loaded, while the other three battalions had to strip themselves of gear and equipment, and then share, in turn, the 30th Naval Construction Regiment's precious line haul trucks to get into position for DESERT STORM's ground campaign.

Kubic therefore realized that bringing the tooth forward and leaving the tail behind, as envisioned in the task force system, was absolutely essential. The distances in Iraq were too vast and the roads too constrained, and the lead task force would have to move very fast and in echelon right behind the Marines and their Engineer Support Battalions. The Seabees therefore would have to be not only *strategically* mobile but *tactically* mobile for the possible invasion. Furthermore, convoy space would likely be extremely limited, with priority given to tools, heavy machinery, weapons, ammunition, and bridging equipment. Consequently, Kubic and his commanders knew up front that the Seabees would have to abandon most of their normal amenities, such as tents, galleys, and showers, just to keep up with the Marine vanguard.

Kubic also made the extremely tough decision to split battalions and their command staffs and assets among the three task forces. Although many Seabees, particularly the chiefs, grumbled mightily about it, Kubic believed that the idea was operationally sound since task organization had long been a hallmark of Seabee operations, with construction battalion detachments and teams routinely deploying wherever they were needed. The admiral wanted to take this one step further though to maximize the MEG's flexibility beyond the detachment level by matching Seabee skills, personnel, and equipment from individual construction battalions to specific jobs throughout the whole battlespace. For instance, Seabees with bridging skills and equipment from a battalion would be assigned to a maneuver task force moving through the Tigris-Euphrates valleys. Likewise, Seabees from the same battalion who specialized in road building and repair would work in the rearward construction task force to keep the logistics trail open.[7]

In DESERT STORM, construction battalion commanders retained operational control over all of their Seabees and equipment despite their relative locations on the battlefield. The new task force command and control scheme though required battalion commanders to relinquish operational but not administrative control of their personnel and assets outside of their respective task forces. If a battalion commander posted to the maneuver task force needed to draw upon either his equipment or his manpower from another task force, then he could not directly do it without having to request it through the MEG command staff. Likewise, the battalion's executive officer, in charge of his respective Seabee elements within his assigned task force, could not call upon his commander for more assets without going through MEG channels.[8]

As many in the Seabee community quickly realized, the battalion's people and resources would be cross assigned and its operational command chains would essentially be altered temporarily, while preserving administrative unity of command. Unfortunately, this somewhat chaotic matrix organization structure was absolutely necessary, given the unprecedented circumstances the Seabees faced, and the complex, extremely difficult mission they would have to undertake to execute their TOP SECRET orders. Since Kubic and his commanders were not free to discuss these highly classified planning matters, they could not fully explain their organizational rationale nor their intended tactics, techniques, and procedures to the Seabees and their immediate leadership. As a result, the next several months would prove to be difficult for many officers and NCOs who were tangentially involved in the planning and training without knowing the classified details.

Marine Resistance to the MEG

The first exercises, including DESERT SPEAR in June, KEDGE HAMMER in July, and the MEFEX in October, suggested that Kubic's task force scheme would work very well. But the new commander of the 1st Force Service Support Group, Brigadier General Edward G. Usher III, nearly brought the whole MEG plan to a screeching halt when he openly announced that he opposed the MEG in general, and Seabee command of Marine bridging companies in particular. He and his subordinates reasoned that a Seabee admiral just did not have the proper training to lead Marine engineers in combat situations. Usher and Kubic met several times with Brigadier General James Mattis, who was now the deputy commander of the 1st Marine Expeditionary Force following his successful Joint Task Force 58 mission in Afghanistan. Mattis hammered out a compromise whereby the Army and Marine bridging units would be welded into Task Force Romeo (for River) for one final exercise to be held late in the summer, which would evaluate the MEG's continued command over those units.[9]

The MEG exercise was held as scheduled. Its outcome seemed to confirm Kubic's contention that the complexity of the engineering mission and the need for "synchronization" of all non-organic engineer units demanded a single battlespace manager from the Seabee community. Since Marines traditionally maintain a very strong sense of "command ownership," no doubt even stronger than the Seabees, they simply could not accept the idea of moving Marine units into larger Navy units. Hence, Usher and his Force Service Support Group logisticians remained thoroughly unconvinced and continued their resistance to giving up any Marine engineer units to the MEG.[10]

A change of command within I MEF exasperated the stand-off with the 1st Force Service Support Group after Hagee was selected to become the Marine Corps' new commandant in August. The commanding general of the 1st Marine Division, Lieutenant General James T. Conway, was selected to replace him as I MEF commander in November, with Mattis moving up to become the new commanding general of the 1st Marine Division. When Kubic asked I MEF for Marine Corps staff from the 4th Force Service Support

Group's Command Element to serve on the MEG staff, Usher took advantage of the overall command shuffle by resurrecting the old arguments against the MEG, which Hagee had settled two years earlier at the Camp Pendleton Validation Conference. Weeks of circular discussion ensued as Usher argued not only against sending any Marines from the 4th Force Service Support Group to support the MEG, but also against attaching the 8th Engineer Support Battalion and its Marine and Army bridging companies to Task Force Romeo. Both Conway and Mattis grew somewhat irritated at the endless haggling, but fully supported the Marine Corps Planning System, and agreed to submit the renewed MEG question to an Operational Planning Team (OPT) session supervised by the I MEF G3 (Operations) Colonel Larry Brown and his Force Engineer, Lieutenant Colonel Peter Ramey.

To represent the Seabees, Kubic assigned Commodore Bill Rudich as the senior MEG representative to the session, and also asked Task Force Romeo commander Colonel Pete Kole to attend as well. As it happened, Rudich and Kole walked straight into a Marine ambush, and they were thoroughly outgunned during what turned out to be a disastrous session for the MEG. At its conclusion, the Operational Planning Team not only determined that the 8th Engineer Support Battalion could single handedly manage all the bridging operations as part of the Force Service Support Group for the 1st Marine Division, but also decided that Kole's 265th Engineer Group and its two Army Engineer Battalions were no longer needed for the mission. Colonel Kole departed the Operational Planning Team session abruptly, and was not pleased by the way he and his soldiers were treated after many months of MEG planning and exercises, pre-dating 9/11. Even worse, the team's recommendations indirectly questioned the need for a MEG and reached Hagee's desk without review by the major subordinate commanders, including Kubic and Mattis. Hagee, who was preparing to leave his post for his new job as Marine commandant, accepted the recommendations at face value, thereby leaving the MEG in "shambles."

Kubic was upset at both the session's outcome and how the Marine logisticians and engineers had rammed the Operational Planning Team recommendations straight to Hagee without Major Subordinate Command review. Mattis was also concerned that the Operational Planning Team recommendation went to Hagee without his review and comments, and Conway was likewise disappointed in how the team had handled the issue. To address these valid concerns, upon assuming command of I MEF, Lieutenant General Conway authorized a subsequent review of the Operational Planning Team's decision with the major subordinate commanders. But, serious damage had been done to Kubic's plans and the MEG was set back many months.

Fortunately, the damage to the MEG was not mortal. Kubic first moved to repair the Seabees' relationship with Kole, who had traveled home to Georgia disappointed by the Operational Planning Team's shabby treatment of the 265th. It was now impossible for the 265th to lead Task Force Romeo since the unit's Time-Phased Force and Deployment Data (TPFDD) personnel and equipment transport plan was moved significantly down the priority scale after the session. In short, Kole's unit could never arrive in time with all of its people and equipment to spearhead the bridging mission. However, planning for possible Phase IV Civil Military Operations in Iraq was then underway, and Kubic envisioned placing the 265th at the core of Task Force Echo (Endurance) to lead stabilization and more permanent construction efforts in southern Iraq while the two other Seabee task forces advanced northward behind the Marines. Moreover, the 265th could then remain behind to transition and support the Army's reconstruction efforts while I MEF redeployed after "kicking the door down" and soundly defeating Saddam. Kole liked this idea, and agreed to come back aboard if we could revive the MEG as a Major Subordinate Command.

Kubic then concentrated on overturning the Operational Planning Team's indirect recommendations against the MEG. He had Rudich, ever resilient and much the wiser after his rough handling by the Marine logisticians and engineers, restructure the MEG, with the 265th forming Task Force Echo, while Rudich's 30th Naval Construction Regiment would move into Task Force Mike (Mobility). Rudich also rewrote the MEG's Concept of Operations and prepared a new "hard-hitting" briefing for Kubic to deliver to Hagee. However, as it turned out, Kubic was never able to schedule his brief for the I MEF commanding general until after the Change of Command took place. A "prebrief" for "principals only" was scheduled in October 2002, as the various staffs were deploying to Kuwait, on the day before Kubic's scheduled brief to the new commanding general, Lieutenant General Conway. At this point some in I MEF, including the new Chief of Staff Colonel John Coleman, the Chief of Operations (G3) Colonel Larry Brown, and of course 1st Force Service Support Group commander Brigadier General Usher, were openly questioning whether they even needed a MEG for the pending operation. They had circled the wagons and locked down on their desire to limit the influence of a Seabee flag on their internal Marine Corps command and control structure.

Rear Admiral Kubic went to the meeting by himself with Rudich's brief and was amazed (and disappointed) by the hair-trigger emotions in a room that was filled with MEF staff (without the commanding general's presence) despite the billing as a senior "principals only" meeting. In this hostile atmosphere, the admiral carefully made his points over the course of a difficult two hour meeting and ultimately gained group consensus in his favor on everything except command and control of the bridging companies. Later, during the war, it became very apparent to Kubic that the 1st Force Service Support Group's interest in the bridging mission was focused not on synchronizing Engineer operations, but on seizing the Engineer's trucks at the earliest opportunity to support its overextended long haul mission. During this planning phase though, the Marine engineers successfully obscured the real reason for their intransigence on this particular issue and forced the awkward arrangement.

At the end of the meeting Kubic faced a dilemma – should he force the bridge command and control issue to his good friend Lieutenant General Conway and give him a serious administrative headache in his first week on the job? Or, should he consolidate his gains after two largely successful hours of discussion by a lone Seabee against thirty-plus-Marines, and graciously agree to drop his bridging command and control concern and to turn the controversial decision brief into a consensus confirmation brief?

At that point, resolidifying the MEG concept was key and Kubic felt that he would have other opportunities to work the command and control issue – so he chose the path of gracious consensus. The next day, Conway responded very well to the confirmation brief and, most importantly, he clearly instructed his staff that "we will have a MEG" for this operation, settling that debate (again) once and for all. However, Kubic was never able to resolve with any clarity the command and control issue regarding the bridging companies, leading to continuing strain with the G3 Colonel Larry Brown, Force Engineer Lieutenant Colonel Pete Ramey, and 1st Force Service Support Group commander Brigadier General Ed Usher as they worked up to D-Day. (This lack of command and control clarity ultimately caused some very close calls on the battlefield during the war which required "intense leadership" and a number of "one-way discussions" to resolve, as Kubic later put it.) But, at the end of the day, the MEG survived with three task forces, Mike (Mobility), Charlie (Construction) and Echo (Endurance) and the 265th still on board – it was a good day in Kubic's opinion. Indeed, he thought that it was the best decision possible at that time, and the critical turning point in establishing the MEG as an operational Major Subordinate Command of I MEF.

The 1st Naval Construction Division Stands Up

While grappling with the Marine engineers and logisticians at I MEF headquarters, as the commander of the 3rd Naval Construction Brigade, Kubic also had his hands full dealing with a global "realignment" of all Seabee forces. For the previous ten years, the Seabees had been organized into a dual brigade command structure, with the Atlantic Fleet Seabees under the control of the 2nd Naval Construction Brigade in Norfolk, Virginia, and the Pacific Fleet Seabees under the 3rd Naval Construction Brigade in Pearl Harbor. Both brigades reported independently through their respective four-star Fleet commanders to the Chief of Naval Operations in Washington, DC. Before 9/11, the Chief of Naval Operations, Admiral Vernon Clark, launched a massive global reorganization of all naval forces and shore facilities to streamline and reconfigure the Navy in accordance with its new joint global strategy, called *Sea Power 21*. As part of the reorganization effort, Clark commissioned a naval construction force alignment study to determine how the Seabees should best be organized for *Sea Power 21*.[11]

The study was completed late in 2001 under Rear Admiral Mike Shelton. It recommended that all 18,000 Navy Seabees from both brigades should be unified under a single division-level command structure. Clark accepted Shelton's plan and ordered both naval construction brigades decommissioned and replaced with a new unified division to better organize, train, operate, and maintain the naval construction force. Consequently, the 1st Naval Construction Division (NCD) "stood up" on August 9, 2002, with Kubic as its first commander. As a result of the realignment, and his prior promotion to Rear Admiral (Upper Half) on October 1, 2001, Kubic found himself in the unique position of being in command of all Seabees worldwide as well as the I MEG commander. This made it somewhat easier to fight the internal battles that still had to be fought to bring the MEG finally to life as the admiral began shaping the Seabee role for the oncoming war.[12]

CHAPTER 4

The Road to War

The creation of the 1st Naval Construction Division coincided with a general escalation of rhetoric emanating from the Bush Administration concerning Iraq. In his speech at the West Point graduation ceremony on June 1, Bush had announced a controversial new doctrine of "preemption." No longer would the U.S. wait for future attacks upon itself or its allies from a "few mad terrorists or tyrants" before acting against them. At this point, the Taliban had been routed in Afghanistan and Al Qaeda's beleaguered leadership had retreated into the rugged mountains inside Pakistan. And although he did not name Saddam in his speech, Bush strongly hinted that Iraq was moving into America's crosshairs, arguing that deterrence and containment were no longer possible when "unbalanced dictators with weapons of mass destruction can deliver those weapons on missiles or secretly provide them to terrorist allies."[1]

Bush removed any doubt that Saddam was America's next target in the Global War on Terrorism when he delivered a scathing address at the United Nations on September 12. During his speech, the President outlined a litany of Saddam's failures to abide by a long series of U.N. resolutions, including those that required him to stop supporting terrorists and to destroy his weapons of mass destruction. After taking the U.N. to task for its spinelessness in dealing with Saddam over the years, Bush put both the world body and the Iraqi dictator on notice: "The purposes of the United States should not be doubted. The Security Council resolutions will be enforced — the just demands of peace and security will be met —

or action will be unavoidable. And a regime that has lost its legitimacy will also lose its power."[2]

Five days later, Bush approved the new *National Security Strategy of the United States of America*, which formally institutionalized his preemption doctrine. It stated:

> The United States has long maintained the option of preemptive actions to counter a sufficient threat to our national security. The greater the threat, the greater is the risk of inaction— and the more compelling the case for taking anticipatory action to defend ourselves, even if uncertainty remains as to the time and place of the enemy's attack. To forestall or prevent such hostile acts by our adversaries, the United States will, if necessary, act preemptively.[3]

Based upon Saddam's prior history of regional aggression, his past use of weapons of mass destruction, his flaunting of U.N. resolutions, and support for terrorists, the new strategy effectively placed America on the road to war once again.

With preemption now firmly grounded into his foreign policy, the Bush Administration began laying the political and military groundwork for a potential new war against Saddam, beginning with America's allies in the Middle East. Although they had no love for the dictator, the Saudis could not be counted on this time. They had been staggered by the internal implications of 9/11, and were under sharp criticism in America for their perceived coddling of Al Qaeda and other terrorist organizations. Fearful of fueling their own political troubles further, they were decidedly cool to the idea of a preemptive war against Iraq and refused to allow any of their bases or facilities to be used for the purpose, at least overtly.

The Kuwaitis, on the other hand, were more compliant, but without much enthusiasm. Indeed, both the Bush Administration and CENTCOM had planned from the start to use Kuwait as a staging base for U.S. and Coalition ground and air forces. To expand the U.S. logistics base there and to facilitate the movement of prepositioned weapons and equipment from Qatar, infrastructure improvements had been first on the agenda, even before Bush had announced his new preemption policy at West Point in early June.[4]

"This Is Going To Be Hard"

For its part, MARCENT needed sufficient facilities to bed down all of the Marines' strike and fighter aircraft that would be supporting I MEF before any ground movement north into Iraq could occur. When CENTCOM officials approached the Kuwaitis with a request to build temporary air basing facilities for the task, the Kuwaitis made it clear that they wanted permanent facilities like those in Saudi Arabia, beginning with an enormous new aircraft apron at Al Jaber air base. CENTCOM, backed by the Bush Administration, agreed. To get the job done as quickly and quietly as possible, MARCENT planners calculated that the Seabees would be the fastest and most efficient builders for the task. Hence, Lieutenant General Hailston's early need to get some Seabees into Kuwait.[5]

Although the MEG framework was still in development and being questioned by some at that time, Kubic knew from the outset that he needed a regimental sized Seabee element to meet Hailston's immediate needs. But he did not necessarily want to move whole battalions from deployed or homeport sites all at once. Kubic therefore decided to bring about two hundred fifty Seabees slowly into Kuwait from their forward base in Rota, Spain, and two hundred fifty more from Guam. His intent was to build up forces, as required, as the construction materials began arriving. This type of re-deployment was fairly typical for the Seabees, he later recalled. All he had to do was "task them, resource them, make sure they knew this was the real thing, point them in the right direction, and then get out of their way."

Before doing that, Kubic decided to visit Kuwait in August 2002 to get a first-hand feel for what needed to be done and where the prospective Seabee work sites would be located. He had been in Kuwait before, in 1983, to help build a logistics complex for the Kuwaiti Air Force at Ali Al Salem Air Base, and so he already had some idea of the construction task ahead. After landing, Kubic and his staff went to scope out the proposed site for the Marine's aircraft apron. Looking at the vast untouched desert, he suddenly realized, "Wow! This is going to be hard." The project was going to take longer, cost more, and consume more manpower than anyone at MARCENT and CENTCOM had estimated, but Kubic and his commanders began to appreciate how important this work really was if the U.S. was going to go to war again.

While out in the desert, Kubic determined that the Seabees were going to need a base and headquarters camp from which to work on the parking apron. After visiting Al Jaber Base and Ali Al Salem Base, the admiral traveled to Kuwaiti Camp Commando at the base of the Mutla Ridge. I MEF was considering establishing their Headquarters there, and he needed to decide whether or not to place the MEG command element with MEF Headquarters or to locate it with the Seabee projects at Al Jaber or Ali Al Salem.

As Kubic walked the ground at Camp Commando, he ran quite unexpectedly into Lieutenant General Conway, who was doing a similar site recon. They were both pleasantly surprised to see each other, and took the opportunity to conduct an impromptu planning session together. Conway wanted the MEG command element with him at Camp Commando, and so Kubic quickly made the decision to locate the MEG headquarters there. Their recon focus was then directed toward how to build the camp properly, and on how "permanent" the construction would be.

General Conway saw Camp Commando as a temporary tent camp with only minimal creature comforts. He wanted the camp to be functional, but did not want to invest in too much infrastructure. Kubic thought that they might find themselves there for many months and offered suggestions to make the camp more functional while retaining an "expeditionary" price tag. Once they agreed upon a basic "bare bones" concept, Kubic solicited Conway's agreement for a MEG area at Camp Commando. In the heat of the dry Kuwaiti summer, it was hard to visualize how drastically the desert climate could change by winter. But Kubic knew from previous experience that the weather would change for the worst in the months ahead, and could see that the proposed camp area would flood during the rainy winter season unless the Seabees constructed a drainage system. With the General's permission, Kubic promptly staked out an area of high ground for the very first I MEG headquarters near what would become the Camp Commando main gate.

Unfortunately, the rains did come in winter, and without proper drainage many Marine areas did flood. Although Seabees were "high and dry" themselves, they got "plenty wet" digging trenches to drain the area for the Marines on the low ground. This was a harbinger of events to come as Seabees responded on the fly to deliver whatever support the Marines needed, whether it was planned or not.

With the MEG headquarters site selected, Kubic and his staff moved on to the staggering projects which the Seabees had been assigned to build. After walking the site, they were convinced that they had a solid plan for the Al Jaber parking apron. The Kuwaitis had already planned a C-130 pad as part of their master military infrastructure plan at Al Jaber, and the U.S. had already committed itself to assisting in the pad's construction before the focus of the Global War on Terrorism had shifted to Iraq. Because a C-130 pad could easily be adapted to support Marine F/A-18 strike fighters, the Seabees had a very real project that they could use as a cover to shield its true purpose.[6]

In accordance with the Defense Department's unspoken strategy of "dribbling out force deployments," as journalist Bob Woodward later put it, Seabees could move into Kuwait in small low profile detachments without raising any eyebrows at home or in the media. The new 1st Naval Construction Division also had the ability to redirect deployed resources from the Atlantic and Pacific Fleets to the critical MARCENT/CENTCOM projects without raising any questions regarding the actual intended use of the parking apron and other Marine Aircraft Wing bed down facilities. And if the U.S. managed to oust Saddam without attacking Iraq, the Seabees would still leave behind a useful piece of infrastructure for possible future operations in the Middle East. The Seabee plan started to come togther in early September 2002 as a "win-win" situation for MARCENT, CENTCOM, the 1st Naval Construction Division, and the U.S.' Kuwaiti allies.[7]

Already behind schedule and needing to get started quickly, Kubic returned to the Seabee Bunker in Hawaii and had his engineers quickly prepare additional site plans and cost estimates for the initial work. Based upon the preliminary requirements for infrastructure to support Marine aviators and the Marine ground force that would have to launch a "go early and ugly" attack on Saddam's forces, Kubic's team expanded initial project scopes to include refueling and ammunition depots, rotary wing pads, and berthing. With the plans drafted, the admiral visited Hailston again in Bahrain, briefed him on the projects which his team had planned, and told him "If you can give us the money, then we can sneak some Seabees in."

The Seabees "Sneak" Into Kuwait

Lieutenant General Hailston liked Kubic's proposed course of action. Based upon their earlier discussion, he had already initiated a request for forces from CENTCOM calling for two 125-person Seabee Air Detachments and fifty Seabees from a Naval Construction Regiment to deploy to Ali Al Salem and Al Jaber Air Bases in Kuwait. He had told his CENTCOM superiors that he needed them to "complete infrastructure improvements to operate Marine fixed wing aircraft in support of Operation ENDURING FREEDOM and future contingencies, due to insufficient parking ramp and ammunition storage area to support USMC aircraft." CENTCOM forwarded Hailston's request to the Joint Chiefs of Staff on August 13, 2002, and on September 2, the Joint Chiefs issued the necessary deployment order requiring both Air Dets to enter Kuwait and start work at Ahmed Al Jaber and Ali Al Salem within two weeks.[8]

As Kubic had originally planned, the Air Detachments (Dets) from NMCB 5 at Rota and NMCB 40 from Guam were tapped to undertake the early construction efforts in Kuwait. Equipment shipped from Rota would support both detachments, with select pieces of additional equipment and tools coming from Guam and the continental United States (CONUS). The Air Dets would also rent or lease other necessary equipment from Kuwaiti suppliers to hasten construction, and in certain cases, to get work started before the sea lifted materiel arrived.

Since the anticipated Kuwait/Iraq Theater of Operations lay within the designated area of responsibility of the 30th Naval Construction Regiment, Commodore Rudich and his staff at Pearl Harbor would provide overall project management and command support for the Detachments. Therefore, Rudich sent a small team led by Lieutenant Sean McNelis from the 30th Naval Construction Regiment to Kuwait to make preparations for the Air Dets' arrival and to expedite material procurement. McNelis subsequently arranged for the Dets' initial berthing, and successfully resolved final site and design issues, and also began identifying sources for select fill, concrete, and other items that were necessary to complete the project. Arriving on September 6, McNelis and his team became the first Seabees officially to "sneak" into Kuwait as part of Operation ENDURING FREEDOM.

The Joint Chiefs of Staff deployment order required both Air Dets to arrive on September 15. However, NMCB 40 had been scheduled to rotate home in mid-October. Its replacement would be the "Fearless" NMCB 74, which was about to deploy to Guam under Commander Clifford M. Maurer, an outstanding officer who, measuring just under six feet, eleven inches in height, had been a standout Naval Academy basketball player before entering the Civil Engineer Corps in 1984.

Rudich and Kubic both worked with MARCENT, CENTCOM, and the Pacific Command to have the deployment order adjusted to reflect the unit rotation. The Joint Chiefs of Staff subsequently issued a revised order sending an Air Det from NMCB 74 to Kuwait by October 15. It was expected that both units would be deployed for approximately ninety days to complete their work.

Early Seabee Projects in Kuwait

Following the arrival of McNelis and his team, a "forward" command element from the 30th Naval Construction Regiment and the 31st Seabee Readiness Group from Port Hueneme arrived on September 23 to take on-site charge of the bed down operations. That same day, the 1st Naval Construction Division renamed 30th Naval Construction Regiment/ 31st Seabee Readiness Group "Forward" as "Task Force Charlie"—with "Charlie" standing for "Construction"—and handed over operational control (OPCON) to MARCENT. Task Force Charlie then set up its headquarters at Ahmed Al Jaber Air Base, where the more extensive construction was required and would start first.[9]

Once the first two Seabee Air Dets and the 30th Naval Construction Regiment/ 31st Seabee Readiness Group forward command element arrived in Kuwait, MARCENT ordered them to complete a total of seven initial beddown projects. At Ahmed Al Jaber Air Base, the Seabees had to build the huge C-130 parking apron that would beddown the Marine F/A-18 fighters, and a munitions storage area (MSA) to store ordnance such as bombs, missiles, and ammunition.

Additionally, the Seabees had to make site preparations for the special aluminum matting (AM-2) parking areas needed to base Marine AV-8B Harrier attack jets. The AM-2 matting was an improved version of the heavy pierced steel planking used in World War II. Portable and tough enough to survive the rigors of flight operations, AM-2 matting consisted of steel rectangles coated with an epoxy nonskid material, and was available in both six and twelve foot lengths at one half inch thick and two feet wide. Construction crews assembled AM-2 in a brickwork pattern to form runways, taxiways, parking and other areas required for aircraft operations and maintenance. The Air Force had adopted it in 1965 for use in nearly all of its South Vietnam air bases, and AM-2 remained state of the art in expeditionary airfield construction. The Seabees, of course, were masters of its use. At Ali Al Salem Air Base, Seabees had to start similar projects, including a Munitions Supply Area and more site preparations for AM-2 matting for helicopter pads.

The aircraft apron and Munitions Supply Area at Ahmed Al Jaber were large military construction (MILCON) projects and funding had to be rerouted from other MILCON projects elsewhere in the world, requiring both Defense Emergency Relief Fund (DERF) authorization and Congressional notification. Once Congress was notified, a statutory fifteen-day waiting period ensued, during which Congress could either comment or object to the redirected funding. If fifteen days passed without congressional objection, then the Seabees could use the money. Both military construction projects cost $6.7 million and $1.4 million, respectively, with the cost for all seven projects totaling $8.85 million. MARCENT did not expect any problems on the money front, but the wheels of bureaucracy ground slowly. Congress was to be notified on August 18, with expected approval by September 1, but the Pentagon failed to send its formal notification until October 16. As a result, the required funding only became available on October 31, and was released the next day.

The release of the Defense Emergency Relief Funds finally allowed the Seabees to start work on all of their projects. This sixty-day delay required considerable acceleration of the construction effort to meet the December 31 completion deadline. Unfortunately, a combination of the standard Kuwaiti bureaucracy, security issues, material shortages, and climate would eventually push the projects' completion dates into January.

The Kuwaiti government seemed to miss no opportunity to impede the Seabees' work. The Kuwaitis insisted upon formally reviewing the scope and sites for all projects to ensure that they were compatible with their master plans for both bases. They then closed all of their open pit quarries from November 5-13, ostensibly for environmental reasons, thereby causing a serious shortage of local select fill needed for the parking apron's sub-bases. On December 26, the Kuwaitis once again slowed progress by impounding some four hundred HESCO (Hercules Engineering Solutions Consortium) blast protection barriers, which were filled with a mixture of sand, dirt and gravel and designed to defeat suicide vehicle bombers. Its timing was suspicious, and many Seabees believed that this petty act of bureaucracy was part of a larger Kuwaiti effort to pressure the Air Force into paying customs duties on imported materials. This issue was not resolved until January 10, 2003, when Kuwaiti officials finally released the anti-terrorist barriers.

U.S. Air Force security requirements at Ahmed Al Jaber caused further delays. Because of the asymmetric nature of the Islamic terrorist threat, and with the 1996 Khobar Towers truck bombing still fresh in Air Force minds, the Kuwaitis and other Arabs and foreigners working near the project sites were immediately suspect. Consequently, the Air Force ordered every civilian contractor entering the air base to be searched and escorted by his sponsor. During the early phases of the aircraft apron project, this requirement severely impacted the completion schedule by diverting Seabees from their construction work to security escort duty. The security regime became so onerous that Kubic ultimately had to send, on November 23, another one hundred and fifty Seabees from NMCB 74 to Kuwait from Guam and Puerto Rico to pick up the slack.[10]

Unprecedented foul weather also played havoc with the construction schedule. The months of October, November, and December were exceptionally wet and the area received three times the yearly average rainfall for the period. Both earth preparation and concrete work on the aircraft parking apron project necessarily had to be shut down intermittently as a relentless succession of cold fronts passed through the region.[11]

An acute materials shortage resulted in one final delay. Ongoing commercial construction of buildings and roads in Kuwait required a lot of concrete, and this was a material Maurer's Seabees desperately needed in vast quantities to complete the apron. As a result, local vendors were unable to supply enough concrete to meet both the Seabees' military demand, which was on the order of one thousand cubic yards per day, and Kuwaiti demand for private construction. The four local contractors, whom we had working concurrently, would bring as much product as they could each day, but it was never enough. One of the site's foremen, Chief Builder Wayne Jensen, later told Navy journalists that "we poured as much as they supplied." "At one point," echoed Chief Builder Ray Roberts, "we actually had some down time because they just couldn't bring us the material as fast as we could place it."[12]

The Ahmed Al Jaber parking apron and taxiway was the largest concrete placing project since the construction of an enormous aircraft carrier pier and an adjoining 8,000 foot runway at Subic Bay in the 1950s. It absorbed most of the Seabees' manpower and resources in Kuwait during this time, with the actual direct labor on the project requiring on average between one hundred fifty and one hundred eighty-five Seabees on a daily basis. Given sixty days to complete the project, our Seabees had to work twenty-four hours per day, seven days per week (excepting an eighteen-hour Christmas holiday), to try to meet the December 31 deadline.[13]

The project had actually started on November 6th once funding had been approved, and the site had required two weeks of excavation, grading, and filling. During this process, the Seabees moved over one and a half million cubic feet of earth and laid down and compacted over one hundred thousand cubic feet of fill for the apron's base and sub-base. To ensure proper drainage, they had to build the entire apron with a 0.5% slope, requiring them to elevate the west end more than five feet above initial grade, working only in six inch lifts at a time. The tedious procedure called for them to place the fill material, roll it flat, check its compaction, and then move on to place another six inches of material.[14]

The first concrete pour occurred on November 25, with regular pours continuing nonstop through January 9, when the last concrete truck finally rolled offsite. To place the magnitude of this job in perspective, a big pour for Seabees is over one hundred cubic yards per day. However, by the end of the project, Maurer's crew was literally placing over one thousand cubic yards a day, and once even did over fifteen hundred cubic yards.[15]

The working conditions for NMCB 74's Air Det Seabees were tough as well. Aside from the wet and frigid weather, their working days were extremely long, averaging sixteen to seventeen hours. To keep them going, Maurer had food delivered directly to them at the job site. Kubic and Rudich were simply amazed at their perseverance and valor under such adverse circumstances, especially after they saw a photograph of a young Seabee who had fallen asleep at the apron while sitting knee deep in wet concrete.

The aircraft apron ultimately measured twenty-two acres (720 feet by 1,156 feet) in size and was twelve inches thick, with two 450-foot by seventy-five foot taxiways connecting it to Ahmed Al Jaber's runway. It had consumed some 38,500 cubic yards of concrete and over 55,000 feet of reinforcing steel. After the final concrete pour on January 9, Maurer's Seabees had to spend another three weeks finishing it. This entailed over twenty-three miles of saw cuts and joint sealing before Maurer declared it complete on January 31. On February 2, Groundhog Day, Rear Admiral Kubic accompanied a number of Kuwaiti dignitaries to the site and led a ribbon cutting ceremony for the new aircraft apron. The first Marine F/A-18's landed there shortly thereafter.[16]

While NMCB 74's Air Det persevered to complete the Ahmed Al Jaber aircraft apron, NMCB 5, under Commander David L. Fleisch, tackled the other projects. NMCB 5's initial 125-person Air Det had flown from Rota into Kuwait from September 27 through 30. After the Kuwaitis had approved the planned bed down projects, the Det had broken ground on a "hot pit" refueling pad project at Ahmed Al Jaber on October 2, using equipment that had been flown in along with its personnel. Following a three-week voyage from Rota, Spain, the Merchant Vessel (MV) *Greenwave* finally arrived in Kuwait on October 22 carrying NMCB 5's heavy equipment, eleven days after its Air Det had started building the Munitions Storage Area at Ali Al Salem.[17]

"Material Breach"

The work soon took on new urgency as political indicators began pointing increasingly toward war. On October 16, 2002, President Bush signed the hotly debated House Joint Resolution 114 into law, which authorized the U.S. to use force if necessary to disarm Iraq. Armed with this blank check, Bush tightened the screws on the U.N. and Iraq even further. After an intense round of diplomatic and political maneuvering, the U.S. and Britain pushed Resolution 1441 through the U.N. Security Council on November 8. The resolution held Iraq in "material breach" of all previous resolutions, beginning with 687 from 1991, and gave Saddam a last chance to disarm under the threat of "serious consequences." He had thirty days to openly declare all of Iraq's nuclear, biological, and chemical warfare programs, and forty-five days to re-admit U.N. weapons inspectors into Iraq with unimpeded access to his palaces, laboratories, and other potential weapons facilities.[18]

Saddam responded by allowing weapons inspectors, led by the head of the United Nations Monitoring, Verification and Inspection Commission (UNMOVIC), Dr. Hans Blix, to reenter Iraq on November 27. On December 7, Saddam also released a 11,790-page dossier supposedly outlining the information required by Resolution 1441. However, on December 19, Secretary of State Colin Powell called it "a catalogue of recycled information and flagrant omissions" and all but pronounced Iraq in material breach of the U.N. resolutions. The inspections would take time though, and the Bush Administration was prepared to go along with them for the time being to buy itself some more time to deploy and prepare a sufficient combined joint invasion force to Kuwait.[19]

An "Internal Look"

As domestic and international political tensions over Iraq escalated, CENTCOM quietly continued its preparations. In November, General Tommy Franks transmitted to Secretary of Defense Rumsfeld and to the Joint Chiefs of Staff CENTCOM's official request for deployment of the "Pre-N-Day" force, which comprised those troops that President Bush would have to commit to the region before he could make any decision to go to war. To avoid any unwarranted media attention, Franks planned this initial deployment to occur as a series of training exercises and troop-level increases, ostensibly because of increased Iraqi intransigence in the no-fly zones. In retrospect, the Defense Department and CENTCOM really did not fool anyone with their "discreet" build-up since the mainstream media was so focused on Iraq at that time. The request was necessarily large, totaling some 128,000 Soldiers, Sailors, Airmen, and Marines, all of whom who would be slated to arrive in the region by February 15, 2003. Additionally, Franks requested that the Pre-N-Day force be "augmented," beginning on N-Day, by Special Mission Units and additional Navy and Air Force personnel, bringing the total up to over 200,000 troops before "G-Day." To keep all options open, he also asked the Defense Department to alert the U.S. Army's 101st Airborne Division, follow-on support units, and more Special Forces to be able to deploy by March 20, 2003.[20]

General Franks' requests for forces required a number of incremental deployments of between 25,000 and 35,000 active duty personnel each, as well as an initial call-up of some 20,000 reservists. The Defense Department scheduled the first of these to occur after Christmas to lessen the impact upon service families. In the meantime, Franks continued honing OPLAN 1003 at his CENTCOM headquarters in Qatar, which had recently been constructed with the help of a detachment of Seabee reservists from Construction Battalion Maintenance Unit (CBMU) 303. There, Franks conducted a four-day high-tech computer and communications war game called INTERNAL LOOK that was billed to the press as a routine exercise previously held in 1990, 1996, and 2000. But it was really a dry-run of his latest war plan revision to determine what would theoretically happen if he invaded Iraq using his current command, control, and communications configuration, as well as his projected force levels.[21]

The results were decidedly disappointing. Analysis showed that his troops, which were significantly lighter than those used in DESERT STORM, were neither flexible enough nor fast enough to achieve their military and political goals quickly in the event of war with Iraq. It was obvious that a lot more work needed to be done before CENTCOM would be ready to take on Saddam any time soon.

Camp Construction

War was becoming increasingly more likely, perhaps coming as early as January 1st, but more probably within the February 15 timeframe. Marines and other forces were encountering deployment delays, and Kubic and his staff began making further preparations for the expected influx of Seabees that would be needed to support CENTCOM's planned build-up. During his August 2002 site visit with Conway, he had realized that the Seabees would eventually need a logistics base as well as a headquarters.

Kubic looked at both Ahmed Al Jaber and Ali Al Salem air bases since both were strategically positioned just outside of Kuwait City. The more developed, more crowded Ahmed Al Jaber was nicer, having supported the United States Air Force as it enforced Iraq's southern "no-fly" zone. It would also be the construction site for the intended Marine aircraft apron and the 3rd Marine Aircraft Wing's Combat Operations Center. But from his earlier time in Kuwait, the admiral was more familiar with Ali Al Salem, which was more suited for rotary wing aircraft and air cargo operations. He thought it would be a better camp site for the Seabees since its runway could handle very large cargo planes such as C-17 Starlifters and C-5 Galaxies. It was a better air head, a little closer to the port, and had more wide open areas where the Seabees could build their own camp, "out of sight, out of mind." Moreover, it was adjacent to the base's "diamond" shaped helicopter parking area and would share a common boundary with a future tent camp that would house 3rd Marine Aircraft Wing personnel.

With this preference in mind, Kubic consulted with the Kuwaitis and the U.S. Air Force base commanders at both Ahmed Al Jaber and Ali al Salem, and then formally chose the Ali Al Salem site for the Seabees primary logistics and follow-on training base. Since NMCB 74 was busy building the Ahmed Al Jaber parking apron, the 1st Naval Construction Division issued, through Task Force Charlie, a Fragmentary Order (FRAGO) to NMCB 5 on October 26 to build the new tent camp at Ali Al Salem. Plans called for it to accommodate 250 Seabees initially, and Rudich's Seabees proposed naming it "Camp Moreell," after Rear Admiral Ben Moreell, the World War II founder of the Seabees. This was a most appropriate name in Kubic's opinion and he immediately approved their recommendation. While construction proceeded, a temporary encampment at Ahmed Al Jaber would be used until NMCB 5 completed the new Camp Moreell.

The recent arrival of Seabee reinforcements from NMCB 74 to bolster the aircraft apron project required additional berthing and logistics facilities. The 1st Naval Construction Division therefore issued another fragmentary order to NMCB 5 through MARCENT on December 23, ordering the enlargement of Camp Moreell to accommodate up to 500 Seabees. This work was completed by mid-January 2003. Task Force Charlie also built another camp eighteen miles north of the city of Al Jahra, very near the Iraqi border. The Seabees named it "Camp 93" in memory of the passengers of United Airlines Flight 93, who rallied against their Al Qaeda hijackers on 9/11, and prevented the terrorists from flying their plane into either the White House or the Capitol, at the cost of their lives. Camp 93 would become the MEG's "Southern Bridge Park," in which Class IV construction materials and bridging equipment would flow from the port in Kuwait City. From Camp 93, the materials could then be staged, loaded, and transported by convoy into Iraq and ultimately to MEG units from an anticipated Northern Bridge Park, later known as "Bridge Park Davisville," after the Seabees' former Rhode Island base.[22]

Later described by one young Seabee as "a collection of large tents in the middle of the barren desert," Camp 93 would later become famous in the media for the sign posted on its front gate bearing the slogan, "Let's Roll!" These were the last words uttered by Flight 93 passenger Todd Beamer before he took part in the doomed counterattack against his plane's hijackers. Their inclusion on the sign, as well as the camp's provocative name, reflected the Seabees' fundamental belief that what they were doing in Kuwait was an important part of our Nation's larger war on global terror. Further, by helping rid the world of Saddam Hussein, many of them felt they were participating in a greater cause that would change the course of history, and make the world a much safer place for them and their families.[23]

Additional Equipment Arrives

While managing the initial construction projects in Kuwait, the 1st Naval Construction Division began sending additional equipment into theater. Fortunately for the Seabees, the process was based upon the "lessons learned" from the last Iraqi war and Kubic's Seabee Light Regiment concept. Previously, when the Seabees had deployed to Saudi Arabia for DESERT SHIELD/DESERT STORM, their Table of Allowance gear and equipment had been moved from main body deployment sites in Guam and Roosevelt Roads and also from Prepositioned War Reserve Material System (PWRMS) warehouses in Gulfport and Port Hueneme. The flow of equipment had ultimately met mission requirements, but it was slow and awkward in coming. For example, NMCB 40 had packed up its Table of Allowance on Guam and was unable to work productively while they awaited shipping to Saudi Arabia. Once they left, another Table of Allowance had to be shipped from Port Hueneme to Guam to support reserve NMCB 23 that had been mobilized and deployed to Guam as a replacement battalion. Basically, two Tables of Allowance had to be moved just to get one into the Gulf Theater of Operations. As a result, two Battalions had endured low productivity periods awaiting shipping of their gear and equipment.

The Maritime Prepositioned Force (Enhanced) – MPF(E) – fixed this problem and increased the speed and agility of Seabee contingency response exponentially. Through the efforts of many dedicated individuals within the Naval Construction Force, the Naval Facilities Engineering Command, and the Chief of Naval Operations staff, Seabee gear and equipment had been loaded on MPF(E) ships in the decade since Operation DESERT STORM. As a result, it was all ready to go without having to shuffle Seabee units and their Tables of Allowance inefficiently around the globe when deployment orders came.

Seabee employment of MPF(E) Tables of Allowance was made even more agile by an innovative modular packing and loading concept in which battalion Tables of Allowance were standardized into six modules and spread loaded among two or three MPSRON ships. Each Table of Allowance included three Core Modules (CMs) which would support 250 Seabees. Each Core Module had an imbedded Air Det Table of Allowance (MCA) designed to support a heavy Air Det of 125 Seabees. The Table of Allowance also included a Basic Module, designed to support camp sustainment, and a Heavy Module, designed to support and sustain expanded horizontal operations. Finally a Fly-In Echelon was configured to include the basic gear, weapons and equipment that would not be loaded onboard the MPSRON, so that it could fly in with the Seabees to join up with their MPF (E) gear and equipment.

The Modular Table of Allowance and the MPF (E) were the fundamental innovations that clearly enabled Seabee speed and ultimate success in Operation IRAQI FREEDOM. Initially, two Core Modules were shipped from Rota Spain to Kuwait to enable two 250-man detachments from NMCBs 5 and 74 to move into theater. The Table of Allowance in Guam was not moved, and the two Core Modules from Rota were quickly and efficiently replaced by moving assets from Gulfport.

As a consequence of the Modular Table of Allowance innovation, the lead elements of two NMCBs were positioned in Kuwait with gear and equipment by initially moving less than one Table of Allowance, in sharp contrast to the former Concept of Operations that required two full Tables of Allowance to be moved to position initial Seabee forces during DESERT STORM. It remained to be seen how well the new system would work when CENTCOM ordered a more substantial deployment of Marines and Seabees.

That deployment order came in October, when Request For Forces/Deployment Order 164 sent I MEF's tactical and rear command posts to CENTCOM's Area of Responsibility (AOR). General Conway offered each MEF subordinate command the opportunity to sea lift equipment and gear to support their efforts as part of this deployment order. At this point, I MEF had not formally recognized the MEG as a Major Subordinate Command despite Conway's standing order that there would be a MEG for this campaign. Consequently, the Seabees were left out of the loop. Kubic raised the alarm about this oversight, and Conway ordered that Seabees be given space alongside the other subordinate commands during the shipment. Because of the delay though, the Seabees at Gulfport and Port Hueneme found it nearly impossible to locate and prepare the necessary command gear in time for the ships' departure.[24]

To make the most out of this fleeting opportunity, Kubic approved Rudich's recommendation that embarking three echelons of the Reserve Naval Construction Support Force Unit (NCFSU) 2, based in Port Hueneme, was the best option under the circumstances. Each echelon consisted, respectively, of long haul trucking, earth moving, and various logistics/headquarters equipment. The admiral approved them for immediate shipment because they were heavy and could not be flown into Kuwait if needed on short-notice. In all, 272 pieces of equipment were prepared and moved in very short order from Port Hueneme to San Diego, California and from Gulfport to Charleston, South Carolina.

The cost to unpack, clean, and reactivate the heavy construction equipment and to purchase repair parts was roughly $2 million. The Pacific Fleet Command (COMPACFLT) came through with strong support for the deployment, and supplied the necessary funds in less than twenty-four hours after Kubic requested the money. On 24 October, the Seabees loaded this heavy equipment aboard the fast sealift ship, USNS *Bellatrix* (T-AK-288), which subsequently arrived in Kuwait City's harbor on November 16 after a three-week voyage. This equipment complemented the twenty-eight other pieces of equipment that the Seabees had loaded aboard the same ship to augment the pre-positioned gear already in Bahrain.

The 1st Naval Construction Division originally meant for the Bahrain-bound equipment to be pre-positioned in the Middle East on a contingency basis. But it was apparent that all pre-positioned equipment would be critical for a possible early ground war since the Maritime Pre-positioning Force and other shipping resources were suffering persistent movement and off loading delays, leaving the Seabees in Kuwait without sufficient equipment to support a sudden Marine movement north. Needless to say, the Seabees working in Kuwait were ecstatic when the *Bellatrix* arrived with their own long-awaited heavy equipment. More would be shortly forthcoming.

In early December, the 1st Naval Construction Division sent word to Task Force Charlie that two Maritime Pre-positioning Ship Squadrons from the U. S. Navy's Military Sealift Command would be arriving shortly in Kuwait harbor loaded with additional equipment. To meet the delivery, Maurer pulled Chief Equipment Operator Charles "Chuck" Hair from the aircraft apron project and sent him to the port, which had never seen ships like those before, to supervise the offload. Because all available Seabees were needed for the apron, Hair took a group of Marines that had never done this kind of work before, plus a few Seabees posted at the port, and began offloading the first MPSRON that the Navy had employed since DESERT SHIELD/STORM.[25]

He had sixty-eight Marines and Seabees with him, and over the next six weeks, managed to offload 327 pieces of equipment and 114 containers from five ships. He moved it all fifty-eight miles inland to Camp Moreell for assembly, and then forwarded it on to the Camp 93 assembly area near the Iraqi border. After completing this monumental task, Hair returned to Ahmed Al Jaber and helped put the finishing touches on the aircraft apron.

Despite some external complications and occasional friction, the new Modular Table of Allowance system worked very well for the Seabees. The Naval Construction Force shipped the complete Table of Allowance from Rota and backfilled in due course with another Table of Allowance from Gulfport. Two NMCB Tables of Allowance were offloaded from MPSRON ships, and an NMCB Table of Allowance and part of the NCFSU 2 Table of Allowance were shipped from Port Hueneme. In accordance with the emerging MEG Concepts of Operations, the incoming Tables of Allowance were then assigned to specific units to manage administratively, while the modules were deployed as required to the various task forces to support their respective missions. The MPF (E) initiative, combined with the modular Table of Allowance concept, was ultimately a huge operational success in Kubic's estimation, with credit due to all those who labored so hard to make it work.

CHAPTER 5

Bridging Issues

While the Seabees labored in Kuwait during the late autumn and early winter of 2002, the 1st Naval Construction Division and the 30th Naval Construction Regiment focused on planning for future operations. Commodore Rudich had arrived in Kuwait from Pearl Harbor in mid-November, but Rear Admiral Kubic's headquarters was still at 1st Naval Construction Division in Little Creek, Virginia. The MEG staff at this point was comprised of Rudich's 30th Naval Construction Regiment command element as well as an ad hoc "pick-up" team from four or five different active and reserve interservice commands. Field-grade Marines were conspicuously sparse, and Kubic's plan to have a joint MEG staff of Seabees and Marines did not come together very well as they moved into Kuwait. As a result, the bulk of the work fell upon the 30th Naval Construction Regiment, and it had to plan and execute Task Force Charlie's ongoing construction work in Kuwait and staff the advance cadre of the MEG command element tasked with planning for potential war in Iraq.

Furthermore, Rudich found himself having to wear essentially four hats—as commander of the 30th Naval Construction Regiment, commander of the current Task Force Charlie, commander of the future Task Force Mike, and the deputy MEG commander. Keeping four balls in the air was daunting, to say the least, and Rudich was later quoted as saying, "I am so busy, I don't know if I'm coming or going...I was going out the gate and I met myself coming in." Kubic was sure if asked how he did it, Commodore Rudich would deflect credit from himself and praise his "Can Do!" staffs for handling all of those simultaneous and chaotic taskings. But from the admiral's perspective, Rudich was the leader in Kuwait during this period, and did a heck of a good job building and getting Seabees ready to fight.[1]

Semi-Permanent Bridging & Class IV Material Procurement

During most of the Operational Planning Team (OPT) sessions and MEF exercises conducted in the late summer and fall of 2002, the 30th Naval Construction Regiment necessarily functioned as the nucleus of the joint MEG staff, which altogether numbered less than fifty Seabee and Marine personnel at this point. The OPTs centered on several key issues, the most important of which was the procurement of Class IV heavy construction materials and semi-permanent nonstandard bridging for a number of key waterways located along the Marines' expected axis of advance within the Tigris-Euphrates valley. Although these material and bridging procurement issues had been raised in every exercise for over a year, it took an immense Seabee effort to help I MEF and MARCENT "snatch victory from the jaws of neglect" since no one wanted to spend any money until they were sure Marines were really going to war or at least until they were sure their budgets would be reimbursed.

The MEF Engineer had assembled (without Seabee input) a massive list of class IV requirements during the MEFEX held in August 2002. This list was apparently compiled using "better safe than sorry" criteria, and outlined all the raw materials that the Marine engineers believed would be needed to support projected bridging operations in Iraq. In reality, this material list was not tied closely to actual or projected work, was not vetted very well, and was frankly quite excessive. Nevertheless it became the official MEF list and created a huge funding hurdle that no one wanted to jump. In late November, the Seabees submitted an updated list showing the material essential to cross the Line of Departure (L/D). Total requirements, including bridging, were estimated in excess of $60 million for a worst case scenario, while less than $20 million was needed immediately to ensure the MEG was combat capable by February 15, 2003.

Adding to Kubic's concerns, I MEG did not have a fully executable plan for crossing the seven potential river crossing "wet gaps" (rivers, deep streams, and canals) on Iraqi Highways 1 and 7 which either the Iraqis or Coalition forces were likely to create through demolition of existing bridging. By Western standards, the roads to Baghdad were in poor condition. The state of the roads, with their severe washes and unfinished construction, aggravated the already looming threat of bridge destruction. Gaps scattered along major avenues of approach could effectively impede the Marines and endanger their mission of defeating Saddam's forces and reaching Baghdad quickly under the evolving OPLAN, now called 1003 Victor, or 1003V.[2]

The bridging problem, interestingly enough, was reminiscent of an earlier military campaign in the region that has largely been forgotten over the past two or three generations. This was the disastrous British 'Basrah to Baghdad' campaign against the Turks during World War I, which had resulted in the destruction of an entire British division at Al Kut and ultimately cost over 80,000 British casualties, with nearly 29,000 dead. Marine Reserve Colonel Michael C. Howard, commanding officer of the 4th Combat Engineer Battalion, who had been on the MEF staff when Gen Zinni first created the MEG and would later augment the MEG staff, had recently written an excellent *Marine Corps Gazette* article about the debacle, and it was very much on Kubic's mind during this planning period.[3]

Although the anticipated Marine and Army axes of advance toward Baghdad would be farther west than the old British route from Basrah, Howard's historical analysis offered three important lessons for the MEG planners. First, the British military leadership had stayed in India and was out of touch with real time operations in Mesopotamia. Second, their field logisticians had remained in Basrah, and as British forces moved away from that city and into the Mesopotamian interior, their supply lines became overextended and eventually snapped. And finally, Iraq's rivers "kicked their butts," and without sufficient engineers, they had trouble coping with both high and low water areas.

Needless to say, the Marines and Seabees earnestly wanted to avoid the same mistakes made by the British in 1916, and so MARCENT and I MEF resolved early on that additional bridging would be required to support the Coalition attack. The overall bridging plan that ultimately emerged called for 2nd Force Service Support Group's 8th Engineer Support Battalion to span critical gaps immediately during the attack and while under fire with its assault bridging, including AVLBs (armored vehicle launched bridge), Ribbon Bridges (also known as Assault Float Bridges), and Medium Girder Bridges (MGBs).

I MEG, which would follow directly behind the attacking 1st Marine Division and Task Force Tarawa, would then replace the assault bridges with a more robust and semi-permanent "line of communication" bridging. This bridge tactic would allow heavier follow-on forces to move north quickly in support of the advancing attack. The MEG would then recover 8th Engineer Support Battalion's assault bridges and push them forward where they could be re-utilized. This system of "leap-frogging" would be repeated throughout the attack. However, intelligence was sketchy about the rivers and waterways, and MEG planners knew next to nothing about their currents or bottoms, which made the anticipated bridging operations extremely uncertain and perilous.

Unfortunately, the early Seabee effort to solve the semi-permanent bridging problem with a single solution was more difficult than first anticipated. Detailed engineering work on this problem started in the summer of 2002, when Kubic "exercised" NAVFAC's Pacific Division engineers to demonstrate their contingency responsiveness by recalling them to work over a weekend. The engineers had a "hypothetical" problem to solve – design an expeditionary, semi-permanent river crossing. Kubic suggested the use of culverts, much like those which NMCB 3 had used in the wide flood plains of Tunisia in 1990 when he had served as its commanding officer. During that deployment, NMCB 3's Air Det, during a disaster recovery operation dubbed, Operation ATLAS RAIL, was sent to Tunisia to repair a rail line breached in several locations by a flash flood. The Det successfully repaired all the breaches, small and large, using culvert and fill construction techniques, which required horizontal, side-by-side emplacement of large pipe culverts into the gaps to provide conduits for the water. These culverts were then covered with sand and soil to make roadways.

For obvious reasons, the Pacific Division engineers did not fully appreciate that this exercise was a real effort in support of the "road to war" in Iraq. Believing their weekend work was only in support of an exercise, they quickly prepared a culvert-based river crossing design, without any real analysis, and turned in their "homework assignment." Kubic and the leadership of the 30th Naval Construction Regiment, caught up in the MEG's early "growing pains," evolving Seabee maneuver doctrine, and the logistics of Seabee Force redeployment, did not rigorously proof the design and just accepted it at face value. With no constructability review conducted, and hence no objections, the most critical element of the primary Seabee mission in support of the Marines in Iraq was put "on the shelf" as a flawed solution.

Unfortunately, the MEG then used the culvert design during subsequent OPTs and war games and sold it to the Marines as the preferred solution for all large wet gaps. This approach was perfectly acceptable for the vast majority of potential wet gaps on the road to Baghdad, but it was inadequate for the wide and deep crossings of rivers and major canals. But without other readily available expeditionary solutions on the table, the Seabees and Marines pressed on and began procuring the pipe culverts they would need to muscle themselves across the hundreds of wet gaps that would exist if Saddam blew every bridge and culvert along the way and flooded the Iraqi lowlands with water released from his dams.

When it came time to procure the pipe culverts, some innovative Seabees identified corrugated plastic culverts from a local supplier in Kuwait that were smaller than what they needed. They then talked the Kuwaiti vendor into manufacturing much larger, one-meter diameter culverts, and procured a virtual mountain of one-meter "white pipe" that would be necessary to support the Marines in the worst case scenario and without any other nonstandard bridging assets. Some Seabees also searched the internet and found 72-inch diameter corrugated metal pipe culverts which shipped in two sections and were bolted together on site. These "mini Quonset Hut" sections were procured in bulk as well. It was not the best solution in Kubic's view, but if the Seabees did not get any bridging, the Marines could still make it to Baghdad even under the worst of cases with these two types of culverts.

"Make the Rivers Fit the Bridges"

In late October 2002, the 30th Naval Construction Regiment sent the flawed river crossing design to NMCB 5 and NMCB 74 for planning preparation. Red flags immediately shot up from both battalions through the MEG command chain when they recognized that this solution would deteriorate quickly if the rivers were more than two meters deep or more than forty meters wide or had currents in excess of 0.5 knots. As a result, the 30th Naval Construction Regiment fired immediate and serious questions back to Hawaii about the construction feasibility and structural integrity of the pipe culvert "course of action (COA)." As the problem was studied more closely, the 30th Naval Construction Regiment's concerns were amplified further throughout the month of November 2002, and it became apparent that the Seabees (and by extension, the Marines) had a BIG problem. To address the more complex river and canal crossings which they would face, Kubic ultimately commissioned a bridge Operational Planning Team (OPT) to expand the available options so that the Seabees would not have to rely simply upon the pipe culvert Course of Action. This OPT was tasked to begin just after Thanksgiving once a quorum of principal leaders (both officers and senior enlisted) from NMCBs 5 and 74 had arrived in Kuwait.

Kubic had been pushing the Marine leadership to provide bridging funds since the summer of 2002 with no success. But now, time and money were really critical issues, and time was quickly running out. Steel bridge sets were expensive, and were not readily available. If bridge sets were to be used, the purchase, packaging and delivery to Kuwait needed to be scheduled immediately with the bridge manufacturers. In addition, operational units would have to be trained on assembly techniques, since bridge sets from various manufacturers are unique in their components and assembly. As of late November 2002, if the "go early and ugly" strategy that General Hailston had previously warned Kubic about was executed, with a January 2003 step-off date, the Seabees would not have had a viable means to cross all rivers and canals and, in his opinion, would most certainly have failed in their primary Marine support mission.

Realizing how critical the situation really was, Commander Maurer, commanding officer of "Fearless" NMCB 74, had discussed this problem informally with his civilian engineer friends from the U.S. Army Corps of Engineers, and had come up with some good ideas, including the use of mole piers (earthen structures protruding into the rivers) and "erector set" style nonstandard steel bridging. Right after Thanksgiving, Kubic returned to the U.S. for a short time and then planned to return to Kuwait via Bahrain where he would attend meetings with Generals Hailston and Conway. As he was departing Kuwait, Maurer and Lieutenant Commander Patrick Garin (NMCB 74's Operations Officer) met with him at the transient VIP quarters at Ahmed Al Jaber Air Base. There, they discussed the pros and cons of both the pipe culvert and possible mole pier bridging strategies. Kubic listened intently to Maurer's discussion on the merits of a mole pier approach, and encouraged him to advance his ideas further through the OPT process. Before adjourning their impromptu meeting, Kubic also asked Maurer and Garin to do everything in their group's power to develop more viable river crossing options quickly.

The admiral then returned home briefly to Little Creek to make final preparations for shifting his flag to Kuwait in anticipation of a possible "Go" order from I MEF. The new bridge OPT began on November 26, 2002. It was held at the 30th Naval Construction Regiment's camp at Ali al Salem Air Base inside a Southeast Asia Hut (Seahut) that was built as a field SCIF (Sensitive Compartmented Information Facility), where classified information could be openly displayed and discussed. The leadership teams from both battalions and regimental staff officers and chiefs toiled over improving the pipe culvert Course of Action, and diligently explored other ideas, such as placing pre-fabricated timber bents, using shipping containers as bents, and constructing concrete box culverts. But each option they considered had major shortcomings, and they kept coming back to a more viable approach to cross Iraq's wet gaps using nonstandard steel bridging.

Once the OPT was under way, Maurer requested permission from Rudich to consult formally with his engineer friends at ERDC (Engineer, Research and Development Center) in Vicksburg, Mississippi. Maurer had worked with this Army Engineer organization while serving as Operations Officer of NMCB 40 in 1996 during Operation JOINT ENDEAVOR in Bosnia, and found that they were undoubtedly America's foremost experts on military bridging solutions.

Rudich granted permission for Maurer to consult formally with ERDC. With the assistance of Lieutenant Colonel Gary Grey (USA) of the Combined Forces Land Component Commander (CFLCC) – located at Camp Doha, he was able to arrange a secure video-teleconference on December 3, 2002, with ERDC's Tele-Engineering Operations Center (TEOC). During the teleconference, Maurer described the bridging mission that confronted the Seabees and the multitude of unknown physical conditions of the Iraqi waterways which would be critical in developing a single solution that could be universally applied to the wet gaps. With remarkable response, only two days later, two engineers from ERDC, Dr. Rick Olsen (specializing in soils and foundations) and Mr. Geraldo Valezquez (a structural/bridge expert) arrived in Kuwait for further consultations.

Immediately after his teleconference, Maurer briefed Kubic via telephone, and the admiral approved his request for on site Corps of Engineers support with the condition that three engineers (Melvin Tsutahara, Kirby Hong, and Keith Kayashi) from the Navy's Pacific Division also come to Kuwait since they would be the MEG's enduring reach back support from Seabee Bunker in Pearl Harbor. Together, the five civilian engineers reviewed the Operational Planning Team's work and confirmed that the culvert solution was not viable for all potential wet gaps, given the known information on the particular Iraqi waterways the Marines would face as they moved north. The unknown soil conditions of the Iraqi rivers and their banks became the most vexing issue, with the key question being, "How would we bridge a wet gap if that gap was greater than 160 feet across, as many of them were?"

Dr. Olsen poured over multitudes of intelligence photos of the bridges and probable river crossing locations, both satellite photos and pictures taken from recently flown UAV (unmanned aerial vehicle) missions. He astutely concluded that the Iraqis' use of mole piers as work platforms when constructing their permanent bridges could indeed be replicated by U.S. contingency engineer forces such as the Seabees. Olsen's observations, coupled with his assurance that Seabees could achieve adequate bearing strength to support the reaction points of a 200-foot steel bridge, stimulated the thinking of Maurer and a few other Seabees, but did not immediately lead to another, more viable Course of Action.

When Kubic returned to Kuwait a couple of weeks later, he went immediately to Ali Al Salem to receive the Operational Planning Team's "out brief" on all the issues it had considered and the options it had analyzed. During the meeting, which took place on December 19, 2002, Maurer and the ERDC and Pacific Division engineers briefed the admiral on the six different wet gap crossing Courses of Action which they had come up with since his last discussion with Maurer. Since the Marines' required a "line of communication" bridge that could support their 70-ton Abrams main battle tanks, the only viable solutions that his group presented were those incorporating sixty meter Class-70 "Compact 200 Super Logistics Support Bridges" manufactured by the Mabey & Johnson Company in Britain, along with various ideas for river bank and mid-span abutments and supports. These pre-fabricated, modular, steel bridges were essentially updated versions of the old World War II military bridges designed by Sir Donald Bailey, which were most famously used by British and U.S. Army engineers during the Rhine crossings in March 1945.[4]

Kubic had been pushing MARCENT to buy Mabey & Johnson Bridges (MJBs) for many weeks by this point, and most recently at a General Officers' meeting in Bahrain in early December 2002. But,

MARCENT did not have the funding to commit to a Mabey & Johnson bridging solution. Unfortunately, the Operational Planning Team did not offer any other, more innovative approaches. The bottom line was that the rivers were too wide and too deep and the conditions too uncertain to develop a reliable expeditionary crossing solution for the targeted wet gaps without substantial amounts of Mabey & Johnson bridging. And even then, they did not have a plan for how to employ the limited lengths of Mabey & Johnson bridges the MEG Seabees might be able to procure to cross the many different widths of wet gaps they would face, including many gaps that were wider than the standard sixty meter logistics support bridge. The Operational Planning Team did an excellent job within the constraints they faced, but basically told Kubic "No Can Do!" The admiral was especially disappointed to learn that not much had happened with the mole pier idea.

Kubic quietly queried Maurer during a break about why his ERDC and Pacific Division group had not followed-up on their Thanksgiving meeting and moved forward with a solution incorporating the mole pier approach. He replied, quite cryptically, that he was "not at liberty" to discuss the matter with Kubic. The admiral had known Maurer since he was a Lieutenant and this sounded strange to him – in Kubic's opinion, he was no "shrinking violet." Kubic suspected that others who were more senior to the NMCB 74 commander had not seen the potential in the mole pier idea, and had remained focused on simply improving the pipe culvert plan when other "out of the box" ideas did not hold up well under close engineering scrutiny. Also, it appeared to Kubic that the Operational Planning Team was too large (over twenty officers and chiefs and civilians) and had been unable to develop any breakthrough ideas since it apparently conducted itself as a deliberating committee rather than as a focused engineering design team. So, attempting to hide his disappointment and frustration, Kubic thanked the team members for their hard work and for their briefing and then disbanded the OPT.

Based upon later recollections of what happened during the OPT, it appeared that Commodore Rudich had agreed with the team's findings and recommendations regarding Mabey & Johnson bridging, but was apparently unwilling to challenge the pipe culvert Course of Action since the MEG did not have funding to execute a Mabey & Johnson bridging Course of Action. Maurer, knowing the current pipe culvert Course of Action was a recipe for certain failure, sought permission to make the case directly to Kubic for a composite mole pier/Mabey & Johnson Course of Action, which Rudich granted.

Essentially, Maurer's plan incorporated mole piers of varying lengths with Mabey & Johnson bridges of varying lengths to ensure that the particular wet gap could be spanned using available materials and equipment - assuming of course that the MEG could get the required bridging. This approach would allow Seabees to reduce the wet gap distance and then select a Mabey & Johnson bridge that would span the existing gap.

The Mabey & Johnson Bridge & Mole-Bridge COA

Bailey bridging has always been a favorite logistics solution for American and British military engineers since World War II, and has withstood the test of time very well, with many still standing throughout Europe. Strong, reliable, and battle-tested, the bridges were originally designed to be erected quickly, using manpower alone, and allowed varying span lengths and carrying capacities. Though the original Bailey bridge was designed to support loads of up to only thirty tons (the weight of a Sherman tank) it could be configured to handle more modern requirements demanded a higher load capacity, sufficient to support a 70-ton Abrams tank.[5]

Accordingly, two former Royal Engineers, who founded the Mabey & Johnson Company and bought the rights to the Bailey design, dramatically improved it using modern techniques and capabilities, such as superior metallurgy and computerized structural analysis and modeling. For example, the bridge's panel chords and transoms were constructed of Grade 55C steel and all structural components were hot dip galvanized. It was capable of carrying loads of up to eighty tons (tracked) or one hundred ten tons (wheeled), and could withstand extremely harsh environments.

The modern Mabey & Johnson bridge could also be constructed as a single span up to sixty meters long, or in a multi-span configuration using intermediate piers or floating pontoons as supports. Further, it contained a simple bolt inventory (only six types), versus over forty different bolts in other bridges from competing manufacturers, and its heaviest piece weighed only 700 pounds (while other bridges contained 1,600-pound parts), meaning a six-man team could easily handle Mabey & Johnson bridge components. A Mabey & Johnson bridge was therefore relatively easy to transport and assemble and could easily be returned to stock after use. In fact, many Seabees were already quite familiar with it and fond of it, since NMCBs 1 and 4 trained with Mabey & Johnson bridges in the Philippines in previous deployments.

Despite the Mabey & Johnson bridge's obvious benefits, Kubic was displeased with the now-disbanded Operational Planning Team's recommended Course of Action since the Seabees did not have any bridging, had already committed to the original culvert design with the Marines, and had already started purchasing the materials to execute this particular, flawed Course of Action. The admiral was looking for innovation and did not find any. Moreover, it appeared that there simply was not enough time to purchase the new bridge sets, have them delivered to Kuwait, and train the Seabees destined for Task Force Mike on how to assemble them in a combat environment before the start of the impending operation. So, Kubic felt like they were stuck with the pipe culvert Course of Action and just had to live with it.

Seabee Jedi

At this point, disaster was clearly looming. It was almost January and the MEG had neither a solution nor money nor materials to support its primary mission. Kubic thought that it would be OK if this was just a drill, but bridging would become a showstopper if the attack actually proceeded. It was time to call upon Maurer directly with a small group of innovative young CEC officers and enlisted chief petty officers whom the admiral eventually titled, with great respect, "Seabee Jedi" after the "Jedi Knights" of the *Star Wars* movies whom these young Seabees admired in their even younger days. These "go-getters" would ultimately prove that "the force was with them" during Operation IRAQI FREEDOM.

The following Sunday afternoon, Kubic convened a design session at the MEG Command Operations Center (COC) at Camp Commando with a small, hand-picked engineering team that included "Master Jedi" Maurer, Lieutenant Commander Russ Seignious (a former Marine), Lieutenant Dave McAlister (Kubic's former aide), Lieutenant (Junior Grade) Eric Ulmen, and Chief Equipment Operator James Moran. McAlister and Seignious were the MEG's first real bridging experts since they had previously attended, along with a number of other Seabees, the annual I MEF Exercise (MEFEX) at Camp Pendleton, California in July 2002. This particular MEFEX was based on one of America's potential combat scenarios, and required a tremendous amount of bridging, which gave these two officers from the Future Operations cell a great deal of experience in that particular field and made them valuable additions to the MEG staff.[6]

Before getting down to business, Kubic told the team members that "You need to think like Expeditionary Engineers. Throw out the traditional designs and get creative!" They then rolled up their sleeves and went to work. The Seabee Jedi bounded the problems quickly, and developed a solution matrix for all possible crossing widths and water depths, and also developed a range of solutions for the most probable cases. The toughest possibility was unfortunately the most probable – crossing a one hundred-meter gap with three meters of water and a standard river current below one knot.

The team Kubic assembled soon confirmed the ERDC/Pacific Division group's original findings that the sixty-meter, Class 70, Compact 200 Mabey & Johnson bridge was their most flexible non-standard bridge component. Moreover, by constructing thirty-meter earth moles on either bank, the team also showed that a forty-meter wet gap could be achieved, which could then be spanned by a sixty-meter Mabey & Johnson bridge with ten meters of overlap on each mole. This design approach would provide a factor of safety against erosion, and created a wet gap that was still wide enough not to create an excessive venturi effect in the narrowed channel. In other words, instead of tailoring Mabey & Johnson bridging to fit each particular wet gap, Seabees could select a standard sixty-meter bridge, and by using appropriately sized earth moles, they could "make the rivers fit the bridge." This sounds like a rather simple concept, but it was very profound in its impact, and it had eluded the Seabees in all their prior discussions. Up until the time the Jedi convened, they were all too focused on the more standard approach of erecting customized bridges of various lengths for each potential gap.

The remaining problem, in addition to minimizing the actual amount of bridging components they would need, was how to construct and stabilize the earth moles. Sheet pile was the obvious answer if they could get equipment employed at the site and had sufficient time. But the MEG possessed only limited pile-driving equipment, making traditional construction of earth moles with sheet pile difficult. So the team needed an expeditionary solution as well. Ultimately, to facilitate stabilization of earth moles, Senior Chief Equipment Operator Charles Zimmerman, of NMCB 5, suggested buying standard sheet pile and placing it with an innovative MOVAC vibratory hammer.

This easily portable piece of construction equipment could be affixed to the end of a hydraulic tracked excavator's arm, in lieu of the bucket, and could be used to drive sheet piles. This simple solution would allow the Seabees to use their tracked excavators to prepare the soil at the bridge sites, to construct the sheet pile retaining walls for the mole piers, and then to serve as lifting cranes for the bridge erection. The ability to use a single piece of equipment for multiple functions allowed for redundancy without increasing overall equipment numbers, which was vital for high speed, maneuver warfare.

Unfortunately, sheet piles and MOVACs were not immediately available, and therefore could not be counted upon at that point to help get the Marines to Baghdad. But, what the MEG lacked in sheet piles and pile driving assets, it made up for in 36-inch plastic and 72-inch steel pipe culverts. The team started by exploring whether or not our 72-inch steel pipe culverts could be used in some fashion to construct temporary retaining structures for the river face of the earthen moles. During a much needed break, Lieutenant McAlister sat down and thought about this problem while playing with several empty toilet paper tubes. In the spirit of Archimedes, he had a sudden epiphany. He returned to the design session carrying six of the empty toilet paper rolls, tied them together in sets of three, and set them perpendicular on a table.

"What if we tied culverts together and placed them vertically along the mole's water edge? Would their weight keep them in place and allow them to serve as temporary sheet piles?" he asked. Elaborating further, he suggested that they could use the steel 72-inch steel sectional culverts (which had already been located for purchase in the U.S. and were to be flown into Kuwait by strategic airlift), bind them together in groups of three (or maybe four) with cable, place them vertically, and fill them with sand or dirt to form an expeditionary sheet pile barrier to protect the mole from erosion. Kubic immediately realized that this was the breakthrough the Future Ops team needed, and thus Dave McAlister's sand-pile-culvert-module, or SPCM (pronounced Spick-Um), was born. When SPCMs were added to the river bank at the water's edge of an earth mole, the "Mac Mole" was created.

Sand Pile Culvert Modules (SPCMs), Mac Moles, and MJBs

Over the course of the next few days, the Future Ops cell and the rest of the MEG staff developed the SPCM and Mac Mole concepts further. Through the 1st Naval Construction Division (Forward) Command Operations Center (Seabee Bunker) in Pearl Harbor, they requested that the Pacific Division's Civil and Structural Engineers provide "reach back" technical support and advice on the issue. During Christmas week, the Pacific Division engineers developed and supplied more detailed designs for the SPCM earthen moles. The designers originally envisioned the SPCM as modules of four culverts, fastened together at the center using all-thread bolt stock and linked between modules with angle iron clips.[7]

However, the construction details proved particularly challenging, as the engineers expressed three major concerns: first, the potential forces imparted on the SPCM's by the river current during construction (water flow at some locations approached two meters per second (3.9 knots)); next, the unknown soil and environmental conditions at the site (preliminary reports indicated that the river bed consisted of a soft silt layer over a clay base); and finally, the potential for excessive settlement and scour, especially at the now narrower river gap opening. To address these concerns and to ensure that Seabees could ultimately construct the SPCM within time constraints and using available materials, the MEG and Pacific Division conducted an iterative design process, and frequently exchanged e-mail and voice communications via Seabee Bunker.

The concept was refined even further over the next month, both through engineer analysis at the Pacific Division and hands-on training in Kuwait, wherein the Seabees would construct a bridge over a dry gap in the desert. In its final form, the SPCM design incorporated cells of three culverts bolted together to form one unit, which allowed both a tighter nestling of the components and reduced the chance of water infiltration. Bolts were placed directly through the culvert walls and external wrappings of high-strength steel cables replaced all-thread bolts from the original design. The engineers then incorporated a series of cross-laced steel cables to fasten the modules together. The SPCMs could then be lifted with a tracked excavator acting as a crane, placed one by one along the perimeter of the earth mole, and tied back into the earth mole itself.

Following emplacement, the SPCMs were then filled with spoil and the entire mole area was backfilled. Once filled with on-site material, the SPCMs formed a stable, integrated armor protecting the earthen mass. To alleviate scour concerns, the SPCMs had to be embedded at least 500 mm (eighteen inches) into the river bottom. Additionally, at the head of the narrowed gap, a second row of

SPCM's was placed on the outboard face to provide enhanced toe protection. Since placement of the SPCMs would be an expeditionary effort, on-going inspection and maintenance of the units were required for the duration of the crossing's use.

To ensure just-in-time procurement and delivery of the necessary Mabey & Johnson bridge sets, Kubic appointed McAlister as the Navy's representative in a joint Navy-USMC engineer delegation that toured Mabey & Johnson's sales center in London and the company's factory in Gloucester, England, in January 2003. There, McAlister and the Marine engineers met with Mabey & Johnson executives, who expressed a true desire to help I MEF and the other Coalition forces in any way they could. The company's management, comprised largely of retired Royal Engineers, offered to re-prioritize the bridges they were manufacturing to support I MEF with "head of the line" privileges. They also explained the quality control processes, and showed the Navy-USMC delegation what packaging options were available. The company would ultimately go so far as to send a couple of representatives to Kuwait to train the Seabees on particular bridges in different situations and configurations.[8]

A Comedy of Errors

During his visit, McAlister confirmed once and for all that the Mabey & Johnson product, in comparison to similar bridges made by competing companies, would be ideal for the expeditionary bridging that the Seabees and I MEF needed and was the best product choice for the anticipated mission inside Iraq. In the meantime, Kubic briefed the Mabey-Johnson bridge/SPCM plan to the I MEF commander, Lieutenant General Conway. Once he saw the whole solution laid out in clear and simple terms he realized how much the Marines needed this capability and approved the plan immediately. MARCENT followed suit and quickly provided the money to begin procurement. The MEG now had a fighting chance to get all of the necessary class IV materials and the Mabey & Johnson bridges required to cross the Line of Departure (L/D) by mid-February. But then the bureaucracy kicked in.[9]

The MEF Engineer decided to split the MARCENT Class IV material and bridging money between the Seabees and the Defense Logistics Agency (DLA) without consulting with the I MEF G4 logisticians, or MEG engineers. With good intentions, the MEF Engineer staff placed an order with the Defense Logistics Agency in Philadelphia that led to a comedy of bureaucratic errors, but no substantial Class IV material until well after the war's major combat operations were over. Fortunately, no Mabey & Johnson bridging was ordered through this source.

On the other hand, Seabee material procurement was handled either locally in Kuwait or by the Construction Battalion Center in Gulfport and managed by a Seabee Materials Liaison Officer (MLO). The Seabee MLO system was very efficient, had been perfected over decades of contingency construction experience, and began almost immediately to flow critical material to Kuwait by air and sea, all the while the MEF engineers' procurement remained stalled with the Defense Logistics Agency in Philadelphia. In some cases, materials ordered through the Defense Logistics Agency by the MEF had to be purchased again locally by Seabees to meet combat capability deadlines. Again, the Seabees muscled through the Class IV procurement process, assisting the MEF wherever possible. Due to intense effort by Seabees and Marines, the MEG went "fully green" for Class IV only a couple of days before D-day. "It was a good thing we didn't attack until March 20, 2003," Kubic later commented.

Bridging procurement was a different story and required great determination on the part of the MEG to overcome institutional resistance toward buying British Mabey & Johnson bridges. After the MEG decided to go with the SPCM/MJB plan in December, the Seabees were ready to order the bridging sets immediately upon receipt of funds through the Gulfport Construction Battalion Center. The Seabees had recently purchased the same type of bridge for training in the Philippines, but on the advice of a Marine Sergeant, a Marine Comptroller ruled that Mabey & Johnson bridges were "equipment" rather than "material" and could only be purchased with procurement rather than Operations and Maintenance (O&M) dollars. The Seabee comptroller was much more "construction-savvy" and recognized that the Mabey & Johnson bridge steel was merely a component in a non-standard bridge, and he was therefore ready to buy steel for construction with O&M dollars. The Marines still insisted on the more strict interpretation, and their financial managers caused significant delays while "the system" resolved the funding types and sources with which to pay for the bridges.

If this were not bad enough, once the procurement dollars were finally released, the Marine Corps Systems Command determined that a similar U.S. bridging system had to be procured rather than the British Mabey & Johnson system. The MEG went to great lengths to show the difference between the two systems, to point out that the Mabey & Johnson design could be erected without a crane using pins and six types of bolts while the American version used over forty different bolts and required a crane to erect – a good bridge, but not expeditionary. When the Marine Corps Systems Commander, Brigadier General William D. Catto, told Kubic that the contracting officer had concluded that the U.S. bridging was to be bought despite MEG objections, the admiral sent a "determined" e-mail to all concerned citing the high risk of failure associated with that approach. Ultimately, with General Catto's assistance, the logisticians and contracting officers listened to the engineers (possibly with some encouragement from their bosses), cancelled the order for the U.S. bridges, and ordered the Mabey & Johnson bridges.

Kubic's joy was short-lived when Murphy's Law kicked in and he found that somewhere in the Marine logistics system, someone had ordered the wrong bridge configurations. He or she had used an old list provided by the MEF Engineer without review by the MEG. But, not to be stopped at this point, the Jedi tackled the problem and quickly developed a list of Mabey & Johnson bridge components that the MEG needed to reconfigure the order to meet projected requirements as closely as possible. By this point the Marines had learned to trust the Seabee Future Operations cell, and they worked closely with them to negotiate a modification to the order.

At this point, Mabey & Johnson and the Seabees took over. Out of a strong sense of patriotism, the retired Royal Engineers who ran the Mabey & Johnson Company shipped the needed components on an expedited basis. The Seabees, for their part trained quickly and ultimately crossed the Line of Departure with Mabey & Johnson bridges without further incident. As it happened, the Marine Corps ultimately contracted for a total of 1,100 meters of Mabey-Johnson bridging, which was in turn broken down into two 300-meter bridges, two 200-meter bridges and one 100-meter bridge. Additionally, pontoons for a float bridge capability were purchased from the Flexi-Float Corporation in Texas. This package included eighty 40-foot and forty 20-foot pontoons. After a contract modification, the MEG received Mabey & Johnson bridge components that could be assembled into two 200-meter floating bridges, two 120-meter floating bridges, and eight 60-meter fixed bridges. All told, the two bridge contracts were funded at a bargain price of $15 million.

As a post script to the Class IV and bridging procurement debacle, the MEG ended up with too much floating bridging and too little fixed bridging. Also, too much culvert was ordered when it appeared that Mabey & Johnson bridges would not be bought and delivered on time. It would have been much better, in Kubic's opinion, to have given the engineers the money they needed early on and let them buy what they needed through Seabee procurement channels, which were very skilled and experienced in buying Class IV construction materials and bridges. Instead, Marines and Seabees had to muddle through the standard peacetime procurement system, which was not tuned to meet the timelines and specifications required to procure and construct the necessary "bridges to Baghdad" under intense combat conditions.

The MEG Stands Up

In addition to planning the Operation IRAQI FREEDOM missions and dealing with the Class IV and bridging issues, the 30th Naval Construction Regiment had to prepare to split its thirty-five member staff between what would become Task Forces Mike and Charlie. The MEG's need for mobility, combined with the expectation that all logistics, including construction material and spare parts, would have to come from Kuwait, drove the creation of the new Task Forces Mike and Charlie. Kubic tapped Commodore Will McKerall and a small staff contingent from the 22nd Naval Construction Regiment from Gulfport to lead the new Task Force Charlie. Unfortunately for Rudich, the MEG needed the bulk of the 30th Naval Construction Regiment's administrative, logistics, and equipment management personnel to remain behind in Kuwait to supervise the primary communications and logistics management systems needed to support the operation.[10]

This left Rudich with the exceedingly difficult task of deciding which staff members would stay with him in Task Force Mike and which ones would move to Task Force Charlie. Rudich understood that Mike's success would depend upon how well Charlie supported it, and so he knew he had to achieve skill and experience balance between the two task forces. Therefore, he had to distribute his small cadre of personnel so that the right people would land into the right jobs in both task forces.

McKerall's arrival in early January finally allowed the much-dreaded staff division to occur. McKerall's new Task Force Charlie, which incorporated incoming NMCB 133 and detachments from NMCB 5, NMCB 74, NCFSU 2, and CBMU 303, would assume responsibility for the continued MPSRON debarkation and the completion of Camp 93 in Kuwait. Rudich's Task Force Mike, freed from the static bed down projects in Kuwait, would begin focusing more upon their anticipated maneuver mission behind the growing Marine invasion force inside Iraq.

January 1 had come and gone, and CENTCOM had established February 15 as the new planning date for certifying all in-theater units as combat ready. However, the MEG still did not formally exist as a Major Subordinate Command within I MEF. The big fight with the Marine logisticians and I MEF staff in late summer and early fall of 2002 had effectively derailed a Memorandum of Agreement that had been in the works, despite Conway's directive to the contrary.

With the MEG still hanging in the wind, Rear Admiral Kubic used some "administrative back channel" work to bring the new MEG organization to life. He first asked MARCENT, through his Seabee Liaison Officer, to send a message to I MEF transferring operational control of all Seabees in theater from MARCENT to I MEF for assignment to I MEG. MARCENT agreed and set the command shift date for January 26. However, I MEF's G3 Operations Officer and Engineer failed to generate the required fragmentary order to facilitate the changeover.

Kubic therefore seized the initiative and by-passed I MEF temporarily to achieve his aim, specifically by invoking his authority as the commander of the 1st Naval Construction Division. As I MEG commander, he sent a message to himself and courtesy-copied it to "the world," asking the 1st Naval Construction Division to stand up the MEG with a command element built around Rear Admiral Kubic, and to create Task Forces Mike, Charlie, and Echo. As 1st Naval Construction Division commander, Kubic responded to the I MEG commander (i.e. Rear Admiral Kubic), again copying "the world," by issuing I MEG Execution Order #001, dated January 26, 2003. The order dissolved Rudich's old Task Force Charlie and formally placed Rudich in command of Task Force Mike, while McKerall took command of the reconstituted Task Force Charlie.[11]

Colonel Pete Kole's 265th Engineer Group, which had participated in the DESERT SPEAR, KEDGE HAMMER, and MEFEX 02 exercises in 2002, was then making preparations to deploy to Kuwait. Therefore, in accordance with the revised MEG organization plan, Execution Order #001 also activated Task Force Echo for long-term contingency construction. Since Kole would not be in theater for some time, Kubic placed Task Force Echo under Commander Jim Worcester of NMCB 4, who provided the Task Force command staff and served as its commander.

In the grand scheme of things, the 1st Naval Construction Division's Execution Order #001 provided all of the MEG's subordinate commands and units with command and control legitimacy. However, it necessarily left the relationship between the I MEG commander (Rear Admiral Kubic) and the I MEF commander, Lieutenant General Conway, a bit fuzzy. Conway, who was then preoccupied with many other important planning issues, did not question Kubic's method in raising the MEG up to Major Subordinate Command status within I MEF. He simply accepted it as *fait accompli*, with their future command relationship based primarily on "respect, friendship, and a warrior's handshake." Thus, the MEG was born. A week or so later, the G3 realized the oversight, and messages were exchanged to execute MARCENT's tasking and to commit formally to writing the I MEG reporting relationship to I MEF.

In the meantime, Rudich's two subordinate battalions, NMCBs 74 and 5, had retrieved their equipment and tools from the MPSRONs. They were ready to begin the next training phase of the emerging war plan as Task Force Mike. McKerall's Task Force Charlie too began making its own plans, focusing on possible second-echelon construction projects, such as enemy prisoner of war camps, bridge sustainment and replacement, road improvements, and equipment repair and logistics support for Task Force Mike. Worcester and his staff had to supervise Task Force Echo's initial projects in Kuwait until Kole and his 265th Engineer Group arrived in March. These included construction support for the U. S. Air Force's "Red Horse" Civil Engineer Squadron at Ahmed Al Jaber Air Base, barracks and mess construction for the 3rd Marine Aircraft Wing, and bed down facilities for the 2nd Force Service Support Group of the Marine Logistics Command at Logistics Support Area (LSA) Fox.

The MEG's stand-up signaled the end of the Seabees' first phase of pre-hostility planning and operations in Kuwait, and the beginning of a new, more intensive phase focused on the more practical problems attendant to a Marine Expeditionary Force advance into Iraq. With the "single battlespace engineer manager" concept still emerging, and Kubic's joint task force division of Seabee labor firmly embodied within the MEG framework, the Seabees would now encounter a series of new challenges that would test their collective engineering and logistical skills to their fullest as the U.S. moved even farther down the road to war.

CHAPTER 6

Learning Curves

While the I Marine Expeditionary Force Engineer Group (I MEG) and its task forces were standing up in January 2003, events on the geo-political stage were swirling toward an almost inevitable conclusion. After United Nations weapons inspections had resumed on November 27, 2002, Saddam Hussein and his minions had played a tense game of cat-and-mouse with the inspectors, led by Dr. Hans Blix, and the Director General of the International Atomic Energy Agency (IAEA), Mohammed El Baradei. Blix hinted at trouble on January 9 when he announced that the Iraqis were not being as cooperative as they had promised and that they had not disclosed all of Iraq's WMD capabilities as required by U.N. Resolution 1441, and the sixteen other U.N. disarmament resolutions that preceded it, dating back to 1991. As a result, his team had not yet found a "smoking gun" with which to condemn Saddam. But it would continue searching Saddam's laboratories and palaces for another two weeks before he issued his final sixty-day report to the U.N. Security Council, pursuant to Resolution 1441.[1]

The mandated report was released on January 27. Although Blix couched his and El Baradei's findings in diplomatic nuance, he criticized Saddam's regime for limiting access to certain key facilities, harassing the U.N. inspectors, impeding interviews with Iraqi scientists, intimidating witnesses, and preventing aerial surveillance during inspections. Moreover, evidence existed that the Iraqis had moved or hidden important materials and equipment at various sites before the inspectors had arrived, and that top secret information had been concealed in private residences and out of the inspectors' reach. Blix concluded that the regime had failed to provide active, immediate, and unconditional cooperation with his inspection team as required by Resolution 1441, and that "Iraq appears not to have come to a genuine acceptance, not even today, of the disarmament that was demanded of it."[2]

Further weapons inspections would continue, but Blix's report gave the Bush Administration the formal *Casus belli* that it had been seeking to build a case for liberating Iraq. On January 28, the day after Blix issued his report to the Security Council, President Bush delivered his annual State of the Union Address, amid widespread global protests against another war with Iraq. In his address, Bush echoed Blix's findings and outlined an entire litany of U.N. resolution violations as well as numerous internal atrocities that Saddam's regime had committed against his own people. The President also explicitly tied Saddam's regime to the ongoing terrorist threat against America, asserting that "Evidence from intelligence sources, secret communications, and statements by people now in custody reveal that Saddam Hussein aids and protects terrorists, including members of Al Qaeda. Secretly, and without fingerprints, he could provide one of his hidden weapons to terrorists, or help them develop their own."[3]

"The world has waited twelve years for Iraq to disarm," he continued. "America will not accept a serious and mounting threat to our country, and our friends and allies." The United States therefore will "ask the U.N. Security Council to convene on February 5th to consider the facts of Iraq's ongoing defiance of the world," and "Secretary of State [Colin] Powell will present information and intelligence about Iraq's illegal weapons programs, its attempts to hide those weapons from inspectors, and its links to terrorist groups." For those who sought to thwart or stall the U.S. through the U.N. bureaucracy, President Bush warned that "We will consult," but "If Saddam Hussein does not fully disarm, for the safety of our people and for the peace of the world, we will lead a coalition to disarm him."

As Bush promised, Secretary Powell appeared before the U.N. Security Council and a world-wide audience via live television on February 5th. During his smooth but controversial presentation, he laid out the U.S. case against Saddam's regime, using secretly collected tape recordings of Iraqi military officials, satellite imagery of research laboratories and weapons munitions facilities, and evidence of weapons inspection evasion. Along with a comprehensive catalog of resolution violations and internal atrocities, Powell emphasized Iraqi connections to the Al Qaeda network, particularly through the Palestinian/Jordanian terrorist Abu Musab Zarqawi, an associate and collaborator of Osama Bin Laden, who specialized in poisons and explosives. Zarqawi, the U.S. believed, was a primary link between Saddam and Bin Laden and had helped establish a terrorist training camp in northeastern Iraq for the vicious Ansar al-Islam organization.[4]

Before ending his presentation, Powell asked the $64,000 question, "Given Saddam Hussein's history of aggression, given what we know of his grandiose plans, given what we know of his terrorist associations and given his determination to exact revenge on those who oppose him, should we take the risk that he will not some day use these weapons at a time and the place and in the manner of his choosing at a time when the world is in a much weaker position to respond?" His answer was grim: "The United States will not and cannot run that risk to the American people. Leaving Saddam Hussein in possession of weapons of mass destruction for a few more months or years is not an option, not in a post-September 11th world."

Although Powell's testimony and evidence was compelling, and despite backing from Great Britain and Spain, the U.S. failed to convince several of its erstwhile allies to support another resolution that explicitly authorized the removal of Saddam's regime from power and the liberation of Iraq. Among those countries that actively opposed American diplomatic efforts to get U.N. authorization for war were Germany, Russia, and France, all of which would later be implicated in the subsequent "Oil-for-Food" scandal. The French opposition to the U.S. was particularly onerous, since many Americans still remembered the tens of thousands of doughboys and G.I.s who died while fighting on France's behalf in both world wars, many of whom remain buried there today.

Even more galling was a *Washington Times* report, published in early March, in which U.S. intelligence sources revealed that France had been secretly selling spare aircraft parts to Iraq to help Saddam stock-up in the event of an American attack. As a result, it seemed that France, always the source of good cheese and surrender jokes, was now actively working to secure America's defeat, both politically and militarily, despite its past reliance on American military support to ensure its own liberty.[5]

With France holding veto power in the Security Council, along with Russia and an always reluctant China, the U.N. was clearly a political dead-end for the U.S. But since the U.S. military was not yet ready to strike, the Bush Administration allowed the inspections and political machinations to continue through February 2003 and into March. However, Saddam's time was obviously running short, as the American build-up continued unabated in the Kuwaiti Theater of Operations (KTO).

"TPFDD by RFF"

While the U.S. was making its case to the U.N. in February, the 1st Naval Construction Division ordered the remainder of NMCBs 5, 74, and 133 to deploy to Kuwait. They arrived at the end of the month, joining their Air Detachments (Air Dets) and a small 30-person detachment from CBMU 303, a reserve unit that had been working at CENTCOM's Qatar headquarters since September 2002 before moving north as directed by Kubic. The 1st Naval Construction Division also sent warning orders to two Heavy Air Dets from NMCB 21 (Reserve) and individual Air Dets from NMCB 15 (Reserve) and NMCB 25 (Reserve) for deployment in February, and scheduled NMCB 7 to deploy in late March. Additionally, NMCB 4 began making preparations for a regular rotation with NMCB 5, also scheduled for March. Two other Seabee units, PHIBCB s 1 and 2, had already moved to Kuwait Naval Base and were then building a joint, 4,500-person field camp there called Camp Patriot. However, they fell under the operational control of the Maritime Prepositioning Force, under Rear Admiral Clyde W. Marsh, and remained outside of I MEG's command chain.[6]

The Amphibious Construction Battalions are an integral part of the Navy Beach Groups and provide the ship to shore bridge for Navy Amphibious Ships plus construction and operation of expeditionary camps ashore. In Kuwait, the PHIBCBs were tasked with construction of temporary and semi-permanent facilities ashore that far exceeded their normal mission capability. But they excelled none the less, and when it became necessary to intensify their work effort, called upon willing Seabees from nearby 1st Naval Construction Division units, including the always versatile CBMU 303.[7]

As it happened, the overall deployment process was both difficult and chaotic. Well before American and Coalition combat troops began arriving in Kuwait, Defense Department and CENTCOM planners had worked tirelessly to develop the Time

The MARFORCENT leadership gathers in Bahrain in December 2002 to plan the "Road to War."

Front Row, Left to Right: Major General Jim Mattis, Lieutenant General Earl Hailston, Lieutenant General Jim Conway, Major General Jim Amos. *Back Row*, Left to Right: Brigadier General Rich Natonski, Rear Admiral Chuck Kubic, Brigadier General Mike Lehnert, Brigadier General Ed Usher, Colonel Tom Waldhauser.

(Official U.S. Navy Photograph)

NMCB 74's Air Det built an enormous twenty-two acre aircraft apron for USMC F/A-18 jets at Al Jaber air base in Kuwait in the Fall of 2002. (U.S. Navy Photographs by Photographer's Mate 2nd Class Eric Powell)

NMCB 5 built the Munitions Supply Point at Ali Al Salem Air Base in the fall of 2002 to support potential Marine air operations against Iraq in the event of a "go early, go ugly" scenario. (Official U.S. Navy Photograph)

Rear Admiral Kubic conducts his weekly MEG War Council with his staff and Task Force Commanders and their staffs at Camp Commando, Kuwait, prior to the war. (Official U.S. Navy Photograph)

In February and March 2003, the Seabees trained for both their expeditionary engineering and job site defense missions.
(Official U.S. Navy Photographs Taken by Photographer's Mate 2nd Class Eric Powell)

Immediately upon arrival in Kuwait, the U.S. Navy Seabees began constructing the camps and infrastructure necessary to support Marine ground and air operations against the regime of Saddam Hussein.

(Official U.S. Navy Photographs Taken by Photographer's Mate 2nd Class Eric Powell)

MEF Engineer Group
Task Organization

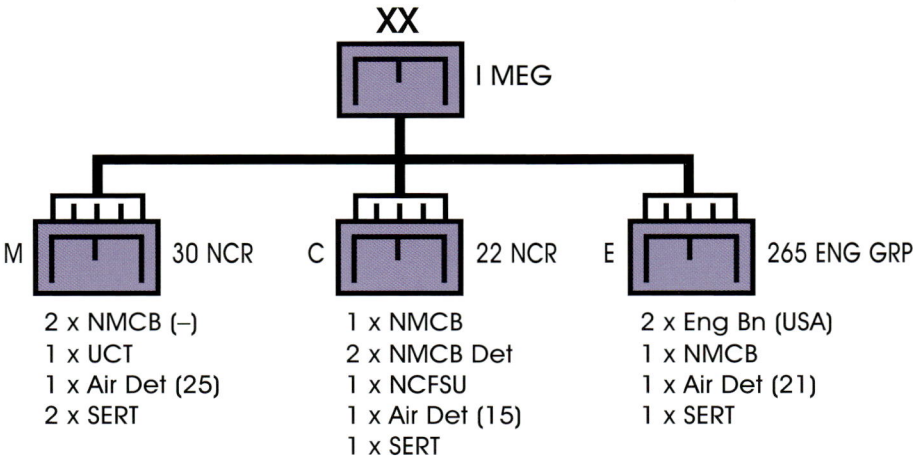

The MEG's Order of Battle as originally planned. Task forces were augmented and elements reassigned as required to "flex" to changing requirements.

A SERT element in training at Camp 93 in Kuwait.
(Official U.S. Navy Photograph)

Seabee "Jedi" of the MEG's Future Operations Cell. From left to right: (Standing) Lieutenant Junior Grade Eric Ulmen, Lieutenant Kent Hendricks, and Lieutenant Dave McAlister, and (seated) Lieutenant Russ Seignious, and Chief James Moran. (Official U.S. Navy Photograph)

In early 2003, the Seabees began training for the berm-reduction operations that would be necessary for an attack into Iraq from Kuwait.
(Official U.S. Navy Photograph)

During the lead-up to the war, the MEG chose to use a bridge design from the British Mabey & Johnson Company, based upon its simplicity, light weight, and durability. No single Mabey & Johnson Bridge component weighed more than seven hundred pounds, enabling a six-man Seabee team to lift, move, and emplace it with relative ease.

(U.S. Navy Photograph by Photographer's Mate 2nd Class Eric Powell)

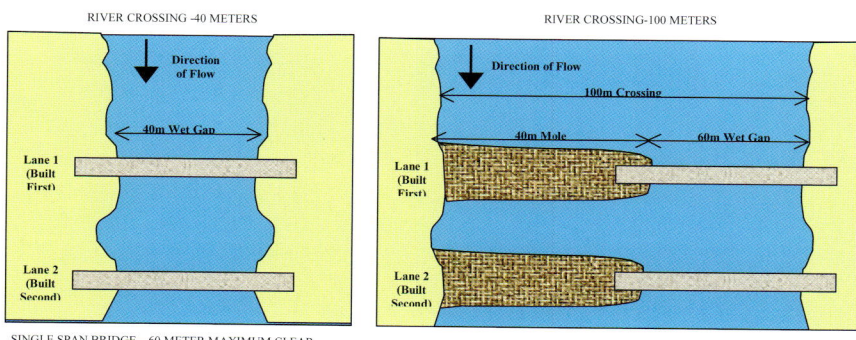

(Left) A typical Mabey & Johnson bridge emplacement across a 40-meter wet gap under ideal conditions. (Right) Making the "river fit the bridge" using 40-meters of earthen moles and 80-meters of Mabey & Johnson bridging.

Sand-Pile-Culvert-Modules (SPCMs) were used to construct "Mac-Moles" and proved to be the solution for bridging wide "wet gaps" with fast moving currents.   (Official U.S. Navy Photograph)

The "Great Wall of White Pipe" at Camp 93.
(Official U.S. Navy Photograph)

Throughout March 2003, Seabees had to endure countless Nuclear-Biological-Chemical drills and false alarms while awaiting orders to advance north into Iraq with the Marines.

(U.S. Navy Photograph by Photographer's Mate 2nd Class Eric Powell)

Another Seabee checks the time during a Nuclear-Biological-Chemical drill.
(U.S. Navy Photograph by Photographer's Mate 2nd Class Eric Powell)

Task Force Charlie's "Jiffy Clean" Nuclear-Biological-Chemical Decontamination Team. (Official U.S. Navy Photograph)

Task Force Echo takes cover in Expeditionary trenches during N-B-C drills at Camp Fox, Kuwait in March 2003.

(Official U.S. Navy Photograph)

Rear Admiral Kubic and members of Task Force Mike with Israeli-loaned D-9 "Zionist Monster" Armored Dozers, affectionately named "Ziva," "Golda," "Natasha," and "Matilda" by the Seabees. (Official U.S. Navy Photograph)

After an embankment collapsed during the assault into Baghdad, the 62-ton "Zionist Monster" Ziva lay "mired up to her gills" in the Diyala River for several days. She was later rescued by a M-88 Hercules tank retriever anchored to her sisters Golda and Natasha. (Official U.S. Navy Photograph)

The last pre-attack meeting with senior MEG staff on March 19, 2003 inside the MEG Command Bunker. A day later, Patriot Missiles (right) zoom toward incoming Iraqi Ababil 100s at Camp Commando.
(Official U.S. Navy Photograph)

The impact of the Iraqi Seersucker missile at Camp Commando on March 20, 2003. (Official U.S. Navy Photograph)

Phased Force Deployment Document (TPFDD) and to synchronize the flow of troops and their equipment with the war plans. The theory was that all personnel and equipment movements would flow in an orchestrated fashion once the National Command Authority (NCA—i.e. the President and the Secretary of Defense) gave the order to attack. However, due to the ongoing song-and-dance routine at the U.N. and the resulting geo-political sensitivities involved in the decision making process, it quickly became apparent that the National Command Authority wanted more direct control of the troop movements and was unwilling to simply say "Go!" Consequently, all troop movements were authorized personally by Defense Secretary Rumsfeld in response to individual Requests for Forces (RFFs) issued by CENTCOM. This approach set aside all of the careful deliberate planning, created an inter-service free for all, and overwhelmed the Nation's limited sea and airlift forces.

The U.S. military ultimately muscled its way through the RFF process, but as the volumes of "lessons learned" attest, it was not pretty. Many units arrived late, troops arrived long before their equipment, ports were overwhelmed, and long haul assets could not even come close to meeting demand, causing major back-ups at the single SPOD (Sea Port of Departure) and APOD (Air Port of Departure). The Seabee theater plan for movement of troops and equipment from the SPOD and APOD envisioned using significant Army long haul equipment supplemented by contract support. When it became apparent that "TPFDD by RFF" was going to overwhelm the limited theater support available, the Seabees shifted all available internal resources to get themselves and their incoming additional equipment out of the port quickly.

Initially, I MEF and the Military Logistics Command (MLC) planned to move all equipment to Tactical Assembly Area (TAA) Fox and then trans-ship only what was needed for the initial attack to camps being built farther north at Tactical Assembly Area Coyote. This did not make much sense to the MEG given the times and distances involved, but no amount of persuasion could convince the logisticians to alter their plan initially. Since the Seabees were capable of operating within the system with a high degree of expeditionary experience in moving troops, equipment, gear and supplies, the MEG finally decided that it could take care of itself and announced that it was hauling all its own material directly north to Camp 93 at Tactical Assembly Area Coyote.

Ultimately, Seabee determination and hard work carried the day. All MPF equipment, with the exception of two Rough Terrain Container Handlers (RTCHs) which required movement on Army Heavy Equipment Transporters (HETs) due to their size, was moved by Seabees with Seabee tractor-trailers with little external Army or Marine support. During this effort, the Seabees effectively moved into their assembly areas – a major success achieved with an all hands, around the clock effort. This proved to be the right move and was quickly emulated by I MEF and the Military Logistics Command. The complete Seabee offload was executed ahead of schedule and without incident.

Army Engineers were required to supplement the skills and capacity of the Seabees and the Marine Engineers. The 265th Engineer Group of the Georgia National Guard provided an additional regimental command element, along with combat engineering skills, including breaching and employment of mines. The 265th and its commander, Colonel Pete Kole, were already familiar with the MEG concept and had previously trained with the Seabees during exercises in Korea. The 478th Corps Mechanized Battalion of the Kentucky Army Reserve provided mechanized capability to support river crossings and force protection, while the 1092nd Engineer Battalion of the West Virginia National Guard provided heavy horizontal construction and convoy capability. These units were carefully integrated into the MEG Concept of Operations and Task Force structure during the initial planning process. However, TPFDD by RFF failed to get these units to theater on time and did not deliver their specialized equipment until weeks after the soldiers arrived, frustrating everyone concerned.

In hindsight, Rear Admiral Kubic believed that including Army Engineers in the MEG was a sound concept that could have been executed better. Severe competition within the Army and MEF for equipment lift, once the flow shifted to TPFDD by RFF, significantly delayed arrival of these units and their equipment. In particular, the delay of the 478th Corps Mechanized Battalion deprived the MEG of mechanized hardened vehicles during its movement north and during independent bridging operations. When it became apparent during the TPFDD review that the equipment of the 130th Corps Wheeled Battalion of the Puerto Rico Army National Guard was in a poor state of readiness, that unit was relieved by the 1092nd Engineer Battalion, further delaying the closure of Army units in the MEG. Also, the Army's unwillingness to move part of the 265th Engineer Group as an advanced party left the MEG Command Element understaffed with Army personnel and required Seabee Commander Jim Worcester (the commanding officer of NMCB 4) to take interim command of Task Force Echo.

This last issue was particularly vexing for Kubic as MEG commander. After the 265th had slid down the TPFDD totem pole because of the disastrous "River" OPT the previous summer, the admiral now had to move mountains of Army bureaucracy to have Kole and his staff immediately deployed to the Kuwait Theater of Operations for duty in the MEG. After much effort, Kole was given his deployment orders, but his staff members were not. So Kubic and his "MEGsters" ended up butting heads with a particularly obstinate Army civilian logistics clerk over their delayed deployment. Kubic first reminded her that the MEG had a war brewing and that he needed all of his staff members to fight it once it started. But when this failed to impress her, Kubic demanded to speak with the first two-star flag officer in her command chain about the issue.

This contact, along with a personal discussion with the Coalition Land Forces Component Commander, Lieutenant General David D. McKiernan (USA), broke the log jam. But even then, the Seabees had to send their own buses from the Gulfport Construction Battalion Center up to Marietta, Georgia, to pick up Kole's people and then transport them to Kuwait via Gulfport since the Army refused to supply the necessary vehicles for the task. As a result, Kole's team arrived in Kuwait really late, but at least the MEG had them on site and just in time for the war.

"Beds and Butts"

As the various Seabee and Army engineer units converged on Kuwait via TPFDD by RFF, the MEG had to find places to both feed and bed them down. In August 2002, the Atlantic Division (at the request of the 1st Naval Construction Division) had the Construction Capabilities (CONCAP) contractor (Brown and Root) prepare a master plan to build a temporary camp for up to five thousand troops at Commando Camp. The plan was tiered, included utilities, and used the available space very efficiently. Unfortunately, it was briefed to MARCENT before Kubic had a chance to review it, and the Navy Commander who presented the proposal jumped too quickly to the final $22 million solution without showing the $5 million first step, which would have been easier for the Marines to swallow. Needless to say, the briefer was thoroughly skewered, and the proposal was dead on arrival.

This was very unfortunate in Kubic's opinion because the MEF then opted for what proved to be a very expensive tent-leasing strategy that ultimately cost significantly more than the CONCAP proposal. In fact, the tents were contracted for by logistics officers who later had trouble accounting not only for projected costs but also for the actual costs incurred during the chaotic construction of what turned out to be a large expeditionary camp that supported over eight thousand troops. The MEF chose not to seek assistance with its facilities services contracts either from the Naval Facilities Engineering Command or its own Force Service Support Command specialists. The Marines' approach instead was to use a series of small purchase contracts with little or no specifications, and then quickly muscle their way through the process, accepting sole source prices from local contractors. This approach ultimately worked, but quality of life for the arriving troops suffered for it. But then, this was war and war is hell, as far as the Marine commanders were concerned, and in the final analysis they got the job done.

Food service was the most serious example of flawed service contracting. At the outset of the pre-war assembly period, food was adequate and somewhat better than some expected for field conditions, but it was very expensive, not very appetizing, often cold, and usually delivered in insufficient quantity. The MEG looked into the MEF contract at the request of I MEF commander, Lieutenant General Conway, who had just eaten at a Seabee galley run by the same contractor and noticed a difference in overall quality. The Seabee contracting officers found that all food service for the MEF was being provided based only upon a purchase order with a six line specification requiring a given number of meals per day for a given time period. When more people showed up (based upon estimates against firm counts) the contractor borrowed from future meal days. If the contracts ran past the time when the attack would occur, the contractor "kept the change" since they were firm fixed price contracts with mobilization costs spread over the contract period in the per meal cost.

When the quality began to deteriorate further, at Conway's request, Kubic asked one of the Seabees' Navy food service teams to take a look at the whole process. Its report was shocking, with a strong emphasis on the totally unsanitary conditions in the kitchen where the food was cooked and then trucked over to the Marine galley tent. After seeing what was going on, Seabees volunteered to take over leadership of the food service operations. The Marines initially rebuffed their offer, until it made its way to Conway, who once again remembered the dinner he ate at the Seabee galley at Camp Moreell and the marked difference in quality achieved from the same contractor with better management and continuous oversight.

Lieutenant (Junior Grade) Terri Gabriel, the S4A from NMCB 133, and her team moved in and quickly turned around the existing service at Camp Commando, writing and awarding a replacement contract that provided far superior food at less cost. Kubic later doubted if many Marines knew or appreciated the effort that Seabees made behind the scenes to ensure that everyone had high quality chow for the balance of the time at Camp Commando. But, as Kubic recalled, Lieutenant Gabriel and her Seabee cooks sure were proud of the work they did, and took their reward from the smiling faces of Marines every day at chow.

In addition to food problems, basic camp bed down remained a critical issue. At first, it was not obvious where the camps should be, or how large they should be. Planning continued on an ad hoc and iterative basis. The MEF's original concept was to bring all Maritime Pre-positioning Force gear from the port to Tactical Assembly Area Fox. Fox was an ugly piece of desert given to the Marines no doubt because no Kuwaiti really wanted to go there. Kubic did not want to double stage the Seabees' gear but wanted to move directly north to the area where the MEF planned bare bones camps and where the troops would spend a week or two before they attacked. This was initially planned on the cheap and ultimately grew into a very costly solution when D-Day was delayed until late March. Early in the game, the 30th Naval Construction Regiment found and staked out a "very nice piece of desert" with hard, stable sand near the main highway going north to Iraq. This piece of desert became Seabee Camp 93. The Seabees bermed a full grid square and then hauled all of their equipment and containers there about sixty miles from the port. This is the camp where Task Force Mike Seabees would form their convoys and then move into their pre-attack positions.

At Ali Al Salem, the MEG began to build up Camp Moreell, from which Task Force Charlie Seabees would stage, with strong back tents, Seahuts, and shower trailers with full plumbing. The MEG also built Camp Castle at Tactical Assembly Area Fox when it became apparent that Army units and NMCB 4 would arrive before the attack occurred and needed bed down spaces of their own. In contrast to the soft, nasty sand at Fox, Camp Castle was very comfortable and served as the main camp for Task Force Echo. In total, the MEG had about 140 spaces at Camp Commando, 1,500 at Camp 93, 1,200 at Camp Moreell and 1,000 at Camp Castle — 3,840 spaces for an engineer force expected to grow to over 4,500 (not counting the Korean Battalion that later pushed the MEG to over 5,000 troops). As a result, planning for "beds and butts" became almost more complex than planning for the war. This was especially true since the MEF never allocated sufficient rental tent spaces for the MEG troops due in large part to no one having the numbers straight at a key decision meeting run by the I MEF Chief of Staff in January. In the end, it all worked out, but looking back on it, Kubic decided that it was good that I MEF attacked before all the troops arrived.

At the command and staff levels, the MEG slowly improved its Combat Operations Center and berthing area, but it was a constant struggle with the I MEF staff to meet the Seabees' basic needs for space, communications and berthing. When the MEG command staff could not get a tent to expand its Command Operations Center, the Seabees began erecting a seahut, but were quickly ordered to stop building something permanent in the Marines' "temporary" camp. The Seabees complied and received the tent they asked for in the first place. Kubic later observed:

> I don't think the MEF leadership ever realized how much more expensive the temporary camp was becoming as they continued to haul water in and sewage away. It was a great day when Seabees took care of themselves and finally got a shower and a laundry trailer installed near our berthing area. It was even better when we hooked into "free" base power and water while the MEF continued to buy water and fuel for its generators. Sometimes you just have to let Marines be Marines and Seabees be Seabees.

Ultimately the MEF Camp Commandant staff finally recognized the value of the Seabees when Kubic brought CBMU 303's Air Det into camp to rescue a failing maintenance contractor. After the war, Kubic was sure that many Marines were commended for their work at building and running Camp Commando – and given their situation, it was a really good camp and reasonably comfortable for desert field conditions. But the admiral never shook the nagging feeling that the approach taken to building, operating, and maintaining this camp was harder and more expensive than it really needed to be.

"One Big Pot"

As the additional Seabees and engineering soldiers arrived in theater, the MEG staff divided them up and distributed their component elements, personnel, and assets among the three task forces. This was done in accordance with the MEG's emerging operations plan, which sought to match the right equipment and the right number of people with the right missions in a way to best support the Marine Corps. The dispersal of resources proved to be difficult for Seabees whose units had traditionally operated as cohesive battalions under single commanders ever since their glory days of World War II. Although the battalions had been known for task organization throughout their history, with various detachments routinely deployed around the world away from their main formations at any given time, the commands themselves had never before been split. Therefore, without the benefit of written doctrine and proper training in the new organizational system, and compounded by the sudden rush get the Seabees from the U.S. to Kuwait through the RFF process, the seeds of confusion were sewn right from the start.[8]

But again, war is hell, and Kubic needed to adopt a new, lighter, faster organization structure using the people and equipment resources that had made it through the "TPFDD by RFF" process. He had to support the lead units in Task Force Mike with resources from Task Forces Charlie and Echo until all of the MEG's people and gear showed up. In retrospect, this approach was further complicated by the need to keep the still evolving battle plan and mission classified. Many of the incoming troops and their officers and NCOs did not initially know the war plan or the timing and simply could not understand the need to break up their units.

Like many deploying Seabees during that period, Equipment Operator First Class Frederick Kyriss, of NCFSU 2, realized something was different as soon as he landed in Kuwait. He remembered that the first thing his commanders did was to have him list his real-world skills down on a piece of paper, regardless of his rating. He soon found out that I MEG was matching skills to specific jobs within the task forces, and assigning individual Seabees on that basis. Within a week, Kyriss and several of his comrades were assigned to Commodore McKerall's Task Force Charlie, while the others from his unit ended up in Commodore Rudich's Task Force Mike, such as Chief Equipment Operator Rudolpho Santiago, who was assigned a truck for Mike convoy duty. Kyriss later characterized the process as simply throwing key personnel into "one big pot" and then mixing them up.[9]

One of Kyriss' officers, newly commissioned Ensign Jerome Arabe, submitted a particularly nice resume to NCFSU 2's commanding officer. After outlining his experience as a former senior chief with military instructor experience with the Marines, he found himself attached as a construction officer to a Marine Force Recon unit for Task Force Tarawa, which would ultimately see some of the heaviest fighting in Iraq. Similarly, Steelworker 1st Class Michael Hill had been a weapons and tactics instructor for the previous three years before joining NMCB 74 in Kuwait in early February 2003. He reported to battalion commander Cliff Maurer and Command Master Chief Perone, who asked Hill how he was doing, where he came from, and what he did there? Hill replied, "From the regiment Master Chief," and that he had "taught weapons and mortars, and tactical skills." Perone said, "Great! Welcome to Task Force Mike!" He then proceeded to inform a slightly confused Hill that he would "be going forward with the Marines as soon as [President Bush] instructed [them] to do so.[10]

Not surprisingly, the battalion commanders and their chiefs were wholly unprepared for and ultimately frustrated by the MEG's interference with their command authority and the dissolution of unit integrity. They found that under the MEG system, a battalion's skipper would be placed in charge of its Task Force Mike element, while his executive officer would take charge of the remainder in either Task Force Charlie or Echo. Any changes that the battalion commanders wanted or needed to make, such as changing out a truck, adding tool kits for mechanics, or bringing forward or swapping out Seabees from another task force, would have to be approved by the MEG senior staff. Commodore Bill Rudich later commented that "it was almost like a Request for Forces (RFF) through the MEG."

The loss of control over their respective battalions' Tables of Allowances was particularly irksome since battalion commanders were still nominally responsible for their units' equipment, even though the MEG had effectively pooled it. For example, NMCB 7's commander, Commander Christopher J. Honkomp, who was assigned to Task Force Echo, later remembered that Task Force Mike commandeered most of his line-haul equipment. He also had to fight Task Force Charlie for the return of his remaining trucks and personnel every time he sent them north in a convoy. Additionally, the NMCB 15 and NMCB 21 Air Dets took about two-thirds of his Table of Allowance with them when they moved northward, leaving him with only a few pieces of heavy equipment and communications gear with which to execute his own mission.[11]

Other Seabees had similar stories. Senior Chief Builder Troy Kellerman of NMCB 133 later recalled that "we did not get everything we wanted" since "we all had to share the equipment that came off the ship." Chief Equipment Operator James Mellow of NCFSU 2 echoed her account, stating that "everything [was] up for grabs" and the task forces [took] what they needed. His colleague, Senior Chief Equipment Operator Charles Cox, added that their unit's gear had already been "scattered all over Kuwait" by the time that they arrived in theater. "We actually had no ownership of anything," said Cox, and to his chagrin, "much of NCFSU 2's equipment nomenclatures had been painted over with either task force designators or host unit numbers, such as 5, 74, or 133.[12]

Gathering up and reclaiming the "fragmented" personnel and equipment to reconstitute the battalions after the campaign would be painful. Moreover, the system would cause the battalions' officers innumerable personnel headaches since, being spread out among the three task forces, they would have no way of judging the relative contributions of their Seabees or ranking them while handing out awards and promotions once they returned to their home ports. Without being able to see the full picture, they could not "play the honest broker" in resolving disputes among the various companies and departments that would invariably arise during and after a potential war.

"We Weren't Ready for That!"

The shock of the MEG's task force organizational system aside, other surprises greeted incoming Seabees as they arrived in Kuwait in January and February 2003. The first of these was a long and rigorous training regimen, which the MEG devised to ensure that they were prepared to meet whatever demands CENTCOM and I MEF might place on them. Under CENTCOM's emerging 1003V OPLAN, the distance and the speed of advance at which I MEF planned to attack were unprecedented. To meet the OPLAN's general engineering support requirement for I MEF's advance, the MEG Seabees would have to advance forward in the tactical battlespace farther than they had ever done since the Vietnam War. Consequently, Kubic envisioned the MEG's task forces operating as maneuver elements, advancing, building, and fighting in echelon directly behind the 1st Marine Division and Task Force Tarawa. He therefore fully expected the Seabees to match the Marines' every move and to be able to hit the road running at a moment's notice.[13]

The MEG maneuver plan was heavily influenced by former Marine General Alfred M. Gray's expeditionary maneuver warfighting doctrine, and represented a radical departure from the Seabees' standard way of operating since Vietnam. In the intervening years, Seabees more or less had come to think of themselves solely as static "rear echelon" engineering forces deployed in rear areas, focused primarily on construction, humanitarian relief, or civic action projects. Recent Seabee doctrine decreed that they would only be brought forward to replace assault bridges, repair runways, and build forward bases well after any attack took place. With smaller, more mobile ground combat forces attacking quickly into Iraq, where speed and momentum would be vital, Kubic had to turn this paradigm on its head and compel the MEG task forces to support the Marine maneuver elements not only after, but also during the attack, as NCB 133 had during the World War II battle of Iwo Jima. As Equipment Operator 1st Class Kyriss later observed, "we went back to the traditional Seabee way of going in with the Marines." Unfortunately, he continued, "[we] weren't ready for that."[14]

The MEG staff had already given the previously deployed Seabees of NMCBs 5, 74, and 133 a glimpse of what Kubic expected out of the MEG units, in terms of training, if and when a war got underway. On New Year's Day 2003, Kubic led them, fully outfitted in battle gear, on a ten-kilometer roundtrip foot march to Mutla Ridge, a sandy crest overlooking Camp Commando. The I MEF Headquarters Group and numerous Seabees had already made a "run" there and back on Christmas Day. By emulating the Headquarters Marines in this training exercise, Kubic sent a clear message that the Seabees would be operating alongside Marine combat forces and needed to be prepared to keep up.[15]

Since the MEG Seabees would be maneuvering directly behind the Marine assault forces, they would be under immediate threat of enemy attack and might very well have to engage in heavy combat. Since World War II, the Seabees had always been prepared to defend themselves and their work sites, and had done so repeatedly then, and again during the Vietnam War. During their regular deployments and evolutions over the years, they had been required to maintain proficiencies in a wide range of infantry weapons, small unit tactics, counter ambush techniques, and security measures. Their training was grounded upon the doctrine outlined in the *Seabee Combat Handbook*, first published in 1976, with revised editions in 1985 and 1993, and a published second volume in 1996 covering communications, command, and control.[16]

Further, the Navy had drafted the requirements for an optional Seabee Combat Warfare Specialist (SCW) program in 1990 to encourage Seabees to acquire infantry combat skills. OPNAVINST 1410.1, issued by the Chief of Naval Operations in 1992, formally authorized it, and a December 1998 revision made its warfare qualifications mandatory for all enlisted Seabees beyond the E-5 pay grade. Officers were likewise expected to complete the program in order to compete successfully for promotions and billets. Later in Kuwait, Kubic insisted that everyone on the MEG staff be Seabee warfare qualified, not only to set an example for the troops but also to emphasize that the Seabees' roots were grounded in the operational combat forces and not the logistics combat forces.[17]

All Seabees who earned the coveted SCW designation were entitled to wear a special insignia device, gold for officers and silver for enlisted personnel. It was comprised of a cutlass (representing an officer's traditional weapon and badge of authority) and a Model 1903 Springfield rifle (the first rifle issued to enlisted Seabees during World War II), crossed behind Frank J. Iafrate's original Seabee emblem, all in front of a fouled anchor (highlighting the U.S. Navy) with oak leaves (oak being the traditional building material for the CEC and the Seabees) in the background. Hundreds of Seabees of all ranks had earned their badges before deploying to Kuwait. But many had not since the qualification process, complete with field exercises and written and oral examinations, was stringent and required up to twenty-four months for completion for active duty personnel, and forty-eight for selected reservists.[18]

Although these combined measures had kept the Seabees combat capable, in reality they had not been involved in any actual ground fighting since Vietnam. In DESERT STORM and the various U.S. humanitarian relief efforts and military interventions of the 1990s, including those in Somalia, Haiti, and the Balkans, Seabees generally operated in high threat areas but from stationary locations with strong defensive positions. Therefore, Kubic's insistence that they abandon their traditional emphasis upon defensive combat and integrate into the Marine assault forces was wholly unexpected.

As a result, battalion training officers moved quickly to implement realistic combat training for the incoming Seabees and to accelerate the SCW program, using brand new firing ranges constructed at each of the main camps. They first compiled lists of qualified Seabees, and after enrolling them, assigned subject matter experts to instruct them in key SCW topics, establishing a rigid training regime in the process. This was on top of their daily construction assignments. Command Master Chief Kevin J. Eichman of PHIBCB 1 reported early in its deployment that five of his Seabees had already become SCW qualified, with another nine preparing to appear before their examination boards. He expected the number to increase ten-fold in his unit alone over the length of its stay in theater.[19]

The combat training extended throughout all of the Seabee units in Kuwait. Senior Chief Builder Jeffrey Weigel of NMCB 74, who helped supervise the battalion's Charlie company and its 120 Seabees within Task Force Mike, recalled doing a lot of "regular military and familiarization training" in different "fighting positions" and planning for "every [possible] scenario" while moving forward. Senior Chief Builder and SCW specialist Troy Kellerman of NMCB 133 later described, in preparation for a "worst case scenario," how the combat training program was "hands on" with a "lot of weapons training" and that every Seabee was armed, even the chaplain. She added that E-6 petty officers and below generally wielded a variety of infantry weapons such as M-16 automatic rifles, M-60 and .50 caliber machine guns, mortars, M-19 grenade launchers, and regular hand grenades, while senior and master chiefs and officers packed nine-millimeter pistols.[20]

"We're Lost!"

Since the Seabees would have to line-haul all of their equipment northward into Iraq should CENTCOM issue orders to attack, convoy operations as well as combat skills would be key to completing their missions successfully. As a result, convoy training consumed a great deal of the Seabees time during the six-week period from mid-February until late March 2003. Because of the rather ad hoc organization that arose from the sudden splitting of the battalions and units, the various elements adopted whatever training procedures worked best for them and their respective task force assignments.

In the absence of any prior Seabee doctrine concerning task force convoys, those of NMCB 133's Charlie element was typical of the ad hoc and occasionally unorthodox planning measures that the lower Seabee echelons had to undertake to prepare for an advance northward. NMCB 133 Air Det Chief Kellerman, based at Camp 93, later described the old school methods her Seabees used to plan and practice their specific convoy movements. In the absence of suitable computers and simulation software, they first took surplus soap bars from care packages, wrote the names of vehicles on them, lined them up on the sand, and, using them as models, discussed how they were going to move out.

Following the model exercises, Kellerman's Seabees then hiked out into the "middle of nowhere" without their vehicles, lined up, and practiced their movements in real time. Kellerman thought that the "soap bar" models were actually more beneficial for the troops rather than the high-tech simulations, war games, and Power Point briefs, which were the current rage in the U.S. military, since she could not physically "get one hundred people around a computer to show them what we're going to do." Moreover, the process let everyone in her unit get involved in the planning, as opposed to a few key principals, and by combining it with their combat and weapons training, they even took it so far as to practice their perimeter security arrangements, with great success.[21]

Some outfits, like NMCB 74's Mike element, were more daring and actually took their trucks and vehicles out into the trackless desert to practice night convoys using night vision goggles (NVGs). Sometimes these exercises resulted in some interesting adventures. Steelworker 1st Class Michael Hill later recounted his first and last stint as convoy commander during one such jaunt. Driving a fifteen-ton commercial-type dump truck loaded with two tons of SPCMs, he and his A-driver Steelworker Constructionman (SWCN) Dusty Horn were placed sixth in a fifty-vehicle convoy, up front near the convoy commander. Their heavily loaded truck was not very fast and was not the easiest thing to drive in the desert because of its weight. The convoy's commander had not told them where they were going, and instead, ordered them to simply follow the lead vehicles.[22]

The two Seabees set out from Camp 93 with their convoy into the pitch black, moonless night, but soon found that when the drivers ahead hit their brakes, the brake lights would come on and overwhelm their night vision goggles, effectively blinding them. As a result, Hill and Horn had to repeatedly back off, and switch their goggles on and off to maintain their bearings and to give the blinding effect time to wear off. After about twenty minutes of this, they noticed that the lead vehicles had suddenly vanished into the night, leaving them and the rest of the convoy behind. By default, Hill became the new convoy commander for the forty-three vehicles in line behind him, and he had absolutely no idea where he was or where he was going. As Hill later told it, he and Horn immediately "[broke] out into hysterical laughter knowing that they [were] leading the entire battalion into nowhere."[23]

Without a radio in their dump truck to alert anyone of their predicament, they continued driving across the barren desert with the remaining convoy vehicles following in tow. A few more minutes passed, and Hill finally pulled over to consult with the number seven vehicle commander next in line, telling him, "Hey man, I can't find anybody else and we're lost, so that makes you lost; so let's figure out what we're doing here." While commiserating in their plight, they both saw a tractor-trailer, with a massive D-9 bulldozer on its back, passing by about one hundred meters off to their right. Jumping back into their vehicles, they quickly caught up with the driver, a young construction man, and found that he too was lost. After another round of intense discussion, the construction man agreed to lead the convoy since everyone present believed that he probably would not make it to the rear without losing his way again. So, he drove forward, and Hill and the rest of convoy followed.

Unfortunately, the construction man did not get very far before he drove his tractor-trailer onto a sand berm and got stuck in the sliding sand. Seeing that the situation had hardly improved, Hill made a "command decision" to break off and reform his convoy, and led it in a new direction, leaving the tractor-trailer behind on the berm. A few miles later, either Providence or kind fate intervened, as Hill began seeing huge mud-puddles ahead. He soon learned that a tanker truck carrying eight thousand-gallons of water had made them after its driver had accidentally hit the tanker's release lever, thereby giving Hill a guiding trail straight back to Camp 93. Thinking "Oh my God, we're going to find our way home," he followed the puddles, which got progressively larger and deeper as they neared the camp. Finally, he saw the Camp 93 lights in the distance, and after a few more miles, he safely led the convoy back into the camp's compound. In the aftermath of their jaunt, Hill and Horn kept their story largely to themselves, and the convoy's commander never knew what happened since he never bothered to come back and check on them. "It was a learning curve," said Hill, "and boy did we learn to make sure that we never lose sight of vehicles in front of us again."

In view of the MEG's final decision in December to employ Mabey & Johnson bridging and "Mac Moles" for executing the anticipated bridging mission toward Baghdad, the Seabees and Soldiers of the MEG likewise began a rigorous and continuous regimen of Mabey & Johnson training. By mid-March 2003, over 1,500 Seabees and Soldiers from five Naval Mobile Construction Battalions and one Army Corps wheeled battalion were "Mabey & Johnson Bridge Qualified" ("MJBQ'd," to the MEG duty experts). Not only were they trained to assemble the bridge, they became proficient in constructing various types of mole piers to support the Mabey & Johnson bridges. The bottom line, said Kubic, was that when the MEF called the MEG forward to "span the gap," Seabees, Soldiers, and Marine "MEGsters" were ready to go.

The "Slime" Threat

The threat of nuclear, biological, and/or radiological attack loomed large over the Seabees in Kuwait, even more so than during DESERT STORM. Even before Kubic's initial meeting with Lieutenant General Hailston, the broad consensus among President Bush and his cabinet, and running throughout the Defense Department and CENTCOM, was that Saddam still maintained stockpiles of nuclear, biological, and chemical (NBC) weapons of mass destruction. Further, most Defense Department and CENTCOM analysts were equally certain that he would use them against Coalition forces at some point before or during a potential campaign. Indeed, I MEF commander Lieutenant General James T. Conway grimly told Marine Corps field historians in March 2003 that "we've got to face for the first time probably in 90 years…an NBC threat and a guy that we think has every intent to use it." Consequently, I MEG moved to ensure that the Seabees were fully prepared to meet the threat in case Saddam decided to "slime" them.[24]

Seabees generally train for defense against Nuclear/Biological/Chemical attacks as part of their routine home port operations, and have done so regularly since the early Cold War years. During field exercises, they practice getting attacked with Nuclear/Biological/Chemical weapons, and familiarize themselves with their gas masks, Military Operational Protective Posture (MOPP) suits, and decontamination gear. As NMCB 133's Chief Kellerman later said, "we want to be prepared and we don't want to get there and then start training." Every Seabee therefore is grounded in the basic tenements of Nuclear/Biological/Chemical defense before ever deploying on a contingency or expeditionary construction mission.[25]

However, this deployment was different and the threat of getting "slimed" was seemingly more immediate. The MEG accordingly ordered Task Force Charlie to develop and implement an aggressive new training program to develop the additional skills needed to perform thorough equipment decontamination for MEG units maneuvering in the battlespace. Commodore McKerall complied, and his Charlie staff quickly developed a program to Kubic's liking that included a full-scale "proof of capability" exercise, which took place at Camp Moreell on February 20.[26]

The exercise's goal was to process twenty vehicles through a Detailed Equipment Decontamination (DED) line within three hours. During the exercise, which began at nine o'clock in the morning (local time), McKerall's Charlie Seabees ran every type of vehicle available in the Moreell Alfa yard through the DED line, with the exception of a large crane. This was done to give the Seabees the experience of working with a variety of trucks, Humvees, road graders, bulldozers, and other pieces of heavy equipment, should an actual incident involving multiple, dissimilar vehicles occur.

During planning, McKerall's staff estimated that between 250 and 500 gallons of water would be required to decontaminate one vehicle, depending on its size, and so the decontamination team used water from six 6,000-gallon water bladders to conduct the exercise. The team then set up a series of stations, through which each vehicle would pass in turn until it was fully "decontaminated." The clock started ticking as soon as the first vehicle reached Station One, and for the next three hours, the decontamination team thoroughly scrubbed down an eclectic procession of trucks, transports, and heavy construction equipment as they passed through the stations, one by one.

The final vehicle departed from the site just over three hours after the exercise started. As the vehicles moved through, the team members noted a number of problems, such as vehicles getting stuck in the sand, logistical shortfalls, personnel and vehicle limitations, and mobility restrictions. But they developed solutions as they went, which were ultimately incorporated into the MEG Nuclear/Biological/Chemical plan.

An added benefit of the exercise was that a core group of Seabees became proficient in the principles and techniques of Nuclear/Biological/Chemical decontamination. After the exercise, the MEG's CBR/NBC department developed a comprehensive plan equipping each task force with operational decontamination capabilities, through the use of a "Jiffy Clean" truck concept. These trucks would be set up using organic equipment from each Task Force's Table of Allowance and would be dedicated solely to decontamination while the task forces were on the move. In case of a large attack, the plan called for the Jiffy Teams to quickly converge on one large site if necessary. The MEG also ordered Task Force Charlie to train similar Jiffy teams within the other two Task Forces. In keeping with the MEG's planned maneuver operations in the battlespace, these teams would quickly but only partially decontaminate vehicles on site to keep the Seabees and their equipment able to move and maneuver until the situation permitted their return to a forward Detailed Equipment Decontamination site near a water source for the full treatment.

Bunker drills likewise became a crucial part of the Seabees' daily Nuclear/Biological/Chemical training in Kuwait. I MEF had been hardening Camp Commando and building concrete box style bunkers around the camp since early January. Once the drills started, I MEG made sure that all of its personnel took them seriously, with Seabee chiefs checking tents and accounting for all hands whenever the camp's siren and loudspeaker alert system sounded. During the drills, it became readily apparent that there were more Seabees and Marines in camp than available bunker spaces, and on more than one occasion Seabees running into their assigned bunkers discovered that they were already fully occupied by Marines. Consequently, I MEG began pushing for more bunkers, but with only limited success.[27]

The bunker drills also presented Kubic with a difficult command and control problem, which was shared by nearly all of the other I MEF commanders. Whenever the siren sounded, the admiral found that the bunkers effectively knocked him out of the command loop and left him isolated from the MEG task forces for considerable amounts of time.

Consequently, Kubic had a large, heavy timber Seabee command bunker built next to the MEG's command and control tents. Seabees from NMCB 133 did the work, and Kubic thought that it was the very best bunker he had ever seen—half buried and the rest completely sandbagged. It was rigged with a full communications suite and connections for the Secret Internet Protocol Network (SIPRnet), and the admiral rigorously drilled his staff in breaking down the MEG's communications gear in the Combat Operations Center and quickly moving it all over to the bunker. The MEG's staff and watch officers became quite proficient in transferring operations between the command tents and the bunker and back again during the drills. Accordingly, Kubic would not be offline and out of touch with the task forces for long in the event that Saddam began launching weapons of mass destruction at Camp Commando.

It was during this period that Kubic also realized he needed a new style gas mask with a voice amplifier and bifocal inserts. When the war started, others needed to be able to shoot – he needed to be able to read computer screens and to talk. The Seabee logistics system quickly responded and his new gas mask with voice and bifocals arrived quickly well before the start of the war. With his special gas mask and modulated voice amplifier, some of the Seabee Jedi and MEG staff thought he looked and sounded like Darth Vader. But, from the admiral's perspective, it was absolutely critical for maintaining command continuity and clarity during the seemingly endless bunker drills.

Aside from the drills, Kubic's most extreme challenge throughout the build-up was to sustain global command and control (C^2) of the 1st Naval Construction Division while commanding the MEG. The Seabee Bunker was the C^2 node in Pearl Harbor that was created in the immediate aftermath of 9/11. Seabee Bridge was the main 1st Naval Construction Division Command Operations Center in Little Creek, Virginia. Seabee BUG was Kubic's onsite "Battle Unit Global" in Kuwait. It was manned by two officers (initially Lieutenant Commander Robyn Eastman and Lieutenant Dave McAlister) at the MEG Command Operations Center (at Camp Commando) who kept the admiral plugged into both Bridge and Bunker, and who stayed linked with him twenty-four hours a day, seven days a week through his Aide, Lieutenant Jeff Lengkeek, no matter where he was or what he was doing.

It was this global command net that cracked the "TPFDD by RFF" code. Constant communication combined with working "the system" from the inside out by "embarkation masters," such as Senior Chief Clarke at Seabee Bridge, made the difference for the

Seabees. Kubic remembered that I MEF was continuously amazed at Seabee knowledge on ship, plane, and troop movements. In an arena where knowledge was power, the Seabees had embarkation power. Reserve mobilization and logistics support were also managed with equal success by the "wizards of the Bridge, Bunker and BUG," as Kubic called them, who kept the Seabees personnel and equipment pipeline flowing throughout the critical period leading up to the war.

CHAPTER 7

Concept of Operations

Because of the ongoing haggling at the United Nations and in Baghdad concerning weapons inspections, and the "TPFDD by RFF" system of deployment imposed by the National Command Authority, the expected February 15 attack date came and went without a "Go" order. A new jump-off date of February 28 was set and then pushed back once more to March 15. This was probably fortunate in as much as CENTCOM commander General Tommy Franks and Defense Secretary Donald Rumsfeld were still working out the final details of a comprehensive battle plan that would enable U.S. and Coalition forces to move quickly into Iraq, seize Baghdad, and topple Saddam Hussein with minimal destruction and loss of life. CENTCOM's initial plan, OPLAN 1003, had been developed in the 1990s and was essentially DESERT STORM II in terms of strategy, tactics, and troop levels (with over 500,000+ from all branches), with an anticipated five divisions crossing the Line of Departure (L/D). It called for a "generated start," characterized by a deliberate ninety-day build-up, followed by a ninety-day ground and air campaign against Iraq.[1]

Secretary Rumsfeld, of course, was then in the early stages of his military "Transformation" program. Needless to say, Rumsfeld found this OPLAN wholly unacceptable and believed that a much lighter force, based upon greater maneuverability and lethality, could do the same job much more efficiently. As a result, Rumsfeld and Franks had spent the greater part of 2002 revising 1003 and integrating a number of other plans that had been floating around

Concept of Operations

CENTCOM to meet different contingencies. In the end, the Defense Department and CENTCOM whittled down the size of the anticipated attack force from over 500,000 troops (which were not available anyway due to 1990s "Peace Dividend" downsizing) to below 200,000.

Because of political uncertainties, the plan's original "generated start" was superseded by a "running start," as entailed in General Hailston's "go early, go ugly" strategy, in which a light force of perhaps only two brigades would cross the Line of Departure if Saddam did something stupid. The running start was problematic though since it would require one or more operational "pauses" to allow incoming heavy Army and Marine reinforcements to catch up with the brigades before moving against Baghdad. Moreover, as Naval War College professor and historian Colonel Nicholas E. Reynolds (USMC, Ret.) pointed out in his book *Basrah, Baghdad, and Beyond: The U.S. Marine Corps in the Second Iraq War*, it would be difficult to determine an optimal attack time, considering the trade-offs between strength and surprise.[2]

The Defense Department and CENTCOM ultimately agreed upon a compromise "hybrid" plan that would incorporate the best features of both the "generated start" and the "running start" plans. It was called OPLAN 1003V, and unlike DESERT STORM, which entailed a grinding thirty-day air campaign followed by four days of ground combat using overwhelming force to achieve the very limited goal of evicting the Iraqis from Kuwait (under the so-called "Powell Doctrine"), 1003V envisioned something very different. Based upon the hyperwar theory of warfare outlined in the book *Shock and Awe: Achieving Rapid Dominance*, written by Harlan K. Ullman, and James P. Wade and published by the National Defense University in December 1996, OPLAN 1003V sought to destroy the Iraqis' morale with powerful air strikes using technologically superior weaponry against a wide variety of targets, followed shortly thereafter by a lightning, multi-directional ground attack toward Baghdad by U.S. and Coalition ground forces. Overwhelmed and paralyzed by the resulting chaos and the sheer speed of the action, CENTCOM hoped, the Iraqis would quickly be "shocked" and "awed" into surrendering, with minimal casualties and limited destruction of the country's infrastructure.[3]

While the aerial "shock and awe" portion of the extremely complex OPLAN 1003V was self explanatory, the plan's primary ground attack would be executed by the U.S. Army's V Corps (out of Germany), which would sweep north through the lightly defended central Iraqi desert and then deliver a synchronized "left hook" by attacking Baghdad from the west. Well before the attack, U.S. and coalition Special Operations Forces would quietly infiltrate Iraq and lay the ground work for major military operations, performing reconnaissance missions, identifying key command and control centers, locating Saddam's mobile SCUD launchers, and making contact with and organizing various Iraqi dissident groups, especially the southern Shi'ia and the northern Kurds.[4]

CENTCOM also planned a secondary ground attack into northern Iraq out of Turkey by the U.S. Army's 4th Infantry Division, under Major General Raymond T. Odierno. The heavily mechanized division was then moving eastward through the Mediterranean in the expectation that the Turkish government would allow it to disembark and open up a northern front when the attack order came. Unfortunately, on March 1 the Turkish Parliament refused to allow the 4th Infantry Division to land, and it and its equipment remained offshore on ships while multi-billion dollar offers of additional U.S. economic aid failed to change Turkish minds. With this part of the battle plan scuttled, General Franks ultimately ordered the division to Kuwait, via the Suez Canal and the Red Sea, where its lead elements would be integrated into V Corps.[5]

Although its role was also defined as a supporting one, I MEF's mission was perhaps more hazardous than that of the V Corps. The Marines not only had to chew up Saddam's regular and irregular forces along the way, but they also had to secure the southern Iraqi oil fields, pumping stations, and pipelines and their lines of communication (LOCs) before attacking Baghdad itself from the east. Acting in concert with V Corps, Lieutenant General Conway's intent for I MEF was quite plain, "Remove the regime and provide initial stabilization until control could be turned over to another authority."[6]

Historically, the Marines had never attacked this far inland before. The last comparable instance was 1st Lieutenant Presley O'Bannon's six hundred mile overland attack from Alexandria, Egypt to the "shores of Tripoli" during the First Barbary War in 1805. Conway's understated aim therefore was truly daunting.

At this point, I MEF's organization for battle included the 1st Marine Division, the 3rd Marine Aircraft Wing, the 2nd Marine Expeditionary Brigade (christened Task Force Tarawa), the 15th Marine Expeditionary Unit (Special Operations Capable), I MEG, the

Concept of Operations

1st Force Service Support Group, and the 1st United Kingdom (U.K.) Armoured Division. Just like it had done in Desert Storm, I MEF would support the U.S. Army's flanking attack by marching "hey diddle-diddle, straight up the middle" into the teeth of the Iraqi defenses, this time within the Tigris and Euphrates valleys rather than in Kuwait. The 1st Marine Division, under Major General Mattis, would spearhead the Marines' attack, taking on all comers and generating as much mayhem as possible among Saddam's troops as it marched up Highways 1 and 7 toward Baghdad.[7]

Since the Defense Department and CENTCOM believed that Saddam would torch his own vitally important southern oilfields at the first sign of an invasion, the 1st Marine Division's initial mission was to save them from destruction. After quickly securing them, the 1st Marine Division would swing to the west and Task Force Tarawa would then move north, filling the gap between the 1st Marine Division and the 1st U.K. Armoured Division. The 1st Marine Division would then have a very tough way to go, fighting through the desert from the Kuwaiti-Iraqi border to Jalibah Airfield and then swinging toward the hotbed city of An Nasiriyah, which proved to be a tough nut to crack. The 15th Marine Expeditionary Unit (MEU), fighting initially with the 1st U.K. Armoured Division, would help secure I MEF's right flank, isolating and then taking the Iraqi port cities of Umm Qasr and Basrah and securing the Shi'ite south.[8]

I MEF's Concept of Operations consisted of four phases. Phase I (Setting Theater Conditions) involved the deployment of sufficient forces and equipment into theater to get the job done. Phase II (Shaping Operations) would commence when I MEF was in a position to target its designated Iraqi objectives. This phase would also include cross-border reconnaissance, the forward passage of lines with the Kuwaiti forces at the border, and the continued flow of forces into the theater.[9]

Phase III (Decisive Maneuver) was divided into two parts. Phase IIIA would begin with MEF ground forces crossing the line of departure, advancing into Southern Iraq and seizing key Iraqi oil infrastructure south of the Euphrates River. During this "sub phase," the MEF intended to make an example of the Iraqi's 51st Mechanized Infantry Division by forcing it to capitulate or by destroying it completely, sending an unequivocal signal to remaining Iraqi Army units that "If you choose to fight, you will die!" Phase IIIB entailed an attack north of the Euphrates to destroy the Baghdad

Division near Al Kut and the Al Nida Division east of Baghdad. Phase III would end with the 1st Marine Division staged east of Baghdad, ready to help the Army's V Corps seize the capital city when the time came.

Phase IV (Regime Removal/Transition) was also comprised of two parts and would begin with I MEF supporting the Army's V Corps' attack into Baghdad. While the MEF was supposed to play a supporting role in this attack by isolating the eastern and southern approaches to the city, no one truly doubted that the Marines would have to attack into the city. During Phase IVB, I MEF's focus would shift away from combat operations to post-hostility operations and preparations for redeployment. Its new priority would be the security of its forces, its lines of communications, and key Iraqi facilities as well as conducting Civil Military Operations (CMOs) for the benefit of the newly liberated Iraqis. Phase IV would end entirely when responsibility for further restoration of Iraq was transferred to appropriate international agencies. At that time, I MEF forces would redeploy to Kuwait and then return home.

The MEG's Battle Space

Under OPLAN 1003V, I MEF's operational battle space ultimately extended from the Iraqi city of Tikrit (Saddam's hometown) in the northern part of the country, to Kuwait City in the south. This Area of Responsibility covered more than six hundred linear kilometers and encompassed a number of major cities, including Tikrit, Baghdad, An Numaniyah, An Nasiriyah, Al Kut, Jalibah, Basrah, Um Qasr, and Kuwait City. Highway 1 (known as Main Supply Route (MSR) Tampa for operational purposes), running north from An Nasiriyah to Baghdad, defined the Area of Responsibility's western boundary. This road was only partially completed and was surfaced with both asphalt and dirt and it featured multiple culverts and wash areas. In the middle of the MEG's battle space and running north to south was the Saddam Canal, which spanned an average width of sixty to eighty meters. East of the Saddam Canal was Highway 7, which connected An Nasiriyah and Al Kut to the north, turning west at Al Kut, where it became Highway 6 and continued to Baghdad. The Tigris River defined the Area of Responsibility's eastern boundary from Basrah to Al Kut; at Al Kut, the Tigris turned west and traced Highway 6 into Baghdad.[10]

As it advanced through its Area of Responsibility while executing its part of 1003V, the MEG would have to contend with a number of potential river crossings, the most likely of which were over the Euphrates at An Nasiriyah, over the Tigris at An Numaniyah and Al Kut; and over several sites on the Diyala River, which guarded the eastern approaches into Baghdad. Additionally, several tributaries branched off the Tigris and undercut Highway 7, creating numerous potential crossing points along that critical advance route.

Following the attack and during the operation's planned stabilization phase, the MEG battlespace was expanded to west of the Euphrates, encompassing the major cities of Al Hillah, Karbala, Ad Diwaniyah, and An Najaf. By the end of the operation, if all went as planned, the entire MEG would be dispersed over an impressive 67,000 square kilometers of territory.

Enemy Situation

In the weeks and days preceding Operation IRAQI FREEDOM, the Iraqi military, while significantly degraded as a result of DESERT STORM, remained one of the largest and strongest in the Middle East. Saddam had largely rebuilt and reorganized his armed forces, particularly his Republican Guard Divisions and his Regular Army. His overarching goal had been to maintain regime security, a function his forces had been particularly successful in performing through the use of regime-sponsored terror and secret police organizations. In rebuilding his combat power, Hussein's emphasis had been on quality over quantity. Specifically, he invested heavily in his remaining armored and mechanized equipment, ultimately making his ground forces smaller and less infantry-intensive. I MEF knew that Saddam's three-pronged strategy was 1) to control his people and troops, 2) attrite U.S. forces, and 3) survive by any means possible.[11]

The Marine commanders thought that the most competent of Saddam's forces were the Republican Guards (and to a lesser extent the regular Iraqi army). Regardless, both the Republican Guards and the regular army lacked the ability to engage in sustained, high intensity combat due to aging equipment, poor logistical support, a limited maintenance capability, and an overall shortage of spare parts. The Marines anticipated that morale and discipline would be severely lacking, especially within the regular forces, which were heavily dependent upon conscripted troops.

Immediately prior to the operation, the Iraqis' force disposition consisted of major concentrations of troops, armor, and artillery distributed across three regions of the country. In the north, facing

Kurdish-held areas, Saddam had positioned approximately 150,000 troops, 900 tanks, 1,000 APCs and 1,000 artillery pieces, all of which came from his I, II, and V Corps (comprised of a total of thirteen divisions, including one Republican Guard and three heavy regular army divisions). Forming a defensive perimeter around Baghdad itself were four Republican Guard divisions, comprised of roughly 30,000 troops, 400 tanks, 500 APCs and 200 artillery pieces. Lastly, in southern Iraq, about 70,000 troops from III and IV Corps (consisting of six divisions, including three heavy regular army divisions) faced Shi'a insurgents in the south.

After the MEG's G-2 Intelligence section completed its analysis of Saddam's military situation in March, Marine Major Chris Brown, working with the MEF G-2, outlined the enemy's most probable course of action (MPCOA) to MEG commanders. The MEF G-2 believed that Saddam would defend the southern approaches to An Nasiriyah with three divisions, using a multi-layered defense while relying on Republican Guard heavy divisions to defend Central Iraq and Baghdad. Additionally, Marine intelligence officers believed that the dictator would use his security forces (Special Republican Guard, Special Security Organization, the Saddam Fedayeen, etc.) to protect his regime and quell any civil unrest that might be generated by an attack, and also employ a variety of asymmetric, unconventional, and improvised terrorist tactics to counter the coalition's significant conventional military superiority.

G-2 also thought that Saddam had taken the lessons of the U.S. experience in Somalia to heart, as widely publicized in the popular book and movie, *Black Hawk Down*. Consequently, G-2 believed that Saddam intended to try and channel MEF units into Iraq's urban areas during the attack by blowing up Iraq's southern dams and "tactically inundating" the battlespace with flood water. Afterward, he hoped to embroil I MEF in bloody street battles with the Saddam Fedayeen and the Special Republican Guard (which had established company-size strong points at key nodes throughout his major cities) and inflict enough casualties to turn U.S. public opinion and bring the attack to a screeching halt. To further slow I MEF and add to the horror, G-2 expected Saddam to destroy key bridges on Highways 1 and 7 and to then "slime" the Marines and Seabees with chemical agents on the near shores as I MEF attempted to bridge and cross the resulting wet gaps. By Saddam's way of thinking, if the Stalingrad-type street fighting did not churn American stomachs and force a cessation of hostilities, then scenes

CONCEPT OF OPERATIONS

of horribly burned and killed U.S. troops via mustard and nerve gas surely would.

Admittedly, this was a grim and potentially realistic scenario. However, as in most wars, the enemy rarely conforms to his own plan or doctrine, and the MPCOA was merely a base of assumptions from which operational plans could develop. The MEF and MEG, therefore, had to be ready for just about anything, no matter how devastating or worse than that envisioned by the MPCOA.

The MEG Mission

Under OPLAN 1003V, I MEF assigned the MEG the challenging and potentially far-reaching mission of providing theater-engineering support in tandem with the 1st Force Service Support Group to the advancing Marine forces. Throughout the planning process, this mission was continuously refined to adapt to I MEF's evolving operations plan as it progressed through successive revisions based on changing geopolitical and military events. Through extensive coordination with I MEF and its MSCs, the MEG's mission eventually coalesced to reflect the following goal:

> Support the I MEF Theater with bridging, mobility and general engineer support to maintain the Divisions' tempo throughout the attack. MEG will complete LOC and infrastructure upgrades to maintain unrestricted flow of logistics and enhance expeditionary airfield (EAF) operations throughout the AO, and provide general engineer support to I MEF. On order, transition to Phase IV Civil Military Operations engineer support and prepare for redeployment.[12]

Simply put, the plan was to meld the Seabees' unique deliberate construction capabilities with the MEF's requirement to maintain the mobility of the 1st Marine Division's attack.

Based on this final statement, Rear Admiral Kubic issued his "Commander's Intent" for successfully completing the MEG's mission during the attack. It was centered on six key points:

1. Focus MEG effort on 1st MARDIV mobility via upgrading roads and building bridges.

2. Coordinate bridging requirements with 1st FSSG and 1st MARDIV to ensure effective battle handover of river crossing sites and identification and execution of emerging engineering missions.

3. Push non-standard bridging forward to ensure rapid replacement of assault float bridging for re-use at the front and to provide unimpeded flow of 1st FSSG logistics.
4. Support 3rd MAW through upgrade and expansion of airfields.
5. Establish, improve and maintain roads for rapid, continuous forward flow of logistics.
6. Provide General Engineering support to I MEF for beddown, camps and civil military operations.

Task Organized

Task Force Mike was structured to conduct route maintenance and to construct Non-Standard Bridges. Because its mission was to provide direct mobility support to the 1st Marine Division, Task Force Mike was designated as the MEG's "Main Effort" unit. As bridging was its primary mission, Task Force Mike carried bridging materials and little else. It had two Seabee Engineer Reconnaissance Teams (SERTs) attached to it and would often maintain operational control of up to three SERTs at any given time. In short, Task Force Mike needed to travel light to keep up with the momentum of the 1st Marine Division's attack.

Task Force Charlie was initially organized with the mission of constructing an enemy prisoner of war/humanitarian assistance (EPW/HA) facility. The Task Force also contained "beefed-up" Main Supply Route crews to conduct road improvements. Because it would have to provide Task Force Mike with logistical and line haul support, Charlie was assigned the only Naval Construction Force Support Unit (NCFSU-2) in theater.

Task Force Echo's mission was twofold: support the 3rd Marine Aircraft Wing and the MEF Logistics Command, while pushing logistics and echelon assets forward in support of Task Forces Mike and Charlie. Echo also continued carrying out the formidable task of training and acclimating newly arriving MEG units that flowed into theater, and preparing for reconstruction and Civil Military Operations in the south, while the battle was still being fought in the north.

Under the command of Commander Jim Worcester, Task Force Echo's initial projects would include construction support to the USAF Civil Engineer Squadron at Al Jaber air base, to the 3rd Ma-

Concept of Operations

rine Aircraft Wing for troop bed down, and to the 2nd Force Service Support Group (MEF Logistics Command) at Logistics Support Area Fox. Additionally, Commander Worcester and his staff continued to refine and "war game" the MEG's and the Task Force's operational plans for supporting the MEF advance into Iraq. Captain Dave Fleisch eventually relieved Commander Worcester and served as Task Force commander. On March 27, the command was transferred to Army National Guard Colonel Pete Kole and the 265th Engineer Group command element, which finally arrived despite many trials and tribulations inside the U.S. Army's logistics system.

After getting on the ground, the 265th Engineer Group's advance party coordinated with Captain Fleisch to learn about the MEG's updated mission and operation plans. After a successful turnover, Colonel Kole took command while Captain Fleisch rotated out. Kole's ad-hoc staff was built around the advance party element from the 265th and a core group of Seabees from various units. Two additional airlifts delivered the main body of the 265th to Kuwait in April, long after the war had started. However, the main body's arrival allowed a general reduction in the number of Seabees assigned to the Task Force Echo headquarters. Many Seabees still continued to hold key staff positions though, including the Chief of Staff of Task Force Echo, which was filled by Captain Dave Phillips. With the Army engineers in place, Task Force Echo was the only MEG task force command element with multi-service component representation on its staff.

A recurring mission for Task Force Echo was assisting newly arriving MEG units in completing the reception, staging, onward movement, and integration (RSO&I) process. These tasks included assisting these units in air and sea port off-loading operations, movement of troops and equipment to assembly areas, and build up of combat power (logistics, training, and personnel). To this end, the Task Force employed a team of personnel dedicated to providing newly arrived commanders with technical advice and "lessons learned." This reception team more than proved its worth. Task Force Echo assisted in the RSO&I of over 4,500 Seabees and soldiers and over 2,500 pieces of equipment into the Kuwait Area of Responsibility.

As noted before, the arrival of the Army Reserve's 478th Engineer Battalion in early March created a significant problem. While the battalion's troops had landed in a timely manner, its equipment was not scheduled to arrive for another month. The challenge for the MEG and for Task Force Echo was to determine how to employ over 450 engineers without the benefit of their organic equipment. Moreover, this would not be the last time such a dilemma presented itself. The 265th Engineer Group and the 1092nd Engineer Battalion also experienced several weeks' delay in receiving their equipment. Additionally, while its soldiers trained for future missions, South Korea's 1100th Engineer Battalion (ROK) waited for over a month while its equipment was shipped to Kuwait. The constant delays between the arrival of troops and the debarkation of their equipment effectively slowed the RSO&I process.

Without their organic equipment on hand, the two Army engineer battalions were assigned a number of combat support missions, including convoy operations support and security at Ammunition Supply Points (ASPs), base camps, and oil fields. These initial assignments adversely affected a number of MEG projects, as the Army's engineer battalions, when properly equipped, were a rich source of engineering expertise and construction labor.

Task Force Echo's combat effectiveness was also somewhat hampered by the limited availability of equipment. This problem stemmed from the constant tasking of NMCB 7 to provide its own Civil Engineering Support Equipment (CESE) to the two reserve Air Detachments (NMCB Dets 15 and 21), to Task Force Charlie, and to the Army engineer battalions. NMCB 7 was, initially, the sole source of Task Force Echo's equipment.

With all of the task forces on the ground and organized, each was assigned one or more SERTs, and Task Force Mike received two special dive teams to ensure that it could conduct independent operations as it encountered both anticipated and unforeseen challenges. In addition to establishing the task forces' general responsibilities, the MEG Staff also detailed specific tasking plans, by phase, for Mike, Charlie and Echo. The majority of planning and operational concepts initially focused on Phase III operations. Phase IV operations were broadly defined prior to the attack and would undergo further refinement following the start of the war.

I MEG's CONOPs

Generally speaking, the MEG maneuver scheme involved the movement of the three task forces, in echelon, behind and in support of the 1st Marine Division's attack. The MEG's most forward elements would consist of three SERTs [from NMCBs 74, 133, and 5 (later replaced by NMCB 4)], which would reconnoiter MEG objectives, identify future engineering requirements, and provide early warning of Iraqi attacks on critical infrastructure and lines of communication. Based on I MEF's planned advance routes, the MEG staff had identified sixteen planned and potential objectives. These objectives consisted mostly of possible river-crossing sites and airfields that I MEF would need to support its air operations. The MEG planned first to move forward, establish a base of operations, then push detachments, as needed, from the base out to work sites. Ideally, the task forces would "co-locate" with the forces they were supporting in order to ease coordination and security. They were, however, prepared to operate independently if necessary. Because there would be instances in which the Seabees would have to provide their own security, the World War II motto, "We Build, We Fight!," remained constantly in the backs of their minds. Lastly, to minimize confusion, the MEG conducted all planning and coordination using the same four-phase system as the MEF.[13]

Phase IIIA

As noted before, Task Force Mike was the MEG's main effort and would receive support priority. Its initial task was to support the reduction of obstacles in preparation for the initial assault across the Kuwaiti border. After crossing and regrouping just beyond the border, Task Force Mike's first job was to advance to the vicinity of An Nasiriyah and support bridge-crossing sites there along the Euphrates River and the Saddam Canal. Following behind the 1st Marine Division, it would hold the bulk of its forces at Jalibah Airfield (in southern Iraq) until called forward. Once the roads were secured, Task Force Mike would begin Main Supply Route maintenance and construction from Jalibah to An Nasiriyah. It would then establish MEG Bridge Park Davisville while preparing concurrently to support the 3rd Marine Aircraft Wing in establishing a forward operating base (FOB) where Marine aircraft could be refueled, rearmed and repaired. The MEG identified Jalibah as the most likely forward operating base site. If work on the site was not complete by the time Task Force Mike was ready to move on, Task Force Charlie would move up and continue the work. The positioning of the MEG forces during the first hours and days of the attack was critical. Task Force Mike needed to push its forces forward quickly to respond to non-standard bridging requirements and to prepare for Phase IIIB, during which it would support the 1st Marine Division's attack up either Highway 1 or Highway 7, or both.

During Phase IIIA, Task Force Charlie's initial tasks were to relieve Task Force Mike of border obstacle maintenance, follow behind the 1st Marine Division and construct an Enemy Prisoner of War holding area near Al Jazair, and provide line haul for Task Force Mike. Task Force Charlie's dozer teams would relieve Mike units at the border, allowing Task Force Mike to maintain unit integrity as it moved north. Because I MEF anticipated massive Iraqi surrenders, the EPW holding area was a time-sensitive mission. The remainder of Task Force Charlie would hold fast in Kuwait to provide initial logistical support for Task Force Mike. On order, this contingent would then push its road and dozer crews forward, maintaining roads south of Jalibah while additional dozer teams closed the border berms behind it to protect Kuwait from an Iraqi counter-attack and a potentially overwhelming exodus of Iraqi refugees. Movement of Class IV materials and Mabey & Johnson bridging assets was also Task Force Charlie's responsibility. As soon as practical, Task Force Charlie would start running Class IV convoys, and also move the stockpiled bridging sets to Jalibah, An Nasiriyah or the Bridge Park, depending on I MEF's initial needs. Additionally, Task Force Charlie had to prepare for a number of other potential missions, including FARP/FOB (Forward Air Refueling Point/ Forward Operating Base) support to the 3rd Marine Aircraft Wing, bridging operations in the vicinity of Basrah, and Main Supply Route/Alternate Supply Route expansion within the Area of Responsibility.

Task Force Echo's Phase IIIA mission would call for the provision of logistical support from Kuwait and for preparation to launch a detachment to repair the port at Umm Qasr. However, Task Force Echo's primary task during this phase remained to receive, train, and prepare MEG and Seabee personnel who were still arriving in theater. Task Force Echo would also provide mission support to Task Forces Mike and Charlie by providing personnel and equipment on an "as required" basis. On order, it would follow behind Charlie, conducting Main Supply Route/ Alternate Supply Route maintenance and expansion along the way, thus keeping Task Force Charlie's Main Supply Route workload manageable. Third, Task Force Echo would complete any needed runway repairs at Al Jaber or Ali Al Salem. Fourth, it was to prepare for potential bridging operations in the vicinity of Basrah and Umm Qasr. Finally, in the event that a MEG unit came under chemical attack, Task Force Echo was to have its own "Jiffy" decontamination teams on standby, ready to augment Charlie's decontamination efforts and to help speed up the cleaning process and reduce potential casualties.

Phase IIIB

Once I MEF's attacking forces crossed the Euphrates River, the MEG's mission would be entirely event-driven. Thus, the Task Forces had to be prepared for the most unforeseen of contingencies. During this phase, all three Task Forces would be maneuvering throughout Iraq with an intense focus on providing mobility. The 1st Marine Division would attack across the Tigris and move to isolate Baghdad; Task Forces Mike, Charlie and Echo would all play key roles in making this happen. Task Force Mike would remain the MEG's main effort and would be focused on bridging, road maintenance, and the support of the 3rd Marine Aircraft Wing's next potential Forward Operating Base, which was expected to be at either Al Kut or An Numaniyah.

The MEG staff and the Future Operations planning team established well-defined decision points concerning the commitment of MEG units to Highway 1 or 7, or both. Due to the fluid situation, the SERTs would play key roles in providing early warning and critical information so the MEG staff could formulate solid recommendations for task force employment. During the planning, Highway 7 seemed the most likely route of advance, and so most of the MEG's objectives were concentrated along this axis. To afford Lieutenant General Conway more flexibility in moving his forces northward, Task Force Mike's primary task during Phase IIIB would involve the construction of a connector route linking Highways 1 and 7. This would give Conway the option of moving his logistics forces to the west of An Nasiriyah and then up Highway 7 if the eastern route through An Nasiriyah could not be secured quickly for his convoy operations.

The standing operational plan called for a relief in place between Task Force Mike and Task Force Charlie at the anticipated Bridge Park inside Iraq before Task Force Mike stepped off on its next mission. Task Force Charlie would then hand over its unfinished tasks to Task Force Echo near Jalibah, in turn assuming all of Task Force Mike's pending work. As the 1st Marine Division advanced to isolate Baghdad, Task Force Mike was expected to conduct a number of bridging operations on the Diyala River, just east of Baghdad. Given this expectation and the speed at which the

Division attacked, Task Force Charlie had to be ready to push on to Al Kut and assume Mike's missions.

Charlie's priority during this phase would be road maintenance. As such, it had to be prepared to assume or support any of Task Force Mike's missions on extremely short notice – no one expected Task Force Mike to be stationary for very long. The MEG expected that the final leg of Phase IIIB would be the most difficult phase of the war, as it encompassed operations stretching from An Numaniyah to Baghdad, a battlespace covering over 150 kilometers. Phase IIIB would conclude with elements of all three task forces supporting the MEF's isolation of Baghdad, while simultaneously securing and maintaining the MSRs from within Iraq.

Phase IVA – Attack into Baghdad and Regime Removal

During Phase IVA, the plan was for the MEG to continue to employ all three task forces in Iraq, while pushing even more personnel and equipment north across the border. Task Force Mike would have the responsibility for all projects north of the Tigris River. Task Force Charlie would take the projects south of the Tigris and north of the Euphrates, and Task Force Echo would cover everything else south of the Euphrates. Bridging, road and air base maintenance, and convoy operations would remain priority projects. Additionally, since the Seabees maintained excellent excavation capabilities, the MEG would participate in the hunt for Saddam's weapons of mass destruction as suspected Nuclear/Biological/Chemical sites were discovered. Finally, by "kick-starting" civil-military projects whenever possible, the MEG expected to take the lead in the transition to the stabilization phase of the operation.

A Special Band of Pirates

The I MEG command element was, in effect, the 1st Naval Construction Division (Forward) (Minus) (Reinforced). In actuality it was an ad hoc staff fashioned from highly motivated Seabees, Marines, and Soldiers ultimately representing over twenty-four different commands. Rear Admiral Kubic believed that it was truly a miracle that this staff arrived in time and formed into such a cohesive unit before combat operations started. It seemed like each time he found new needs on the staff, new MEG recruits were found. Kubic affectionately referred to this staff as a special "band of pirates" for they truly were a diverse cast brought together with the common objective of making the MEG succeed.

Concept of Operations

The admiral's only regret was that he could not convince the Chief of Civil Engineers to assign any Civil Engineer Corps O-5's or O-6's to the command element staff, and he felt particularly vulnerable fighting the war without a Deputy Commander. Had he been injured or just gotten sick, there would have been a leadership gap. But Kubic was fortunate to have an excellent Chief of Staff, Captain Gary Engle, at 1st Naval Construction Division headquarters in Little Creek, Virginia, so that he could concurrently command the Division globally while simultaneously commanding MEG operations in Iraq.

Command, however, was clearly stretched too thin during this period. Kubic needed more senior Civil Engineer Corps officers to augment the MEG staff, but these were not forthcoming. Realizing that he had to play the cards that were dealt to him, the admiral resolved to carry out the MEG's mission with a couple of Marine O-6/5's (most of whom were not Engineers) and his cadre of Civil Engineer Corps Lieutenants and Lieutenant Commanders, several of whom comprised that highly capable group of Seabee Jedi. These young officers ultimately surpassed even Kubic's highest expectations and carried the full operational burden of the MEG Command Element staff. "The "Force" was truly with the Jedi," Kubic later exclaimed, and the subsequent victory "belonged to them more than anyone else at MEG headquarters."

Use of Engineering Work Lines to Define Areas of Responsibility

As previously described, the MEG planned to employ Engineering Work Lines (EWLs), which were combinations of phase line and boundaries, to facilitate command and control of the Task Forces across the battlefield. During the planning phase, the MEG staff established multiple Engineering Work Lines tracing key terrain from Kuwait City to Tikrit; during the attack northward, any of these lines could be put into "effect" at any time. Engineering Work Lines proved critical in shifting the MEG's stance as it adapted to the ever-changing MEF maneuver scheme. In theory, when the MEG put an Engineering Work Line into place, the lead Task Force would assume responsibility for all engineering missions north of it, while another Task Force would take control of all engineer work below it, extending down to the next effective Engineering Work Line established even further back. Finally, a third Task Force would assume everything below the most southern Engineering Work Line and north of the Kuwait/Iraq border.[14]

The process of "snapping," or establishing Engineering Work Lines would begin with the issuance of Kubic's Commander's Intent. Careful coordination and often a formal relief-in-place (RIP) between the task forces would follow and the process would end with the official order to "Snap the Engineer Work Line!" Woe to the poor Watch Officer who gave the "snap" order prior to formal approval, as changes to Engineering Work Lines shifted the entire disposition of the MEG. Proper establishment of Engineering Work Lines demanded proper timing and placement of capabilities. Per the Operations Plan, the MEG would shift its stance three times during the attack phases: from the Line of Departure (L/D) to Jalibah airfield, from Jalibah to the Euphrates River, and from the Euphrates River to Route 27. Task Force Mike, because it was the lead element in the attack, always had responsibility for tasks above the northernmost Engineering Work Line (while Task Force Charlie assumed all work south of that line). During the last fifteen days of the attack, this meant that Task Force Mike's Area of Responsibility spanned from the Route 27 Engineering Work Line to Tikrit. Once Task Force Echo was combat ready, the MEG snapped the third Engineering Work Line. At the beginning of Civil Military Operations, Engineering Work Lines traced the outlines of the seven "Governates" in the MEG area of operations.

Logistics Planning and Organization

Because a template did not exist for the establishment and operation of a MEG logistics activity, a G-4 Logistics section was put together from a variety of commands, active and reserve, just like the MEG command element. None of the team members had ever worked together previously. On December 5, 2002, at Camp Commando, Kuwait, Marine Lieutenant Colonel A.J. Espinoza became the leader of the new team, leaving his permanent billet as I MEF Deputy G-4 to assume his new duties as the MEG G-4. In addition to Store Keeper 1st Class Vicki Houser of 1st Naval Construction Division, who was already working on the staff, Chief Equipment Operator Mark Thomas of the 20th Seabee Readiness Group, also joined the G-4 team. These three oversaw the extensive offload and movement of Seabee equipment and personnel from Kuwait City International Airport and the port of Ash Shuaybah to Tactical Assembly Areas Coyote and Fox, also located in Kuwait. Chief Thomas distinguished himself by training and directing the efforts of an ad hoc Seabee crew at Tactical Assembly Area Coyote to oper-

Concept of Operations

ate a temporary Arrival Assembly Operations Element (AAOE), where offloaded equipment would be staged. This was a significant task, as the actual Arrival Assembly Operations Element was not slated to fly into theater until after the arrival of Maritime Prepositioning Force shipping.

This small G-4 staff managed a number of functional areas, including but not limited to movement control, supply, ammunition, material management and food services. Store Keeper 1st Class Houser was designated supply chief and was assisted by Store Keeper 1st Class Timothy White, of the 1st Naval Construction Division, who joined the staff shortly after the New Year. Store Keeper 1st Class White was responsible for, among other things, ammunition allocation and procurement. Gunnery Sergeant Robert McCarty, a Reservist from the 4th Combat Engineer Battalion, became the G-4 chief upon his arrival on February 9, 2003. Lieutenant Commander Bill Sorenson, from FOSSC, arrived on February 23 and assumed his new duties as the MEG Supply Officer.

To facilitate coordination with external support agencies, a logistics cell, under the supervision of Commander Andrew Clyde, SC, USNR, was established at Ali Al Salem Airbase. This contingent was composed of supply personnel from Seabee units and was responsible for coordinating with the Marine Logistics Command, 1st Force Service Support Group, continental U.S. supply activities and local vendors. It also maintained responsibility over incoming supplies at the Doha support activity as well as at the seaport and airport. Additionally, to maintain effective communications with senior logistics organizations, supply expeditors were trained and attached to both Combat Service Support Battalions (CSSBs) 12 and 18 and the Marine Logistics Command (MLC). Finally, Chief Equipment Operator Daniel Jolin, of the 31st Seabee Readiness Group, was co-located with the MARCENT Contracting Officer to protect Seabee interests in the Marine logistics chain.

One particular G-4 success story involved the G-44, or Material Liaison Office (MLO). Under the leadership of Lieutenant (Junior Grade) Eric Ulmen, of the 22nd Naval Construction Regiment (and one of the Jedi), and Chief Builder Leonard Neal from NMCB-1, a cell was created to plan, order, track, receive and issue Class IV material. The success of this cell demanded close coordination with Kuwaiti vendors, Defense Logistics Agency (DLA), CONUS supply activities and U.S. vendors. Despite being located well away from sources of regular supply, the MEG Logistics Office procured and administered over $11.7 million of MARCENT/I MEF funds, ensuring that adequate construction materials were on hand when the Seabees crossed the line of departure.

The MEG G-42, or Unit Movement Control Center (UMCC), was led by Major Shawn Byrne, a 4th Combat Engineer Battalion Marine and logistics officer by profession. His section was charged with the formidable task of moving hundreds of troops and vehicles and tons of supplies and equipment over unprecedented distances. Under his leadership and guidance, the MEG successfully conducted over two hundred convoys and seventy-five airlifts in support of operations in Kuwait and Iraq.

Each task force had nominally 1,500 troops to support until the Korean Engineer Battalion joined Task Force Echo raising its strength to 2,000. The MEG ultimately peaked at a little over 5,000 troops, but had less than 3,000 when it attacked. Once again TPFDD by RFF presented major command and control challenges and could have led to disaster if the MEG had suffered extensive casualties or had been faced with more extensive bridge damage.

Double "BEEP"

As the March 15 D-Day approached, the MEG struggled with a huge dilemma. Rear Admiral Kubic had to make a decision as to when and where he would relieve NMCB 5 (in Task Force Mike) with NMCB 4 as NMCB 7 arrived to relieve NMCB 4 (in Task Force Echo). The original plan had NMCB 5 attacking with Task Force Mike to the Euphrates before NMCB 4 moved up and conducted a Relief in Place after NMCB 7 had arrived and relieved it in Task Force Charlie. This plan would have allowed NMCB 4 to undergo Mabey & Johnson bridge erection training before moving north.

As D-Day slipped and then slipped again though, it became apparent that the Relief in Place had to take place before NMCB 7 arrived if Kubic did not want to strand NMCB 5 for an even longer deployment. Consequently, he had to make a "gut call" and order NMCB 4 to relieve NMCB 5 before the attack started. Over the course of only two or three days, NMCBs 7, 4 and 5 conducted a double turnover of equipment (or Battalion Equipment Evaluation Program, BEEP for short). NMCB 4 moved quickly to Camp 93 to form up with Task Force Mike for the attack, relieving NMCB 5 less than 72 hours before D-Day, and "BEEPing" equipment that was already staged in convoys for the attack north.

CONCEPT OF OPERATIONS

As it turned out, NMCB 7's Advance Party arrived on D-Day and NMCB 5's departed literally hours before the initial March 19 strike on Baghdad. Unfortunately, NMCB 7 was greeted with continuous Iraqi missile strikes, and its Seabees spent their first days in bunkers outfitted in hot MOPP gear. But, this combat Relief in Place proceeded without a hitch, much to the amazement off the I MEF leadership, which couldn't believe that Seabees were rotating full battalions in the rear while simultaneously attacking north behind the 1st Marine Division.

Task Force Tango

Just when Kubic thought planning could not get anymore uncertain or complex, he received a Request for Forces for two Seabee Air Dets to support the U.S. Army's anticipated bed down in Turkey for the invasion from the north by the 4th Infantry Division. The MEG then executed the first of many JTAMs (Jump Through Ass Missions), and formed Task Force Tango from heavy Air Dets from NMCB 4 and NMCB 26. These Seabees all shifted focus with speed and efficiency, and NMCB 4's 126-strong Air Det flew out of Rota and arrived with troops and equipment on a very aggressive timeline. Unfortunately, this mission became mired in political controversy and Turkey refused to allow the 4th Infantry Division to enter the country.

Kubic remembered that this Air Det had a truly indomitable spirit. Under eight inches of snow, its Seabees had spent its first dull week in Turkey refreshing themselves on Chemical/ Biological/Radiological Defense and Seabee Combat Warfare Training. They soon grew restless though without any real construction work to do. Out of sheer boredom one morning, they helped the Air Force build 30-feet wide by 120-feet long concrete tenting pads without any formal orders.

As Chief Equipment Operator Richard Zylla later recalled, the undermanned Air Force crew had been struggling with the pads when he asked them if the Seabees could help. The astonished Air Force foreman replied, "how many Seabees can you get me?" Zylla said that he "could get him probably eighty-five to ninety Seabees in about fifteen minutes." "The Air Force" said Zylla, "was just shocked." He ran back and mustered his fellow Seabees, who grabbed their hard hats and went to work. "It was like someone kicked over an ant hill," Zylla observed, and that "it was kind of neat to see ten Air Force guys with all this work to do and not enough labor" react to the appearance of an army of Seabees in a matter of minutes to help do the job.[15]

The Tango Seabees also got on very well with the Army folks they encountered in Turkey. They built "head-shed" office spaces and video-teleconference rooms for the soldiers before returning to Rota. Afterward, they redeployed to Kuwait along with the rest of their battalion, and quickly moved into the cities of An Najaf and Karbala, where they later made enormous contributions during the Phase IV Civil Military Operations in the summer of 2003.[16]

3rd ID and 1st UK Division

The MEG's staff members believed that their association with the 3rd Infantry Division during the initial planning of the single Corps attack was professionally rewarding. In their collective opinion, Major General Buford "Buff" C. Blount and his staff officers were true warriors and fine gentlemen who demonstrated extreme flexibility as they planned their attack as part of the MEF. Kubic's Seabees had an outstanding relationship with the 3rd Infantry Division Engineer and, in the admiral's estimation, would have undoubtedly worked well together had the original plan been executed.

After Turkey denied access to the 4th Infantry Division, CENTCOM pushed the attack timeline to late February (and then again to mid-March), and very quickly drafted a two Corps (from the south) attack plan. The 3rd Infantry Division was moved from I MEF and placed within V Corps. With equal speed, the 1st U.K. Armoured Division, including the 18th Air Assault Brigade, the Royal Marines' 3rd Commando Brigade, and the 7th Armoured Brigade joined I MEF and replaced the 3rd Infantry Division. "The speed and professionalism of this switch was truly amazing," Kubic commented, and "a testament to the leadership of the respective commanding generals and their staffs." By the time the attack was launched, it seemed to Kubic as if they had been training as a team for months.[17]

The twice daily conference calls with Lieutenant General Conway were especially entertaining for the MEG officers as the overall Brit commander, Major General Robin Brims, always delighted them with his true mastery of understatement, such as the time when he reported that "we were attacked by a significant force last evening – they didn't shoot very straight – we did." In many respects, Kubic thought that Turkey had done the MEF a favor since the Brits taught the Marines a great deal about urban conflict and

CONCEPT OF OPERATIONS

Civil Military Operations and were, in his words, a "solid force of true warriors" on I MEF's right flank once it stormed into Iraq.

Breach Plan

Key to the initial attack was a rapid breach of the extensive obstacles erected by the Kuwaitis along their border with Iraq. The obstacle belt was a five-meter berm with a five-meter trench, ten kilometers of desert, a chain link fence with an electrified 10-roll concertina fence and another chain link fence, five kilometers of desert, and then another five-meter berm with five-meter trench. Multiple lanes across a wide front needed to be breached simultaneously, most likely under fire, before the ground assault could take place. The dilemma was how soon to start and who would do the breach. The plan ultimately included twenty-four Seabee D7 bulldozers organized into twelve teams along with Marine, Army, and British engineers.

Placing Seabees on the attack with a breaching mission was a bit of departure from their standard post-World War II doctrine. But then much of their previous "defensive-oriented" doctrine was rewritten after that war during a peacetime footing. Kubic believed that it was essential that Seabee dozer power be added to this mission, and if the breach plan remained unchanged, then a Seabee dozer would be the first piece of Coalition equipment to enter Iraq.

Convoy Plans

During planning, the 1st Force Service Support Group was paranoid that the MEG would place a heavy burden on its very limited truck assets, and it ultimately became apparent that a key reason why the Marine engineers insisted on retaining operational control of the Engineer Support Battalions was so that they could control their trucks. Indeed, it came to light that the 1st Force Service Support Group was some 375 trucks short of the number needed to support the Marine advance. MARCENT determined this be a potential "show-stopper," and the 1st Force Service Support Group had to find a quick solution, including the potential use of contract Kuwaiti line haul, which would hardly be ideal (for obvious reasons) in a war zone teeming with terrorists and guerillas.

The Marine logisticians clearly had a big problem with their trucking shortage, and so the MEG committed to hauling as much of it own equipment and material as possible. In so doing, the MEG had to protect its own Seabee trucks from the 1st Force Service Support Group, since it was desperately trying to gain control of as many trucks as it could from I MEF's Major Subordinate Command units and even from the U.S. Army. In the face of this internal MEF brouhaha, the MEG developed detailed plans for hauling all of its own bridging and Class IV materials as well as other supplies and equipment. The plan showed the MEG could handle all of its moves with an aggressive racetrack convoy strategy, with the exception of the floating Mabey & Johnson bridge across the Tigris, if it had to be built as a combat expedient project.

ROC Drills

As the weeks passed, the Marine high command was finally able to open the planning details to its subordinate commanders and their staffs so that they could conduct their own Rehearsal of Concept (ROC) drills. These helped field commanders get a feel for how they would set their orders of battle and the general relationships of units in time and space on the battlefield. But plans were far from firm and no one was given specific knowledge concerning the time of the attack. But they all knew that once March arrived the time was near since Baghdad had to fall before 1 May, the predicted time for temperatures to sore above 100 degrees Fahrenheit.

On February 27, a memorable event occurred at Camp Matilda (named after 1st Marine Division's official song, "Waltzing Matilda") in northern Kuwait. Major General Jim Mattis' 1st Marine Division hosted a number of key MEF staff members at the Division's ROC Drill. Following the drill, the I MEF Engineer, Lieutenant Colonel Pete Ramey, conducted his own ROC evolution, also at Camp Matilda to look more closely at the Engineer mission and to ensure all Engineer units were properly synchronized. All engineer commanders at the O-6 level (Colonel/Captain) and below attended the drill. Using the MEF commander's intent and mission type orders as guidance, the exercise was extremely effective in resolving critical, engineer-specific command and control issues.[18]

On March 2, 2003, the MEG G-3, Colonel Howard, spearheaded the MEG ROC Drill at Camp 93, home of Task Force Mike. All MEG commanders and their staffs spent a long afternoon carefully walking through a detailed terrain model as the various stages of the planned operation were sequentially detailed and discussed. At the drill's conclusion, and in keeping with one of his past practices, Kubic lit up one of his cigars to announce that he was pleased with the planning effort, and that the MEG was ready for war, whether CENTCOM was or not.

CHAPTER 8

"Hitting Pads"

March 5, 2003 was a blustery, wind swept day in Kuwait. Although it was just another cold winter day to most of the other American servicemen and women deployed in the Middle East, to Seabees it was an important holiday. It was their birthday, and Seabees customarily celebrate it every year, except in the most extreme circumstances. 2003 would be no exception. When it became apparent that CENTCOM's attack would not happen before mid-March, the Seabees planned boisterous birthday celebrations in each of their desert camps, complete with cake and ice cream, simulated spirits, genuine cigars and assorted real music. By all accounts everyone had a good time, and enjoyed the much-needed stress relief. At the MEG Command Operations Center, the staff members had fake beer and no bands, but they did cut cakes and talk about their rich Seabee heritage. During the day, Rear Admiral made a point of visiting all of the camps to check on the Seabees readiness and morale. There was no reason to worry, and he was soon pleased to find that Seabee pride was the strongest he had ever seen throughout his career. As the admiral looked each of them in the eye, he knew that "they were ready for whatever was about to happen, and that they now just wanted to get on with it."[1]

Ultimatum

By March 18, it was clear that time had finally run out. Following Secretary of State Colin Powell's February 5th presentation at the United Nations, the United States had allowed diplomacy to run its course. Iraqi stalling tactics and dithering by Chief U.N. Weapons Inspector Hans Blix, who repeatedly insisted that he needed more time to secure full Iraqi cooperation, left the Bush Administration wholly unimpressed. On February 14, Powell chastised both Blix and the Security Council, noting that "1441 is about disarmament and compliance and not merely a process of inspections that goes on forever without resolving basic problems.[2]

Ten days later, the U.S., Great Britain, and Spain had submitted a proposed second resolution authorizing military force against Iraq. But strong opposition from Russia, Germany, and France had forestalled a vote on it, and forced the U.S. to build a so-called "Coalition of the Willing" outside of the U.N. to take on Saddam. On March 17, a day after meeting with the leaders of Britain, Spain, and Portugal at a summit in the Azores Islands, President Bush appeared on live television and effectively set in motion the largest military operation the world had seen in twelve years. "Free nations have a duty to defend our people by uniting against the violent," he said. "And tonight, as we have done before, America and our allies accept that responsibility." Bush then gave Saddam Hussein, his family, and his cronies forty-eight hours to leave Iraq or else face war. In concert with this ultimatum, the British ambassador to the U.N. announced that the diplomatic process for disarming Iraq had ended, and U.N. weapons inspectors and all non-essential diplomatic personnel in the region quickly began evacuating. The "moment of truth" had finally arrived.[3]

The MEG Staff watched the speech live from its Combat Operations Center in Camp Commando, Kuwait. Marine 1st Sgt Dennis Jones, the MEG Watch Chief and a firefighter from Des Moines, Iowa, summed up the Seabees' general reaction to the speech with his usual to-the-point brevity, "It's about friggin' time!"[4]

At the time of the President's ultimatum, the MEG task forces were deployed in northern Kuwait and staged at Tactical Assembly Area Coyote, which functioned as the "jumping off point" for the attack north. Closest to the Iraqi border were Task Force Mike's twenty-four D-7, D-8, and D-9 bulldozers (with their tractors and trailers), which had been collected from various units within Task Force Charlie and had joined Task Force Mike on March 7.1 The dozers and their operator teams were poised at the future border crossing areas (or "breach points") and were on call to support the MEF's mechanized assault breach, which would entail reducing border obstacles and allowing Regimental Combat Teams 5 (5th Marines) and 7 (7th Marines) to attack swiftly into enemy territory. The border obstacles consisted of a series of Kuwaiti berms, anti-tank ditches, concertina razor-wire and high-voltage fences, followed by a similar assortment of Iraqi anti-tank ditches, berms and scattered minefields extending fifteen kilometers north of the border.[5]

The dozer teams were also prepared to employ four newly arrived Israel Defense Force (IDF) D-9R Armored Bulldozers, which were loaded on US Army HET (Heavy Equipment Transport) trucks & trailers. These D-9s took an interesting route in their deployment to Kuwait. Though the basic dozers were manufactured at the Peoria, Illinois Caterpillar factory, they were later modified for combat operations at the Israel Military Industries plant in Tel Aviv. Nicknamed "Zionist Monsters," the dozers quickly gained a reputation as the single most important piece of combat equipment for city fighting, based upon the previous Israeli experience fighting in Gaza and the West Bank. Following MEFEX-02 in August 2002 at Camp Pendleton, California, the MEG G-3, Colonel Mike Howard and the I MEF Engineer, Lieutenant Colonel Pete Ramey, had the foresight to request the dozers, which proved most fortunate for the Seabees and the Marines. Once the dozers arrived in theater, Colonel Howard personally located, inspected, and signed for the D-9s from the IDF, acquiring four for the MEG and five for the U.S. Army. Finally, building upon the D-9s' legacy, Howard affectionately named the four "Ziva," "Golda," "Natasha," and "Matilda."[6]

Both Colonel Howard and Lieutenant Colonel Ramey agreed that the D-9s could be the combat engineers' "ace in the hole" should the 1st Marine Division encounter intense urban combat (also known as MOUT, or Military Operations on Urban Terrain) in Baghdad. However, the dozers would ultimately prove their effectiveness well prior to the assault on Iraq's capital, particularly in direct support of Task Force Tarawa during the Battle for An Nasiriyah, where "Matilda" helped clear the way, performing to expectations like the "monster dozer" she was, and leading Tarawa's commander Brigadier General Richard Natonski to declare that "the D-9 scared the hell out of the enemy." Much later, near the gates of Baghdad, "Ziva" prepared embankments for an Assault Float (Ribbon) Bridge over the Diyala River for the 1st Marine Division. Unfortunately, an embankment collapsed under her 62-ton weight and she was, for several days, "mired up to her gills" in the Diyala. She was later rescued by an M-88 Hercules tank retriever that was anchored to her sisters "Golda" and "Natasha."[7]

Two of the MEG's Seabee Engineer Reconnaissance Teams, SERT 133 and SERT 5, were also positioned north with the lead elements of the Marine Corps attack force. SERT 5 was with Regimental Combat Team (RCT) 1 on the east flank, and SERT 133 was with Task Force Tarawa in the center. Additionally, SERT 74 linked up with the U.S. Army V Corps' 3rd Infantry Division, which would attack to the west of Task Force Tarawa. The SERTs' job was to conduct early reconnaissance of roads and bridges and then send their reports back to MEG Headquarters for evaluation and Future Operations planning.[8]

Next, a number of line haul teams were formed from NMCB 4, NMCB 74, NMCB 133, NCFSU-2 and the Army's 478th Engineer Battalion. The line haul teams consisted of approximately two hundred Seabees (primarily Equipment Operators and Construction Mechanics). Lieutenant Commander Williamson and Lieutenant Zeda of NMCB 74 played key roles in establishing the convoys' standing operating procedures (SOPs). On March 18, as G-Day was drawing near, the first two convoys were formed and "embedded" in Task Force Mike. Their mission was to cross the Line of Departure once Lieutenant General Conway gave the "go" order and then deliver two 60-meter Mabey & Johnson bridges at either Logistics Support Area Viper or the first bridging site. As it happened, they ultimately remained with Task Force Mike, moving all the way to the outskirts of Baghdad before eventually returning to Camp 93 for follow-on missions. During the first three weeks of hostilities, Task Force Charlie line haul personnel would ultimately execute over forty-five convoys and deliver over five hundred tons of materials and critical supplies to Seabees in Iraq.

Because of the delay in the movement into Iraq, and the need to keep all battalions on a reasonable rotation schedule, NMCB 4 had to move north to relieve NMCB 5, which had already been extended from seven to eight months on its deployment. NMCB 4 trained up quickly on the assault and bridging plan, and conducted the final actions of its Relief in Place with NMCB 5 just days before the start of the war. Only hours before the attack, NMCB 4 integrated into Task Force Mike and pushed north to its initial staging area with the help of their departing shipmates from NMCB 5. Armed with Mabey & Johnson Bridges, this battalion, along with NMCB 74, would lead Task Force Mike's advance into Iraq.

On March 19, Kubic attended the send-off of the Seabees from NMCB 5 as they boarded their flight back to Port Hueneme, California, thereby ending their eventful eight-month deployment, highlighted by the construction of the largest expeditionary Ammunition Supply Point (ASP) in Marine Corps history at Ali Al Salem and the construction of Camp Moreell. The MEG would sorely miss Captain Dave Fleisch and NMCB 5 during the upcoming campaign. But those Seabees had worked hard and no one begrudged them their well-earned trip home.

CFLCC Huddle

While the final diplomatic acts had played out on the world stage, and NMCB 5 was returning stateside, the Defense Department, CENTCOM, and the CFFLCC still did not have the agreement of all the key players on a final war plan. CFLCC had constructed a massive sand table model of the Iraq battlespace on the floor of a large warehouse at Camp Doha in Kuwait City. Raised seats for General Officers surrounded the model with bleachers at either end for staff. This was the venue for several planning sessions and ROC (Rehearsal of Concept) drills. This was an extremely effective technique for macro level planning and synchronization and allowed all to visualize and "de-conflict" the battlespace in time and space.[9]

Although the objectives of the pending war were clear and straight forward – protect the oil fields and topple Saddam – the plan had many complexities to it and had been developed through an iterative process. Although time was running out, D-Day always seemed to be pushed forward far enough, just as it reached the projected day (31 December, 15 February, 28 February, and 15 March) to allow for significant revisions to the plan. Later, on the night of the attack, March 20, 2003, an embedded reporter asked Kubic in the MEF Command Operations Center if the war was going according to plan. The admiral replied, "Which plan?" and suggested that the "planning effort was designed to distract us until we were allowed to attack."

CFLCC held one last huddle around the giant sand table in the warehouse at Camp Doha on March 18, 2003. The experience was quite surreal to all who attended. The President had given Saddam and his sons 48 hours to leave Iraq and the clock was ticking. Only principal officers were present and the staff briefs were necessarily short and to the point. Many details were still not resolved but it was clear that the Coalition had run out of time to plan, and everyone had to do their best with what they had from that point on.

There was still no final resolution of assignment of Army Multi Role Bridge Companies (MRBCs) since most had not yet arrived. This presented I MEF with a dilemma since it did not have adequate assault float bridges without the Army's even to make it to the Tigris, let alone to cross that massive river if Saddam blew the bridges en route as Marine Intelligence had predicted.

Even though the 3rd Infantry Division commander, Major General Buford Blount, offered to relinquish his MRBC to the Marines at the Line of Departure or at the Euphrates, no one was able or interested in writing the required fragmentary order (FRAGO) at this point. Kubic asked the CFLCC Commanding General, Lieutenant General McKiernan, about the assignment of MRBCs to the MEF during the discussion, and he responded that "we don't have enough, you'll have to do the best you can." Had Saddam blown the bridges, this failure to obtain and assign adequate afloat bridging could have been the Coalition's undoing, causing an unplanned tactical pause and exposing the MEF to a chemical-biological attack or even worse, political stalemate.

But the MEG had lots of culverts and Mabey & Johnson bridges by this time, and Kubic knew that the Seabees could cross whatever wet gaps they encountered. Throughout this highly classified planning process, it became very apparent to him how far forward Seabees would have to build and possibly fight, and how important it was for him to push SERTs 74 and 5 and Task Force Mike forward as fast as possible. The huddle that day was surprisingly short, and Lieutenant General McKiernan was poised and confident. He said that they would not get together again until after the war, if ever, and so the commanders took a group photo and went back to their troops.

D-Day was finally set for March 19 in Iraq, the expiration of President Bush's 48 hour ultimatum. Special Operations were scheduled to begin on that date, with the ground and air attacks planned to start in Iraq on March 21 (A=G=D+2) (i.e. Air Attack = Ground Attack = 2 days after D-Day (commencement of hostilities) = March 21), with "Shock and Awe" commencing at 2100 Charlie (local time), 1800 Zulu (standard military time, based on local time in Greenwich, England)). If the plan held, then I MEF would cross the Line of Departure at 0400 Zulu time the next day, on March 22, with the Seabee task forces right behind them.

Unbeknownst to the Coalition commanders, but somewhat predictably, the plan would change again even as Marines and Seabees, with Brits to their right flank and U.S. Army soldiers to their left flank, moved to their pre-attack positions just south of the Kuwait border, which were highly vulnerable areas for Iraqi missiles and artillery.

V Corps/I MEF Boundary

When, in early 2003, V Corps had to shift its planned northern attack to the south because of Turkey's intransigence, an operational "boundary" had to be set between V Corps and I MEF. This boundary became the subject of much discussion and ultimately much confusion. Attacking as the main effort, the 3rd Infantry Division was part of V Corps and was to cross the Line of Departure to the west, move through Jalibah, and secure Tallil Air Base to the South of An Nasiriyah. After defeating the Iraqi11th Infantry Division to the southwest of An Nasiriyah, the 3rd Infantry Division would then cross the Euphrates, with afloat bridging if necessary, and secure the north bank, awaiting a passage of lines and Relief in Place by I MEF. After CENTCOM choreographed this plan in great detail and I MEF had made its plans for movement of its three Regimental Combat Teams up Route 7 and across open terrain to Highway 6, the 3rd Infantry Division changed its plan and decided to swing wide to the west, and attack up Highway 8 and across the open desert. Highway 1 thus became I MEF's responsibility, and a Corps boundary was set between Highway 8 and Highway 1.[10]

This last minute change reduced the significance of Highway 7 and its many wet gaps, precipitating a dramatic shift in I MEF's battle plan. This shift required the MEG to adjust its plan as well, and to focus on improving the partially constructed sixty miles of Highway 1 rather than the massive bridging effort that was planned to be done along Highway 7. The carefully choreographed movement to the Euphrates and the anticipated passage of the lines therefore became a much more ad hoc plan, and created a great deal of confusion. The plan was further complicated, of course, by the need for the 1st Marine Division to take down the Ramalyah oil fields and then swing its forces quickly to the west, passing through Task Force Tarawa, which was then given the mission to secure and move through An Nasiriyah.

The MEG's SERTs still needed to get to the Euphrates quickly and Lieutenant General McKiernan decided that they should still follow behind the 3rd Infantry Division at the final huddle on March 18. But the MEF G3, Colonel Larry Brown, and the MEF Engineer,

Lieutenant Colonel Ramey, remained unclear about where the SERTs should go, and they unfortunately issued an uncoordinated FRAGO that assigned the SERTS to the 8th Engineer Support Battalion Area Crossing Engineer who was traveling behind Task Force Tarawa rather than with the 3rd Infantry Division. This oversight led to significant confusion as MEG Seabees crossed the Line of Departure, and it ultimately led to a real breakdown of command and control of SERTs 5 and 74, both of which ended up between the lines and under direct fire by the enemy. Worse, SERT 74 was split up and remained out of contact with the MEG for nearly forty-eight hours as it executed its preplanned mission to recon the Saddam Canal crossing to the north of the Euphrates and to the west of An Nasiriyah.

Also, the boundary shift resulted in the 3rd Infantry Division choosing not to secure the north bank of the Euphrates along Highway 1, delaying movement of the Seabees who were assigned to reconnoiter (SERT 74) and build (Task Force Mike) the connector route from that road across the Saddam Canal to Highway 7. This delay, coupled with the failure of Iraqis to blow the bridges east of An Nasiriyah, led Lieutenant General Conway to order Task Force Tarawa to attack to the east of An Nasiriyah where they engaged in a massive firefight along what became known as "Ambush Alley." It was hard to assign cause and effect in the smoke and heat of battle, but it would have been better to have worked out the boundary shifts and then rehearsed the movements a bit more carefully rather than going "ad hoc" at the eleventh hour. This early movement of Division sized forces through the same avenue of approach and the necessary requirement for a Corps-level boundary shift also caused extensive and exhausting delays as troops sat and waited and then slugged their way under indirect fire through the soft sand of the breach lanes during their initial movement north. This was a clearly case whereby the courage, resolve, and strength of the troops carried the day despite plans that left a lot of key details unresolved.

Shock and Awe

After much debate about when the air war should start relative to the ground war, CENTCOM finally decided that a near simultaneous air and ground attack was required to secure the oil fields while catching Saddam's regime by surprise. This developed into a very sound strategy with a well planned and rehearsed series of opening gambit attacks. The Coalition planned to throw everything it had at Saddam within a matter of hours, creating the kind of "Shock and Awe" that it hoped would throw his plans and his leaders off balance, and allow its forces to move quickly to exploit the chaos and the disruption of Iraqi command and control that would surely follow.[11]

Under the final battle plan, on D-Day and D-Day+1, Special Operations forces (SOFs) would take down Saddam's border watches and disrupt his early warning system. On A=G=D+2 (March 21) at 1900C, just after dark, the first big strike was to commence with a Navy SEAL attack on Iraq's Gas and Oil Platforms (GOPLATS) and on the Al Faw peninsula, to be followed quickly by the supporting attack on the Al Faw by the British 3rd Commando Brigade with the 15th Marine Expeditionary Unit. There would then be a massive air attack on the 480-foot Safwan Hill, the only terrain feature in southern Iraq with direct observation of the breach lanes. Once this observation post was leveled to 470 feet, Recon Marines would land and call in a huge napalm strike on the hill's northeast face as a diversionary attack. This fiery attack would also serve as a signal to Iraqi freedom fighters that the major assault had begun, and that they should seize bridges and oil facilities and keep them from being blown until Task Force Tarawa arrived at first light. At 2100C, just as Saddam was getting word that there was an attack in the south, he would be hit with the full power of air and cruise missile attacks – the full "Shock and Awe" that was planned.

As it happened though, less than two weeks before the attack, it became apparent that the planned Air Tasking Orders (ATOs) for Shock and Awe could not be fully executed because the Navy and Air Force did not have enough tanker planes to support the massive numbers of planned strikes in Baghdad. The only attack aircraft that could "go down town" and return without tanking were USMC F/A-18's flying off Seabee concrete at Al Jaber Base in Kuwait. At one point, someone at CENTCOM proposed that the Marines fly the Air Force's Baghdad missions while Air Force jets flew close air support for the Marine ground forces. "In an amazing display of restraint," Kubic later chuckled, "Lieutenant General Conway politely declined this proposal." Consequently, the degree of air power committed to the initial "Shock and Awe" plan, though substantial, was much reduced from the initial shock and awe theory. Following a night of massive air raids and rapid SOF/Commando strikes, the first units to cross the Line of Departure were scheduled to go at 0700C, first light, about twelve hours into the planned G=A Day. It was a great plan and all the principals understood and agreed on it at the March 18th Camp Doha huddle – but once again, even the "shock and awe" plan was to be revised significantly even before the first shot was fired.

By this time the Seabee dozer teams were in place near the border and Kubic spent the afternoon of March 19th with each of them. Unfortunately and without even thinking about it, three women Seabees and several women Marines were assigned by their officers to the breaching teams in conflict with current U.S law prohibiting participation of women in offensive ground combat operations. After discussing this with the Assistant Commanding General of the 1st Marine Division, Kubic chose to recall each of these Seabees personally. Ironically, the admiral had once predicted to several members of DACOWITS (Defense Committee for Women in the Service) that a battlefield commander would someday have to interpret the intent of the law governing women in combat in a pre-battle moment – never did he imagine that that commander would be him. Needless to say, this was not an easy message for the admiral to deliver, and when he gave them the bad news, none of the three wanted to fall back. Kubic never forgot the fire in Equipment Operator 3rd Class DeWitt's eyes when she said: "Admiral, I understand why you are doing this. But my crew needs me. I'm the best dozer operator in my unit." Not unsympathetic, Kubic told her that he did not doubt her ability, but the law was the law. As he left, he feared that "she might grab a dozer that night and attack Saddam by herself." She was one tough Seabee, he thought, and was clearly on track to be a Master Chief one day.

If Saddam chose to oppose the breach with the full force available to him, the MEG projected casualties as high as 30%. This prediction weighed very heavily on Kubic's mind. Consequently, he wanted to see those Seabees before they literally advanced into the breach and wish them Godspeed in view of the extreme danger that they were facing. Each of them was ready as far as he was concerned– true American heroes in the finest tradition of the fighting Seabees. By coincidence, March 19 was not only D-Day but it was also the feast of St Joseph the Worker, the patron Saint of Seabees. So Kubic thought that it was a good omen for D-day to fall on the 19th. As night fell, he returned to Camp Commando and began watching the clock slowly and steadily count down towards Shock and Awe.

Decapitation Strike

Shock and Awe, as originally planned, was preempted by a massive U.S. air strike in Baghdad at around 0400C or 0100Z on March 20 – which was after Bush's forty-eight hour ultimatum had expired but well before G Day =A Day =D+2 Day was scheduled to start some 39 hours later. The attack came as a complete surprise to all of the I MEF commanders, including Lieutenant General Conway. Apparently, an Iraqi source codenamed 'ROCKSTAR' had given the Coalition hard intelligence on Saddam's exact whereabouts, and with presidential approval, CENTCOM quickly organized and executed a "decapitation strike" to try and take him out. Once again the battle plan had changed dramatically, and this time without any notice. The air attack thus began ahead of the ground attack, and the Iraqis were likely alerted that the Coalition ground attack was coming sooner rather than later.[12]

Although the air attack against Saddam trashed the battle plan's timing, in an odd way it came as a relief to many of the MEG Seabees after months of sitting in the desert and enduring countless grueling hours of give-and-take planning. As Kubic opened the 0930C MEG "Battle Brief" meeting on that first day of the war, he told his staff that "I venture to say I am having a better morning than Saddam." Despite the flippant humor, the admiral was worried. All of the MEG troops were lined up in their pre-attack positions and were extremely vulnerable to missile and especially chemical warfare attacks. With the air attack on Saddam coming before the ground forces were ready to move, an Iraqi chemical attack would have caught them out in the open and inflicted horrendous casualties on them. Fortunately, the Iraqis did not take advantage of the situation and did not "slime" the exposed troops. But, they did respond in another way, one that came perilously close to "decapitating" the MEG.

Seersucker Counterstrike

The Iraqi counterstrike came just as the MEG staff was concluding the March 20th morning Battle Brief. The only warning was a last-second "whoosh" that sounded like a low flying airplane, followed by a deafening explosion, the concussion of which knocked Kubic and the MEG staff members out of their chairs. The missile was a 500 kilogram Chinese-made Seersucker Anti-ship missile. It had flown low over the Mutla Ridge and under the radar of the Patriot missile batteries protecting Camp Commando, and had landed only about 150 meters northeast of the MEG Command Operation Center tents.

The MEG's Senior Watch Officer, Lieutenant Colonel Geoff Gallo, recalled that "It sounded like incoming artillery." Expecting more rounds, he yelled for everyone to 'hit the deck!' Gallo's Watch colleague, Major James Gonsalves later commented that "While it was a little disheartening to know Saddam had aimed that missile right at us, it definitely took the edge off...kind of like the first hard hit in a hockey game. No one was complaining about wearing flaks and helmets after that."[13] Clearly it was now time for "hitting pads."

The range of this strike was dead on target with the bearing only a half degree off – a little more to its right and the missile would have struck the MEG's "ant (antenna) farm" and fuel storage, most likely rendering a crippling blow to Camp Commando's command and control capability at a very crucial time. As luck would have it, no one was hurt and no damage occurred. But, at the time, the MEGsters knew immediately they were under attack and assumed it was a chemical attack.

The MEG had been planning for this very contingency since mid-February 2003. Following lengthy negotiations with MEF and the MEF Headquarters Group (MHG) for the necessary space, NMCB 133 (Charlie) had erected the MEG Command Bunker. Located directly behind the MEG Command Operations Center, the bunker was large enough to house the primary staff during Scud alerts. The MEF Senior Watch Officer would sound the alarm whenever NORAD detected a missile launch in Iraq. The MEG staff would then move quickly into the bunker with computers, maps, and Iridium phones while radio operators would reestablish communications. NORAD would determine the launch grid and projected impact point of each missile and would distribute the information to CFLCC, MEF and the MEG.

In the days leading up to the war, many in the MEG staff had grown weary of repeatedly having to don their gas masks and MOPP suits for the drills and for many false alarms. On the night of March 19, just before the counterstrike, the alarm had once again sounded that a possible Iraqi missile was inbound. Tent mates Commander Billy Sloan, Lieutenant Michael Crafts, and Lieutenant (Junior Grade) Aaron Chetelat roused themselves up and wearily reached for their MOPP gear, while their MEG colleague Lieutenant Commander Robyn Eastman, continued sawing logs. As Sloan later told the tale, they took their time, having been through this drill countless times before without profit and anticipating it was yet another false alarm. They hoped the whole drill would be over before they could finish gearing up so that they could go back to sleep.[14]

As the warning siren kept wailing throughout Camp Commando, Sloan looked over and saw that Eastman remained soundly asleep while Crafts and Chetelat slowly donned their gear. While debating whether or not to disturb Eastman, Sloan heard an ominous roar in the air nearby. Immediately grasping the implications of the airborne noise, he yelled at Eastman to "Get moving, this may be serious!" Eastman was suddenly wide awake. He jumped into his gear and then high-tailed it out of the tent toward the command bunker. While Eastman was stirring, Crafts and Chetelat heard Sloan's warning too and moved even faster to clear out. So fast in fact, that in the time it took for Eastman to sit up from his cot, they had completely suited up and left the tent at a dead run. Laid back as always, Sloan went out, lit a cigarette, and while watching the sky, slowly ambled toward the bunker. There, the other three Seabee officers saw him taking his time in joining them and said "We thought you said this was serious!" In his native Mississippi accent, Sloan drawled, "It was! That was the Patriots firing off!" They all had a good laugh at how quickly they could move when properly motivated. As it happened, it was another false alarm. The Patriot missile landed harmlessly somewhere in the Iraqi desert many miles away.

All of the MEG's bunker drill training paid off a few hours later though, when the Seersucker strike finally ended the laughing once and for all. Kubic scrambled towards his command bunker as he fumbled for his gas mask, while the MEG staff quickly assembled there and brought their phones, radios, and computers online. At Kubic's side during this high stress kick-off event and continuously with the admiral throughout the planning and combat phases of the war were his Aide, Lieutenant Jeff Lengkeek, and his most trusted advisor, Command Master Chief Kevin Timmons. In Kubic's opinion, Lengkeek was probably the "MEGster" who worked the hardest and got the least sleep. He kept the admiral on track and made his schedule and movements work day after day while keeping him tuned in to the Junior Officer perspective as the MEG went to war. The Master Chief was a solid, no-nonsense Seabee who quietly but firmly led the senior enlisted leadership, and kept the admiral focused on the welfare and morale of his troops. Lengkeek sat to Kubic's right in the bunker and had his computer up and singing within minutes of each SCUD launch. Command Master Chief Timmons sat to Kubic's left and kept count of the subsequent thirty-eight SCUD launches with a pencil on the plywood wall as he gave the admiral his counsel during very stressful moments in the bunker and throughout OIF I. Said Kubic, "I could not have commanded the MEG without these two heroic Seabees at my side."

With courage and efficiency the G6 (communications) guys had the MEG command staff up and talking with radio checks to all three task forces within about five minutes of the seersucker strike. The staff was also up on the MEF net and responding to calls on behalf of the MEF, which was no doubt scrambling as well. The Chemical/Biological/Radiological guys were on top of the strike and had it plotted quickly, as well as the other two missiles that were shot at about the same time. Kubic was very proud of the MEG staff that morning, particularly the MEG's Senior Chief Corpsman, "Doc" Reed, who grabbed his field bag and ran towards the missile impact site to see if anyone needed medical assistance. He was the only person in the camp who did this. When Kubic and his MEG staff left the bunkers two hours later, it indeed felt like they had "hit pads" on the face off and were now ready to "advance the puck."

Saddam shot a total of thirteen missiles at Camp Commando that day. The bunker battle staff grew very proficient under that day's extremely stressful conditions. Fortunately, the other Iraqi counterstrikes were either well off their mark or taken out by the Patriots, and none hit Camp Commando, much to everyone's relief.

The Seersucker strike did put a healthy fear in all of the MEGsters, and they took to the bunkers very quickly every time the alarm sounded. The MEG staff grew very proficient at standing up communications and getting intelligence on where the missile originated and where it was projected to strike. They could then compute chemical downwind movement, warn MEG units, and plan any required decontamination assistance should they get "slimed."

The MEG Command Element endured a total of thirty-nine attacks over the next week. In one case Kubic and several of his officers and NCOs were on the road to Camp Fox and heard the Patriots take out a missile overhead. Looking up, they saw the smoke rings and trails. The original thirteen strikes were the most that Camp Commando sustained in a single day. However, towards the end of this prolonged missile assault, the MEG endured a shot every

50-70 minutes, with five shots fired at the camp one very restless night. Sometimes there would be multiple launches toward Kuwait, with most coming from the Basrah area. With alerts occurring almost every few hours, the Staff trimmed the entire battle drill to less than two minutes.

Although the Iraqi missile salvoes ended well before Baghdad fell, there was no way of predicting an end to the threat while experiencing it. It seemed to Kubic like it would never end, but the attacks also hardened the Seabees' resolve to move quickly to topple Saddam.

The Iraqi Seersucker counterattacks made it apparent that it was time to move forward. With both sides now openly shooting at one another, Lieutenant General Conway was not going to wait for the next missile attack before striking back, and so I MEF pushed hard to get G-day accelerated by twenty-four hours. CENTCOM finally gave the Marines the "go" order on the evening on March 20, several hours after the initial Seersucker strike. Despite the strikes, CENTCOM, CLFCCG, and I MEF believed that there might still be a small chance that they could tactically surprise the Iraqis with a quick assault from the south – just like they originally had planned it. G-Day (Ground Attack Day) had finally arrived.[15]

CHAPTER 9

Into Iraq

Early on March 20, CIA Human Intelligence (HUMINT) indicated that an unknown, division-sized Iraqi armor unit had arrived to reinforce the 51st Mechanized Division, and that the oil wells in South Rumaylah were being set ablaze. If true, then this was one of the worst case scenarios that Lieutenant General Hailston had described during his first meeting with Rear Admiral Kubic back in 2002. With missiles flying and the Iraqis now apparently moving to destroy their own oil fields, the Defense Department and CENTCOM needed no further prodding to unleash its ground attack against Saddam. The order came down. G-Day was a "Go!"[1]

On short notice, Regimental Combat Team 5, the most decorated regiment in Marine Corps history, became the first ground force committed to the fight. It crossed the Line of Departure at 1730 Zulu Time (2030 local time) on March 20, 2003 to secure and prevent further destruction of the gas-oil separation plant (GOSP), and to prevent any reinforcement or escape of the possible Iraqi armor forces. This first major combat operation of the war went smoothly, and by 0956Z on March 21, 2003, Regimental Combat Team 5 had secured all of its objectives in the vicinity of the Rumaylah Oil Fields. Likewise, the Navy SEAL attacks on the GOPLATS (Gas-Oil Platforms) and on the Al Faw peninsula also went as planned – the Navy-Marine Corps team was in Iraq and in the fight.

Following sixty minutes of preparatory fire by the 3rd Battalion (Artillery) of 11th Marine Regiment, the remainder of the 1st Marine Division's assault forces crossed the Line of Departure, commencing at 0400 Zulu on March 21, 2003. Lieutenant General Conway closely coordinated the 1st Marine Division's attack with the 1st U.K. Armoured Division, which attacked simultaneously on the Marines' eastern flank toward Umm Qasr. Task Force Tarawa, led by the 2nd Marines, attacked west of the 1st Marine Division, toward the strategic airfield at Jalibah. Finally, the U.S. Army's 3rd Infantry Division attacked in front of Task Force Tarawa and headed directly for Tallil Airfield and An Nasiriyah. At An Nasiriyah, the 3rd Infantry Division was to push west, securing the bridge where Route 1 crossed the Euphrates River. Once relieved by Task Force Tarawa, the 3rd Infantry Division planned to stay well south of the Euphrates and move up Highway 8 toward Baghdad.

As soon as the artillerymen from the 11th Marines' started firing, the Seabees lined up on the road at Tactical Assembly Area Stethem knew that this was it. Construction Electrician 2nd Class Douglas Hoeppner, in Task Force Mike, later recalled:

> We had finally stopped for the night after a long road march. I was on mid-watch when I started seeing rockets. At first I didn't know if they were incoming or out-going. I was told it was the Marine prep fires and I was relieved. They were headed straight for Iraq. It reminded me of when I was here twelve years ago. I now knew the war had started.[2]

Although the breach points in northern Kuwait were well within Iraqi artillery range, Lieutenant General Conway thought it safe enough to accommodate a last minute request by Kuwait's government that the MEG use local civilian contractors instead of Seabees to open the breach points for I MEF. This was a big departure from the original plan, but most of these men were decorated Kuwaiti Army veterans of Operation DESERT STORM. They not only wanted to protect and then replace their billion dollar investment, but this was also a matter of national pride for them, since they wanted to strike back at Saddam for his 1990 invasion of their country.

As previously planned, the MEG's dozer teams had been rehearsing the breaching operation near the front for several days, but they gladly yielded to the Kuwaitis when Kubic explained the situation to them. Instead of leading through the breach, they began maintaining the breach lanes for the massive convoys that started moving into Iraq after the Kuwaitis had opened the berms for I MEF. The MEG thus accomplished its first construction mission of the war.

The MEG staff spent G-Day getting Seabee convoys underway and synchronized with the attack. The MEGsters also had to straighten out a confusing Fragmentary Order that I MEF had issued which significantly changed the employment and command and control of the MEG SERTs without consulting Kubic or the MEG staff. Kubic was anticipating a Fragmentary Order authorizing SERTs 5 and 74 to move north across the Line of Departure, initially with the 3rd Infantry Division, to allow them to get "engineer eyes" on the Euphrates river crossings to the east and west of An Nasiriyah as quickly as possible. This movement had been coordinated and agreed upon with the Commanding General and senior Engineer of the 3rd Infantry Division while they were still assigned to I MEF and had been confirmed again once the division was reassigned to V Corps. Each SERT's Liaison Officer was to remain with Task Force Mike (moving behind the 3rd Infantry Division) to ensure a strong communications link between the SERT recon and security elements (moving with the division) and the MEG Command Operations Center in Kuwait. When the MEF G-3 issued a Fragmentary Order written by his Engineer to attach the SERTs' under tactical control (TACON) to the 8th Engineer Support Battalion, which was assigned to the 1st Force Service Support Group, Kubic was both surprised and concerned. It appeared once again to him that "rice bowls" had prevailed over tactical considerations and effective Engineer command and control. As recounted later, the end result of this poorly staffed Fragmentary Order was potentially deadly command and control confusion during the employment of SERTs 5 and 74 south of the Euphrates in the early days of the war. But, at this point, there was no time to discuss a revised Fragmentary Order, so the MEG just pressed forward, relying on its previous planning and rehearsals to carry the day.

Commodore Rudich and Task Force Mike received the signal to move out behind Task Force Tarawa at around 2110C (1810Z), just minutes into G+1 on March 21, 2003. (G+ days began at 1800Z each day, with G-day beginning at 1800Z on March 20, 2003.) Rudich and his Task Force Mike Seabees began what was a long night of slow stop-and-go movement up the severely congested Alternate Supply Route Aspen, having had little sleep the night before. Task Force Charlie crossed the Line of Departure on G+1 as well at 0600Z on 22 March behind the Marines' Regimental Combat Team 1, moving toward Al Jazair along Alternate Supply Route Dallas. Movement was slow for them as well, but both task forces made efficient use of time while slowly advancing up the ASRs by dropping their road graders' blades and smoothing out the roads for follow-on traffic.[3]

With Task Forces Mike and Charlie now moving forward as part of the I MEF strike force, Kubic issued the following statement to document the historical significance of the event:

> For the first time in history, Seabees crossed the line of departure in regimental formations as part of a Marine Expeditionary Force order of battle. The First Naval Construction Division is proud to serve with I MEF as the main effort of the I MEF Engineer Group. Now it's time to get to work. Can do.

Enemy Prisoner of War Holding Area "Thomas"

Task Force Charlie's first major project of the war was MEG Objective S2, the construction of a temporary Enemy Prisoner of War Holding Area at Al Jazair. This job fell to a 150-Seabee detachment from NMCB 133, led by the battalion's commanding officer, Commander Douglas G. Morton. Code-named "Thomas," the Holding Area was needed quickly since CENTCOM anticipated (wrongly as it turned out) that tens of thousands of Iraqi regular soldiers would surrender and overwhelm Coalition logistics as had happened in 1991. Under the battle plan, Det 133 had to have Holding Area Thomas partially up and running by G+4.[4]

In truth, no one in the MEF wanted to guard the Enemy Prisoners of War. The feeling was that this was a job for Army Military Policemen (MPs), and that the MEF could get bogged down operationally and logistically if it had to divert resources to this mission. Ultimately, the 11th Marine Expeditionary Unit was assigned the thankless job. But, the lack of "staff ownership" at all levels, especially within CFLCC impeded any agreement on both the Concept of Operations for Enemy Prisoners of War and the required design criteria for the Holding Area. Lieutenant General Conway only wanted a bare bones "holding area," but others at CENTCOM were concerned about the need for "less Spartan" facilities to ensure compliance with the Geneva Convention Prisoner of War camp criteria. The U.S. Army Military Policemen insisted that the EPW facility had to be constructed to very high standards and they had a plan to build such a site. However, their plan briefed better than it would execute, and it soon became apparent that they did not really have the necessary Class IV material to build their proposed facility.

Since a short term holding area did not have to meet the same Geneva Convention criteria as a Prisoner of War camp, the MEG ultimately designed a bare bones holding area with concertina wire, guard towers, berms and slit trenches for waste. But, the facility was laid out so it could be progressively upgraded to add water and sewage, guard facilities, dining facilities and security lights. For short term shelters, the MEG staff designed simple lean-to's that could be erected by the potential Iraqi prisoners using plastic tarp material and sand bags.

Det 133 assembled in pre-attack positions behind Regimental Combat Team 1, with SERT 133 in the lead. They were also to travel with the lead elements of an Army MP battalion that had been ordered to reconnoiter a site near I MEF's temporary holding area to construct their own Enemy Prisoner of War facility using Army engineer troops and/or contractors assigned to the 416th Engineer Command, commanded by Army Reserve Major General Bob Heine. Getting Det 133 formed up and moved from Camp Moreell into their attack positions was a challenge. There was the normal construction friction associated with getting all required Class IV assembled and loaded, combined with a tinge of disbelief that the order to attack was eminent. Led by Officer-in-Charge Lieutenant Phil Lavallee, SERT 133 was in place ready to go before the Iraqi Seersucker missile hit, but Det 133 had to be prodded to get moving during the hectic hours after the counterstrike.[5]

To their credit, once they realized the attack was on, Det 133 Seabees responded quickly and were in position in time to move forward, loaded with all of the necessary Class IV building materials for the holding area. It was quite a feat that they were able to launch this mission on time, considering that the Seabee Materials Liaison Officer had to assemble and mobile load all of the Class IV material while holding area scope and material decisions were still being made and with changes still occurring only days before the attack.

On March 21, 2003 Det 133, along with elements from the Marines' 11th Marine Expeditionary Unit (Task Force Yankee) and Combat Service Support Company 119, left Camp 93 and headed up Highway 1 loaded with Class IV materials to begin the construction of Holding Area Thomas. A few U.S. Army Military Policemen moved with them but then quickly disappeared once Det

133 got to the site. Kubic learned later that the MPs checked out the site, decided that it was too "hot" and too deep into the fight, and scrambled back to Kuwait. They then chose a site for their own holding area near Umm Qasr where they could safely co-locate with the British Enemy Prisoner of War facility.[6]

Once underway, SERT 133 completed the initial reconnaissance quickly. It arrived at the prospective site of the Enemy Prisoner of War holding area, and after reviewing it and selecting an optimum location, Lieutenant Lavallee sent the MEG's first combat reconnaissance report of the war detailing a recommended site layout. He also provided soil conditions and other information to aid in mission planning. The DET 133 Seabees arrived shortly thereafter and carried out their mission in the face of hostile action and tremendous environmental adversity. An enormous sandstorm engulfed southern Iraq for some seventeen hours from March 24-25, but Det 133 kept working through it. When Commodore McKerall inquired about the intensity of the storm at Al Jazair, an exacerbated Commander Morton replied, "It's so bad I can't see the phone."[7]

The sandstorm was indeed of "biblical" proportions and became known as the Mother of All Sand Storms, or MOASS to the troops who weathered it. The wind, rain and blowing sand were brutal, and combined with the threat of hostile action, it became a defining period in which each Seabee, and especially their leaders, had to reach deep into their guts for the courage to continue. Tents were blown and destroyed, equipment was sandblasted, and the Seabees could not easily see or breathe. Even worse, they had necessarily left all of their survival gear behind to lighten their loads, so most were caught squarely out in the open with little shelter other than their vehicles or the culverts that they were carrying north into Iraq. It was truly one of the most hostile environments American troops had ever encountered in the annals of U.S. military history.

Seabees throughout the entire war zone had a particularly rough time of it. Senior Chief Jeffrey Weigel of NMCB 74 in Task Force Mike, which had pulled off the road to ride out the storm, later recalled that "it was just insane—I walked up to two kids up on the line and said, "Where's your foxhole at?" And they said, "It's right there," and it was completely filled in." Weigel's NMCB 74 colleague, Steelworker 1st Class Michael Hill added that when they were first warned about the approaching storm, "we're thinking a little bit of wind." However, he quickly found that "it was the worst thing in the entire world." He remembered that:

> You couldn't see, you couldn't breathe. I mean everything you owned in your entire existence had sand in it. Even if you covered your face, your eyes, it was just horrendous; you couldn't see and then when it got dark, whew, you couldn't see your hand in front of your face most of the time. It was that bad; the wind was so strong and the sand was everywhere. It got into our weapons; we couldn't use our weapons—they wouldn't work because the sand was in everything. Even if you had Ziploc bags, sand got in there. I still don't know how that happens.[8]

Construction Electrician 1st Class Alex Semmler of UCT 2 was less restrained in his description of the storm. He commented that:

> It was the most god-awful thing—it was horrible. I mean you didn't have to worry about tactics because it was just incredible. You were hoping to get shot just to get out of there because you're in full MOPP gear, and you're sweating and you can't breathe, and then at times a little rain would come down, so it was like mud was falling on you.[9]

Swarming sand gnats, the unbearable howling noise of the wind, and a night time thunderstorm added to the Seabees' misery. But they persevered and toughed it out, with many in Task Force Mike crawling under overturned sheet metal culverts for shelter. Others rode out the storm in their vehicles, trying to keep as much sand out as they could.

At Enemy Prisoner of War Holding Area Thomas, Senior Chief Troy Kellerman of NMCB 133 hunkered down with another female Seabee in a two-person nylon dome tent. It was barely sufficient. As she latter recalled, she had left her flap open so that she could keep an eye on the other Seabees in her Det. But when she finally stood up and tried to zip the flap closed, the wind came up underneath the back of the tent, picked the whole thing up in the air, and then turned it upside down, dumping her on her head. "That was unbelievable!" she said later, still in mild shock over her experience.[10]

Despite the zero visibility conditions, the suffocating sand intermittently mixed with mud-like rain, and the Martian-like landscape in which they worked, Morton's Seabees quickly completed Holding Area Thomas on March 26 after the storm subsided. Once they got started, they went for the "whole hog," much to Kubic's surprise, since initial plans called only for a first phase for a 7,000

Rear Admiral Kubic reiterates his commander's intent with Lieutenant Commander Mark Edelson (left) and Lieutenant Dave McAlister (right) at the MEG Command Operations Center at Camp Commando, Kuwait. Colonel Mike Howard, the MEG G-3, and Major Doug Mattox (rear) look on.

(Official U.S. Navy Photograph)

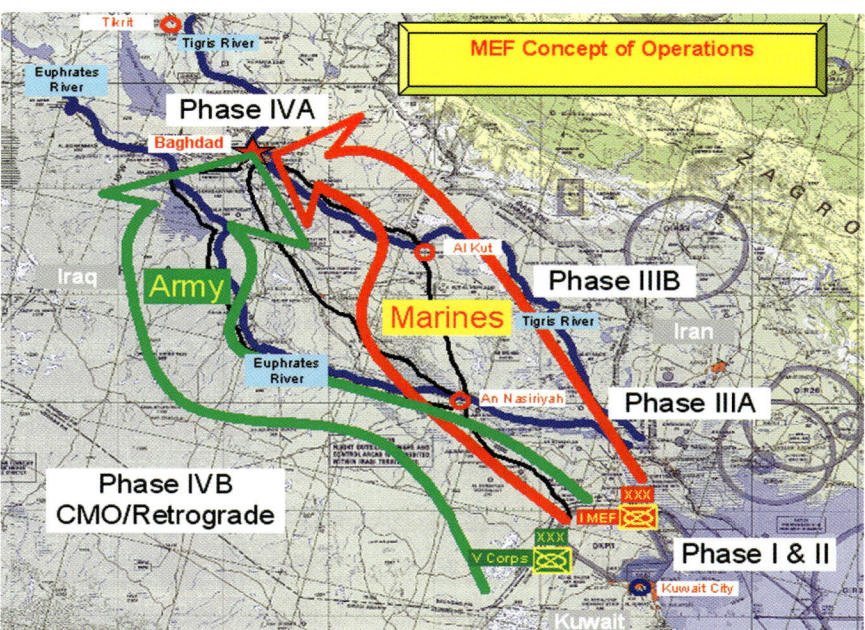

The four phases of Operation IRAQI FREEDOM. Phase I & II occur in Kuwait. Phase IIIA covers the attack through An Nasiriyah. Phase IIIB takes the attack to isolate Baghdad and Phase IVA entails the urban assault into Baghdad.

165

The MOASS took a toll on both the Seabees themselves and their equipment.
(U.S. Navy Photographs by Photographer's Mate 2nd Class Eric Powell)

During the so-called "Night of 1,000 Iraqis," Commodore Bill Rudich ordered Task Force Mike to turn on its flood lights and continue nighttime construction of the war's first Mabey & Johnson bridge despite intelligence reports of a potentially massive Iraqi counterattack.

(U.S. Navy Photographs by Photographer's Mate 2nd Class Eric Powell)

NMCB 74 constructs the MEG's first Mabey & Johnson Bridge across "Gap 5" north of the Euphrates River along Route 1 in Iraq, March 26, 2003.

(U.S. Navy Photographs by Photographer's Mate 2nd Class Eric Powell)

Following the MOASS, Task Force Mike fell in behind the Marines again and continued the drive toward Baghdad, later crossing its own Mabey & Johnson Bridge in the process.

(U.S. Navy Photographs by Photographer's Mate 2nd Class Eric Powell)

Rear Admiral Kubic (call sign "Budweiser") standing over the Euphrates River with Commodore Rudich — all wearing MOPP gear as the attack pressed north (Official U.S. Navy Photograph)

NMCB 4 constructed this 60-meter Mabey & Johnson bridge using "Mac Moles" across the Saddam Canal just north of An Nasiriyah, Iraq. Below is the MEG's third Mabey & Johnson bridge, which NMCB 74 constructed in Iraq along Route 27 over a 40-meter gap on the Saddam Canal.
(Official U.S. Navy Photographs)

During Operation DESERT STORM in 1991, the Seabees had been too "heavy" to maneuver with the Marines. For the impending Operation IRAQI FREEDOM I, they had to shed all of their extra gear and re-learn how to "live like Marines" (i.e. camp and travel light) during the drive to Baghdad.

(U.S. Navy Photographs by Photographer's Mate 2nd Class Eric Powell)

Engineering Aide 2nd Class Oliver Taylor of SERT 74 helps secure a sector of a highway.
(U.S. Navy Photo by Photographer's Mate 2nd Class Eric Powell).

Seabees and Marines of the 4th Civil Affairs Group distribute food and water to more than 1,000 Iraqis in An Nasiriyah in late March 2003.

(USMC Photograph by Corporal Matthew Orr)

Task Force Charlie Seabees from NMCB 133 and NCFSU 2 improve the road surface on one of the main supply routes supporting combat operations in early April 2003 during Operation IRAQI FREEDOM.

(U.S. Navy Photograph by Photographer's Mate 2nd Class Jacob Johnson.)

SERT 4 lines up during a Bridge Reconnaissance mission which took them by the scene of an earlier heavy ambush near Ah Shatrah.

(Official U.S. Navy Photograph)

A Seabee from Task Force Mike stands guard as his battalion (NMCB 4) constructs the Mabey & Johnson bridge over the Diyala during Phase IVA. This bridge would facilitate the 1st Marine Division's ability to quickly secure the eastern part of Baghdad in early April. Marine combat engineers dropped the AVLB bridge (left) during the initial assault into the city.

(Official U.S. Navy Photograph)

With the final battle for Baghdad raging in the background, Seabees from NMCB 4 build a critical Mabey & Johnson "over-bridge" across the Diyala River during Phase IVA. (Official U.S. Navy Photograph)

Flanked by Command Master Chiefs Timmons (left) and Romero (right), Rear Admiral Chuck Kubic (center left) stands with Commodore Bill Rudich (center right) at the Diyala River, April 10, 2003. (Official U.S. Navy Photograph)

Enemy Prisoner of War Holding Area rather than for a 14,000 Enemy Prisoner of War Holding Area that the "Kang'roos" of NMCB 133 actually built. After they completed the project, the Executive Officer of Task Force Yankee, Lieutenant Colonel James P. Gfrerer, exclaimed "This is textbook contingency construction! The Seabees should change their motto from 'Can Do!' to 'Done'." Having finished Thomas, Det 133 moved to Logistics Support Area Viper (at Jalibah airfield) for a short time before continuing north and on to the Davisville Bridge Park.[11]

The MEGsters were very proud of DET 133 as those Seabees completed the MEG's first contingency construction mission. But their joy was soon dampened when the MEF decided not to use the facility. With very few Iraqi prisoners of war to hold, the Marines decided to use the British Facility near Basrah. (They anticipated as many as 40,000 prisoners but captured less than 8,000 in the initial days of the assault.). Clearly those who did not want to be bothered with Enemy Prisoners of War carried the day. But nevertheless, the Desert 'Roos of Det 133 distinguished themselves with this piece of high-end, rapid combat construction, which was the finest EPW holding area never used.

Task Force Charlie also deployed two Main Supply Route repair teams to perform maintenance and make road improvements along MSRs Tampa and Dallas. The first of these teams (MSR 2) launched with the Enemy Prisoner of War team from Camp 93 on March 21. MSR 1 launched two days later on March 23. While the initial work was minimal, these teams, comprised of Seabees from NMCB 133, NMCB 4 and NFCSU 2, would play a vital role in the efforts to keep Main Supply Route Tampa open north of the Euphrates. A third maintenance team from NMCB 74, was sent to improve the border crossing on Maine Supply Route Dallas. This team worked the crossing site on a periodic basis until the Engineering Work Lines were moved north and Task Force Echo took over responsibility for this work.[12]

Battle Rhythm

At the MEG Command Operations Center, Kubic and his staff quickly rolled into a very intense battle rhythm as the MEG Task Forces went to work. They used Video Teleconference (VTC) phones (referred to as "one eyes" for their single lens desk top cameras) wired through the SIPRnet for secure voice-only conference calls with the Commanding General, Lieutenant General Conway, each day at 0600C and again at 1800C. Kubic's Command Group Meeting was at 0800C and he typically received the MEG Operations Battle Brief at 0930C. Operations summaries from the Watch were due by 0530C and 1730C each day and the MEG Situation Report (Sitrep) was due by 2100C each night. In between, there were SIPR and NIPR MEG e-mail accounts and 1st Naval Construction Division e-mail accounts that had to be managed. Sometimes there was a lull between 1100 and 1400, but that just allowed time for the admiral to think about what had to be done next.

Over the next thirty days, when Kubic was not on the move in Iraq, he slept in the command bunker at Camp Commando so that he would be immediately available to the Watch and to minimize his scramble time during missile alerts. He and his team routinely took to the bunkers multiple times on many nights during the thirty-eight follow-on missile attacks Saddam launched their way. He ate all but one meal during that period at his desk, in a plane or helicopter, or on patrol in a Humvee. If not for his driver, Equipment Operator 1st Class Jimmy Gross, who always had a spare Meal-Ready-to-Eat and who figured out how to get take-out from any available galley, Kubic thought that he surely would have starved. The admiral usually got to sleep between 0030 and 0200 each night and was up at 0400, often with a bunker drill interrupting even that short sleep. "Adrenalin is a wonderful thing," he said.

Highways 1 and 7 at the Euphrates

The MEG's pivotal mobility mission in the opening days of the war was first to ensure seventy ton vehicle access across the Euphrates River, and then to construct a connector road from Route 1 to Route 7 across the Saddam Canal to allow attacking forces and their logistics support to bypass the city of An Nasiriyah to the northwest. This effort was critical to the speed of maneuver and was based upon the assumption that the bridges to the east of An Nasiriyah would be blown and that the eastern corridor would be heavily defended. Building a connector route between Highways 1 and 7 had always been a part of the plan, but it had originally been conceived as a logistics corridor that would initially be built by Marine engineers and only later improved by the MEG. MEG planners had reviewed several options for the connector route as well as possible locations for a bridge across the Saddam Canal (which bisected the two highways), which would be needed to complete the connector. Ultimately I MEF assigned this mission to the MEG.[13]

The need for fast construction of the connector road required the attachment of SERT 74 and SERT 5 temporarily to the 3rd Infantry Division's attacking forces so that they could provide Engineer reconnaissance of the Euphrates crossing and connector road route ahead of the advance of Task Force Tarawa and the 1st Marine Division. SERT 5 was to conduct the reconnaissance to the east of An Nasiriyah and SERT 74 was to reconnoiter the west crossing and connector road route as part of the 3rd Infantry Division's movement. The west crossing had a new bridge under construction which the MEG had watched closely with satellite imagery in the months leading up to the operation. Amazingly, Saddam's regime continued to build this bridge right up to G-day, and Kubic suspected that it was almost finished. He hoped that it could be captured intact or that any damage could be over-bridged with a sixty-meter Mabey & Johnson Bridge. But first the MEG had to determine the bridge's condition before making any construction decisions, and that required positioning SERTs 5 and 74 near the front of the fight where their capabilities could be employed, in this case with planned additional force protection from the 3rd Infantry Division.

The Battle for An Nasiriyah

After seizing the Tallil Airfield, the 3rd Infantry Division had attacked toward An Nasiriyah and encountered its first enemy resistance. Fortunately, the contact was light and the division reported that the Highway 1 Bridge over the Euphrates, west of An Nasiriyah, was still intact and secure as of 2130Z on March 22, 2003. This was very good news for the MEG. Unfortunately, however, since all roads running north led to An Nasiriyah, the enemy contact held up the entire movement. Also, I MEF needed the 3rd Infantry Division to clear An Nasiriyah and move on its more southerly route north before I MEF could continue its attack north.[14]

The heaviest action of the war as well as the MEG's first enemy contact occurred on March 23. After completing its Relief in Place with the 3rd Infantry Division near the seized Euphrates Bridge west of An Nasiriyah, Task Force Tarawa focused on the unsecured bridges east of the city. The first bridge crossed the Euphrates, followed by another bridge over the Saddam Canal. One could travel directly through the city or around its east side using these two bridges. The built-up area provided excellent cover and concealment for the Fedayeen fighters who turned this route into what came to be known as "Ambush Alley."

As Task Force Tarawa's G-3 Operations Officer Colonel Ron Johnson later reported to USMC Colonel turned war correspondent Greg Plush, the Iraqis hid out in hospitals, schools, and apartment buildings, which they knew the 3rd Marine Aircraft Wing would not target. In addition to using these structures to conceal their ambushes, the enemy had over fifty Soviet-era T-55 tank hulls staged around these buildings for use as pillboxes. The Tarawa Marines found mortars, staked in and with pre-staged ammunition nearby, in the surrounding building courtyards. They also found a sand table in a schoolyard with Marine positions marked. None of the Iraqis wore uniforms, allowing them to blend in with the local populace, and they frequently used roadblocks to halt and ambush Coalition vehicle convoys and patrols. Much as the Germans had done during the Battle of the Bulge in World War II, they also moved road signs to attempt to confuse MEF convoys or redirect them into kill zones.[15]

Another Iraqi tactic involved sneaking between Coalition units and drawing fire from them to encourage "blue on blue" (friendly fire) casualties. Finally, and most disturbing, the Iraqis often feigned surrender and then ambushed the Marines who moved in to take them into custody. Still, despite these flagrant Law of War violations, the Marines did an outstanding job. Interviewed after the war, the Iraqi Zone Commander for An Nasiriyah (from the Iraqi 23rd Brigade of the 11th Infantry Division) said he was shocked and amazed at the aggressiveness of Marine small unit leaders. He said his soldiers were initially very confident after the first bridge battle, but became dispirited when the Marines kept coming at them.

Saddam Fedayeen, or "Regime Death Squads," augmented the Iraqi Regular Army forces. The Fedayeen attacked in small groups. Post-war interviews confirmed that the Ba'ath Party, and in turn the Fedayeen, were the primary agencies for enforcing Saddam's will on the people. In addition to hundreds of large weapons caches, Task Force Tarawa found torture chambers in former Ba'ath buildings, and the Marine commanders later learned that Ba'athists had threatened to kill Iraqi men's families if they did not join their suicidal cause.

Using similar terror tactics were Kuwaiti "Bedouins." These were collaborators who had returned to Iraq with the Iraqis in 1991. They were even more ruthless than the Regime Death Squads. These units were comprised of criminals and thugs, and were used to keep local populations under regime control. The Fedayeen were usually clean-shaven, often tattooed, and had lots of money, all of which indicated that command and control of these fighters went all the way back to Baghdad.

The weapon of choice for the Regular Army units, the Fedayeen, and Bedouins was the Rocket Propelled Grenade Launcher (RPG), which was generally fired at close range. After the war, Marine tankers said that sometimes the enemy would run right up to within ten feet of a tank and try to fire. In most cases it was pure suicide, but occasionally the fighters would get lucky – in one case they got an M1A1 tank kill when an RPG round ignited an external fuel bladder. In addition to the RPG, the enemy used AK-47s, machine guns, and mortars. The Iraqis staged ammunition and RPGs everywhere. Task Force Tarawa captured more than 2,500 RPGs and more than two tons of ammunition in the An Nasiriyah area alone.

Marine snipers were extremely effective during the battle. The captured Zone Commander's Executive Officer later told Colonel Johnson about the demoralizing psychological effect that the snipers had on his troops. The M1A1 Tanks were also a very effective weapon – the Iraqis were terrified of it, so much so that psychological operations (PSYOPS) vehicles were placed at selected points during the night to broadcast fabricated tank noise, keeping the bad guys awake. One tank had seven dents in it from RPG impacts, and three of the dents had scorch marks where the grenades had detonated and had been deflected. The M1A1, the Iraqi executive officer admitted, became an "un-killable beast" to the Iraqis and had "caused them nightmares."

USMC combat engineers literally plowed the Marines' way through An Nasiriyah at the height of the battle after Brigadier General Natonski asked Major General Mattis to "Please send me one of your four Israeli D-9 Armored Bulldozers ASAP to clear obstacles on Ambush Alley." Mattis replied that he'd be happy to do so, but only under one condition: "That you promise to bury as many of those gutless, sorry-assed, sons-of-bitches with it as possible, because these are the lowest, most cowardly excuses for men that we've ever had to fight."[16]

At Mattis' request, I MEG sent the Israeli D-9 dozer "Matilda" to Task Force Tarawa, and she indeed proved to be a tremendous success at doing what she was designed to do: clear Saddam Fedayeen obstacles and widen the main street of An Nasiriyah by simply and surgically taking out any building in the way. The young 1st Combat Engineer Battalion Marine dozer operator who pushed

Matilda through the city later said that it was "like a knife through butter". Natonski thanked Mattis for the loan, telling the 1st Marine Division commander that "The D-9 scared the hell out of the enemy." Thus, the USMC learned a valuable MOUT (Military Operations in Urban Terrain) tactic that the Israelis had been employing for years, specifically that armored dozers, when properly supported with tanks, infantry, and combat engineers, are the most important piece of combat equipment when fighting in a city. With the D-9 now in the fight, Marine vehicles and infantry could move much more easily and safely through Ambush Alley and secure An Nasiriyah's key bridges.

All told, the Battle for An Nasiriyah saw some of the fiercest fighting of the entire operation. Twenty-nine Marines died in combat on March 23 as they tried to secure this route to Highway 7, marking it as the bloodiest day of the war. The battle demonstrated the type of enemy threat that the MEG's Seabees would face throughout Operation IRAQI FREEDOM: a determined, desperate, often suicidal foe who could strike anywhere at anytime. With their favorite targets being support units and supply convoys, the MEG's Task Forces were extremely vulnerable. This was particularly true for Task Force Mike, which operated in "no-man's land" from March 23 through April 10, in the area ahead of Task Force Tarawa and north of An Nasiriyah, and behind the 1st Marine Division infantry regiments that had pushed north and further west toward Numaniyah.

Indeed, on the night of March 23, the MEG sustained some of its first battle-related casualties when a convoy carrying the MEG's Liaison Officer to I MEF, Lieutenant Commander Billy Sloan, from Camp Justice to Jalibah airfield, drove squarely into the middle of a 1st U.K. Division counterattack along Main Supply Route Tampa between Safwan and Basrah. Sloan was riding in the rear of a seven-ton, six-wheel drive, all-terrain truck, called a Medium Tactical Vehicle Replacement (MTVR), which was towing a trailer. Sloan's truck found itself buffeted by tank battles, mortar fire, and indirect artillery landing all around his convoy. An Iraqi RPG round slammed into Sloan's truck but failed to detonate. However, the force of the impact lifted the truck sideways into the air and to its left, throwing its passengers around like rag dolls.[17]

Sloan was sitting on the right bench above the truck's rear tires and was first tossed upward into the wooden slats of the canvas and then tumbled to the floor. Sandbags were thrown all about, and the trailer in tow turned onto its side and spilled its contents onto the road. The convoy accelerated to clear the area, and then split up, turned around, and returned to retrieve the spilled gear. Sloan was hurt pretty badly, with a broken nose and a couple of broken ribs. A Navy Corpsman bandaged him up to stop the bleeding.

At the scene of the wreck, the convoy's Seabee Officer in Charge decided that it was too dangerous to continue looking for the spilled gear and so he ordered the convoy to reform and proceed to Jalibah. It arrived early the next morning. At Jalibah, the Corpsman attending Sloan called in a MEF physician who arrived and treated the Seabee officer's injuries. Nothing could be done about Sloan's nose, and the doctor could only wrap Sloan's ribs to protect them. A tough Mississippi country boy, Sloan insisted on staying near the action to assist in camp set up until Kubic ordered him to return to the rear to heal. He refused MEDEVAC, but instead took a convoy back to Camp Commando. There were seven passengers in the rear of Sloan's MTVR, and four of them were injured during the incident, but Sloan was the only man who required medical attention.

SERTs Under Fire

As ordered at the onset of the attack into Iraq, SERTs 5 and 74 moved out immediately behind the attacking Army and Marine maneuver forces. SERT 74 moved with the 3rd Infantry Division along Highway 1, briefly stopped at the Highway 1 Bridge, and then fell in behind Task Force Tarawa. SERT 5 initially moved behind Task Force Tarawa, but then followed Regimental Combat Team 1 as it crossed the Euphrates and attacked up Highway 7. SERT 133 moved along Alternate Supply Route Dallas behind Regimental Combat Team 7 and had conducted reconnaissance of the planned Enemy Prisoner of War Holding Area site near Al Jazair before rejoining Task Force Charlie.[18]

Kubic worried a lot about the newly created SERTs. They were essential to the MEG's ability to plan and execute emergent combat construction on a fast moving battlefield, but they were also vulnerable given their forward posture in "soft" Humvees. The MEG developed a training curriculum in the desert that included engineer, communications, and combat skills. During their training Kubic told the SERTs that he wanted them to be able to "move safely, think clearly, and communicate reliably." Their mission to move, think, and communicate would place them into the most demanding situations that Seabees had encountered yet, during this or even any of America's recent wars. Kubic thought at the time, "If it was easy, there'd be lesser human beings doing it."

Under its Officer-in-Charge, Lieutenant Craig Kennedy, SERT 74's initial mission was to reach the Euphrates west of An Nasiriyah right after the assault, determine the bridging requirements there, and then move on to reconnoiter the connector route between Routes 1 and 7 around the northwest of An Nasiriyah.

At An Nasiriyah, the Marines had encountered heavy resistance but Special Operations Forces had already been able to lay eyes on the east An Nasiriyah Bridges and had noted that they were still intact. They could not provide any information on the physical condition of the bridges though or whether or not they would be able to support heavy military equipment (such as the M1A1 Abrams tank). SERT 5's mission, therefore, was to reconnoiter the bridges to the east of An Nasiriyah, if that sector could be secured to allow movement of Marines to the east of An Nasiriyah, and then proceed up Highway 7 to reconnoiter the many bridges and culverts that could seriously impede progress if they were blown by Saddam's forces. Per the un-staffed, errant Fragmentary Order that was released just prior to G-day, both SERTs were to remain under Task Force Mike's operational control, but were directed to travel with the Crossing Area Engineers from the 8th Engineer Support Battalion, which remained assigned to the 1st Force Service Support Group (rather than I MEG), and was in direct support of the 1st Marine Division.

SERTs 5 and 74 needed to travel initially with the 3rd Infantry Division, per the "opening gambit" plan. The I MEF Fragmentary Order that attached them to 8th Engineer Support Battalion, literally only hours before the attack, created unnecessary complexities in command and control. This was especially the case since the 3rd Infantry Division had left I MEF and joined V Corps in January 2003, but retained the mission to secure the Highway 1 Bridge to the west of An Nasiriyah. The Fragmentary Order that the MEG needed and was expecting was to attach SERTs 5 and 74 tactical control (TACON) for movement to the 3rd Infantry Division while retaining operational control (OPCON) of these SERTs with Task Force Mike. From Kubic's perspective as MEG commander, this confusion was a direct outgrowth of the flawed Concept of Operations for employment of Engineers in support of I MEF that arose from the controversial planning sessions conducted during the summer of 2002 at Camp Pendleton. He believed that I MEF and the 1st Marine Division would have been better served with an Engineer Concept of Operations in which all Marine, Seabee, and Army bridging capabilities had been assigned to the MEG's Task Force Mike and placed in direct support to the 1st Marine Division with full "reach back" support, through the SERTs, to the MEG Command Operations Center, and then back to Pacific Division and Atlantic Division for any higher order engineering.

Unfortunately "rice bowls" within the 1st Force Service Support Group prevented this from happening in Kubic's opinion. He believed that this was due in part to both his failure and the failure of the MEG staff. Collectively, they were unable to overcome the general lack of understanding within the MEF G-3 staff on how the overall bridging mission, and the limited resources available to support this critical mission, needed to be integrated within one command structure to be employed with speed, agility, and flexibility in a fast moving battlespace. These collective failures, starting early in the planning and exercise cycle, led to the confusing and incorrect Fragmentary Order that operationally separated (rather than linked) the SERTs' Liaison Officers (attached to Task Force Mike) from their reconnaissance and security elements (attached to the 8th Engineer Support Battalion) just before the attack was launched. Of even greater concern was the fact that it was very unclear as to who exactly had operational control of the SERTs as the attack began. Combined with strained communications, this confusion created a very dangerous battlespace situation for the Seabees of SERTs 5 and 74.

In previous war games (well before the onset of Operation IRAQI FREEDOM), the SERTs always seemed to draw enemy fire, mostly from Special Operations Forces or guerillas, as they moved across the battlefield. In one Korean war game scenario, a SERT was attacked by a Special Forces platoon. Since the SERT had two .50 caliber machine guns, the game registered a SERT victory with 3 friendly Seabees wounded-in-action and nearly twenty enemies killed. The SERTs were now placed in the same position in the real war as in the game, and the game was quite prophetic.

After getting underway, SERT 5 and the 8th Engineer Support Battalion's Crossing Area Engineer 5 advanced to the north, behind the lead combat elements of Regimental Combat Team 5 and through the Iraqi desert to the outskirts of An Nasiriyah. The Seabees of SERT 5 were the first to experience combat action on

March 23, 2003 as they moved to position themselves to reconnoiter the bridges to the east of the city. The team was first directed to move east towards the bridges by Crossing Area Engineer 5. Task Force Mike though, thinking that the decision had been made not to advance up Highway 7 due to the heavy resistance encountered in An Nasiriyah and the securing of the Highway 1 Bridge, re-directed SERT 5 to detach from Regimental Combat Team 5 and head west to rejoin Task Force Mike south of the Highway 1 Euphrates Bridge. This was a mistake, and SERT 5 was quickly ordered to turn around and return east again – quite confusing and difficult for the MEG to monitor, much less control.

Upon reflection, Kubic later decided that SERTs operating in a maneuver environment should remain under the operational control of the senior Engineer commander and act in a fashion similar to the MEF's Force Recon as they gather key engineer intelligence. Task Force Mike did not have the big picture nor did it have the communications capability to control SERT movements. And the confusion over the SERT relationship to the 8th Engineer Support Battalion only made matters worse. Kubic expressed his concern to the I MEF Deputy Commanding General, Major General Keith Stalder, over the errant Fragmentary Order right before the war started. But once the action became fast and furious, the MEG moved on and made the best of it. Kubic feared the SERT command and control fragmentation would lead to combat casualties and prayed that it would not. Fortunately for the SERTs, prayer worked.

When the Crossing Area Engineer eventually ordered SERT 5 to link up with army engineers and escort them to the marshalling position, they were attacked by mortars and small arms. But the team instinctively returned fire and moved through the kill zone without injury. This was first direct combat action engaged in by Seabees since the Vietnam War. By the time SERT 5 rejoined the Marines of Crossing Area Engineer 5 south of An Nasiriyah (this time they linked up with Regimental Combat Team 1), Marine tanks had already crossed the two key bridges in the eastern part of the city across the Euphrates River and the Saddam Canal. SERT 5 was then assigned a position on the maneuver trail and began heading up Highway 7. SERT 5 quickly moved across the Euphrates, east of An Nasiriyah and through "Ambush Alley," where some of the fiercest fighting of the war had just taken place only hours earlier.

Because of the threat of enemy fire in the area, the Marine maneuver commander made the decision not to allow the SERT to exit their vehicles and conduct a detailed survey as they crossed the bridges. Forced to reconnoiter the bridges with notes and photos while on the move, SERT 5 sent a somewhat sardonic report back to the I MEG Command Operations Center that read "As we drove over the bridges, we observed that they were intact and appeared to be in good condition. Due to the fact that tanks had already crossed the bridges and that the bridges were still standing, we believe these bridges can be safely classified as MLC-70."

As the large convoy moved north, the SERT was positioned towards the rear of the formation (where it belonged). When it came time to stop for the night, the Marines directed them to keep moving north until a clear area was located for them to pull off. After a few hours of downtime with little sleep, dawn arrived, and SERT 5 was surprised to find itself near the "point" of the column with other "softer" forces also in their vicinity.

Soon after dawn, the column came under heavy attack by irregular Fedayeen troops in civilian clothes driving taxis and pickup trucks. SERT 5 dug in for a fight. When Marines on the flank of SERT 5 failed to stop an onrushing taxi, the SERT's .50 caliber machine gunner, Steelworker 2nd Class McGibbon, took it out, and then another one that also made a run on the convoy while firing small arms. At some point, the Fedayeen began to move towards a key intersection, and SERT 5 quickly maneuvered to secure it. The SERT was then attacked by a Fedayeen truck with a crew served weapon mounted in the rear. With deadly, accurate fire, Steelworker 2nd Class McGibbon courageously stood his ground, high in the turret, and pumped eleven shots into the Fedayeen vehicle, thwarting the attack. When Kubic asked him later why he only fired eleven rounds, he said "they were coming at us from all sides and I didn't know when I would get more ammo, and besides I only needed eleven shots."

After securing this key intersection, SERT 5 held its ground until the Regimental Combat Team passed through on its way north towards the Baghdad Division on the outskirts of Al Kut. Once the Marines executed this unplanned, yet historic "passage of the lines" through a team of fighting Seabees, SERT 5 fell in towards the rear of the convoy, again where it belonged. Those Seabees obviously should not have been "on point," Kubic said later, "but they showed that they were ready and able to fight in the hottest area of the battlefield during the initial days of the attack north."

Meanwhile, SERT 74, along with the Crossing Area Engineer 1, had advanced on March 22 with elements of the 3rd Infantry Division toward the bridge over the Euphrates to the west of An Nasiriyah. It found that the critical Highway 1 bridge was intact and had not been destroyed or damaged by fleeing Iraqi forces. This was terrific news to I MEG and to the Marines. The first piece of the bridging mission would not be necessary, there would be no need for a delay south of the river, and the likelihood of available military bridging running out before reaching Baghdad was significantly decreased. The 3rd Infantry Division's main force arrived shortly thereafter and secured the bridge site. SERT 74 quickly surveyed the bridge and gave it a load classification of MLC-80, which was more than sufficient to support heavy military equipment such as the M1A1 Abrams tank. The only work needed on this MEG Objective, designated S4, would be to improve the approaches to the bridge.

With the western Euphrates bridge secured and surveyed, Kubic pushed Task Force Mike and SERT 74 hard to get on with the reconnaissance of the connector route. General Conway needed this bypass to ensure his logistics flow if the fighting to the east became protracted. Once again, command and control issues arose when the Crossing Area Engineer directed SERT 74's Officer-in-Charge Lieutenant Kennedy to split off one of his vehicles and to travel with a Marine Light Armored Reconnaissance (LAR) squad to reconnoiter the connector route. Kubic would not have allowed the SERT to proceed with only one vehicle had he known about it since the Recon element by design had two vehicles for depth, communications reliability, and security. Kubic also would have made sure that the Liaison Officer, in this case Lieutenant (Junior Grade) Campbell, was properly positioned with a forward command element before the SERT launched its recon element. None of this happened. Lieutenant Kennedy was given five minutes to make a decision and then load up one Humvee with five Seabees and depart. Given the situation, Kennedy made the only decision he could – he had no choice but to take this risk to carry out his mission. Unfortunately, the MEG then lost communications with SERT 74 for about forty-eight hours. Kubic remembered that it was "a VERY trying time." He feared that "those brave Seabees were lost in battle" and "prayed hard again."

After an exceptionally grueling reconnaissance mission, Lieutenant Kennedy and his Liaison Officer, Lieutenant (Junior Grade)

Campbell, finally rejoined SERT 74 and transmitted a textbook perfect reconnaissance report. The team then crossed over the Highway 1 Euphrates Bridge with Regimental Combat Team 7 to begin its survey of the conditions along Highway 1. The repair of Highway 1 was to become the MEG's largest mission of the war in terms of total man-hours and labor expended. As they advanced along this desolate, dusty and unfinished highway, members of SERT 74 found themselves among the forward most units in the entire MEF. "At one point," reported Lieutenant (Junior Grade) Campbell, "to our knowledge there were no other units forward of where we were."

When Kennedy and Campbell reported in after their hair-raising reconnaissance, Kubic breathed a big sigh of relief, telling everyone in the MEG Command Operations Center that he "was so very proud of those Seabees." The MEG quickly processed the data, determined the route, received Conway's approval to proceed with the connector route construction and FRAGO'd the mission to Task Force Mike, which then passed it to NMCB 4. This was the first full employment of SERT doctrine under combat conditions. It worked like a charm, in Kubic's opinion, notwithstanding the unnecessary command and control hurdles thrown in the Seabees' way and the intense stress his MEGsters experienced as they worried for forty-eight hours about the missing SERT. Said Kubic, "Seabee grit and determination led once again to Seabee success."

Time to Start Bridge Building

With the battle raging on the bridges of An Nasiriyah's east side, it became even more imperative to improve Highway 1 and to build a connector route that could be used as an alternate route to Highway 7. Due to its poor condition, Highway 1 was originally supposed to be only the alternate Main Supply Route north of the Euphrates. But running convoys through "Ambush Alley" in order to use Highway 7 posed unacceptable risks, and so I MEG had to fix Highway 1 quickly, and then build a connector route to Highway 7, as originally planned.19

The MEG staff felt it fortunate that the bridges east and west of An Nasiriyah were intact. It came to light a week later, though, that this was due to the overwhelming speed and shock of the ground attack. The Iraqis had intended to blow bridges and culvert sections to slow the coalition advance, but they never got the chance. Combat Service Support Group 11 sent I MEG the following report on March 28 concerning the Iraqis' intentions:

Today was a very interesting day. We found 4 culverts approx 15 miles North of the Div Main on Highway 1 packed with PE-4 explosives. 1500 lbs were taken out of the culverts by Gunnery Sergeant Roberson's team. All were hard-wired together with a wire leading out approx ¾ of a mile away for the command detonation. There were also mines put down on both sides of the road in front of one of the culverts. It has been marked off with barbed wire and signs by the engineers. All of the PE-4 has been destroyed.[20]

Task Force Mike had stopped near the Al Jalibah airfield and waited for the situation to develop at An Nasiriyah. Initial plans set Jalibah as MEG objective S3, which was designated as a forward operating base for the 3rd Marine Aircraft Wing, and the MEG expected to rebuild it once it fell into Coalition hands. A quick assessment revealed that only minor repairs were needed though.

On March 23, Task Force Mike sent a detachment from NMCB 4 to work on the approaches to the West Euphrates Bridge on Highway 1 (called MEG Objective S4). These repairs were vital to future convoys in maintaining their speed as they crossed the river. While Objective S4 required less work than the MEG had initially prepared, Det 4's completion of these approaches two days later allowed the MEG to turn another MEG Objective "green" on the master project planning map. The remainder of Rudich's Task Force had remained near Jalibah, behind Task Force Tarawa, where it hunkered down and rode out the MOASS on March 24.

After the MOASS passed on March 25, Task Force Mike began to move forward across the Euphrates and up Highway 1(Main Supply Route Tampa). When they reached "Gap 5" on Main Supply Route Tampa, Commodore Rudich recommended building a sixty-meter Mabey & Johnson bridge across an incomplete section of a concrete bridge along Route 1. Kubic approved Rudich's request and the Task Force Mike Seabees prepared to go to work building the first major bridge of the war. Although the 3rd Infantry Division had already emplaced a medium girder bridge approximately eight kilometers north of the river, where an existing gap had formed due to uncompleted construction and a severe wash area, the slopes down from the highway to the medium girder bridge and back up to the main road were too steep for the heavy fuel trucks that had to move quickly forward to support the 1st Marine Division's continuing attack.

During its reconnaissance of the Highway 1 to Highway 7 connector route, SERT 74 had found the best route around An Nasiriyah and a likely crossing site over the Saddam Canal. The site featured a 75-meter gap that would require a construction of a "Mac Mole" pier and a sixty-meter Mabey & Johnson bridge (as opposed to a fifty-meter medium girder bridge that Task Force Mike had originally hoped to use over the Saddam Canal). Despite prior map studies that showed an alternate route and crossing site to the one SERT 74 was proposing, Kubic chose to go with the "guys on the ground" after reviewing the SERT report and the planning data/imagery. Simply put, he trusted the information provided by the SERT on the ground, as they had access to accurate "eyes on" information and could weigh factors that digital imagery and rear planners could not.

During its reconnaissance, SERT 74 had also identified a mineral products staging area (essentially an enormous pile of gravel) on the north and south sides of the west bridge over the Euphrates. The MEG and other Coalition engineer units would use the large pile of material at the site, later named "Mount MEG," for road maintenance throughout the war's major combat operations.

By March 23, the MEG, based upon SERT 74's reconnaissance reports, had identified and developed two active missions for Task Force Mike: 1) emplacement of a Mabey & Johnson Bridge along Highway 1 just north of the Euphrates, and 2) the construction of a Connector Route between Highways 1 and 7. Both missions would be crucial to supporting the Marines' assault as they advanced north of the Euphrates and toward the Tigris.

The Night of 1,000 Iraqis

With the areas parallel to Highway 1 not yet cleared of enemy forces, Rudich's Seabees would have to provide their own security around their construction sites. True to their combat construction heritage, Seabees went right to work constructing a Mabey & Johnson Bridge at Gap 5 along Highway 1 with their weapons locked and loaded, ready to defend their job site if necessary.

Once bridge construction was underway, I MEG had to deal with its first real "fog of war" situation of the campaign. The MEG received a confirmed intelligence report that ten to fifteen vehicles – possibly a bypassed Iraqi tank company – were moving from the southwest behind the 3rd Infantry Division from Main Supply Route Jackson (Route 8) in the vicinity of Al Jalibah towards Task Force Mike, which was now positioned at Gap 5 along Main Supply Route Tampa (Route 1). Almost simultaneously, the MEG received another intelligence report that approximately 1,000 Fedayeen fighters were massing west of An Nasiriyah to attack the Euphrates Bridges and Coalition forces from the east. The MEG staff immediately notified both Commodores Rudich and McKerall, and Task Forces Mike and Charlie braced for the potential heavy Iraqi counterattacks.

Rudich's Seabees were most likely to bear the brunt of any enemy action since they were the most exposed and in the midst of heavy bridge construction. Moreover, to keep building throughout the night, Task Force Mike had to leave its flood lights on. If they stopped building, vital fuel and other logistics could be delayed and Marines could die because of it. With a strict deadline for getting the bridge completed and under serious threat of enemy attack, Rudich called Kubic to discuss the very difficult decision that they had to make. The Seabees either could shut down construction, dig in, and prepare for a night assault that could come from two directions with sizable enemy forces, or they could turn on their lights and continue building throughout the night, while concurrently digging in and preparing to fight the Iraqis if and when they showed up. They discussed their options and the associated risks in a short conversation. This was no doubt the most difficult decision of the war, but the mission was essential. Kubic approved Rudich's recommendation to leave the lights on, continue to build, and be ready to fight if attacked. Rudich's Chief of Staff, Commander Mark Libonate later recounted the situation:

> Heroism comes in many shapes and forms. As our actual combat action was limited, I would like to focus on the heroism of our leader. To me, his heroics came in the form of making the tough decisions, when they matter most, when the lives of his troops were at risk and when the decision may be unpopular. Shortly after we crossed the Euphrates River and were in the process of bedding down for the night at a site adjacent to where one of our subordinate elements was constructing a bridge, we received a call from higher headquarters relating that an attack on our position and the position of one of our subordinate units just to the south of the River, was imminent. The attacking force of 1,000 paramilitary outnumbered our personnel at each site 3 to 1. Additionally, there was also the possibility of attack from

armored vehicles to our west. With amazing clarity of thought, he directed the actions of the Task Force to not only form a proper defense, but just as importantly, to continue construction of the bridge over a gap on MSR Tampa. The bridge construction required lighting, which made us a target from quite a distance. Lesser men would have shut down bridging, turned off the lights and prepared for the onslaught. Fortunately for us and for the Marines who depended heavily on MSR Tampa for logistics support, Captain Rudich is not a lesser man. Despite the risks, despite recommendations to do otherwise, he made the tough call. He is a Seabee at heart who held true to the motto of "We build, we fight."[21]

Task Force Mike dug in deep that night, and Rudich put every Seabee he could spare from the construction into fighting holes with every weapon he could find. The MEGsters all felt certain that the Seabees would take combat casualties that night but agreed that Rudich could not stop the job. In Kubic's daily Situation Report, he commented, "Seabees are dug in along Hwy 1 with berms, crew served weapons, and AT-4's, and will continue constructing the Mabey-Johnson bridge throughout the night. We build, we fight."

Task Force Mike's actions that night were as courageous and as heroic as Kubic had ever seen. Fortunately, the MEG Watch discovered four hours later that the intelligence reports of incoming Iraqi armor and Fedayeen were false. The vehicles turned out to be a U.S. Army convoy moving through I MEF's area that nobody had known about or expected, and the 1,000 massing Iraqis found all they could handle with MEF artillery and 3rd Marine Aircraft Wing bombs. After surviving the so-called "Night of 1,000 Iraqis," Task Mike Force Mike completed the Mabey & Johnson bridge on schedule and prepared to move forward again.

Elsewhere, Task Force Charlie finished the Enemy Prisoner of War holding area at Al Jazair and continued performing maintenance of Main Supply Routes Dallas and Tampa as the tactical situation permitted. Task Force Echo, in the meantime, had finally pushed its first unit, a team to assess the port at Umm Qasr, north into Iraq on March 24.

The Truck Stop from Hell

To support further Mabey & Johnson bridge construction during I MEF's march to Baghdad, the MEG needed a site to store Class

IV construction material and bridge components north of the Euphrates so the Seabees could work a two-racetrack convoy strategy to push their own material north towards Baghdad. Kubic and his staff had various thoughts about where this bridgepark would be located during their pre-war planning.

After a successful reconnaissance by SERT 74, Task Force Mike secured an unremarkable chunk of desert, just off Highway 1 to the south, and just northwest of where the 1-7 connector road would be constructed, approximately 20 kilometers north of the Euphrates. This site was named Bridgepark Davisville after the Davisville, Rhode Island Construction Battalion Center, a former Seabee logistics base that the Navy had opened in 1942 to help support and train its new Construction Battalion forces. It had been closed on April 1, 1994, much to the consternation of many Seabee old timers, following the recommendations of the 1991 Base Realignment and Closure Commission. The site was a convenient place to stage bridges and Class IV material and to base Task Force Mike and then Task Force Charlie while they worked to upgrade Highway 1 and construct the 1-7 connector route. But it was a dusty, nasty place to live, and the Seabees quickly christened it as the "truck stop from Hell," perhaps a more appropriate name due to the amount of traffic and number of vagabond convoys which stopped there on their way to Baghdad. When the MEG ultimately needed to close it, Kubic could not help feel a bit nostalgic about leaving the first Seabee Base Camp constructed in Iraq and defended solely by MEG Seabee and Army forces. In fact, the admiral had a bit of trouble getting everyone to leave as quickly as he wanted. "It is amazing how even a nasty piece of desert quickly becomes 'home' during a war," he said.[22]

With the Davisville Bridgepark now open for business, Task Force Charlie started moving Class IV materials – mainly culverts and bridging – north for forward staging there. An 18-vehicle convoy would be the first of over eighty logistical convoys dispatched north from the bridge yard at Camp 93. The success of these convoys was due in large part to the efforts of Bridgepark Officer-in-Charge Lieutenant (Junior Grade) Gephardt (of NMCB 133), with Chief Builder Mozatos as the on-site technical bridge expert. During the time leading up to the conflict, these two Seabees had worked hand-in-hand with Task Force Mike to prepare for all possible contingencies and to ensure that the right bridging was at the right place at the right time. Chief Mozatos had also worked closely with the Mabey & Johnson representatives, who trained the Task Force Mike Seabees in the proper construction of the bridges. Once hostilities started, Gephardt helped Task Force Mike set up the forward bridge yard at Davisville, and she saw to it that Rudich had all of the bridging and equipment that he needed to complete his mission.

Tactical Pause

In An Nasiriyah, the Saddam Fedayeen continued to harass the Marines, hiding among the local population in civilian clothes, using women and children as shields, and striking at vulnerable supply and logistics convoys while avoiding armored and infantry units. Although An Nasiriyah was still not fully secured, General Franks ordered a tactical "pause" to allow Coalition ground combat units to focus on cleaning out the remaining pockets of resistance in the rear areas before launching the final assaults toward Baghdad. Equipment and vehicles needed to be serviced and refueled as well, while exhausted Marine riflemen, having fought nonstop over the past five days through some of the harshest environments in the world, desperately needed to sleep and to recover from the MOASS.[23]

Back home in the states, immediate cries of "quagmire!" and "Vietnam!" shot forth from the pundits and professional chatterers in the worldwide media, who utterly failed to appreciate the magnitude of what Coalition forces were doing and how fast they were doing it. Even Harlan Ullman himself openly questioned the strategy and tempo of operations, writing in the *Baltimore Sun* that "Shock and awe were promised, but the effects have not yet taken hold," and that "the current campaign does not appear to correspond to what we envisaged."[24]

All of this criticism was ridiculous. During World War II, Patton's drive across France took over four weeks before he too had to stop when his Third Army ran out of gas near Metz. During the opening stages of Operation IRAQI FREEDOM, the Marines and Seabees went half his distance in only six days. As the world would soon learn, Coalition forces were anything but bogged down, although much fighting and bridge building lay ahead over the next couple of weeks on the road to Baghdad.

CHAPTER 10

Across the Tigris

The Iraqis took advantage of the MOASS and CENTCOM's operational pause to regroup and organize a counterattack in An Nasiriyah on March 26. At approximately 1800Z that day, both regular and irregular Iraqi forces attacked the 2nd Battalion of the 8th Marines and the Headquarters of Regimental Combat Team 2. Task Force Tarawa repelled the assault after approximately ninety minutes of heavy fighting, but sustained twenty-five casualties. The Marines inflicted heavier casualties on Iraqis though, destroying several of their mechanized vehicles and a host of smaller civilian model trucks, taxis, and buses. Despite their rabble-like appearance and "spray and pray" shooting style, the Iraqis fought ferociously, particularly the Fedayeen and foreign fighters who took part in the fray. Many appeared to be under the influence of powerful stimulant drugs, and one Marine even told an embedded reporter that he felt like he and his pards were fighting a "drug gang" instead of an organized military force.[1]

Task Force Tarawa became I MEF's main effort until An Nasiriyah could be secured. During the fighting, the Fedayeen were using the bridges east of An Nasiriyah as escape routes for their "hit and run" raids against the Marines and their passing convoys. Consequently, Brigadier General Natonski directed Seabees from Task Force Charlie to reinforce the Marine combat engineers, to fortify his Command Post, and to build counter-mobility berms around the bridges. Led by its Operations Officer, Lieutenant Commander Wilmore, NMCB 133 did the necessary work and significantly disrupted the Fedayeen's movement in and around the city. Natonski was gratified, and a small team from NMCB 133 subsequently traveled along with Task Force Tarawa continuing to Al Kut, and remained with the Task Force until it went home in late May. During a subsequent dinner with the officers and chiefs of Task Force Charlie's Command Element and NMCB 133 at Al Kut, Natonski said, "Task Force Charlie has been with us from the beginning near An Nasiriyah, which at that time was still a hot place, [and] there was something comforting about having those dozers placing the berm."[2]

During the early morning of 27 March, the 1st Marine Division's Regimental Combat Team 5 attacked north along Highway 1 and seized the Hantush Airfield following a brief but intense firefight. The 1st Marine Division had to pull back to the south when I MEF directed it to secure its Lines of Communication - namely, Highways 1 and 7. The Fedayeen were consistently targeting MEF convoys moving along these routes, and so Lieutenant General Conway had finally decided to do something about it. He revised I MEF's concept of operations to "defeat paramilitary forces in zone in order to protect MEF lines of communication and to set conditions for continued attacks north to defeat the Baghdad and Al Nida Regular Divisions."[3]

As a result, the 1st Marine Division's Reconnaissance Battalion secured the strategically located airfield at Qalat Sikar to the east of Highway 7 and set up blocking positions opposite the Iraqi's Baghdad Infantry Division. I MEF also ordered its three Regimental Combat Teams to begin aggressive security and ambush patrols to interdict Iraqi regular army and Fedayeen operations along Highways 1 and 7. While the Regimental Combat Teams began their aggressive patrols up and down the Main Supply Routes, Task Force Mike worked vigorously on the Highway 1 Mabey & Johnson Bridge. NMCB 4, from Task Force Mike, also continued improving that road, while Commodore Rudich established his main command post at the Davisville Bridge Park.

On 28 March, Rear Admiral Kubic flew up to Bridge Park Davisville to visit Task Force Mike and to assess its on-going projects. The highlight of Kubic's trip was seeing NMCB 74's completion of the MEG's first Mabey & Johnson Bridge at the Highway 1 gap. He was pleased by what he saw, commenting later that "these Seabees had made a fine showing, worthy of their World War II forefathers."

ASR Hueneme and the Saddam Canal Crossing

Along with the CONOPs change, I MEF issued a Fragmentary Order formally tasking I MEG to construct the connector route from Highway 1 to Highway 7. This new road would allow convoys to by-pass An Nasiriyah and improve the Marines' maneuver and supply operations in I MEF Area of Operations. The connector route would allow the 1st Marine Division to rearm and refuel, a clear priority since it had already attacked over two hundred kilometers in less than three days with little or no replenishment.

Sustaining the 1st Marine Division became one of I MEF's highest priorities as the Marines needed to continue the attack across the Tigris and towards Baghdad. The by-pass needed to be built quickly, and since the route traversed "bad guy country," the MEG requested additional security support from Task Force Tarawa.[4] A Light Armored Reconnaissance platoon drew the security mission and it moved out alongside Task Force Mike's NMCB 4 on March 29.

The first job was to build a road from Highway 1 to the Saddam Canal. During this construction, NMCB 4 staged all of the SPCM (Sand Pile Culvert Module) and Mabey & Johnson bridging parts at the canal. Once the road was completed, the battalion then built a thirty-meter mole pier, reducing the total gap to fifty meters.

Next, the battalion's Seabees assembled and pushed a sixty-meter Mabey & Johnson bridge across the canal to the other side.

The Seabees' inability to float equipment across the canal at this juncture made the project especially difficult. They also had to contend with the ever-present enemy threat, which on more than one occasion forced them to stop work and man their fighting positions. To prepare for possible attacks on its work site, NMCB 4 registered its 60mm mortars on key approach avenues and coordinated a detailed fire support plan with the Marines, which included on-call air and artillery support. Finally, a number of curious Iraqi locals from a nearby town closely watched the Seabees, slowing the work.

Despite the challenges and harsh conditions, NMCB 4 quickly built both the connector road, which the Seabees christened Alternate Supply Route Hueneme after their West Coast Seabee Center, and the Saddam Canal Crossing in slightly less than four days (about ninety hours). Together, Alternate Supply Route Hueneme and the Mabey & Johnson bridge crossing provided a vital alternate link from Highway 1 to Highway 7 (Main Supply

Route Bismarck) just in case the eastern routes around An Nasiriyah became untenable. The first tactical convoy to cross the canal was a Patriot Missile Battery headed north to cover the 1st Marine Division's push to the Tigris.

SERTS Back on the Move

On March 26, the MEG's SERTs remained extremely busy roving throughout the battlespace. SERT 5 moved north on Highway 7 through Ambush Alley, tracing Regimental Combat Team 1's attack north toward Al Kut. Highway 7 was a difficult route, featuring a number of potential ambush areas in which the Fedayeen, pushed from the An Nasiriyah area, concentrated their efforts against MEF convoys utilizing this route. SERT 5's mission was to conduct route and bridge reconnaissance as it moved north.[5]

As night fell, SERT 5 found itself "dug in" near the front of the convoy awaiting orders to continue the move in the morning. As dawn broke, the Fedayeen attacked the lightly armed logistics vehicle near SERT 5 using civilian tracks and light machine guns. SERT 5 quickly mounted up and Steelworker 2nd Class McGibbon swung into action with his .50 caliber heavy machine gun. After passing over the intact An Nasr bridge (one less engineering obstacle on the road to Baghdad) SERT 5 continued up Highway 7 before stopping and taking position with Marines dug in near the town of Qalat Sikar.

By this time, SERT 7, led by Lieutenant Allen Sullivan and Lieutenant (Junior Grade) Doug Anderson, had arrived in Kuwait and relieved SERT 4 as the MEG Tactical Movement Team (TMT). I directed SERT 4 to head north and conduct a Relief-in-Place with SERT 5 so that the Seabees of SERT 5 could return to Kuwait and retrograde back to the U.S with the rest of their battalion. South of An Nasiriyah, SERT 4 joined a large convoy from the 1st Force Service Support Group, including engineers from 7th Engineer Support Battalion, who were enroute to conduct airfield repairs at Qalat Sikar airfield. On March 27, the convoy, which consisted of over two hundred vehicles, passed through An Nasiriyah and began heading north up Highway 7. SERT 4, with their crew served weapons including M2 .50 caliber and M60 machine guns, occupied a position near the front of the convoy. As the convoy passed through the town of Ash Shatrah, the convoy began to take enemy mortar, grenade, and small arms fire.

The enemy fire continued as the SERT neared the northern edge of the town, where the convoy commander inexplicably gave the order to halt, perhaps not aware that many of his forward vehicles were still in the kill zone. "At that point we were not only laying down suppressing fire with our crew served weapons," reported the SERT Officer-in-Charge, Lieutenant Andrew Cook, "but were able to focus in on individuals and muzzle flashes in the building 200 yards to our right, and take deliberate, targeted shots." Fortunately, the Iraqis were poor marksmen and hit none of the Seabees. Even more amazing, the Seabees watched a donkey that was grazing in the field between their position and that of the Iraqis. Despite the heavy volume of fire being exchanged, neither Seabee nor enemy bullets hit the donkey. Clearly, it had a guardian angel on duty that day.

But the Seabees were not yet out of the woods. The convoy commander next ordered the convoy to turn around, and so SERT 4 drove back through the kill zone along the length of Ash Shatrah and headed south towards An Nasiriyah. The convoy then stopped again, regrouped, and returned north, this time with Marine Cobra gunships and a Light Armored Reconnaissance platoon in support. As it began to get dark, SERT 4 passed through the kill zone for a third time. Over the course of the ambush, the SERT team expended hundreds of .50 caliber and 7.62mm machine guns rounds and 5.56mm M16 rounds in suppressing the enemy. The SERT continued north, driving in the dark using Night Vision Goggles, until it reached a position surrounded by friendly tanks near the town of Qalat Sikar. The next day, March 30, it conducted its Relief-in-Place with SERT 5 near Al Kut.

Meanwhile, SERT 133 linked up with Commodore Rudich in order to support Task Force Mike's current missions and to prepare to move north along Highway 1 and to recon the route for road repairs and potential bridge sites.

Throughout the remainder of the war, the SERTs provided valuable information that guided the disposition and operations of MEG units during the drive to Baghdad. Although they had some initial communications difficulties (and despite the MEF's denial of satellite access), the SERTs' heavy communications capability proved successful, using High Frequency data networks to send imagery, documents, and detailed surveys to the rear. On more than one occasion, Task Force Mike and Task Force Charlie had communications difficulties and one SERT or another served as their sole means of communication back to the rear. More importantly, the reports and images the SERTs provided were used by operations watch officers at the MEG, who relayed these reports and photographs to engineers at the Pacific Division for detailed designs or technical recommendations.

A notable example of the SERTs' effectiveness involved the bridge over the Saddam Canal on Highway 27. The Marines' 2nd Tank Battalion, of Regimental Combat Team 5, was the first unit to cross this bridge on April 1. Marine engineers rated the bridge at MLC-70. However, tankers noted ominous creaking and straining sounds as they drove across the bridge. The MEG sent SERT 74 to investigate and Lieutenant Kennedy's Seabees immediately noted a number of serious cracks and other damage in the concrete supports. They gave the bridge an initial rating of MLC-25. Their report was then sent back to the Pacific Division, where structural engineers evaluated the data and determined that the Highway 27 bridge should be properly rated as MLC-30. Based on this information, the MEF engineer directed the MEG to emplace a Mabey & Johnson bridge adjacent to the existing span that could support military traffic for the remainder of the war.

The SERT teams continued to provide expertise and engineering assessments well into Phase IV of the operation. They later surveyed numerous bridges damaged by either coalition bombing or Iraqi explosives. Divers entered the water at key sites to assess current speeds, depths, and soil conditions. As hostilities wound down, the SERTs were often sent out into communities to assess sites for humanitarian service projects such as schools, civic facilities such as courthouses, jails and police stations, and infrastructure such as roads, electrical, water, and sewage utilities. The contribution of the SERT teams to the success of the MEG both during and after the war cannot be overstated. They resoundingly proved themselves to be a vital element to the Seabee Engineer effort for all future conflicts and operations.

Task Forces Charlie and Echo Get into the Fight

By March 29, the 1st Marine Division and Task Force Tarawa had completed their forward passage of lines at An Nasiriyah. Major General Mattis pushed Regimental Combat Team 5 up Highway 1 toward Ad Diwaniyah, with the 2nd Light Armored Reconnaissance Battalion in the lead and Regimental Combat Team 7 south of the Euphrates, poised to follow. Brigadier General Natonski's Task

Force Tarawa had cleared enough of Ambush Alley to allow Regimental Combat Team 1 to pass east of An Nasiriyah and to resume its attack north of the Saddam Canal along Highway 7.[6]

The next day, Task Force Charlie's Tarawa detachment started construction on Brigadier General Natonski's new command post, which had recently moved into the city of An Nasiriyah. Task Force Charlie also supported both the 15th Marine Expeditionary Unit and the 24th Marine Expeditionary Unit, which had just arrived to reinforce positions near Qalat Sikar. Finally, due to increased security concerns north of the Euphrates, I MEG Task Force Echo, now under (Army National Guard) Colonel Kole, who had just arrived and assumed command on March 28, sent its first combat ready company from the 478th Engineer Battalion to Davisville to secure the bridge park and to free up more Seabees for the high-priority connector route construction.

On March 31, after the MEG shifted its Engineering Work Lines to the north, NMCB 133 relocated to Bridge Park Davisville. The heavy traffic there had created a dust problem along the first fifty or so miles of the route north of the Euphrates, which would present significant challenges in the days ahead.[7]

NMCB 133 quickly went to work to improve the condition of the road, which was the only route currently being used to re-supply forces in their drive north. The route was also critical because the U.S. Army's 4th Infantry Division would use it in the coming days as it advanced toward Baghdad. This route, primarily an unfinished roadbed, contained several open culverts that had been bridged by other engineering units. Within the first three days of the project, NMCB 133 had placed a second lane at five of the crossings and had significantly improved the condition of the road along its entire length. On April 7, all crossings had been improved to double lanes at road elevation. The Seabees used stone located at an abandoned asphalt plant to strengthen the roadbed in areas where it had become soft. An overriding focus of the maintenance effort was dust control. Due to the amount of traffic, dust conditions along the route were severe and at times, treacherous. Several means were used to control the dust, including fuel and water application, each with varying degrees of success. One relatively successful method involved using kerosene, along with cutback asphalt from the abandoned asphalt plant. Task Force Charlie's maintenance and dust control efforts continued until it was relieved by Task Force Echo in May.

Route 1 was the lifeblood of the coalition push toward Baghdad, as it provided a relatively safe passage north. This route had one disadvantage though in that there was only one bridge spanning the Euphrates west of An Nasiriyah. If this bridge had been damaged or destroyed, I MEF would have needed non-standard Mabey & Johnson bridging to keep the route open. Thus, it was imperative that the bridge remain intact. NMCB 133 placed a security team, led by Lieutenant Breitenbach and Chief Steelworker Robbins, at the Euphrates Bridge crossing while Lieutenant Junior Grade Streiter and Chief Equipment Operator Cox headed up a security team at Alternate Supply Route Hueneme's Saddam Canal crossing.[8]

Task Force Echo and Umm Qasr

Once the ground assault began, I MEG had first assigned Task Force Echo the mission of maintaining Alternate Supply Route Dallas from Kuwait into Iraq. NMCB 7 was responsible for maintaining this Alternate Supply Route, which was critical for resupplying Task Force Tarawa during its initial attack on Jalibah and An Nasiriyah. However, Task Force Echo's role quickly expanded as the Coalition's tempo of operations accelerated, and the British 1st United Kingdom Armoured Division and the 15th Marine Expeditionary Unit cut-off Basrah, and more importantly, opened the port city of Umm Qasr. As Iraq's only major port, Umm Qasr had been closed for eight months before the Coalition forces crossed the Line of Departure. This closure was preventing sea-based Coalition humanitarian assistance from getting into Iraq and to its northern cities, and the Navy therefore wanted it open sooner rather than later.[9]

Even before the Brits secured Umm Qasr, NAVCENT called upon I MEG to move in, alongside a Navy Explosive Ordnance Disposal (EOD) Detachment, to begin the reconstruction and Civil Military Operations effort there. This was yet another confusing command and control issue at first since NAVCENT's call for Seabee Air Det support came very late in the game, and the reserve Det to be dedicated to the effort, NMCB 21 out of Lakehurst, New Jersey, had just arrived due to delayed TPFDD flow. Although it seemed like a natural mission for Task Force Echo, since it was in I MEF's area of operations controlled by the 1st United Kingdom Armoured Division, NAVCENT didn't see it quite that way at first, and wanted its own assets to control.

Reason ultimately prevailed, and the mission was assigned to the Seabees via I MEF, and I MEG assigned it to NMCB 21's Air Det. Ironically, these reserve Seabees were from the New York City area and many had been firemen, policemen, or city workers during the 9/11 attack on the World Trade Center. They were now the first U.S. troops to cross the Line of Departure with the specific mission of helping the newly liberated Iraqi people rebuild their country. Mission planning had to happen very quickly, and the suddenness of the tasking caught both Task Force Echo and Det 21 off guard at first. But they quickly recovered and made their necessary preparations. For political reasons, the mission also called for the inclusion of a supporting information/public relations component with embedded reporters to show the world that U.S. forces only intended to liberate the Iraqi people, not to conquer them.

On March 23, Task Force Echo's acting commander, Navy Seabee Commander Jim Worcester, dispatched a four-man assessment team, led by Lieutenant Lance Flood, to Umm Qasr. Flood's team arrived later that day, but unfortunately, the 15th Marine Expeditionary Unit pulled out before the 1st United Kingdom Armoured Division moved in, leaving Flood's advance party and the Navy Explosive Ordnance Disposal Det in a precarious position for a whole day and night in which fighting continued in the port. The Seabees and Navy Explosive Ordnance Disposal Team manned the defenses that night. While coming under repeated artillery and mortar shelling, they returned fire quickly and effectively. After the Brits finally arrived, Flood's team turned security over to them and quickly began their assessment of the power, water, and infrastructure repair requirements for the port.[10]

After Flood filed his report, I MEG quickly organized Det 21 into a twelve-vehicle convoy outside of Camp Commando. The Det Seabees were confident but Kubic was concerned. Not all of the required equipment was ready for this first major move, command and control at the Officer-in-Charge level seemed confused, and the press corps had turned out in great numbers to see the Seabees launch the first Civil Military Operations of the war. After some pointed discussion, the admiral ordered Det 21 to move out – there was no time for further planning or preparation — they were solid, highly motivated Seabees, and he trusted that their training would carry the day once they got going. Kubic later recalled that he "didn't realize until much later in the war that the average age of this first Seabee Reserve Det to enter combat in Iraq was 41, four years older than the average age of the World War II-era Seabees who came before them."

Det 21 arrived in Umm Qasr on March 27 and went straight to work. Over the next month, the New Jersey Seabees executed an impressive list of projects in Umm Qasr, including the construction of water tanks and a landfill, the restoration of electrical and water service to parts of the city, numerous force protection projects in support of British forces, installation of playground and soccer field equipment for local residents, and several "quality of life" projects for U.S. and U.K. forces positioned at the port, including showers and a Reverse Osmosis Water Purification Unit (ROWPU) for fresh water production. Det 21 also built a road and ferry landing to support the logistics flow across to the Al Faw peninsula before Basrah fell.

On March 29, the admiral traveled with SERT 7 to Port Umm Qasr to coordinate the Seabee efforts with those of Commodore Tillison (in command of the Navy's Explosive Ordnance Disposal (EOD) task force) and the 1st U.K. Armoured Division. This was an important day for the people of Iraq, as the first humanitarian relief ship, carrying needed supplies, began offloading its cargo. The Seabees of Det 21 had played a key role in making this happen. The relief ship was offloaded in record time but water was becoming critical. Large numbers of local civilians were in the streets carrying water from the limited sources at the port, and asking all Coalition vehicles for water as they passed by. The local treatment plant was operational, but the water source had been secured by a closed valve currently inaccessible in Basrah. The Brits recognized the importance of this valve and planned to seize and control it as they worked the Basrah security issues.[11]

Perhaps Det 21's most important contribution to the war effort was its initiation of what became a highly successful civil works strategy of seeking out and upgrading the schools that the emerging city leadership deemed vital for recovery. It soon became clear to I MEF's commanders that the deep fight for the future of Iraq was all about the children of Iraq and especially about their education. In early April, Rear Admiral Kubic visited Umm Qasr again, this time with a truckload of embedded newspaper and TV journalists. Det 21 showed the impact of their school reconstruction strategy to the world through I MEG's embedded media, which reported the amazing reconstruction progress in the city. The Det 21 Seabees continued to deal with Iraqi direct and indirect fires around Umm Qasr, while continuing their work around the port and surrounding town. After getting several school improvement projects underway in April, it was time for Det 21 to leave for its next mission, which was farther north in Ah Samarrah. A contingent of Spanish engineers arrived to take over the relief work, and the last Seabees from NMCB 21 left Umm Qasr on April 30. Although it had moved on, the Det's hard work in Umm Qasr not only played a crucial role in the short term goal of opening the port, but it also left an indelible mark on the long term objective of winning the peace in that sector.

As the war progressed and MEG forces moved deeper into Iraq, Rear Admiral Kubic also assigned Task Force Echo other missions involving rear area security. These missions included manning Bridge Park Davisville, providing security at the Ammunition Supply Point back at Tactical Assembly Area Coyote, and assisting Task Force Charlie with convoy operations into Iraq. Concurrent with ongoing combat and engineer support operations, the 478th Engineer Battalion and the 265th Engineer Group rotated back to the port to receive their equipment, which was delayed significantly by Army TPFDD constraints, and to complete the last stages of Reception, Staging, Onward Movement, and Integration (RSO&I). It was discouraging to the Seabees to see the mission effectiveness of these solid Army Guard and Reserve troops compromised by the failure of the fractured TPFDD process to deliver their vehicles and equipment until weeks after their arrival with the war already in progress.

UCT 2

I MEG attached Underwater Construction Team (UCT) 2 to Task Force Mike to give Commodore Rudich in-water bridge reconnaissance and construction capability. Unfortunately the UCT's mission quickly expanded to recover fallen Marines lost in the canals and rivers due to hostile action.

The first of these recovery missions occurred on March 26 after the 6th Engineer Support Battalion installed an expeditionary fuel line to support I MEF as it rolled north. When the Marine engineers came under harassment fire, four of them attempted to swim the Saddam Canal, northeast of An Nasiriyah to outflank the attackers. Two of them, Corporal Evans James and Sergeant Bradley S. Korthaus, didn't make it and drowned. The Marines called UCT 2 for help. After an extensive search lasting a day or so, the Seabee divers recovered the bodies and turned them over to the Marines for return to the U.S. for proper military burial.

This was very important, not only for humanitarian purposes, but also to keep the remains from being exploited by the Iraqis, as happened to members of the U.S. Army's 507th Maintenance Company and the 3rd Combat Support Battalion after their convoy was infamously ambushed at An Nasiriyah on March 23. In that incident, *Al Jazeera* broadcast disturbing images to the world of the American soldiers who had either been killed or captured during the ambush. Outraged, the MEF commanders swore that they would not allow any of their fallen Marines to be so exhibited. So, recovery of their "fallen angels" became a high MEF priority in the battles to come.

On the dark, dusty night of March 25, a Marine M1A1 Abrams tank (nicknamed "Hermes" and belonging to 2nd Platoon, Charlie Company, 1st Tank Battalion, of Regimental Combat Team 7) veered off an unfinished bridge along Highway 8 west of An Nasiriyah, flipped over, and sank in the Euphrates River. Once the Marines noticed the tank was missing, they immediately began an extensive search. Construction Electrician 1st Class Alexander Semmler of UCT 2 later recounted his encounter with two Marine tanks sent back to look for the missing tank and its crew:

> We actually had moved across that bridge, I guess it was a day later, and all of a sudden we see these two tanks rolling south at us. They pulled up to us and asked us if we had seen a tank. We're like…what the hell do you mean? And they say "we lost a tank…we can't find it." We said no, sorry; and then they asked us for fuel. And so we sent them back to where we had a tanker to give them some fuel so that they could continue their search.[12]

Soon afterward, the Marines found three of the missing tankers' sea bags, which had previously been strapped to the outside of their tank's turret, floating down the river. They then saw the broken guard rails at the bridge. Putting two and two together, the armored search party realized that the tank had never made it across. Suspecting the worst, the Marines once again called upon UCT 2 for help. The same Seabee divers who had recovered the drowned engineers quickly located the tank and its crew members' bodies twenty-feet under water at the bottom of the river. They then helped the Marines drag the mud-encrusted tank ashore and recover the remains.[13]

Much later in the campaign, when I MEF was located at its forward headquarters at Hillah (Babylon), the UCT was called into recovery action again when a CH-46 Sea Knight helicopter hit some power lines and went down in the Euphrates River, killing its four crew members. As with the tank, the Seabee divers pulled up the bodies and helped the Marines extract the chopper from the river. In addition to these tragic recovery efforts, the UCT distinguished itself throughout the campaign with its support to Task Forces Mike and Charlie. Much of the UCT's recon knowledge and communications capability served as the basis for development of SERT doctrine prior to the war under the forward looking leadership of Chief Warrant Officer (Diver) Bill Johnson.

Early Reconstruction Efforts in An Nasiriyah

Even before the city of An Nasiriyah was fully secured, the call went out to get electrical power restored to the city. The MEG quickly sent a survey team to the power plant and determined that combat damage had been light to non-existent, but that maintenance had been sorely neglected for many years. The survey team also determined that the gas turbine generators had been shut down and needed electric power to restart them. But, the power line from Basrah had been knocked down and had to be repaired, or else, portable diesel generators would be required to start the plant. Rear Admiral Kubic accordingly recommended that CFLCC purchase or rent two dozen large generators since it was obvious to the MEG staff in late March 2003 that the country would have a hard time getting its power back on.

The MEG contracting officers worked up a cost estimate of $10 million, but there was no available funding source to pay for the generators. The U.S. Agency for International Development (USAID)/Bechtel contract was not ready to go and they could not pass money separately to the MEG for it to use the Navy CONCAP contract with Brown & Root to acquire generators. But, as the local Iraqi power plant workers slowly returned, the Seabees quickly teamed up with them, and despite language barriers, managed to restore limited power using expedient repairs and work-arounds to jump start the gas turbine generators.

It was at this time that the MEG directed Task Force Echo to push NMCB 7 forward. The battalion's commanding officer, Commander Christopher J. Honkomp, led his Seabees first into Jalibah to relieve Task Force Charlie Det 133, and then took his Air Det on to An Nasiriyah, where they established a base camp at Whitehorse – a former camp of the Iraqi 11th Infantry Division. With the sounds of battle still echoing in the distance, Honkomp and Det 7 began to survey hospitals, schools, and water plants along with the U.S. Army's 4th Civil Affairs Group (CAG), which had established a Civil Military Operations Center (CMOC) along the main route through the city. Their approach proved to be extremely effective. With funding plugged up for the time being, Honkomp floated a loan to the Navy for $1,000 out of his own pocket to buy the construction materials that his Seabees needed since he "had guys just dying to do the repairs" but were unable to do so until the funding snafu was cleared up. Soon however, based on Honkomp's $1,000 loan, Seabee-backed projects were underway that clearly demonstrated the Coalition's intentions to liberate rather than conquer An Nasiriyah.[14]

Near the scene of the bloodiest fighting along Ambush Alley, a water treatment plant was repaired. Not only was looting damage repaired, but Seabees, working side by side with Iraqi workers, also restarted pumps and motors that hadn't worked in years. When Rear Admiral Kubic visited this plant, the blue collar Iraqis approached him with their hands over their hearts and tears in their eyes as they thanked the Marines and Seabees for liberating them and working with them to restore their water plant. In a nearby woman's hospital, a roof damaged by an artillery shell was repaired, a water tower was patched, and two useless generators were scavenged for parts by Seabees who then got a third generator working to the total amazement of the hospital staff.

At this point, the MEG was using money left over from Class IV material expenditures to procure parts and building supplies through the local economy via the CONCAP contract, which supplied a buyer with cash. This was the only source of cash, and the MEG justified O&M funding as being appropriate given its use in support of Civil Military Operations which, in turn, was key to ending combat operations and protecting the force. Kubic felt that it was key to put a friendly face on the U.S. forces quickly in the city to avoid the need to return to "kinetic" (i.e. combat) operations. He was a bit concerned about how much would be required to make an impact, and after the buyer and Seabee expediters returned from a successful day of shopping for plumbing and electrical supplies, he asked how much they had spent. When they said "$200.00," he knew that they were on the right track and were truly getting a solid return on their investment. Ultimately, the work in An Nasiriyah expanded to schools and hospitals and government buildings when the MEF/MEG was able to use funds seized from Saddam's regime to fund this much larger reconstruction effort.

Seized Iraqi funds in fact became available in An Nasiriyah following what became known as NMCB 7's "bank job." The 4th Civil Affairs Group, which was also responsible for securing the local banking system and An Nasiriyah's financial assets, decided that it wanted to consolidate funds from all the city's banks. This was a big problem for the bank on the western side of the Euphrates, located along the Seabees' regular route to their job sites. Would-be robbers had broken into it before security had been reestablished, and had severely damaged the main and auxiliary emergency doors of the bank's vault, so much so that they could not be opened anymore. As Honkomp later recalled, the Marines' solution was to blow a hole through the vault with a tube-launched, optically-tracked, wire-guided (TOW) missile. "But," said Honkomp, "they couldn't guarantee that anything would be left inside when they were done. So the Civil Affairs Group thought that was a bad idea."[15]

The Civil Affairs Group then turned to NMCB 7 for help in getting the damaged vault open. As Honkomp later recalled, "CAG had already arranged for some Light-Armored Vehicles (LAVs) to be there, to receive the money, escort it to the central bank, and everything would be fine." Unfortunately, one of the things that Honkomp found out was that everyone involved worked on different times. The Seabees and Marine Light Armored Vehicles operated in Zulu Time while the Civil Affairs Group worked according to local time. Consequently (with daylight savings time now in effect), there was a two-hour time difference in which the Civil Affairs Group and the Seabees thought that the Light Armored Vehicle would be there at the bank ready to go. Consequently, a comedy of errors ensued.

Honkomp's Seabees arrived at the appointed time, but found that the Light Armored Vehicle was no where in sight. The Civil Affairs Group was in a hurry to get the money out, and so it directed the Seabees to begin working on the vault's back door, in the belief that the Light Armored Vehicle would eventually arrive. The Seabees were able to quickly jack up the door, use the bank director's key to unlock it, and then cut off the remaining good hinge, the other one having been damaged during the original break-in attempt. The door fell off, and the vault opened. In the meantime, a crowd of Iraqis had gathered around the bank to watch the safe cracking effort, making the Seabees nervous. Threatening to ignite the situation into something ugly was a sudden shouting match between the bank director, and the director of the bank where the money was supposed to go, over how much was there.

The 4th Civil Affairs Group representatives realized that the situation was about to get out of control. So they directed Honkomp and his Seabees to load all the money up in their Humvee and take it to the designated bank repository, under the protection of their .50 caliber machine gun. Honkomp did not like the idea at all, thinking that "if you weren't a target before, you're a target now" if he took responsibility for transporting all of that money, which amounted to two billion local dinars (equivalent $1.5 million U.S. dollars), across the city to the other bank.

Fortunately, he was backed by his Master Chief, Olin Lacey, who "was a pretty savvy guy and realized things to get into and not to get into." After conferring with Lacey, Honkomp demurred, explaining to the Civil Affairs Group that a soft-backed Humvee was not the best vehicle for the purpose they had in mind. At that point, the Civil Affairs Group people finally figured out the time difference issue and managed to summon the Light Armored Vehicle early to take control of the money. Honkomp and his Seabees decided to leave while the going was good. That evening, as he briefed the Marines on what his Seabees had done that day, Honkomp noted that this was probably the first time that the Seabees had ever broken into a bank. A Marine, wise to the ways of the Seabee world, retorted, "I doubt it!"

The bank job aside, Honkomp and NMCB 7 led the way with Civil Military Operations and began contracting with local builders even before Baghdad fell. A key project to repair the previously looted and burned city hall and courthouse constituted a tremendous boost to the local efforts to establish a town council. With a strong sense of pride and on his own accord, the contractor who won the bid sculpted the scales of justice into the iron gate of the fence he rebuilt at the courthouse entrance. This large, two-story concrete building was completely restored for less than $90,000. It was in An Nasiriyah that the MEG learned the value of restarting Iraqi small businesses and jump-starting capitalism and free enterprise as a way to bring political stability to an area that resisted coalition forces fiercely just weeks earlier. This pattern was to repeat itself in other cities throughout the MEF's Area of Responsibility in the weeks and months ahead.

It was also here in An Nasiriyah that the Army's 265th Engineer Group quickly learned the MEG's approach to Civil Military Operations and then led a very aggressive restoration effort that eventually included a Korean Engineer Battalion and medical company which were assigned to I MEG – the first forces to join the coalition Civil Military Operations effort once major hostilities ended. The Koreans brought highly skilled military engineers to An Nasiriyah who could also build and fight. These Korean Engineers renovated schools and major hospital facilities which they then staffed with their own medical forces. This coalition effort freed NMCB 7 to move up Highway 8 to Ad Diwaniyah in late June to relieve NMCB 4 – again a very successful Civil Military Operations strategy that served to stabilize areas in the south and created the conditions for the MEF to turnover operations to other coalition forces (e.g. to the Italians in An Nasiriyah) and redeploy from Iraq. The Seabees and Marines established and refined their CMO tactics, techniques and procedures for Iraq in An Nasiriyah – which became a textbook example of CMO success, resulting in a level of electrical and water services that had not been experienced by the city's population since before the Iran-Iraq war of the 1980s.

I MEF Attacks across the Tigris at An Numaniyah

On April 1 at 0500Z, I MEF resumed its attack north. The plan was to have Regimental Combat Team 1 attack first and fix the Baghdad Infantry Division at Al Kut. At 1500Z, Regimental Combat Team 5 would attack up Highway 27 and secure river crossings over the Saddam Canal and the Tigris River. Once across the Tigris, it would move west toward Baghdad and stop. From there, it would block any enemy reinforcements coming down Highway 6 from Baghdad. At 0300Z on 2 April, Regimental Combat Team 7, the main effort, would attack across the Tigris, then swing back to the east and destroy the Baghdad Infantry Division from its flank and rear. It was a very bold scheme of maneuver and the Marines executed it perfectly.[16]

After Regimental Combat Team 1 halted just south of Al Kut, the Regimental Combat Team 5 attack was moved up six hours and it attacked northeast along Highway 27. The Saddam Canal crosses Highway 27 about halfway between Hantush and An Numaniyah. Unfortunately the bridge was MLC 30 at best. Still, in order to maintain the momentum of the attack, Regimental Combat Team 5 pushed its lead tanks and some vehicles across. The 8th Engineer Support Battalion pushed forward and flawlessly constructed an assault floating bridge, which carried the rest of Regimental Combat Team 5 and eventually Regimental Combat Team 7 when they attacked later on April 2. Since the likelihood of multiple future assault bridge missions was extremely likely, it was important that this temporary bridge be replaced as soon as possible so it could be used closer to Baghdad. Again, Task Force Mike arrived to make it happen. As SERT 74 raced forward to reconnoiter and analyze the site, I MEF reported terrific news that "Tanks Across the An Numaniyah Bridge over the Tigris. Bridge is intact."

This was indeed incredible news for the MEG. Kubic thought this would be the one bridge that the Iraqis would definitely destroy. Still, the MEF tasked the 8th Engineer Support Battalion with another Assault Bridge mission since it would take time to analyze the existing An Numaniyah Bridge, and also because the MEF wanted alternate crossing routes if the existing bridge was targeted. Despite intelligence that said otherwise, the Baghdad Division did not put up much of a fight. This allowed Regimental Combat Team 7 to attack early as well and advance across the Tigris without incident, giving the 1st Marine Division two regimental combat teams advancing on Baghdad from the east along Highway 6. Regimental Combat Team 1 remained in place as Al Kut was not secure. The Republican Guard's Al Nida Division would be I MEF's next target. It supposedly lay between Baghdad and Al Kut along Highway 6.

The MEG Employs all three Task Forces in Iraq on April 2

With the 1st Marine Division attacking north of the Tigris on April 2, the MEG needed to shift its stance for the third time since the beginning of the war. While Task Force Mike's NMCB 4 focused on finishing up the 1-7 Connector Route, NMCB 74 began its move north to replace the assault floating bridge at the Highway 27-Saddam Canal Bridge intersection and support engineer operations at An Numaniyah Airfield. The plan was for Task Force Mike to relocate to An Numaniyah so it could be in place to support the 1st Marine Division's attack to isolate Baghdad. In order to do this, it would need to turnover Bridgepark Davisville, Highway 1-7 Connector, and Highway 1 repairs north of the Euphrates.[17]

On 2 April, Task Force Mike-Main moved from Bridge Park Davisville to the An Numaniyah Airfield, which was named Logistics Support Area Chesty (after the legendary Marine General Lewis Burwell "Chesty" Puller) in order to support I MEF's attack. Logistics Support Area Chesty, just south of the city of An Numaniyah and the Tigris River, needed much work to turn it into a suitable Forward Operating Base.

In addition to the specified task of deliberate runway repairs and Main Supply Route Maintenance, Task Force Mike tackled basic quality of life projects as well as the large dust problem, which was interfering with air operations. The move also placed Commodore Rudich in the best position to command and control the current projects underway, while at the same time providing him with a springboard north of the Tigris in which to support the final push on Baghdad. While Task Force Mike's NMCB 4 stayed at Davisville to finish the 1-7 Connector Route, NMCB 74 tackled the numerous projects at Logistics Supply Area Chesty, continued maintenance on Main Supply Route Tampa, and prepared for the MEG's next Mabey & Johnson bridge project at the Highway 27/Saddam Canal Bridge.

The SERTs were also busy on April 2. Out ahead of the MEG task forces, the SERTs continued to earn their pay with SERT 74 providing a load classification of the existing bridge over the Saddam Canal on Highway 27, SERT 4 beginning their recon for a suitable new bridge site, and SERT 133 pushing forward to recon the airfield at Logistics Support Area Chesty. SERT 5 returned to Camp Commando for redeployment.

Commodore McKerall's Task Force Charlie moved its forward element north to the Davisville Bridge Park and took over all of Task Force Mike's projects, except for the 1-7 Connector Route. This put McKerall's Seabees in a better position to support Task Force Mike with its line haul operations, which were then in full swing. Finally, Task Force Echo, now under Colonel Kole, moved a detachment from NMCB 7 into Task Force Charlie's positions at Logistics Support Area Viper and took over the ongoing projects there, including Main Supply Route maintenance south to the border, the construction of defensive positions for a Patriot Battery at Viper, and the reduction of bunkers along Alternate Supply Route Dallas, which the enemy was using to snipe at friendly convoys.

All in all, Rear Admiral Kubic considered it another historic day for MEG. In the Daily Situation Report, he commented that

"Task Forces Mike, Charlie and Echo are all now deployed in Iraq and will continue to move north in echelon to support maneuver forces and to improve LOC's, bridges, and airfields."

The Route 27 Bridge over the Saddam Canal

Regimental Combat Team 5 attacked from Highway 1 northeast along Route 27 toward the Tigris River Bridge near An Numaniyah. The Iraqi gun position overlooking the bridge was destroyed by air, and the Marines were able to establish a bridgehead after a short fight. The existing bridge over the Saddam Canal was in poor shape. SERT 74 classified it at MLC 25. While the initial forces made it over the bridge, it quickly degraded under the stress. The 8th Engineer Support Battalion emplaced a floating assault bridge on the day of the attack, but removed it two days later to be used in the attack on Baghdad. The MEF called the MEG forward to emplace a Mabey & Johnson bridge as soon as possible. After a successful SERT mission and leader's reconnaissance, Task Force Mike chose a suitable bridge site at the canal and NMCB 74 went to work on their second Mabey & Johnson bridge in Iraq. The Route 27 bridge site was located approximately thirty kilometers southwest of An Numaniyah and involved a forty-meter wet gap. After some reach-back recommendations from the Pacific Division, a sixty-meter Mabey & Johnson Bridge supported by a sheet-pile mole was chosen. This would be the first bridge built in Iraq using sheet-pile by the Seabees.[18]

While a construction detachment was sent to work at the bridge site, the rest of the battalion settled into its new home at Logistics Support Area Chesty, which became the major forward base for the MEF as it maneuvered to isolate Baghdad. I MEG also tasked NMCB 74 with building another connector route. This road off Route 27, named Pearl 3, was needed to connect traffic from Route 27 to the 8th Engineer Support Battalion floating bridge over the Tigris. The Iraqis failed to destroy the An Numaniyah Bridge, so the Marines rushed across and established positions north of river. They now had two routes across the Tigris. Once the existing Numaniyah Bridge was deemed safe for movement, the floating bridge was recovered for potential use near Baghdad. Still, NMCB 74 completed their work on Pearl 3 on April 9 and focused on finishing the Saddam Canal bridge on Route 27 and battling the dust at the An Numaniyah Airfield.

The Fourth Shift

On April 6, Task Force Mike's command element moved forward from Logistics Support Area Chesty to Logistics Support Area Daly at Salman Pak Air Base on the outskirts of Baghdad to support the 1st Marine Division's final assault. The Marines quickly called the Seabees forward to bridge the Diyala River. Task Force Mike sent NMCB 4 to do the job. As Task Force Mike shifted north of the Tigris, Task Forces Charlie and Echo shifted their focus north as well and the MEG readjusted the Engineer Work Lines. The MEG ordered Task Force Echo to assume all general and specified engineering tasks south of the Euphrates River. Integrated into this mission was the maintenance of Highway 1 and Alternate Supply Route Dallas, improving the road network leading to Logistics Support Area Viper, providing engineer support in order to establish airfield and logistics operations at Logistics Support Area Viper, and digging-in Patriot batteries that had been repositioned forward on the battlefield. Task Force Echo units also found themselves performing the first of many jobs relating to the re-establishment of public utilities in An Nasiriyah (led by NMCB 7) and the destruction of captured enemy munitions and equipment.[19]

Along with on-going Engineer missions directly supporting the war, elements of Task Force Echo continued to train and prepare for additional missions. Back in Kuwait, Seabees from NMCB 7 trained and staffed a back-up "Jiffy Decon" team capable of conducting a thorough decontamination of a company plus sized unit. They also conducted Mabey & Johnson bridge training for a "Be Prepared To" mission to erect non-standard fixed bridging in case they had to be thrown into the fight. Work also continued at Logistics Support Area Fox and Al Jaber air base on various rear echelon construction and road projects.

Early April marked the introduction of the 1092nd Engineer Battalion (Corps Wheeled) from the West Virginia National Guard into Task Force Echo's operations. Due to the delay of its equipment arriving in country, the 1092nd was not certified as combat ready until April 9. Although it may have arrived late in country as Task Force Echo's Corps Wheeled battalion, its presence essentially doubled the Task Force's capabilities to perform horizontal construction and line haul operations. The 478th Engineer Battalion, from the Kentucky Army Reserve, provided a mechanized element to the Task Force with highly motivated and skilled combat engineers. But they were very limited as to what they could do when it came to expeditionary construction because that was not their wartime mission focus. However, despite their dearth of construction equipment, these soldiers continued to provide timely assistance requested by the Task Force. These troops ultimately demonstrated their character and Engineer capability at a critical juncture, as the U.S. Army, I MEF, and the MEG finally closed in on Baghdad during the first week of April. The end was drawing near for Saddam's regime.

CHAPTER 11

Babylon Falls

The Diyala River guards the eastern and southern approaches into Baghdad. Although the Marines were now north of the Tigris, the Diyala posed a significant new obstacle that needed to be breached prior to any ground assault into Baghdad. The Marines found their primary routes over the three existing bridges impassable due to accurate enemy artillery fire and direct heavy weapons fire from the western shore. The Iraqis had done a good job registering their guns on and around the bridges to slow any attack and they were well dug-in to defend them. They had also damaged the two southern bridges, and the Marines found the northern-most bridge still under construction.[1]

On April 6, Major General Mattis reported to Lieutenant General Conway that the 1st Marine Division had reconnoitered some sixty kilometers of the Diyala River northward from the Tigris but had found no viable crossing. The levees and roads leading up to the river would not support the necessary Marine vehicle traffic and both southern bridges were covered by indirect artillery fire. The Marine engineers believed that the newest concrete bridge, albeit damaged by Iraqi sappers, was the most viable despite missing a twenty foot span. The 1st Marine Division was now focused on finding and securing crossing sites across the Diyala.

The moment of truth had finally come. The MEG had spent most of its pre-war planning energy on figuring out how to bridge the Euphrates and the Saddam Canal, as well as all of the culverts and potential wet gaps along Highway 7 from An Nasiriyah to Al Kut.

To a lesser extent the MEG also planned on how it would emplace a floating bridge across the Tigris. But I MEF and the MEG had put very little planning effort into how they would actually take down Baghdad. Kubic later commented that "it was almost like we felt we would have time to plan that later once we actually got to the city. There were just too many variables and too much to accomplish before we had to face that challenge. And we thought a prolonged siege would be required before the front line Republican Guard Divisions surrendered their capital and their leader."

Also, the Marines and Seabees all believed the Iraqis would "slime" the U.S. troops with chemical weapons once they crossed the Tigris, turned west, and reached Baghdad's outer environs, and that they would have to deal with a major decontamination effort before launching the final assault. In the meantime, the basic plan was simple—Baghdad would be pounded by air until I MEF was ready to move forward again. It was comforting for the MEG staff to remember at that point that Marine F/A-18's could sortie from the Seabee-built parking apron at Al Jaber Base in Kuwait and go to "Downtown Baghad" without refueling. But as NMCB 4 assumed perimeter defense responsibilities at Salman Pak, and once again locked in its 60 mm mortars (Kubic wished they still had the 81 mm mortars from Vietnam days at that point), the Seabees' days of pouring concrete on Christmas Eve in Kuwait seemed a distant memory.

Since the MEG had assumed that most bridges and culverts would be blown during the movement towards and across the Euphrates, the Saddam Canal, and the Tigris, it did have a bridge plan to deal with those threats. But the MEG staff never planned exactly where and how to bridge the Diyala River. This river served as the natural boundary protecting Baghdad from assault along Highway 6 from the east. Improvisation and seat-of-the-pants expeditionary engineering would be the standard mode of operations from this point forth in the campaign.

Into Baghdad

As it happened, the assault moved forward very quickly, following the same tactics that I MEF had planned for the Euphrates and resulting in the most significant combat construction accomplished by the MEG. Once Marines crossed the Tigris and secured Salman Pak airfield, Lieutenant General Conway suddenly needed a plan to attack Baghdad. Knowing that bridge conditions were crucial to keeping his ever-lengthening supply lines open, Conway ordered the MEG, through a personal call to Kubic, to give him some options. So SERT 4 became a key element to this effort. Unfortunately, the "fog of war" had set in, and the MEG fumbled this tasking. As the battle moved closer to Baghdad, Commodore Rudich decided to move his Jump Command Post forward from Salman Pak closer to the Diyala River using SERT 4. He executed this move at night before his rear Command Post, which was still at An Numaniyah, rejoined his Main Command Post at Salman Pak. This action split his command element into three parts ("Jump, Main, and Rear" command posts) at a very critical time. He also employed elements of SERT 4 (leaving them "not mission capable") to make this move, without order or concurrence from I MEG, which had operational control of SERT 4 at that time.[2]

In the confusion, tactical communications with both Task Force Mike and SERT 4 completely broke down. There was a period of time, in fact, when I MEG "lost" SERT 4 and could not contact Task Force Mike. While the global communications network, administered through the Seabee "Bridge, Bunker, and Bug" worked very well, the lack of sufficient tactical communications staff and equipment was by far the MEG's greatest deficiencies throughout the campaign. Although the MEG had satellite communication (SATCOM) capabilities, the Marines did not allow the Seabees to use the satellite frequency (due to competing demands) for any period of time to communicate with one another within the battlespace.

Due to communications constraints and sparse assets, Kubic's ability to jump the MEG Command Operations Center forward was severely limited. The best he could manage was to field a small "jump Command Post," which was located at An Numaniyah in Logistics Support Area Chesty, as the assault moved into Baghdad. After the war, a number of SERT members reported that their operations had in fact been adversely affected by the communications trouble, especially after they outran the limited range of the High Frequency (HF) and Very High Frequency radio sets in their Humvees due to the speed of the advance north. Fixing Seabee tactical communications was Kubic's number one "lesson learned" and his top recommendation to the Chief of Naval Operations, Admiral Vern Clark, when he briefed Clark and the CNO War Council after the campaign.

Despite repeated appeals to the MEF G6, to the MEF Deputy Commanding General, and even to General Conway himself, the MEG ended up existing, building, and fighting with minimal tactical communications. Kubic and his staff had to rely heavily on "borrowed" SIPR and NIPR drops, High Frequency radios, and iridium phones, which sometimes worked, but usually did not. More dangerously, the MEG had no Blue Force tracker sets despite its extensive convoys, and Kubic considered it a miracle that no Seabees were lost to friendly fire in the fluid, rapidly changing battlespace. He found this situation extremely maddening, especially when Seabee and Marine lives were on the line.

A full-day passed before Task Force Mike regained stable command and control and the MEG reestablished contact with SERT 4. It was an extremely trying period for all concerned, and precipitated a heated Iridium phone conversation between Kubic and Commodore Rudich once communications were finally reestablished. Without SERT 4, the MEG was unable to provide the I MEF Commanding General with the fully reconnoitered river crossing options he had requested. Lieutenant General Conway was a tremendous leader and a great boss as far as Kubic was concerned. With the campaign now reaching a crescendo, the Seabee admiral was personally embarrassed that the MEG had failed to respond to Conway's call for help. When Rear Admiral Kubic joined Commodore Rudich at the Diyala a day or so later, they walked together and reviewed the "fumble." They fixed the problem and both learned from this disastrous communications breakdown.

In the meantime, on April 7, the 1st Marine Division rolled boldly across the Diyala at multiple locations to avoid both a big traffic jam and another operational pause while sitting within the range of the heavy Iraqi artillery. The Marines were low on artillery shells and their food was reduced to one ration per Marine per day. Nevertheless, Regimental Combat Team 7 attacked across the damaged bridges, while Regimental Combat Team 1 attacked across floating bridges. Major General Mattis first called his Marine combat engineers forward to Bridge #3 (the new concrete bridge), where they laid an Armored Vehicle Launched Bridge (AVLB), enabling Regimental Combat Team 7 and some of its heavy vehicles to get across the river and then fight their way into East Baghdad. The combat engineers then moved to Bridge #1 and laid an AVLB there as well. In order to keep as many Marines as possible from having to cross over these pre-targeted kill zones, the 8th Engineer Support Battalion also emplaced two float bridges while under fire next to the extreme southern and northern most bridges, relieving some of the pressure. Still, the Marines needed more routes into the city as well as more durable bridging to ensure the uninterrupted flow of Coalition forces and supplies into Baghdad. The Marines once again called upon the Seabees, staged just twenty kilometers to the rear at Salman Pak, for help.[3]

Saddam's Regime Falls

The MEF's intention was to avoid block-by-block urban conflict in Baghdad. As it happened, the city fell quickly on April 9 once its outer defenses were breached and the senior officers of the Hammurabi and Nebuchadnezzar Divisions deserted their commands. The U.S. Army's "thunder runs" through western Baghdad proved devastating to Iraqi morale, despite televised assurances by Saddam's hapless Information Minister, Mohammed Saeed al-Sahaf (universally derided as "Baghdad Bob") that American forces were no where near the city. Characterized by one British commentator as "extended drive-by shootings," the heavily armored thunder runs shattered Baghdad's ground defenses in the western part of the city. With the end of Saddam's regime clearly in sight, the Marines decided to stay on the attack and to clear their whole zone once they got across the Diyala.[4]

The 1st Marine Division attacked Baghdad with extreme courage and on empty stomachs. Artillery rounds were severely depleted, and rations were reduced to one Meal-Ready-to-Eat (MRE) per person per day just prior to the attack. But Mattis could not wait for resupply given the threat of enemy artillery. When the 1st Force Service Support Group found itself stretched too thin, given low truck maintenance availability, the 3rd Marine Aircraft Wing began flying emergency artillery rounds, food and water to Salman Pak on the outskirts of Baghdad, where Seabees dropped their bridge components, reloaded their convoys, and hauled "beans and bullets" to the front line Marines.

On April 9, Saddam fell from power, not with a bang (like Hitler in his Berlin bunker), but with a whimper. For all his prior bluster, he quietly discarded his ubiquitous olive-green uniform and black beret and donned the garb of a Bedouin so that he could ignominiously sneak out of the city before he was captured. That evening, the Marines reached Al Firdus (Paradise) Square in Baghdad, where a large crowd of Iraqis were trying to topple a thirty-nine foot tall statue of Saddam with sledge hammers and people power. A Marine M88 armored recovery vehicle, called a "tank retriever," rolled up to the statue and, in images beamed live around the world, twenty-three year-old Corporal Edward Chin of Bravo Company, 1st Marine Tank Battalion, climbed precariously up the vehicle's boom and draped an American flag over Saddam's face. Perhaps realizing his faux pas, Chin quickly replaced Old Glory with the Iraqi national flag.[5]

The Marines then helped the Iraqis by attaching cables around Saddam's figure and throttling up the 1,300 horse power recovery vehicle to pull the statue down. Once the statue was toppled, the Iraqis beat it with their shoes, a grave insult in Islamic culture, and broke it apart as expressions of their joy over their liberation. Although Chin's action with the American flag was not exactly the message that CENTCOM and the U.S. government wanted to broadcast to the Islamic world, the symbolism was gratifying considering all that the U.S. and its armed forces had been through since 9/11, and even before, with the 1991 Persian Gulf War.

The Twin Diyala Bridges

After receiving I MEF's urgent request for bridging support, and now that communications were reestablished, I MEG ordered SERT 4 to reconnoiter the damaged bridges. The MEG then alerted Task Force Mike to get ready to emplace new Mabey-Johnson bridges once I MEF gave the MEG the go head. SERT 4 moved forward quickly. Arriving at New Diyala Bridge (Bridge #3), the team found that one lane of the far side span was completely blown and that the second lane of the same span was damaged beyond repair. The Marines had over-bridged it temporarily with an AVLB that was supported only by the sagging pre-stressed cables on one end and a damaged bridge pier on the other.[6]

This bridge represented a big challenge for the Seabees. It was a prestressed concrete box girder bridge, and had an unusually complex structure. SERT 4 therefore had some difficulty in determining its load bearing capability. At MEG Headquarters, Kubic's staff downloaded SERT 4's engineering report and accompanying high resolution digital images of the bridge through I MEF's satellite data communication link. After looking at the data and the images, the MEG staff became immediately concerned about the span adjacent to the blown one. Since the pre-stressed cables had been relaxed, potentially degrading the load bearing capacity on other bridge spans, the negative moment capacity of this continuous concrete structure was reduced to zero at a key pier adjacent to the blown span (to use structural engineer jargon).

In other words, the bridge was dangerously unstable. If this span could not carry seventy tons (to continue the movement of M1A1 Tanks and fuel trucks), it was obvious that the MEG needed to build a new bridge rather than fix both lanes of the damaged bridge. However, with the Marines continuing to fight it out with the Iraqis in East Baghdad, time was against the MEG. Kubic made the tough decision to build a Mabey & Johnson bridge to "over-bridge" the totally blown span using the existing concrete bridge structure. It was hardly ideal, but for the time being, it would have to do. So, the MEG sent NMCB 4 up to the Diyala on April 8 (the day before the Saddam statue came down in Baghdad) to begin construction on the Mabey & Johnson over-bridge to provide for at least for one-way movement of fuel and logistics vehicles and tanks into East Baghdad.

This bridge went in quickly as NMCB 4 worked throughout the final battle for Baghdad, despite nearby Iraqi direct and indirect fire. Many of the Seabees from this crew would earn combat decorations for their valor while building under fire in the coming days. On April 10, two days after NMCB 4 had arrived and the day after they had started building the Mabey & Johnson bridge, Rear Admiral Kubic visited this job site himself. It was still not fully secured and so NMCB 4 worked during the day while manning defensive positions both day and night. Unexploded ordnance (UXO) was cooking off as a result of lingering fires, there was sporadic small arms fire from the near-by housing area, and two incoming mortar rounds landed close enough to cause the Seabees to take cover and assume a defensive posture. Also, the MEG had hard intelligence that suicide bombers had new explosive vests that looked like a fashionable outer garment. Since the MEG didn't want to stop pedestrian flow over this key bridge, Kubic's team had to deal with this serious threat with Seabee security while construction on the Mabey & Johnson over-bridge proceeded.

When Kubic saw the damaged bridge for the first time, he knew that the Seabees had an even bigger problem than previously realized. The Mabey & Johnson over-bridge would support seventy tons, but the rest of the existing concrete bridge was highly suspect. At one point the Pacific Division engineers concluded that the bridge had totally failed and should be abandoned.

After more detailed survey work to define the bridge's composite construction of pre-cast concrete girders, formed into box girders by fully integral cast-in-place top and bottom slabs with pre-stressed, post-tensioned cables (and 106 pages of detailed calculations and lots of solid engineering work by the "Seabee Jedi" in the Future Ops cell), Kubic concluded that the remaining spans could support a thirty ton load with properly routed one-way traffic. He then determined that the Seabees needed to build a new bridge at a site selected by SERT 4 and Task Force Mike and that it had to be a two-lane, seventy-ton bridge. This new sixty-meter Mabey-Johnson bridge would span an eighty-seven meter gap with a twenty-five meter and a seventeen-meter mole. The new bridge was located near the totally destroyed Old Diyala Bridge (down stream about four hundred meters from the new Diyala Bridge) and near the still-standing foot bridge where the Marines charged across the Diyala a few days earlier. The moles were subsequently built with sheet pile using the MOVAC attachment to a tracked-excavator. Once completed, these bridges became known as the Twin Diyala Bridges.

The twin Diyala Bridges were a marvel of design-build combat construction. During construction, Seabee crews worked the road approaches and earthen moles from both sides, and launched the Mabey & Johnson bridges from the Baghdad side of the river. When the Marines turned this area over to the Army in the middle of the construction effort, the Seabees assumed full responsibility for site security and for patrolling the housing area adjacent to the job site. Since the U.S. Army arrived in Baghdad with a far fewer dismounted infantry from its 3rd Infantry Division than the Marines had in the 1st Marine Division, there was no other option but for the Seabees to hold the turf while building the bridges. With Seabee snipers on the rooftops and Seabee patrols running day and night through the village, NMCB 4 clearly executed the top end of the Seabee "We Build, We Fight" mission, while building the last bridges to Baghdad during the final days of I MEF's march into Iraq in March and April of 2003.

All in all, NMCB 4 completed the work in less than ten days and fully restored the main access into Baghdad along Highway 6. The earthen moles with sheet pile bulkheads worked superbly. As Kubic saw this construction underway on Easter Sunday, April 20, he reflected on the fact that two weeks before Christmas he did not even have a design solution for the MEG's bridging mission, let alone any funding for the bridges, and no bridging material was purchased or staged in theater. Kubic later recalled that as he stood there on the Baghdad bank of the Diyala River, he was never prouder of the Nation's Seabees, who true to their heritage, had just done the impossible without even taking a "bit longer."

Task Force Tripoli's attack on Tikrit

The 1st Marine Division soon established a command post in Saddam's palace and immediately began to work CMO projects with the new Office of Reconstruction and Humanitarian Assistance (ORHA) cell set up in the Palestine hotel. The streets of Baghdad were not filled with cheering Iraqis, but they were not heavily contested battlegrounds either. There were a lot of young Iraqi males walking around town with close haircuts and ill-fitting civilian clothes who were not smiling – no doubt former members of Saddam's elite Republican Guard reflecting upon their defeat in their own capital city by the U.S. Army and the U.S. Marine Corps.[7]

Following Baghdad's capture, CENTCOM ordered the Marines on April 11 to advance rapidly north to Tikrit. Saddam and his minions had fled Baghdad, and intelligence suggested that he might seek refuge in his hometown, located about a hundred miles northwest of Baghdad in the heart of his Sunni tribal power base. Since the Turks had refused to allow the U.S. Army's 4th Infantry Division to move south into Iraq from Turkey, this entire region remained wide open for escape by Saddam and Ba'athist members of his regime, many wanted for war crimes committed during the Iran-Iraq War of the 1980s and his 1990 invasion of Kuwait. This additional, extended mission was meant not only to snuff out the remaining organized Iraqi resistance up north, but also to corner and capture Saddam before he had time to organize a Sunni guerilla force to operate against the Coalition during Phase IVB operations, as was widely feared.

To carry out the mission, the 1st Marine Division organized Task Force Tripoli (named after the early 19th century USMC campaign in which Lieutenant Presley O'Bannon's task organized unit advanced some six hundred miles from Cairo across North Africa, against the Barbary pirates in Libya). Consisting of elements of 1st, 2nd, 3rd, and 4th Light Armored Reconnaissance Battalions and commanded by the 1st Marine Division's Assistant Division Commander, the newly promoted Brigadier General John F. Kelly, Task Force Tripoli made amazing progress. By April 13, Task Force Tripoli had reached Samarra and rescued seven American Prisoners of War.

Five of them were survivors from the U.S. Army's 507th Maintenance Company that had been ambushed at An Nasiriyah nearly three weeks earlier and the other two were captured Apache pilots. The Task Force arrived at Tikrit on April 15 and destroyed five Iraqi tanks and killed at least fifteen Iraqi soldiers just outside the town limits. Once inside Tikrit, the Marines began actively patrolling largely deserted streets but encountered no further resistance. Saddam was no where to be found, and no new leads on his whereabouts were immediately apparent. However, organized Iraqi military resistance was crushed once and for all, and the Task Force was relieved about a week later by the 4th Infantry Division, which had just arrived from Kuwait after being turned away by the Turks in February.[8]

Throughout this operation, Task Force Mike stood ready to provide engineering support if necessary. In his daily report to I MEF on April 11, Rear Admiral Kubic wrote:

> Route 1 between Baghdad and Tikrit crosses numerous bridges/culverts that would not be easily by-passed if destroyed. Task Force Mike has Class IV available at Daly and Chesty for culvert crossings and has called forward additional Mabey-Johnson Bridges. The MEG will be prepared to support 1st MarDiv mobility during move to Tikrit if required. TF Charlie will launch excavation team 11 Apr to link up with TF Tarawa in the vicinity Qalat Sikar to move east to excavate suspected sensitive sites.

While the last vestiges of the military campaign to destroy Saddam's regime and liberate Iraq wound down, the rest of I MEF began to settle down into a stabilization mode in which the Marines ran aggressive patrols and Seabees began repairing key infrastructure such as power and water lines. Basic services and the restoration of normal aspects of life became the new focus of the Coalition's occupying forces. In this arena, the U.S. Navy Seabees were in their element. Seabees had already laid claim to the soccer stadium at the Rashid Military Academy, the so-called "West Point" of Iraq. This happened to be one of the very few large grassy areas in Baghdad and the first such green terrain that the Seabees had seen in many months. As they moved into the city, they helped secure this key terrain, cleared the runway, and set up a base camp there. Tents went up quickly and uniforms were stripped off for some well-deserved sun bathing on the grass.

Although the Seabees could now afford a little rest and relaxation, there was still much work to do. By April 20, the MEG had accomplished all of its pre-planned objectives and then some. In fact, as the MEF moved into the next phase of IRAQI FREEDOM, the MEG was already jumping out in front by coordinating, planning, and identifying processes with the military and civilian officials charged with winning the peace as part of the new Phase IVB stabilization operation.

Easter Sunday 2003

Holy Saturday, April 19, 2003, was not a good day for the MEG. A young Seabee, Mess Specialist Seaman (MSSN) Halloway, had been hit by an Army truck whose driver was confused by the heavy dust still plaguing Route 1 near Bridgepark Davisville. At the time, she was standing security watch along Highway 1, and was now in a coma fighting for her life. Rear Admiral Kubic's jump Command Post was at An Numaniyah air field and NMCB 74 had planned an Easter sunrise service. Kubic continued to operate on only two or three hours of sleep per night, and he rose early that morning to participate. The turnout was sparse but devout and the chaplain captured the moment for all of the Seabees present. Kubic quickly realized that no one knew of the terrible accident the day before, and at the appropriate time he told the group about the gravely injured Seabee and asked the Chaplain to lead them in a special prayer.

As Kubic later recalled, it was during that prayer that the first light of dawn began to break and it was about twenty-four hours later that Mess Specialist Seaman Halloway began to move her hand and fingers. Over time she recovered, and Kubic believed those Seabee prayers played a role in her recovery. Following a Seabee-cooked hot Easter Sunday breakfast with Commander Cliff Maurer and NMCB 74, Kubic traveled out to the twin Diyala Bridges to check on their progress. After returning to camp, he took a few hours off that afternoon and walked around camp talking to Seabees.

Kubic had been saving a very large cigar to smoke as a "victory dance." Although President Bush would not declare the end of major hostilities until May 1, Kubic knew on April 20 that Saddam's forces had been fully defeated. He declared victory that Easter Sunday afternoon and lighted up his victory cigar. It was an exhilarating feeling, he later said, matched only by the pride he felt as he shared thoughts and war stories with active and reserve

Seabees on that calm afternoon while walking around Logisitics Support Area Chesty at the An Numaniyah airfield, just south of the Tigris River.

Harry Wong and the Boys

While Kubic reflected on the campaign at An Numaniyah on Easter Sunday, the MEF learned that the Army would assume responsibility for the entire Baghdad sector and that the MEG would quickly realign its position to the south and east and would assume responsibility for Karbala, An Najaf, Al Hillah, Ad Diwaniyah and As Samawah from the Army. The MEF looked at alternate sites for its Command Operations Center during Phase IVB operations and chose Saddam's Babylon Palace on the bank of the Euphrates near the town of Al Hillah following a reconnaissance that the MEG participated in. By this time Rear Admiral Kubic had developed great confidence in CBMU 303's Detachment, which, among other tasks, had operated his jump command post throughout the war.

CBMU 303 had been mobilized after 9/11 to provide security for Navy Region-Hawaii, specifically to guard Pearl Harbor. These Seabees, hailing from San Diego, San Jose, and Hawaii, willingly executed this less than exciting mission but often expressed the desire to "get into the fight." They formed a highly skilled and extremely professional Det that gained the respect of everyone who encountered them. One particular crew within CBMU 303 was led by a superb Officer-in-Charge named Lieutenant Harry Wong. Wong was young, extremely energetic, very talented, and well respected by his Seabees. Raised in Phoenix, Arizona, he had earned his bachelor's degree in Engineering from Arizona State University in Tempe, and was a project manager in Boeing's Satellites Division in El Segundo, California. He was also a reservist for the Los Angeles Police Department as well as a Naval Reservist. While Harry Wong's "boys" were older than active Seabees, averaging between forty-five and fifty-five, they brought tremendous skill, unbelievable energy, and total dedication to every assignment. They were absolutely terrific, hardworking Seabees who just plain knew how to "get stuff done." They never seemed to stop playing ball and just kept hitting "homers" every day.[9]

Before the Iraq War, while CBMU 303 was deployed to Pearl Harbor, Kubic occasionally ran into Wong. Tired of the boring guard duty and chomping at the bit to do meaningful construction, he often asked, "Admiral, do you have another mission for us?" Usually, Kubic found some other work for them besides standing security watches. Finally, in August 2002 when they were about to demobilize and go home after a year-long deployment, a very important mission materialized, this time to prepare the command center for General Franks in Qatar. Kubic thought to himself, "This is a perfect mission for CBMU 303."

Although their initial deployment was over, Harry Wong and his boys eagerly agreed to extend on active duty to go to Qatar. This would be the first time that Seabees had ever worked directly for a CENTCOM organization. Once there, they earned the high praise of the CENTCOM leadership. Among their achievements was the construction of adjoining high tech offices for the Commander and Deputy Commander within the CENTCOM Sensitive Compartmented Information Facility (SCIF) area.

Surprisingly, many of the British and Australians who arrived in Qatar had never heard of Seabees before. As Wong later recalled, "one of my guys brought over a stencil, and everything we built, we spray-painted it with a Seabee logo." "We wanted to make sure that everyone knew the Seabees were here," he laughed, and that "the Navy was here building stuff for the front command." CBMU 303's branding extended even to General Franks' personal toilet, the lid of which proudly boasted a Seabee logo on its underside, visible when it was lifted up for business.

When their assigned work was substantially complete in Qatar, Kubic visited Wong to see how they were doing. They had all volunteered to stay beyond their first year and were into their second year and were then preparing to demobilize. Some of these Seabees hadn't been home for a long time. A couple of them, including Wong, talked among themselves, and approached Kubic with the same old question. They said, "Admiral, do you have another mission for us?" Kubic replied, "How many of you would be willing to stay on?" And Wong said, "Well, it depends. Are we going to go back home, or are we going North?" "No, we'll send you North," Kubic said, because at that point in time, the MEG saw the need to build facilities at the Kuwait Navy Base to help support the amphibious Seabees who were building a pier there, and a camp for the Navy ashore. And Kubic needed to augment the Phib Seabees. And so he said to Wong and his boys, "OK, I need to know right now, how many guys would be willing to stay on for another couple of months and go up to Kuwait?" It was akin to William Travis drawing a line in the sand at the Alamo, as Kubic later commented.

About half of them stepped forward. Wong's crew was thus cut in half, but it was still sizeable. And so Kubic brought Lieutenant Wong and his Seabees up to Kuwait Navy Base, where they worked for a while, grading beaches for Marine Landing Craft Air Cushion (LCAC) hovercraft and building the Camp Patriot tent city there for staging Marine combat units. After successfully finishing up those jobs, they wanted to stay on even longer. At the time, Camp Commando (I MEF HQ in Kuwait) was riddled with problems. Instead of letting the Seabees build the camp from the beginning, the Marines had hired some fly-by-night contractors to do the job, poorly as it turned out. Much work needed to be redone there. And so, much to the sorrow of Beach Group 1 at the Kuwait Navy Base, which had come to rely on Wong's Seabees, Kubic sent Wong's crew to Camp Commando to help clean up the mess. Not surprisingly, they impressed everyone they met there.

Under Wong's leadership, the hard-working detachment from CBMU 303 built two seahuts at Camp Commando to establish their work spaces, and stood up a Camp Maintenance headquarters. Additionally, they erected two AT&T phone strongback tents which improved the morale of over 4,000 Marines at the base, who suddenly had more convenient facilities for calling and communicating with their families back home. Wong's equipment operators then helped build SCUD bunkers the "Seabee Way", that is, buried in the ground. In fact, Wong and his boys finished their personal "high-speed" L-shaped SCUD bunker just in time for the Seersucker missile strike at Camp Commando. After the attack though, they found their new bunker stuffed full of Marines, leaving room for only five of Wong's Seabees.[10]

After I MEG crossed the Line of Departure on March 21, Wong visited Kubic and once again asked "Sir, do you have a mission for us in Iraq?" Kubic replied, "Well, Harry. I'm going to have to jump my command post up closer to Baghdad. And we really don't have anybody to build it, set it up, and maintain it. You can put together a crew—split your platoon in half again and form up two squads, and then pick a squad to go with you and leave a squad here. You should travel with the folks who will build and operate the new jump command post. You now have the mission to jump my command post up to just south of the Tigris River."

As usual, Wong's crew just jumped right in. Before he left Camp Commando, he approached Kubic once more and asked, "Was there anything special that you want, Admiral?" After some thought

Kubic told him, "I'll tell you what...even though this is a war, would you build a proper "head" so that we can have just a little bit of Seabee convenience?" At the time, Kubic was thinking about just some modest little box or outhouse situated somewhere discreet near the command post. Much to his surprise, he wholly underestimated Harry Wong and his boys in this endeavor.[11]

When Kubic first arrived at the new jump command post just south of the Tigris in early April, he jokingly asked, "Well, where's the head?" Somewhat sheepishly, they pointed it out to him. It was dark and Kubic couldn't see much except the outline of some sort of structure. So he walked toward it as Wong turned on the light switch, and to Kubic's complete astonishment, found they had installed fluorescent lights. Not only were there fluorescent lights but also a burnout head, a stainless steel sink, running water, a mirror, and a shower...everything that anyone could want in terms of comfortable toilet facilities, right out there, in the middle of no where. Once again, in Kubic's opinion, Lieutenant Wong and his guys had excelled. Indeed, Wong's personal philosophy was "when you're fighting a war, if you have a Flag Officer making life or death decisions, then you've got to make it comfortable for him so that he can have a clear mind when he makes those decisions." Out of sincere gratitude, Kubic opened the "flag head" to the crew.

After Baghdad fell, Kubic planned to move the MEG command post forward since it was obvious that the Seabees were going to be staying in theater for a while until the dust literally settled. Lieutenant Wong and a couple of his "boys" came to him and asked, "Sir, could we go to Baghdad with you?" Laughing, Kubic replied, "Harry, you've been with me the whole way from Hawaii to Qatar to Kuwait and Iraq. Jump in." So, as Kubic later recalled, "Lieutenant Harry Wong finally made it from Pearl Harbor to Baghdad – just leading 'his boys' to do what Seabees did best, job after job."

Soon afterwards, the MEG Headquarters moved to Al Hillah, about sixty miles south of Baghdad and the site of the ancient city of Babylon. There, Harry Wong and the "boys" found the MEG staff a fantastic bed-down place at Saddam's Babylon Palace. It had been looted and stripped of all furniture, light fixtures, bathroom fixtures, and anything else that was not securely anchored. But in short order, the Seabees mounted new lights, installed air-conditioner units, and retrofitted the plumbing system to work off a water bladder/pump system. CBMU 303 likewise rewired the palace's numerous bed rooms as living spaces for the Marines posted there.

Wong also laid claim to several of Saddam's support buildings, including his kitchen and some shop facilities. He turned the kitchen facility into a first class Command Operations Center with berthing and offices. CBMU 303 even provided an indoor shower and a flush toilet – albeit with a double flush mechanism that only a Seabee could have conceived. The MEG staff became very comfortable in this forward HQ from late April until early September. Eventually, NMCB 15's Air Det was also assigned to Camp Babylon and made significant improvements, including the re-start of Saddam's fishpond as a swimming pool, complete with a circulating source of fresh water and a jury-rigged filtration and chlorination system. To the Seabees, this was Club Med compared to where they had been for so many months. Once the food contractor moved in, the chow was even better than Club Med and to many of them it was uplifting to sit along the bank of the Euphrates and eat breakfast or dinner wondering what Saddam was doing while they were enjoying his palace.

Seabees in Babylon

Saddam's Babylon Palace was a manifestation of his self image as Nebuchadnezzar III and a self proclaimed demigod. It sat high on a man-made hill and overlooked the reconstructed ruins of the ancient city of Babylon. It was stone and marble with massive rooms and ornate decoration. Around the exterior were bas-relief stone panels with scenes depicting Saddam in various glorious roles of statesman, teacher, patron, sportsman and demigod. But as Rear Admiral Kubic toured these panels for the first time during a site survey accompanied by reporters from ABC TV, he was taken back when Lieutenant Wong pointed out a panel showing Saddam as a great military engineer, with one hand raised summoning troops carrying weapons in one hand and construction tools in the other, while his other hand held a drafting triangle and rested on a drawing table. Thinking aloud, Kubic said, "the SOB thought he was a Seabee!" To which the reporter responded, "How do you know he didn't have Seabees?" Kubic replied, "Because if he had Seabees, he would have won!"[12]

The restored city of Babylon and the nearby ruins of the foundation of the tower of Babel were magnificent. The Seabees found that the museum curators and resident archeologists were very proud that they saved much of the site and many artifacts from looters, but there was damage to the museum area that Seabees volunteered to repair. One Seabee even repaired a large model of the tower of Babel and the city Babylon. As the archeologists guided the Seabees through the city and shared its history, many found that they were essentially hearing the same Bible stories that they had learned in their youth. The hanging gardens were not replanted but the structure itself was still there and so was Daniel's lion den, which the Iraqis had rebuilt. The archeologists had no love for Saddam since they did not want new structures built on old walls. But from the Seabees' perspective it was very easy to tell the old from the new, and in their opinion, this restoration may have been one of the few good things that Saddam ever did.

Lieutenant Harry Wong accompanied Kubic on one particular tour. He stood in awe of where he was and what the Marines and Seabees had accomplished. He later described his impression of the moment.

Babylon is an ancient city that goes back thousands of years. There are still ancient ruins there. It is where the first laws were written by Hammurabi and appropriately named the Code of Hammurabi. It is the place where Nebuchadnezzar ruled and where he created the Hanging Gardens, one of the Wonders of the Ancient World. When we walked the grounds of the ancient ruins with Saddam Hussein's Palace in the background, a British reporter asked us how we felt as Americans about being here in Babylon. He said many great armies fought here over the centuries, and at that point I started to realize the significance of the American military presence here in Babylon.[13]

Mission Accomplished

Once it was apparent that the war was won and the MEG would be "shifting gears" quickly into more stabilized positions for the next several months, Rear Admiral Kubic began planning the Seabee draw down in Iraq, the demobilization of reserves, and the retrograde and reconstitution of their gear. Kubic had already brought reserve Captain Al Garcia, 1st Naval Construction Division's N9 and former commander of the 9th Construction Regiment (based in Fort Worth, Texas), to Camp Commando in mid-April to serve as an interim deputy. But Kubic really needed Garcia to become the enduring in-country "senior man" as he worked to shift the Seabees back into their peacetime jobs. So on Easter Monday, Captain Garcia relieved Commodore Will McKerall at An Numaniyah as Task Force Charlie Commander. Having led Task Force Charlie with strength and determination through RSO&I, the breach of the Iraqi border, and consolidation at Al Kut, McKerall returned to Camp Commando to assume new duties as the MEG Deputy Commander.

This change allowed Garcia to manage the transition in Iraq while McKerall pulled together the Seabee retrograde in Kuwait. It also permitted Kubic to make a quick trip out of theater to meet with his Navy bosses in Norfolk and Hawaii and to check the Pentagon's pulse concerning the continued service of Seabee Reserves.[14]

Kubic landed at Dulles airport on April 26 and was met by his wife, Anne, holding a small American flag. Once home, Kubic went quickly to work and maintained SIPR, NIPR, and telephone contact continuously with the MEG Command Operations Center in Al Hillah. Ultimately, senior-level discussions in Norfolk, Washington, DC, Hawaii, and Iraq led to the Seabee re-deployment plan known as the "redeploy, constitute, surge" plan, or simply the "down, set, hike" plan. It proved to be difficult to close the deal on the plan, and further visits to the Pentagon were required before the 1st Naval Construction Division could publish it. The big issue was OPNAV's desire to demobilize all reserves by September 30, leaving the 1st Naval Construction Division with only two battalions to cover the globe from September 2003 to February 2004. But Kubic and his superiors finally worked out a solid plan that worked very well.

On May 1, 2003, while Kubic was negotiating with OPNAV to bring the Seabees home, President Bush capped the National victory celebration in a particularly flamboyant way. He donned a naval aviator's flight suit, strapped himself into the co-pilot's seat of a S-3 Viking (piloted by the Executive Officer of VS-35, Navy Commander John "Skip" Lussier), and in the only naval flight ever to use the call sign "Navy One," landed aboard the USS *Abraham Lincoln*. Live worldwide video feeds captured the moment as it happened, with Bush jumping out of his aircraft and "high-fiving" the *Lincoln*'s crew, much like Tom Cruise's "Maverick" character in the 1980s movie *Top Gun*. That night, on the *Lincoln*'s flight deck, under a sign famously emblazoned with the message, "Mission Accomplished!," Bush addressed both the nation and the world:

> Major combat operations in Iraq have ended. In the Battle of Iraq, the United States and our allies have prevailed. And now our coalition is engaged in securing and reconstructing

that country....Operation Iraqi Freedom was carried out with a combination of precision, and speed, and boldness the enemy did not expect, and the world had not seen before. From distant bases or ships at sea, we sent planes and missiles that could destroy an enemy division, or strike a single bunker. Marines and soldiers charged to Baghdad across 350 miles of hostile ground, in one of the swiftest advances of heavy arms in history. You have shown the world the skill and the might of the American Armed Forces.[15]

President Bush reiterated that the U.S. military still had difficult work to do in Iraq, and that it was bringing order to parts of that country that remained dangerous, all the while pursuing and finding Saddam's thugs and henchmen, who would be held accountable for their crimes. After noting that "We have begun the search for hidden chemical and biological weapons," Bush told his worldwide audience that "We are helping to rebuild Iraq, where the dictator built palaces for himself, instead of hospitals and schools. And we will stand with the new leaders of Iraq as they establish a government of, by, and for the Iraqi people." "The transition from dictatorship to democracy will take time," he warned, "but it is worth every effort."

Once again, even before Bush made his dramatic landing and speech, Seabees were ahead of the power curve and were already beginning Phase IVB Civil Military Operations with the hope that we would all be home by Labor Day 2003 – two years after their American homeland was attacked.

Blair Airfield & Cemetery at Al Kut

Air movement was key to Phase IV operations and repairing the runways at Blair Airfield in Al Kut was crucial to the MEF's air bridge between Ali Al Salem in Kuwait and Al Hillah in Iraq. There were two runways, a taxiway and an alternate taxiway at Blair, all of which needed a good deal of heavy equipment and concrete work before planes could take off or land. Blair had been designated as the MEF's primary runway for fixed-wing aircraft. But Saddam's troops from the Baghdad Division had done a superb job cratering its two runways. Marine ESB engineers had made some expedient rapid runway repairs (RRRs) to one asphalt runway. Sustained fixed wing operations required a better, more enduring repair of the concrete main runway though. It had been blown at every key location so that no useable 3000-foot strip could be re-opened without considerable work. The concrete was over a foot thick and heavily reinforced.

On April 15, the MEG ordered Task Force Charlie to perform deliberate runway repairs (DRR) at Blair Airfield in Al Kut. The idea was that these deliberate repairs would make the field capable of handling C-130s and eventually C-141s. NMCB 133 arrived at the field on April 17 to begin work. The 8th Engineer Support Battalion also lent a hand, providing demolition support and clearing some damaged concrete panels using explosives, which created surface blasts and helped expedite the process.

The Seabees quickly compiled and presented a Bill of Materials for the project to Task Force Tarawa. The biggest problem, as in pre-hostilities construction, would be the availability of concrete – the project required 1,440 cubic yards. Although MEG buying agents identified and did business with a local contractor, he was not able to meet the initial demand required to keep the job going. To supplement the contract, the MEG purchased five thousand bags of cement in Kuwait and shipped them north with additional concrete trucks. Eventually, local sources were able to meet the demand for concrete and the pace of the work accelerated.

At first, the job was tough. The Kang'roos initially tried every easy technique in the Seabee book to clear the craters, including blasting, but they were stymied. They soon learned though that using a "bull prick" and an excavator and other various pieces of heavy equipment was the only way to get the job done.

Despite the slow and arduous work required to clear out the mess, Task Force Charlie planned the construction extremely well, allowing C-130 traffic an open runway at all times and permitting critical air operations to flow unimpeded. On May 4, the MEG declared the north runway mission capable.

On April 30, before finishing the north runway, NMCB 133 began work on the north taxiway and completed that project within a week. The south runway, on the other hand, was problematic. The 2nd Marine Aircraft Wing used this runway as a parking apron for C-130s and as a landing zone for helicopter operations. The Seabees were not granted access until May 8, when the 2nd Marine Aircraft Wing let the 'Roos partially begin repair work on the east end on May 20. They completed the project two days later, and Blair Field became fully operational on May 24. As an enduring reminder of their achievement, NMCB 133 put their "brand" in a large concrete slab right in the middle of the runway. Lieutenant General Conway lauded the completion of the Blair Field project during a video teleconference on May 24. He exclaimed, "Over 1000 cubic yards of concrete, thirty huge craters, two runways, a taxiway – just a fabulous job by the Seabees. God Bless the Seabees!"[16]

While the runway work was in progress at Blair Airfield, NMCB 133 and the MEG G3, Marine Reserve Colonel Michael Howard, set out to locate a WWI British cemetery in the city of Al Kut. Rumor had it that it was desecrated years earlier by Saddam's thugs and was in need of major restoration. The MEG's idea was to find and restore this cemetery as a tribute to the 1st U.K. Division who fought so gallantly on the Marines' right flank throughout the war.[17]

During the Mesopotamian Campaign in WWI from 1914-1918, British forces fought from the Kuwait border to Baghdad – much the same fight that I MEF had just completed but along a different route of attack and at considerably slower speed. The MEG had used this example back during the summer 2002 planning phases to avoid making the same mistakes that the Brits did in World War I.

The Turks had trapped the British 6th Division in Al Kut during WWI, and it had eventually surrendered with severe losses. Many of the British soldiers were buried in war cemeteries that had been cared for by Iraqis for many years until Saddam sought retribution after DESERT STORM. One of these cemeteries was located in a slum-district in central Al Kut. The final resting place for 420 British soldiers who perished there, it was totally desecrated with garbage, debris, animal carcasses, and feces. Marine and Seabees set to work to clean it up and to re-erect as many tombstones as possible. In the process of doing this work, a middle age man showed up with photos of the cemetery when it was a well-kept grassy lawn. His father had been the caretaker and he had helped him as a boy. He said the people of Al Kut knew this was a sacred place and they never felt good about its desecration. His photo showed a cross and a British flag in the center of the cemetery. The monument itself was an inverted broad sword, or crusader's cross, and was called the "Cross of Sacrifice" by the Brits.

The group set out to reconstruct the monument. The NMCB 133 Kang'roos took on the job of casting a large cross in reinforced concrete and then embedding a smaller iron cross on its face, as shown in the Iraqi photo. As word spread of these efforts, senior officers at CENTCOM Headquarters in Qatar soon expressed concerns about the project, considering its Christian character. They felt that the Seabees might offend the Moslem sensitivities of the local Iraqis with the cross, and ordered NMCB 133 to stop. When the caretaker's son learned of the decision, he convened a "huddle" of senior local leaders. After some discussion, the leaders announced that "the free people of the liberated city of Al Kut would respect all religions and would the Seabees please get on with the job of completing the restoration of the cross" – which they did, with Iraqi help. The MEF then held a rededication ceremony with the 1st U.K. Division, attended by an Anglican bishop representing the Archbishop of Canterbury.

The solemn ceremony, complete with bagpipe and bugle calls, took place on May 8, 2003. I MEF commander Lieutenant General Conway and Task Force Tarawa commander Brigadier General Richard E. Natonski spoke on behalf of the U.S. Marine Corps, while the commander of the 1st U.K. Armoured Division, Major General Robin Brims, represented the British. Rear Admiral Kubic also took part in the ceremony as the I MEG commander and as commander of the 1st Naval Construction Division..

The event attracted hundreds of applauding Iraqis who lined the walls of the cemetery and the windows and roofs of building overlooking the cemetery. As the ceremony started, there was a cloud cover. As the British flag was hoisted, a breeze passed through, snapping the flag into the top right quadrant of the cross with the sun streaming through it. Kubic later recalled that it was truly an inspiring moment and clearly reinforced to him what they were all fighting for. It was also clear to him there was a lot more work like this to be done if the U.S.-led Coalition was to secure peace with freedom for generations to come in Iraq and throughout the region. Phase IVB Civil Military Operations (CMO) projects were next on the Seabees' platter, and the MEG attacked this challenge with the same intensity in which the MEF attacked Baghdad.

CHAPTER

12

Stabilization and Civil Military Operations

Following Saddam's downfall and the capture of Baghdad and Tikrit, military operations quickly shifted gears as Coalition forces, after vanquishing the Iraqi army and the Fedayeen, began working to win the peace in Iraq. Having fought bravely in places like Ramalyah, An Nasiriyah, Al Kut and Baghdad, and having lived spartanly in camps at An Numaniyah and Salman Pak, the Marines and Seabees had never paused long enough to establish basic health and comfort services. As such, the need for quality of life items such as "burn outs" (toilets) and showers became quickly apparent. Additionally, planners readily admitted that Civil Military Operations (CMOs) would be essential to building and maintaining a lasting peace in Iraq. Thus, on April 20th, 2003 (Easter Sunday), the MEF, and combat tested MEG, formally entered the stabilization Phase IVB of Operation Iraqi Freedom.

The MEF's first priority was repositioning its forces within pre-established "governates," which were formed for purposes of rebuilding Iraq. This "shuffling" demanded significant effort, as it required the MEF to swap responsibility with the U.S. Army for Tikrit and Baghdad in exchange for the southern governates. Task Force Tarawa maintained its position in the central governates, basing its operations at Al Kut and An Nasiriyah. The 1st U.K. Division expanded its Area of Responsibility north to the Maysan Governate and established its headquarters in Basrah. The MEG's

I MEF leadership gathers for a "General Officers Huddle" just south of the Tigris to plan Phase IVB Civil Military Operations (CMO).

Left to right: Major General Keith Stalder, Brigadier General Rich Natonski, Brigadier General Mike Lehnert, Rear Admiral Chuck Kubic, Lieutenaant General Jim Conway, Major General Jim Amos, Major General Jim Mattis, Major General Robin Brim, Brigadier General Ed Usher.

(Official USMC Photograph)

On 20 April, Rear Admiral Kubic delivers a "Job well done!" and victory message to NMCB 74 at the An Numaniyah Airfield, Iraq.

(Official U.S. Navy Photograph)

Task Force Mike Seabees constructed sheet pile earthen moles to "make the Diyala River fit" a 60-meter Mabey-Johnson bridge.

(Official U.S. Navy Photograph)

NMCB 4 constructed the MEG's fifth and sixth Mabey & Johnson bridges in Iraq across the Diyala River east of Baghdad.

(Official U.S. Navy Photograph)

This Task Force Mike Seabee is hammering away on a Mabey & Johnson bridge near Baghdad. (Official U.S. Navy Photograph)

Harry Wong and the "Boys" on the bank of the Tigris River at An Numaniyah. Lieutenant Wong stands second from the right, holding the Seabee flag.
(Photograph Courtesy of Lieutenant Commander Harry R. Wong, CBMU 303)

As part of I MEF's Civil Military Operations (CMO) in the summer of 2003, Task Force Charlie constructed a 205-meter floating pontoon bridge across the Tigris River at Zubidayah. The pontoon bridge replaced a similar bridge sunk by Marine aviators to cut off the Iraqi Al Nida Division as Marine ground forces moved towards Baghdad in April 2003. (Official U.S. Navy Photograph)

Seabees from Task Force Charlie install 1,200 yards of concrete to repair the runway at Blair Airfield, Iraq, on April 25, 2003.
(Official U.S. Marine Corps photo by Cpl Shawn Rhodes)

Task Force Charlie spreads MC-70 along Highway 1 and water (left) at An Numaniyah to fight the dust problems in Iraq.

(Official U.S. Navy Photograph)

Rear Admiral Kubic (center) with Seabees from NMCB 133 who had reconstructed and erected this iron "Cross of Sacrifice" at the rehabilitated World War I British Cemetery in Al Kut. (Official U.S. Navy Photograph)

Task Force Charlie tackled this project at Sarabadi Bridge in May 2003. The first MEG Mabey & Johnson Bridge built over the Tigris River, it was a dangerous mission due to the complexity and height of the damaged span.

(Official U.S. Navy Photograph)

Sarah Habes, a 12-year old Iraqi girl, was a surprise guest-speaker at a dedication ceremony at the Al Amarkeziyah Secondary School in Ad Diwaniyah, where she thanked the Seabees and the Marines for building new schools in Iraq and giving Iraqi women and children a brighter future.

(Official U.S. Navy Photograph)

A Seabee gun truck with improvised steel armor turret secures an intersection near Fallujah during OIF II.

Seabees repaired IED damage to roads and bridges to sustain combat and logistics mobility during OIF II. (Official U.S. Navy Photograph)

Seabees from NMCB 74 build HESCO barriers during Operation Vigilant Resolve in April 2004, as the Coalition surrounded and attacked insurgents during the first battle of Fallujah. (Official U.S. Navy Photograph)

Seabees from NMCB 23 secure a severely damaged school in Fallujah, Iraq. The Seabees were forward deployed from Fort Belvoir, Va., in support of reconstruction efforts in the city.

(Official U.S. Navy Photo by Journalist 1st Class Jeremy L. Wood)

A night time convoy passes by Seabees from NMCB 40 as they provide security for a road repair project in Fallujah, Iraq, May 20, 2004.

(Official U.S. Navy Photo by Petty Officer 3rd Class John P. Curtis)

challenge was to position its assets in such a way as to best support I MEF. On April 8, before the battle for Baghdad had even ended, Task Force Mike had begun working on what amounted to the first real CMO project in Baghdad, the twin Diyala bridges. Task Force Mike would also continue supporting the 1st Marine Division, which was assigned its own Governates.[1]

Task Force Charlie continued in its efforts to spread dust palliatives on the Main Supply Routes, especially on Highway 1, where dust significantly reduced visibility and presented a serious hazard to convoy operations. Additionally, Task Force Charlie began working a suspected Weapons of Mass Destruction site in the vicinity of Al Amarah and also assisted Task Force Tarawa with force protection operations at Al Kut and An Nasiriyah. Task Force Echo, which had actually initiated Phase IV operations in Umm Qasr and An Nasiriyah, well before the rest of the MEF, continued to improve the cities' infrastructure through school repairs and water supply maintenance.

As Phase IVB ramped up, enemy activity gradually waned. There was, however, a continuing threat from small paramilitary factions banding together and calling for attacks on Coalition forces. They generally met their fates after taking pot shots at our troops. At one point, on April 18, Major General Brims reported to Lieutenant General Conway that the British sector was "mostly quiet" but "we had one drive-by shooting." With typical British wit, Brims observed that "He missed, we didn't."[2]

These "dead enders," as Defense Secretary Rumsfeld later infamously called them, were primarily concentrated in the Al Basrah, Wasit (Al Kut) and Dhi Qahr (An Nasiriyah) Governates. Occasionally, they got lucky and did real damage. Just after Saddam's regime collapsed, a U.K. 3rd Para soldier was severely wounded by a "dead ender." Fortunately, he was saved using twenty-eight units of American blood, leading Lieutenant General Conway to comment that "He is now more American than British."[3]

The Coalition Forces Land Component Commander (CFLCC), U.S. Army Lieutenant General David McKiernan, began to set the stage for Phase IVB by first announcing that the Port of Umm Qasr was open to the maritime community for limited humanitarian support operations. Notably, McKiernan's announcement would not have come without the previous stabilizing efforts of NMCB 21 and British forces. Second, in order to stem the potential transborder flow of Iranian troublemakers, CFLCC removed the buffer zone along the border and I MEF directed Task Force Tarawa to assume border security operations (which Force Recon had been conducting for some time).[4]

From the MEF's perspective Phase IVB was planned as a 120-day transition period in which MEF forces would withdraw and be relieved by other U.S. Army or Coalition forces. Ideally, during this bridging period, troop reconstruction efforts would be replaced by contractors hired by the Office of Reconstruction and Humanitarian Assistance (ORHA).

The 1st Marine Division distributed its units throughout the southern Governates as its Command Element completed a Relief in Place (RIP) with the U.S. Army's 82nd Airborne Division in Al Hillah (Babylon). By the time Phase IVB began, 1st Marine Division units were operating from the Al Muthanna (As Samawah), Babil (Al Hillah) and Ad Qadisiyah (Ad Diwaniyah) Governates.

The 1st Marine Division had to move farther than any unit in the MEF. Task Force Tripoli went from Tikrit to Samarrah in order to relieve Regimental Combat Team 5. This would allow Regimental Combat Team 5 time to get in place in As Samawah and Ad Diwaniyah. In both of those places, Regimental Combat Team 5 was to conduct a Relief in Place with the 82nd Airborne Division. Regimental Combat Team 1 was to turn over its sector of Baghdad to the 3rd Infantry Division, then return south in order to assume control of Al Hillah from the 82nd Airborne. Regimental Combat Team 7 was also to turn over its sector of Baghdad to the 3rd Infantry Division and return south to assume control of An Najaf and Karbala.

The MEG's role during Phase IVB would be critical in ensuring the MEF's and the United States' long term stabilization of Iraq. The Seabees were also indispensable in improving the Marines standard of living in theater while facilitating the retrograde of the MEF from Iraq and Kuwait. However, while quality of life and retrograde efforts were important, Civil Military Operations would prove to be the most essential weapon in winning this phase of the Iraq war.

The Three Tier System

Starting with the initial work in Umm Qasr, Kubic instructed MEG project assessment teams to conduct a 3-tier assessment of each requirement. Tier 1 was the work that needed to be done on an *expeditionary* basis to solve the immediate crisis and could be accomplished principally by troops for $100,000 or less. Tier II was the work that would be needed to be done on a *deliberate* basis to repair the damaged or deteriorated infrastructure and would be done by both troops and Iraqi small business contractors with projects estimated to be less than $5 million. Tier 3 projects were large *developmental* projects that required investments greater than $5 million, and would be done by the large follow-on U.S. contractors with Iraqi subcontractor support.[5]

For example, the water system at Umm Qasr needed a Tier 1 "expeditionary project" to provide dispersed water tanks that would be filled with fresh water from tanker trucks to mitigate water shortages quickly. A Tier 2 "deliberate project" was needed to fix the existing water treatment plant and filtration system to begin delivering non-potable water throughout the community similar to pre-war conditions. Finally, a Tier 3 project was needed to replace the entire water treatment and distribution system in the city of Umm Qasr to provide reliable, fresh, potable water – something the local Shi'ite residents had never had under Saddam's regime, resulting in a poor quality of life which Phase IVB had the opportunity to improve dramatically.

The MEG quickly assembled a plan with over $130 million worth of Tier 1, 2, and 3 projects. The idea was to avoid the need for follow-on military or civilian contractor infrastructure teams to re-survey the projects – they could start with the plans which the MEG developed and then build from there. But, despite significant effort, the MEG received less than $4 million of seized money, and combined with other assets (e.g. Mabey Johnson bridges), put $7.2 million worth of work in place during the 120 days of its Phase IVB CMO work. In Rear Admiral Kubic's opinion, the MEG could have done so much more with more money. But political forces, including the MEF's mandate to wrap things up, and go home without the need to turnover long-term projects, marginalized the MEG's efforts. However, the MEG selected projects carefully to achieve the "most bang for the buck," within the time and money allotted, and executed them all very well. By using contractor support, MEG CMO projects also served as the initial jump start for the Iraqi small business construction industry.

The MEG's 3-tier assessment system was reviewed by many and was sufficiently robust in its planning detail to serve as the basis for the way in which the Coalition could plan and execute its long term CMO work. The 3-tier assessment process also made it clear that Seabees were not going to fix everything immediately, and kept the scope of the effort focused on expeditionary success. This process also allowed the emerging Iraqi leaders to see how U.S. troops were approaching reconstruction, and helped gain their trust and support.

Shortly after Phase IVB began, the MEF also made significant efforts to establish a formal process by which units could identify, gain approval, and receive funding for CMO projects. The process eventually coalesced into a workable plan and MEF units quickly began utilizing it. The 1st Force Service Support Group identified and placed Paying Agents, each with authority to purchase up to $2,500 in materials per project, at the infantry battalion level. Task Force Tarawa absorbed the 4th Civil Affairs Group (CAG) and immediately went to work on a number of critical projects in An Nasiriyah and Al Kut. Civil Military Operations Centers (CMOCs) were established in every Governate. The Civil Affairs Group also teamed up with Seabees and began working with local Iraqi leaders, focusing on power restoration, water resources, legal programs, and food and fuel supplies. This encouraged Iraqi citizens to seek out CMO representatives and to request help proactively, occasionally even providing fruitful intelligence leads.

Projects outside of the Civil Military Operations Center's funding or scope of work capabilities had to go to higher headquarters for further adjudication and funding – in this case, the MEF. Once prioritized by a Civil Military Operations Center, the MEF "Fusion Board" would review projects and take action as appropriate. The MEG Liaison Officers (LNOs), who had helped coordinate and plan the war with the MEF, now assumed additional duties as members of the Fusion Board.

The MEF Chief of Staff, Colonel John Coleman, chaired the Fusion board, while MEF Force Fires facilitated it. Their role was subsequently handed off to the 358th Civil Affair Brigade. The group's purpose was to provide Lieutenant General Conway with weekly forecasts on Civil Military Operations, prevent stove-piped planning and execution, permit complementary action, and allow the MEF to optimize economies of scale. The board maintained a mid-term vision, looking at projects that were scheduled for weeks or months in duration. Through this process the MEF was able to prioritize and synchronize multiple efforts throughout the Southern Iraq MEF zone. As active members of the Fusion Board, the MEG Liaison Officers ensured that the submitted projects were feasible and also expertly evaluated those that were not submitted through the Seabees. If a submitted project was beyond the scope of the Fusion Board, then the MEF forwarded it to the new Office of Reconstruction and Humanitarian Assistance (ORHA), which was quickly becoming a "black hole."

"Everything is the Usual State of Chaos."

The Office of Reconstruction and Humanitarian Assistance was established on January 20, 2003 to serve as a transitional "caretaker" government once the Coalition liberated Iraq. The Defense Department appointed retired Lieutenant General Jay M. Garner to serve as the Office of Reconstruction and Humanitarian Assistance's director based on his prior experiences during Operation Desert Storm and his reconstruction efforts in northern Iraq during Operation Provide Comfort. Under Garner, who arrived in theater on April 21, the Office of Reconstruction and Humanitarian Assistance's primary mission was to begin reconstruction of the country using the American contractor Bechtel with appropriated funds from the U.S. Agency for International Development (USAID). Planning had been tightly compartmentalized in Washington, D.C. under the direction of the Defense Department rather than the State Department, and the office was not synchronized with military Phase IVB plans until the MEF set up camp at An Numaniyah, just south of the Tigris. The Office of Reconstruction and Humanitarian Assistance wrongly assumed that the post-war environment would be totally permissive, and so it was not prepared to deal with continuing armed threats during reconstruction. Consequently, the Office of Reconstruction and Humanitarian Assistance and its contractors sat out the war and then the first several months after Baghdad's fall in the Hilton Hotel in Kuwait City. The office did not even have a firm plan to move into Iraq.[6]

When it became apparent that the Office of Reconstruction and Humanitarian Assistance needed to get moving, the office first planned a "safer" move into Basrah. During this time, ORHA staff members were unwilling to cooperate with the construction troops and could not get their money flowing into task orders to Bechtel – the whole process for using appropriated funds to start reconstruction quickly became very "constipated," as Kubic put it.

During a hastily arranged I MEF "General Officer huddle" at An Numaniyah prior to the fall of Baghdad, the Office of Reconstruction and Humanitarian Assistance revealed to the MEF and the MEG that there was no agreed upon command relationship among the Defense Department, CENTCOM, ORHA, and CFLCC. In fact, in response to Kubic's direct question asking "who's in charge?" the briefer stated that the senior people (Rumsfeld, Franks, and Garner) in these organizations were all friends and "would work it out together." Initially, CENTCOM/CFLCC would have the Phase IVB lead, and then over time the lead would transition to the Office of Reconstruction and Humanitarian Assistance. The ORHA briefer further stated that "the senior leadership would not be structured in a formal chain of command but would operate as colleagues on a hand shake basis." The admiral was exasperated, later exclaiming that "anyone who is familiar with the inner workings of the Defense Department and the Armed Services will appreciate the utter foolishness of this poorly conceived, un-structured command and coordination scheme." In short, it was a recipe for disaster and never did work. CFLCC was not interested in moving from Kuwait into Iraq, and neither was the Office of Reconstruction and Humanitarian Assistance for that matter. A frustrated Major General Mattis reported on May 14 that "Everything is the usual state of chaos." Lieutenant General Conway, who was at first inclined to cut the Office of Reconstruction and Humanitarian Assistance a bit more slack, finally concluded on May 28 that there was "No way to put lipstick on this pig."[7]

Indeed, the Office of Reconstruction and Humanitarian Assistance was an organizational train wreck in April and May 2003. Its first director, Jay Garner, was abruptly sacked on May 11 by an impatient Defense Secretary Rumsfeld, only three weeks into his tenure. Garner's transgression was his insistence on early elections and his refusal to implement an immediate "de-Ba'athification" policy in Iraq, similar to the Allies' deNazification of Germany after World War II. Garner's replacement, L. Paul Bremer, former ambassador to the Netherlands, an associate and protégé of Henry Kissinger, and late Chairman and Chief Executive Officer of Marsh Crisis Consulting, was named U.S. Presidential Envoy to Iraq. In effect, Bremer was the designated leader of Iraq, and was given the clear mandate to rid Iraq of its Ba'athist institutions and to get the country back on its feet economically.[8]

Under Bremer, the Office of Reconstruction and Humanitarian Assistance gave way to a new Office of the Coalition Provisional Authority (CPA), and CENTCOM in turn created the Combined Joint Task Force (CJTF) 7, led by U.S. Army Lieutenant General Rick

Sanchez, to provide a unified military command in Iraq. Both quickly established themselves in Baghdad at Saddam's Palace in what became known as the "Green Zone." There, Bremer carefully studied the history of German deNazification and attempted to apply that model to Iraq. But he began running the country much like a Roman proconsul, centralizing all decision-making in Baghdad and creating numerous funding logjams and bureaucratic headaches. It was an inauspicious start.

Not surprisingly, considering the circumstances, money was the biggest stumbling block for the early reconstruction effort. A limited amount of appropriated Operations & Maintenance (O&M) funding could be justified based upon the "operational nature" of this work since U.S. troops were looking to win hearts and minds quickly with Civil Military Operations to avoid further kinetic operations. But these funds were limited (e.g. the MEG used some residual funds provided for class IV materials to get started). USAID and CFLCC were unable and unwilling to provide funds appropriated by Congress for this purpose to the MEF/MEG, since "their" money was already committed to Bechtel's contract. Despite Kubic's high-level discussions with CFLCC leadership, this rice bowl could not be cracked.

So, several weeks into Phase IVB, not one of the MEF's proposed projects had been funded by higher authority, much less started. Recognizing a potentially devastating trend, the MEF took the bull by the horns and issued new instructions to its subordinate units, encouraging them to identify and prioritize projects that were low in cost and high in potential impact, thereby sliding under ORHA/CPA's radar. The thinking was that the more projects that MEF was able to fund itself, the more Seabees and Marines could accomplish for the Iraqi people despite the inept ORHA/CPA.

"Maybe Next Time"

Project identification and selection, while fairly complex, required more administrative skill than engineering savvy – the real challenge lay in funding and execution, all of which would benefit the Iraqi people. MEF Operating and Maintenance (O&M) funds were available, via the 1st Force Service Support Group paying agents, for project purchases under $2,500. The major problem, however, was that most projects which were classified Tier 1, because of their size and scope of work, required much more than $2,500. A two-fold solution became apparent. First, the regular business relationship between the Seabees and Brown & Root — the Navy's CONCAP (Construction Capability) Contractor — offered a contracting option allowing the use of MARCENT's O&M budget as a funding source. The second solution was slightly more creative. Throughout Iraq, millions of dollars in currency were being discovered and seized on a weekly, if not daily basis, having been stashed away by Saddam Hussein, his family, and the regime in various banks around the country. "What better way to use these seized monies than to fund school and infrastructure repairs for the people of free Iraq," the MEG staff members asked themselves? The 4th Civil Affairs Group and NMCB 7 had already shared this epiphany in An Nasiriyah, resulting in Commander Honkomp's "Bank Job." Kubic hoped that their success could be extended throughout the entire MEF.[9]

In order to best utilize MARCENT funds on a contracting basis, the MEG turned to Brown & Root (now Kellogg, Brown and Root or KBR). Mr. Patrick Overaker, a Brown & Root representative, joined the MEG Command Element at Camp Commando during this time. Along with the MEG's CONCAP Team, which consisted of Gunnery Sergeant McCarty, Construction Mechanic 3rd Class Azzi (an Arabic-speaking Seabee), Sergeant Deti, Corporal Pulaski, and Lance Corporal Kratz (security personnel), Mr. Overaker would visit the Task Forces with cash in hand. The Task Forces would provide vehicle transportation and crew-served weapon security, and take the team as close to the market areas as the streets would allow. Overaker's team would then proceed on foot to meet and do business with local vendors. With the assistance of a Seabee (for technical knowledge of the required materials), the KBR Representative and the interpreter would negotiate a fair price, in US dollars, for the materials selected. Meanwhile, the Marines would provide security on the narrow streets, as there were always potential threats from hostile locals who might realize that Overaker was carrying large sums of US currency.[10]

The CONCAP team went on purchasing missions throughout southern Iraq, in cities like An Nasiriyah, As Samawah, Ad Diwaniyah, Al Hillah and Al Kut. Iraqi adults were generally cautious when they first encountered the team. Children, however, were very friendly and curious. For most of them, CONCAP members were the first Americans they had ever seen. They hailed the United States and praised George Bush, and thanked the team profusely. Like most kids, they loved to be photographed.

Gunnery Sergeant McCarty recounted a story about one of their greatest finds from these trips:

> In the city of Hillah, the team discovered a very large warehouse complex that was surrounded by barbed wire and guard towers. We were told that we could purchase materials there only with a "letter from the Government." It was property of the former regime, which explains why it had not been looted. Permitted access to only three of the more than one hundred warehouses, the team noticed ornate fixtures, western style toilets with gold leaf designs, lumber, sheets of polished marble, and tons upon tons of reinforcing steel for concrete. It appeared that this was a material storage facility for the construction of a palace. After reporting the location to the local ORHA office, the team was informed that while we were there, we should have seized the location. Maybe next time.[11]

All told, Overaker's CONCAP team successfully purchased over $25,000 in critical construction materials from the Iraqi vendors.

In terms of regime funds seizure, Coalition forces soon uncovered millions of dollars of U.S. currency hidden in banks and the homes of Ba'ath party officials and other regime thugs. When the Defense Department and CENTCOM authorized the MEF to seize the money, the CONCAP team was ultimately dispatched on two separate occasions to Al Qadisiyah University in Ad Diwaniyah to pick up seized cash for CMO projects. Protection of the money fell to the small Marine security contingent, assisted by the SERTs. This was just the tip of the iceberg. Through April and May, the MEF collected nearly $800 million in "seized funds" and dutifully turned all of this cash (mostly U.S. $100 bills) over to CFLCC for redistribution, as instructed.

The MEG thought that much of this "non appropriated" money could be used quickly to start large infrastructure work in the south, like the completion of Highway 1 northwest of An Nasiriyah for $67 million, and to employ Seabees, Marines, Soldiers, Koreans and Iraqis on a large project neglected for years by Saddam. Such work was critical for military movement and civilian commerce – not to mention jobs for hundreds of former Iraqi soldiers. However, Kubic soon learned that both the U.S. Office of Management and Budget (OMB) and the Congressional Budget Office (CBO) quickly got involved and all the seized money disappeared (at least in the near term) into the bureaucratic ether. Consequently, no cash flowed back to the maneuver units for Civil Military Operations during the first "golden 120 days" after the fall of Baghdad, much to the detriment of the immediate "hearts and minds" campaign.

The MEG was quickly running out of CMO steam when the MEF suddenly found another $6+ million in seized funds. Kubic sent a Marine Gunny and a Seabee Storekeeper Chief to get the MEG's initial allotment. They returned to his tent late that night with a seabag full of $100 bills, and told the admiral they couldn't carry this bag very far it was so heavy. When they said it contained $1,742,000 in hundred dollar bills, Kubic joked that he could carry that bag a long way, but for now they could dump it on his desk.

As he recounted later, he then picked up a bundle of hundreds in each hand and gazed upon the biggest pile of cash he had ever seen. After enjoying fifteen minutes of simulated wealth, Kubic and his men re-counted the money and locked it in the MEG safe, with two-person accountability and an oversight audit team for the duration of the MEG's CMO effort. The MEG now had money, and Class IV materials, especially concrete, could now be bought in the local market. Moreover, CMO projects could be quickly scoped, funded, bid, and then awarded to Iraqi contractors, breathing life into the local economies. By early May, the MEG had Phase IVB Ops underway with a new head of steam.

Power Plants & Water Works

Restoring electricity and water were the MEG's first priorities in the south. Phase IVB started in Umm Qasr and An Nasiriyah while Phase III kinetic operations were still underway in the north. The MEG restarted generators and water systems in Umm Qasr and launched an assessment team to the main power plant and water treatment plant in An Nasiriyah to work with the local Iraqis to restart these plants. In most cases there was very little battle damage. Most of the damage was due to years of neglect and lack of maintenance. In the case of the large gas turbine generators at An Nasiriyah, the staff had shut them down to avoid damage and they could not be started without an electrical jump from a power line that had been knocked down during the war and subsequent looting.

The MEG requested $10 million before the war to buy emergency generators but according to Kubic, it was denied funding by those who simply did not understand how critical emergency power would be during Phase IVB. Also, many key parts had been looted from power and water plants. But a good day of local shopping always resulted in successful "buy back" of parts, which appeared in local markets soon after the looting took place.

The MEG quickly learned that skilled Iraqi blue-collar mechanics had all the capability needed to fix and restart key plants. What they lacked were parts and the authority to make repairs. In many cases Saddam wanted the plants to remain down to conserve resources and punish Shi'ites. The Seabees learned that these were good people who had been terribly oppressed for decades and just needed a helping hand to get back on their feet.

Unfortunately, the speed of the MEG's help was continuously constrained by lack of money and an emerging new bureaucracy in Baghdad that quickly isolated itself from the people in the southern provinces whom we professed to have liberated. It was good that the dollar was strong, Kubic later commented, and the MEG was able to do a lot of good work in those early days with limited money.

Schools & Hospitals

The MEG, in conjunction with Civil Affairs folks and the 1st Marine Division, also targeted key schools and hospitals for repair. In some cases the MEG repaired battle damage, but the Seabees mostly repaired schools that had been trashed by Saddam's troops as a punitive action against local communities or for use by Fedayeen as military barracks and torture chambers. The local population was amazed at the skill and determination of the Seabees. In many cases they had never seen nor heard of military troops doing good deeds. This was particularly true in the schools where the children watched in amazement as Seabees fixed their water and power and added lights and fans and a coat of new paint to cover Saddam's propaganda. Saddam had painted all of the country's schools a dirty, dusty, brownish yellow, similar to his military facilities. One surprise came when a local leader asked the Seabees if they could have the schools painted brighter colors. Kubic said "no problem as long as we can find the color you want," and in a preview of coming democracy, local leaders "huddled" together and came up with a blue and white scheme for the first new paint job for a school. After that, every school had a different paint scheme chosen by their local leaders.

The MEG ultimately focused the bulk of its contract effort on school renovation, and even bundled schools together in packages for bid. By mid-May, Seabee Det 4 in An Najaf was doing "best value" source selection contracting with seized funds. By mid-June NMCB 7 was receiving bids at the Iraq Contractor's Association Hall in Ad Diwaniyah and in one case received nearly sixty bids for a bundle of school renovation projects.

In one school, there was a flagpole in the courtyard where a Seabee began to raise an Iraqi flag he had bought in a local market. Apparently this was a pre-Saddam flag. The workers immediately stopped working, fell into a small formation and saluted their flag. It was a spontaneous display of underlying patriotism from workers who had fought for their country against Iran decades earlier in the Iran/Iraq war.

School ribbon cuttings were major community events and drew local television by July and August. A major ceremony was held on August 23 at the Al Amarkeziyah Secondary School, the largest boys high school in Ad Diwaniyah, to commemorate the completion of four schools, all built by the British in the 1930's and last rehabilitated by Germans in 1958. The ceremony was held on a stage in a large assembly hall, packed primarily by blue-collar Iraqi men. After Rear Admiral Kubic spoke, a young Iraqi girl named Sarah Habes approached the stage while another male speaker was talking. When he finished, Sarah moved to come on stage with a paper in her hand. The stage director tried to stop her as the crowd shifted nervously. Kubic intervened, stating that they should allow her to speak, and they obliged, even though this appeared to be a somewhat awkward cultural breakthrough in the making. She was twelve years old and was dressed in a long bright flowery dress with a black and gray shawl modestly covering her head. She started by giving praise to Allah (in Arabic with an interpreter), thanked the Seabees and Marines, and then stated that today was very important to different people for different reasons.

After discussing some of these, she said it was important to her because now her mother and sister were free to teach. At this point, Kubic recalled, you could have heard a pin drop in the hot stuffy hall. She then went on to say that the real significance of this day was that now all of the women of her generation would be able to pursue their dreams as they grew up in a free and liberated Iraq. By this point, the audience was a bit teary eyed and erupted in thunderous applause for this brave young girl. In any case, Kubic saw that day that the MEF's Phase IVB deep fight for the future of the children of Iraq had been won, at least in that place at that time.

Shopping

Once the MEG had money, it was only a matter of shopping until required construction materials were located. The MEG canvassed its troops and found two Arabic speaking Seabees. One female had studied the more formal Arabic and one male had grown up speaking street Arabic – they made a good team. Soon the Seabees and Marines learned their way around the shops and found reliable brokers. They could also see capitalism sprouting up all around us as money was infused from the bottom up in communities where MEG contractors and Seabees were shopping. They also saw emerging business leaders beginning to show local political leadership as well, sometimes with encouragement from the MEG. By early August it had become apparent to Kubic that the Coalition's civilian leadership seemed to be pursuing an unarticulated political and economic model that was patterned after Saddam's strong centralized political control, supported by a socialist economic bureaucracy. Many of Kubic's MEGsters became convinced that a better model for the future of Iraq would be a decentralized democracy rooted in the provinces and supported by small business capitalism. Although it was easier for Bremer's Coalition Provisional Authority to pump money into the economy through the established Ba'athist ministries and their state owned contractors, this approach looked pretty much like Saddam's system to the man on the street in Ad Diwaniyah in August, and he was worried that continued employment would require "tribute" once again to the powerful men in Baghdad. This approach also led to fast acceleration of prices, as labor and material costs were inflated and the various layers of CPA bureaucracy all charged fees for overseeing the work.

Later on during a return trip in November 2003 to one contractor job site where a military compound was being renovated for the new Iraqi Army, Kubic asked about the price of the contract, the length of the contract, and the average workforce. A quick calculation indicated that the Coalition Provisional Authority was paying about $90 a day for an Iraqi worker – quite a deal by U.S. standards until you realized the average Iraqi worker was only taking home between $2 and $5 per day. The rest disappeared into the overhead black hole. Shopping is fundamentally a capitalistic sport – in the early days, it seemed to Kubic and the MEG that if Iraq was to succeed as a capitalistic democracy, it needed to rely on a political and economic model with more shopping and less price setting.

Task Force Mike and the "War on Dust"

During the early planning stages of the war, the MEF designated Highway 1 as the primary Main Supply Route. A 240-kilometer, six-lane super highway from the Iraqi border to just south of the Euphrates River, Highway 1 was a near perfect Main Supply Route on which the MEF could prosecute a battle plan built around speed of advance. The highway also offered 150 kilometers of six-lane superhighway from Ad Diwaniyah to the Baghdad International Airport. Additionally, heavy fighting in An Nasiriyah and frequent attacks on convoys moving up Highway 7 reinforced the conclusion that Highway 1 offered the best route for movement. The one potential hindrance to a speedy advance was a 109 kilometer section of unfinished road that lay between the two sections of completed highway.[12]

According to the local populace and recent intelligence, over the past six years, the Iraqi government had worked only occasionally on this section of Highway 1. Moreover, as money became tight under the weight of international sanctions, work slowed to a crawl and the regime eventually stopped making payments to its contractors and sub-contractors. Needless to say, the mission of maintaining this roughly sixty-mile stretch of hot, dusty, and uninviting highway fell to the MEG. Initial maintenance efforts involved grading and compacting the road surface, facilitating the speed of the initial drive to Baghdad, and ultimately ensuring an unimpeded northward-moving logistics train. Almost before the first Regimental Combat Team traversed this unfinished portion of the Main Supply Route, dust had proven itself not only a detriment speed but also as a potentially fatal hazard, as the road became quickly choked with thousands of combat and logistics support vehicles.

Eliminating dust in a desert was a job best left to the Seabees. Given Task Force Mike's previous and fruitless efforts to water down the highway that routinely saw temperatures of well over 100 degrees Fahrenheit and choking dust that hampered air operations, the MEG resolved as early as April 1 to locate and procure special dust palliatives in Iraq and Kuwait. By April 7, the MEG began negotiating with a Kuwaiti contractor to supply MC-70 road oil.

While the cost of the palliative was high at $5 per gallon, it was a cost well worth bearing, given the importance of the road to the MEF's operations.

On April 6, Task Force Mike, acting on information provided by the MEG Staff, located an asphalt plant just two kilometers north of the Highway 1 Bridge over the Euphrates River. This plant, owned by none other than Uday Hussein (Saddam's psychotic elder son), was to become the key asphalt production hub for Highway 1 maintenance efforts - its aging tanks held over 50,000 gallons of asphalt. On initial inspection, however, the Seabees determined that the plant could not be restarted without some outside assistance and certain critical parts, all of which would have to come from Kuwait. The MEG Staff immediately set to work procuring the equipment and expertise necessary to make the plant functional again. In the meantime, Task Force Mike began spreading over 100,000 cubic meters of "seized gravel" (the pile of which was proudly named "Mount MEG"), providing temporary stability to the road as countless Coalition convoys traversed its length.

The MEG eventually managed to contract for Kuwaiti emulsion and began making tangible progress on Highway 1. Costs, however, started to mount and were soon draining MARCENT's Operations & Maintenance budget. Having already located an abundant source of emulsion (at Uday's asphalt plant), the MEG Staff realized that there was a much more cost-effective solution to the problem. Once enemy attacks subsided, the MEG would hire the Kuwaiti emulsion contractor, which by April 18th had supplied over 40,000 gallons of MC-70 (at a cost of $200,000), to restore the asphalt plant to operation. The MEG put the plan in effect, and by May 1, the plant was operational, and it ultimately proved to be a resounding success. Rather than paying over $1,000,000 in Marine Corps money for dust palliative, the Seabees, working with their Kuwaiti counterparts, were now producing MC-70 in Iraq at $1.67 per gallon. The asphalt in the plant, when cut with kerosene, would allow the MEG unfettered access to over 150,000 gallons of MC-70 at a fraction of the previous contract price. The only costs borne by the Marines came from the money spent to restore the plant infrastructure and to procure and transport the kerosene.

Interestingly enough, the plant resumed operation, several enterprising entrepreneurs showed up at the plant's gates, claiming ownership of everything from the plant equipment to the sheep grazing in nearby pastures. These claims, difficult to prove in a country like Iraq, were not substantiated. As most persons living near the plant contended, and as the investigation of these claims concluded, the Iraqi government owned the plant, making it legitimately seized United State property. Ownership debates aside, the plant proved critical to ensuring the Marines' maneuver speed during Phase III operations and the safety of Coalition convoys during Phase IV and subsequent retrograde operations. By July 2003, the MEF estimated that upward of 55,000 vehicles had traveled this section of Highway 1 during Operation IRAQI FREEDOM.

In addition to improving Highway 1, the MEG made a similar assault on dust at forward airfields. In the midst of operations against Baghdad, dust was significantly hampering air operations at An Numaniyah and Salman Pak. Initial efforts to spray fuel were making little impact on the dust. The situation was getting critical. The solution was one that had been proven in Afghanistan in 2001 and 2002 — "Rhino Snot" — which created a rubberized coating that, in low traffic areas, is extremely effective, as NMCB 133's Air Det had proven at Camp Rhino in Southern Afghanistan.

Using CONCAP funds and product information based on prior experience, the MEG purchased its first batch of Rhino Snot concentrate and rushed it into the Kuwait. The initial shipment was eight 55-gallon drums. When cut at an 8:1 mixture, this produced 440 gallons of emulsion. It was immediately shipped to the airfield at Tactical Assembly Area Coyote and then flown north to An Numaniyah on the next available flight, which was the next morning. NMCB 4 unloaded the Rhino Snot from the transport and immediately went to work mixing and spreading it, with outstanding results. The remaining thirty-two barrels were trucked north and used at An Numaniyah and the airfield at Salman Pak, just east of Baghdad. This quick action allowed the 3rd Marine Aircraft Wing to provide seamless air support to the 1st Marine Division during its drive into Baghdad.

The success of these efforts was a result of quick action, the application of "lessons learned" from other operations (particularly Operation ENDURING FREEDOM in Afghanistan), and the CONCAP relationships with Kellogg Brown & Root. Air and ground operations therefore became much safer throughout the MEFs Area of Responsibility due to Rhino Snot, Saddam's asphalt, and the Seabees.

The Sarabadi Bridge

On April 1, the Coalition had destroyed several bridges over the Tigris River to cover the flanks of the 1st Marine Division as it assaulted towards Baghdad from Al Kut and other points to the south. Unfortunately, for nearby residents who regularly used the bridges, the destruction was a major disaster in their lives and not simply a necessity of war. Repairing the bridges, from the Seabees' viewpoint, was an act of commitment to the future of the people of Iraq. Within a very short time after the fall of Saddam's regime, Seabee effort to construct key bridges to Baghdad became both the physical and symbolic signs that Iraq had been liberated (not conquered) by a Coalition focused on building bridges for and with the Iraqi people, and building a better future for a free Iraq.[13]

One particular bridge located in the town of Sarabadi, while not completely destroyed, had become a hazard to local traffic. Kubic decided that it needed to be fixed immediately, and gave the job to Task Force Charlie, which would now get the chance to build its first Mabey & Johnson Bridge. In consultation with the MEG, Commodore Garcia decided to keep the damaged span intact even though it slanted at a dangerous angle. The Seabees of NMCB 4 and 133 went to work and within fifty hours had completed a single-lane, thirty-five meter bridge span, rated at MLC-70. Life in the vicinity of the Sarabadi Bridge soon returned to some semblance of normalcy, and Task Force Charlie moved on to other high priority Phase IVB projects.

The Mighty Tigris

Bridges were the most formidable military engineering obstacles which the MEG identified during the planning for the Iraq War. They also turned out to be one of the most formidable challenges to sustaining the peace in the immediate aftermath of the fall of Baghdad. Rear Admiral Kubic knew that several bridges had been blown during the MEF's advance north, and where possible, Marine aviators tried to do this with surgical precision to facilitate quick repair. This did not always happen as planned.

The MEG staff fielded reports about a bridge on Highway 6 east of Al Kut just inside the Brit sector that was totally destroyed. One span was dropped into the river below, but cars could pass carefully on the other span by avoiding major craters, and buses crossed after unloading their passengers and saying a short prayer. But heavy trucks could not use this bridge, and reports indicated that this damage was preventing farmers from hauling their vegetable crops to market, threatening local stability.

Kubic went with a recon team from NMCB 133 to view the damage and to plan the repair. The bridge was a real mess and to Kubic's surprise, a group of Iraqi structural engineers from an Iraqi public works ministry was there conducting the same type of reconnaissance. As it turned out, this was the angriest group of Iraqis the admiral had personally encountered yet. Their leader had been educated at Stanford, and by all accounts was a seasoned bridge engineer. He shouted at Kubic, "look at this – look at this – look at what you have done!" The admiral replied that the destruction was necessary to liberate Iraq from Saddam. Kubic quickly learned though that the Iraqi chief engineer was apolitical and could have cared less about Saddam. His loyalty was to his bridges, and this major one over a tributary to the Tigris had been destroyed.

The engineer continued his white-hot tirade, exclaiming that "the U.S. had destroyed 127 bridges during the last war, and we had just completed repairing the last one several months ago after more than ten years of hard work. Now look at this – we must start over again." Kubic assured him that the Seabees were there to help, and slowly won over a little of his trust. Kubic and the Iraqi soon agreed that his ministry would start the permanent repair by replacing the span that was totally dropped, while the Seabees would emplace a Mabey & Johnson bridge over the other partially destroyed span to maintain one lane access during reconstruction. They shook hands, sealing the deal, and Kubic departed, leaving the Iraqi engineers staring at their mangled bridge, that once again, they had to rebuild, but this time with Seabee help.

NMCB 133 mobilized quickly and worked double shifts to erect the Mabey & Johnson bridge. This effort allowed trucks to get to market and cars and busses to use Highway 6 (a well traveled four-lane road) more safely, despite the inconvenience of single-lane, one-way traffic across the bridge. Kubic figured it would be a long time before the Iraqis even started their construction, and that proved to be true. As soon as NMCB 133 completed this bridge, an even greater challenge presented itself - bridging the mighty Tigris.

The Euphrates was a good sized river, but a bit of a disappointment to most Seabees when they first crossed it west of An Nasiriyah. It was simply not that wide or deep. The Tigris, which flowed parallel to Highway 6 between Baghdad and Al Kut, was much wider and deeper than they had imagined – it was truly a mighty river with massive bridges, most of which survived the war.

But, as the MEF engaged the Al Nida Division in its push north to the Tigris, the decision was made to sink a floating bridge over the Tigris to cut off the Iraqis retreat and impede any reinforcement of Baghdad. When two five hundred-pound bombs missed their target, Cobra gun ships strafed the bridge, sinking most of the pontoons. When Kubic first saw this, he thought that they overdid it. One or two sunken pontoons would have done the job and made repair much easier in his opinion.

The MEG had the pontoons and Mabey & Johnson bridge components at Camp 93. Fortunately, the Seabees did not have to construct this "monster floating bridge" during the actual assault north. But, the destroyed pontoon bridge needed to be reconstructed to reconnect several villages to Highway 6 and to restore commerce and free movement to Baghdad. Once the MEF leadership understood the adverse impact this destroyed bridge was having on the local community, this critical bridge replacement project was authorized as a major CMO effort.

Under the leadership of NMCB 133's Commanding Officer, Doug Morton and his Operations Officer, Lieutenant Commander Charlie Willmore, plans were assembled and a task force that included Army bridge units with supporting boats was formed. Seabees and U.S. Soldiers established an expeditionary camp on the north bank of the Tigris west of Al Kut, and went right to work. This was still a dangerous area with many former Republican Guard soldiers still armed and acting as thieves (or "Ali Babas" as the locals called them) and insurgents. So, the construction force built a proper perimeter, and after some careful instruction by senior Seabees and Marine advisors, emplaced heavy weapons at the job site, thus bringing yet another Seabee Camp to life – practically a replica of the many camps Seabees had built during field training exercises for past several decades.

A major tactical convoy operation then began to haul pontoons and bridge components and heavy construction equipment from Camp 93 in Kuwait to the Tigris River, well over three hundred miles one way. At the site, Seabee Divers and U.S. Army boat operators hauled and anchored pontoons using designs forwarded from the Seabees' reach-back engineering support at the Atlantic Division in Norfolk, VA. These pontoons had been modified before the war by Seabee steel workers in Camp 93 to attach the Mabey & Johnson bridge components as easily as possible. Seabee ingenuity and pre-planning paid huge dividends as they constructed the bridge over the swift moving Tigris. Once they emplaced the pontoons, they erected the bridge components very quickly.

The Seabees did not work double shifts for this project since this was not an exigent combat operation and safety was their biggest concern. Nevertheless, in only about two weeks a beautiful floating bridge once again spanned the Tigris, and the nearby villages were very happy and extremely impressed by the capability of American military engineers. Kubic recalled that the bridge components spanned 205 meters from shore to shore. But like a good fish story, the length of this bridge kept growing as the Seabees and their Army counterparts added ramps and approaches. Kubic later commented that in the end this impressive bridge was "stretched" up to 240 meters, "depending on who was telling this story."

The MEG sponsored a press day at the bridge site, and had two CH-46s haul many TV and news reporters to see the completed project in mid-August 2003. It was a beautiful day, and many Iraqis and two Sheiks turned out from the local communities. Jane Arraf from CNN was among the reporters who interviewed the Seabees, and then surprised everyone by speaking to the Sheiks in Arabic. Hearts and minds had been won by the U.S. forces and media that day, Kubic believed, and he felt the good will in the air. The Seabees involved in the project likewise felt that this last and longest bridge to Baghdad was truly a tangible sign of their commitment to rebuild Iraq. And on that day, even the press agreed, as Kubic wryly noted.

Rumaylah Oilfield Security

Key to the long-term economic viability of Iraq was the return of the oil infrastructure and trade to the Iraqi people. To accomplish this, civilian contractors came to Camp Commando and gradually began moving into the Rumaylah oilfields of southern Iraq. Because fighting was still underway in the country's central regions, the Marines were hard pressed to provide a security detail. The MEF turned to the MEG for its Army engineer units, which had begun arriving in theater in mid-April. Thus, the Army's 1092nd Engineer Battalion, as part of Task Force Echo, undertook the MEG's first infantry mission. On April 16, the battalion sent a company (minus) to Camp Commando to carry out its orders.[14]

In short, the 1092nd's mission consisted of providing sufficient security personnel to protect the contractors working in the Rumaylah oilfields. In addition to providing escorts, the company conducted patrols, which were for the most part uneventful. Occasionally, groups of people (especially in Safwan) would interfere with the effort, throwing rocks and in one instance breaking the window of a vehicle. On May 18, however, the threat level escalated. While conducting routine perimeter security in the British sector of the oilfields, Specialist Brandon Long was injured when an Iraqi child, approximately eighty feet away on a berm, began playing with a grenade, causing it to detonate. Long was treated quickly at a US Army Combat Surgical Hospital (CSH), where doctors removed one piece of shrapnel and closed his wound with several stitches.

The 1092nd's mission soon expanded to include security of civilian teams traveling to oil platforms in the Persian Gulf. One such mission had four Army engineers and a Brown & Root contractor steaming up the narrow Shatt al Arab waterway to the Maabot oil platform at port of Mina el-Bakr in 30-foot boats. After completing work on the platform, the team was to move to a location on the northern tip of the Al Faw peninsula (in Iraq). Fully understanding that this would entail coming extremely close to Iranian waters, the contractors had hired two Iranian-born guides to assist them in the event of a confrontation. Nevertheless, two Iranian gunboats spotted the team and halted them. Prudence being the better part of valor, when faced with gunboats armed with heavy machine guns and with civilian lives at risk, the soldiers did not engage the Iranian patrol. The Iranians took them all into custody, blindfolded them, and moved them to an undetermined location in Iran, where they were held and questioned for twenty-six hours before being released.[15]

During the interrogations, the Iranians accused the U.S. soldiers of being SEAL commandos. They were big, strong West Virginia mountain boys who insisted that they were only simple soldiers who got lost. They told their captors they were not SEALs. SEALs, they said, "were really BIG guys who would have killed the Iranians at night before they were even seen." The soldiers' calm behavior and quick thinking worked, and they were released after only two days in captivity. Kubic speculated that "the Iranians let them go because they couldn't afford to feed these big guys."

The Hunt for WMDs and Mass Graves

Throughout the war, the MEG had hard intelligence that Saddam had chemical weapons and possibly biological weapons, and that he was predisposed to allow his field commanders to use them. The Seabees and Marines acted accordingly and prepared themselves to be "slimed." The Marines and Seabees were so convinced of his capability that they had over 90% confidence that he would unleash chemical weapons as soon as they crossed the Tigris and turned towards Baghdad. Fortunately, none of this came to pass.[16]

After the fall of Baghdad, the Marines, Seabees, and U.S. Army engineers expended a great deal of effort and energy on identifying and investigating "sensitive sites" where chemical weapons were thought to be hidden or buried. Coalition intelligence officers identified these sites from past records and also from current human sources, mostly local Iraqis living in nearby villages and towns. One site near Al Amarah east of Al Kut was particularly promising, and the MEG moved to investigate it even before the fighting had stopped. Local civilians had told investigators that several weeks before the war, Saddam's troops had shut down their power for several days and had not let anyone out of their village. The Iraqi soldiers had then excavated a site outside the city, allegedly buried truckloads of containers, covered them with concrete, and then backfilled the pit. When the solders left, they had turned the power back on for the villagers.

Task Force Tarawa had initially investigated the site and reported back that it indeed looked "hot." The Brits had looked at this site too but did not want to pursue it any further given their shortage of troops for their expanded Area of Responsibility. Consequently, the MEG directed Task Force Charlie to support the resulting mission to excavate and secure any potential WMDs uncovered there. A detachment from Task Force Charlie, led by Lieutenant Phil Lavallee of SERT 133, quickly moved to the site, taking sporadic small arms fire from Iraqi "dead enders" along the way. The Seabee inspection and excavation was delayed though because the area was then being turned over from Task Force Tarawa to the 1st U.K. Armoured Division as part of the Phase IVB shuffle. Because of this confusion, with Lavallee awaiting further orders, the MEG sent its Nuclear/Biological/Chemical warfare officer, Chief Warrant Officer (CWO3) Al Dailey, to the site.[17]

After Dailey arrived, the Det Commander, Lieutenant Lavallee, positioned his team to await the 16th Air Assault Royal Irish Brigade, southwest of Al Amarah. Once the 16th Air Assault Brigade was on site, Lavallee conducted a helicopter reconnaissance with the Brits. From the air, Lavallee's team saw evidence of recent digging, with five dug-in but abandoned T-55 tanks guarding the perimeter of what was obviously a filled-in pit. After completing their recon, Dailey, Lavallee, and the Brits moved forward to the site. There, CWO3 Dailey immediately called back for a Ground Penetrating Radar (GPR) Team to analyze it. By the time the GPR Team arrived, the rest of Lavallee's Det had arrived and the Brits had begun security operations and working the town to gather additional information.

With support from the Brits, the Seabees began to re-excavate in full MOPP gear. This was done in a very deliberate manner over several days, since the MEG feared that its heavy equipment could damage the containers, causing a chemical release. Despite the hard intelligence, the team found nothing except for some scrap metal and medical waste. Daily and Lavallee determined that the Iraqi soldiers had done the excavation merely to dig in the tanks, and possibly to plant fake human intelligence that Weapons of Mass Destruction had been buried there hoping to entice the weapons inspectors into embarrassing themselves before the war as they investigated yet another "dry hole." The Det from Task Force Charlie then returned to continue with other CMO and Quality of Life improvements for Division. Over the next couple of weeks, the MEG supported several more sensitive site investigations, but did not find any chemical or biological weapons.[18]

One issue that received less attention, but which was arguably of equal importance, was the fate of Kuwaiti prisoners of war and of thousands of missing Iraqis. During its invasion of Kuwait in August 1991, the Iraqi army transported hundreds of Kuwaiti prisoners north back into Iraq. These captives were never to be heard from again. It was also widely known that Saddam Hussein had committed a number of atrocities against his own people. Entire families had gone missing during his suppression of the Shi'ite rebellion that occurred shortly after Desert Storm. Once the regime was removed, the time had come to search for the missing Kuwaitis and Iraqis, and to bring closure to their families. Seabee equipment and manpower would be required in this massive effort.

While the search for WMDs in the MEF Area of Responsibility went on with little success, reports from locals of mass gravesites quickly began to surface. Unfortunately, these reports turned out to be true, and the severity of Hussein's crimes against Kuwaitis and his own people became all too apparent. Two of these mass gravesites were discovered near the cities of Al Hillah and As

Samawah, and Seabees were called upon to support this most sobering of missions. At Al Hillah, the remains of more than twelve thousand Iraqis were unearthed. The MEG soon learned that at this site alone, Hussein's henchmen had tortured and executed Shi'ite Muslims for thirty consecutive days, killing an average of nine hundred people per day. Even though the bodies were in varying stages of decay, the means of execution were quite obvious. Many had been killed with single gunshot wounds to the head. Others, with their arms and legs bound, were decapitated with chainsaws. The search for Kuwaiti prisoners met a similarly gruesome conclusion near As Samawah. DNA tests from remains matched those of a number of Kuwaitis known to have been taken prisoner during the 1991 Iraqi invasion of Kuwait.

ROK Engineers

The U.S. was counting on its Coalition partners to assume much of the post war security and reconstruction burdens. The very first country to render such assistance after Baghdad fell was the Republic of [South] Korea (ROK), which offered to send an Engineer Battalion with a Medical Company to repair and operate hospitals and clinics in the southern part of Iraq. The MEG was uniquely structured to attach such a capability into its Task Force Endurance. As an added benefit, this Coalition approach would serve to establish and strengthen bonds between the MEG and the ROK Engineers that were so important under Korean OPLAN 5027.

The ROK engineers brought an impressive handpicked force that trained hard in Kuwait and did everything with a bit of a flare. Before they departed north to An Nasiriyah, they put on a singularly impressive martial arts display and gave Rear Admiral Kubic the opportunity to address their whole formation. They had been schooled to shout in unison "OOH –RAH!" "CAN DO!" and the MEG Motto "FORWARD TOGETHER!" and did so repeatedly throughout his speech, astounding him with their enthusiasm for the mission.

Once in Iraq, the ROK engineers showed themselves to be very skilled at both construction and public relations as they took on school and hospital projects and engaged the local population and its leaders with frequent visits and trips throughout the town. They also donned distinctive blue ball caps, to indicate they came in peace. But they also established solid lines of defense with disciplined troops when they needed to control crowds and protect job sites.

When Kubic later visited their camp at An Nasiriyah, he was treated to a Korean MRE dinner complete with Kim Chi. After dinner, the Korean soldiers entertained him with a traditional Korean folk dancing show. The Seabees could not help but note how the Koreans operated with confidence and a flare for bold approaches, both on and off duty. This boldness did get the Koreans into some trouble when they signed a contract for support to their hospital project without any commitment of MEG funding. They did a great job, but the MEG was not very happy with their contracting flaw. Kubic eventually got the money for the project and bailed them out, and they were very careful to follow MEG financial rules from that point forth. All in all, the Seabees and Marines found the ROK soldiers to be solid coalition partners who stepped forward boldly and made significant civil-military contributions during Phase IVB in southern Iraq.

"Beating Retreat" in Basrah

As Rear Admiral Kubic later observed, "no one tops the British for fighting with pride, grace, and flare steeped in deep tradition." Just a week after Baghdad's fall (on April 17), Major General Robin Brims of the 1st U. K. Armoured Division had warmly congratulated the Marines, telling Lieutenant General Conway that "This has been little short of a miracle. We are so proud to be a part of I MEF." When it came time for Brims to relinquish command, after having been extended for the war, the Brits planned a great celebration in Basrah. It was a twilight ceremony called "Beating Retreat." It was not the actual change of command, but an opportunity for festive and formal celebration with their American Coalition partners, with whom they had just help achieve the near miraculous.

The MEF leadership loaded up into two C-130's and flew a short hop to Basrah International Airport, which had been captured substantially intact with damage to only one outlying building. Prior to the war, Kubic recalled, no one really wanted to commit scarce troop resources to capture this airport given the heavy artillery protection Saddam had dug into community facilities in Basrah, and also because Coalition forces could easily isolate and by-pass it. But it was symbolically important to capture the Basrah airport, and the Brits did it in quick fashion with limited damage when the time came to move into the city. As the MEF commanders walked into an atrium leading to a marble lounge area with operating fountains, the Brits handed them beverages, which looked like Seven-

Ups, but were actually a bit stronger. Inside there were also large cans of other "seized beverages" with lids popping open. It seems the Brits captured the airport with duty free shops intact, and consistent with their Royal traditions, put on quite a festive display of food and drink. Many of the MEF officers proceeded with caution (at least initially) since it had been many months since they had last hoisted a "cold one."

The party moved outside and was treated to a fabulous display of precision music and marching. First by the Division Band, whose members were all trained as Hospital Corpsmen and went into combat with both their medical supplies and musical instruments. Then the Pipe and Drum Corps put on the most inspirational show Kubic had ever seen as the sun set over Basrah. The pipe and drum corps musicians were all part timers and had full time jobs in the various combat arms specialties. Yet they all went to war with their instruments packed for quick employment should the occasion arise. Jokingly, Kubic asked a British General how they marched into battle without the pipes since their pipers were all combat soldiers. In the best formal British response, he said "that did present a bit of a dilemma but we found sufficient officers to pipe the lads into battle." He was dead serious, Kubic thought.

As the evening ended, the MEF commanders could not help but feel a sense of total inspiration. That night and the events of the preceding months were truly historic in their estimation, and they felt that they had been very fortunate to have had the British fighting on the Marines' right flank – the Brits' professionalism and courage were clearly steeped in centuries of military tradition, and during that evening soiree, it was an emotional experience for all who attended.

Tragedy at Al Kut

At the onset of the war, Kubic told the Seabees that they would face three types of danger. Enemy action was anticipated against them, and the admiral was confident that the MEG troops were well trained and would give a good accounting of themselves in battle. Chemical weapons were possible, but Kubic was confident that the Seabees were ready to deal with the possibility of being slimed. His biggest concern though was that their work, even in peacetime, is inherently dangerous. Day to day, Operational Risk Management (ORM) and basic safety awareness were key to countering the biggest threat they would face—on-the-job accidents.

The MEG faced a number of these accidents during the build-up and the war, with cuts, bruises, and broken bones being the most common injuries. In a more serious accident (described previously), a Seabee was run over by an out-of-control Army fifteen-ton truck but fortunately survived. In another serious accident, a Seabee was electrocuted and severely burned, but survived and recovered. There were fingertip amputations and broken backs from falls and broken feet from vehicle accidents. All in all, the MEG suffered about eighty non-hostile wounded-in-action casualties during its deployment with less than ten of these accidents being serious. All accidents are bad, but with nearly five thousand troops in the field, their casualty record was good until early June at Blair Airfield in Al Kut.

A crew of Seabees from NMCB 133 was building a seahut cooling house so that Marines returning from patrols could cool down and relax. The site was next to a former Iraqi barracks that now housed the Marines. On the morning of June 6, the Seabees reported to the job site as they had been doing over the previous few days. Several of the Seabees spotted an object that looked like a machine part with a threaded shaft on a pile of broken glass. Rather carelessly, they picked it up, examined it, and then set it down on a workbench for later tinkering. No one knew what it was.

During a break, Builder 3rd Class Doyle Bollinger saw the object and began to examine it himself. Unknowingly, he was handling an expended Iraqi 57-millimeter high-explosive anti-aircraft round – it was unexploded ordnance, not a machine part. As he began poking at it with his knife, it detonated, killing Bollinger instantly and seriously wounding three other Seabees. His crew mates responded to what they thought was an attack but then they realized it was a tragic accident. The other three Seabees ultimately recovered with little residual physical impairment. But, as Kubic later said, no Seabee ever fully recovers from the loss of a shipmate, particularly someone as well liked and respected as BU3 Bollinger. He was a typically solid Seabee of good nature who was doing his job to make life better for others in a very dangerous environment. His was the first battle death for the MEG and for Seabees since Vietnam, and ultimately, he was the only Seabee killed in Operation IRAQI FREEDOM I. Bollinger's sacrifice served to motivate the rest of the Seabees to work even harder to build for "peace with freedom" in his memory, even as they began preparing to go home.[19]

CHAPTER

13

Homeward Bound

Retrograde, Regeneration, Reconstitution, and Redeployment, or "R4", was shorthand for all the work necessary to move back from Iraq to Kuwait, repair and clean our Civil Engineering Support Equipment, reload the Maritime Prepositioning Force ships into unit sets ready for the next war, and then move troops and equipment back home in an orderly and controlled fashion while turning over territory and work to Coalition partners. In many ways, this was more complex and more difficult and certainly more expensive than moving into Kuwait and getting ready for war.[1]

By the end of April 2003, Kubic and his MEG staff knew that the time was rapidly approaching for the Seabees to go home. The MEF already had an R4 plan that would involve gradually moving all of its personnel, including the MEG Seabees, out of Iraq and eventually, out of Kuwait entirely. The schedule dictated that by June 15, the MEF would downsize to a Marine Expeditionary Brigade, the 1st Marine Division to a Regimental Combat Team, the 1st Force Service Support Group to a Brigade Service Support Group, and the MEG to a single Task Force. In accordance with this plan, the MEG decided to disestablish Task Force Echo, transferring the Army and ROK units to V Corps on June 22. All Seabee units would then become part of Task Force Charlie. Finally, on June 25, the MEG Command Element would stand down, leaving Task Force Charlie, under Commodore Al Garcia, with command and control of all Seabee operations in theater.

MARCENT initially tasked the Marine Logisitics Command with the R4 responsibilities once the MEF retrograded from Iraq. The MEG proposed to construct the wash racks and maintenance facilities, but the MEF declined the offer in the name of cost savings. But as reality set in, the Marine Logisitics Command had to rent space at the local Nestle's plant and pay for contract labor to wash all the vehicles. Faced with spiraling costs, the Marine Logisitics Command then backtracked and asked the MEG to contract with CONCAP to build temporary maintenance facilities at Camp Fox. The MEG accepted the job and accordingly entered into the necessary CONCAP contract. Although the iterative planning process had encountered this bit of unnecessary friction, R4 moved ahead relatively quickly from that point forth once MARCENT found its bearing, set a course, and funded the MEG's proposal.

Ultimately, the MEG had to process between 1,200 and 1,600 pieces of Civil Engineering Support Equipment and six hundred containers during the R4 effort, which it synchronized with the Maritime Prepositioning Force shipping plan. The Seabees washed and repaired all of their gear and Civil Engineering Support Equipment themselves in a controlled withdrawal that saw the final tasks passed on to the newly arrived Air Det from NMCB 40.

While R4 continued at Camp Moreell, the MEG closed Camp Castle at Fox and eventually returned it to the Marine Logistics Command (MLC) under the terms of the original contract. The MEG then completely dismantled Camp 93 and returned the site to its original open desert condition.

Reserve Demobilization

When it became apparent that the war would be over quickly and the MEF would begin the journey home in May, the Defense Department halted the Seabee reserve mobilization at 1,781 troops, out of a planned build-up of 2,400 troops. Although this meant sending some NMCB 22 Reservists home part way through their mobilization training, Kubic later observed that it showed the great flexibility and responsiveness of the Seabee reserve units.

The MEG soon began to demobilize troops from Iraq and Kuwait in conjunction with the redeployment of active troops, and had all of its reserves out of theater by the end of August, with all but the medical holds demobilized by September 30, consistent with Chief of Naval Operations guidance. To ensure proper manning of the Seabee deployment sites at Rota and Guam, the 1st Naval Construction Division asked that NMCB 26 be extended on active duty for a few more months, but the Defense Department denied this request. This placed a bit of a strain on Seabee strength in Europe, and required NMCB 1 to cover both Rota and Guam sites from

August 2003 to February 2004. But, active duty Seabees spread out and fell in on the reserve Seabee sites with a seamless transfer, and the Okinawa and Guam battalions covered the world until NMCB 74 was ready to deploy once again in February 2004, re-establishing the peace time deployment cycles of three NMCBs.

MPF Backload

The MEF backload was smooth and seamless. The ship schedule kept changing but the Seabees' N43 team was up to the challenge. The Civil Engineering Support Equipment was swapped among Tables of Allowance as required to ensure that the best machinery and tools were loaded on the Maritime Prepositioning Force ships. The MEG also shipped the Civil Engineering Support Equipment which needed more extensive repair, and all of its containers, back to the continental U.S. (CONUS) for Integrated Logistics Overhaul (ILO). The Seabees' Table of Allowance system was sufficiently mature that they quickly had new containers packed and ready to go for the Maritime Prepositioning Force upload. All in all, Rear Admiral Kubic believed that the MPF crews had done a superb job, and from his vantage point in the MEG Command Element, "it almost seemed like it all happened over night by magic."

Task Force Mike Moves South

Once the MEF shifted into its Phase IVB positions with its Command Element posted at Saddam's Babylon Palace in Al Hillah, Task Force Mike began standing down after a brilliant campaign in trace of the 1st Marine Division on the attack. Rudich's Seabees started moving south at the end of the first week in May. NMCB 74 returned home to Gulfport in late May, as did Commodore Rudich and the 30th Naval Construction Regiment's Command Element, which arrived in Honolulu to the joy and boisterous cheers of their loved ones.* The MEG was left with Task Forces Charlie and Echo, and split its Area of Responsibility accordingly, with NMCB 4 as-

---

* On December 19, 2003, Rear Admiral Kubic presented Bronze Stars to both Commodore Rudich and his Chief of Staff, Commander Mark Libonate, for distinguishing themselves through "heroism, outstanding achievement, or by meritorious service while serving with the armed forces of the United States in a combat theater." The awards were the highest given to any Seabees for service in Iraq up to that point. Commodore Rudich subsequently retired from the U.S. Navy in April 2004.

signed to Task Force Charlie, responsible for Ad Diwaniyah and An Najaf. By this time, Kubic observed, the MEG was getting pretty good at "shifting gears" and its Reliefs-in-Place (RIPs) were becoming smoother and more seamless.[2]

Task Force Echo CHOPS

As planned and on schedule, the MEG's Army units were "chopped" to Task Force Echo under the command of the 265th Engineer Group. Task Force Echo was then chopped back to CFLCC in late June. The plan was for these units to complete their retrograde with Army support and then return to the continental U.S. The Army followed through with this plan for the 478th Corps Mechanized Battalion since it did not feel it needed mechanized support any longer. But, in a morale busting move, the Army extended the 265th Engineer Group and the 1092nd Engineer Battalion, first for three months, then until December, and then finally to February, for a full year in theater. Rear Admiral Kubic felt very bad for those soldiers and objected mightily to their treatment. However, Army ears were deaf to Navy protests and he had no success in getting their deployments shortened. They were caught up in the Army's emerging deployment policy and logic, and so equity and fairness were not decision factors at that point, as Kubic later lamented.

The MEG Command Element Stands Down

Early in the pre-war planning process, Kubic told the MEG Command Element members to be prepared mentally for the war to be over in May, for them to anticipate going home by the 4th of July, and for their headquarters gear to be shipped back to Naval Amphibious Base (NAB) Little Creek, Virginia, by Labor Day. At the time those projections seemed a long way in the future, but he believed that they helped everyone on his team mentally pace themselves. Little did he know that the true dates would not be too far off from his projections. As it turned out, Kubic sent most the MEG Command Element staff home in late June and had Task Force Charlie assume the watch as a paired down MEG Command Element. By this time NMCB 4 had redeployed to Guam, and Reserves had started flowing home as well. Kubic kept MEG (Forward) at Hillah under the able leadership of Captain Al Garcia, who became affectionately known as the "Commodore of Babylon," and his R3 staff. MEG (Main) remained at Camp Commando with Commander Curbello as Chief of Staff, and MEG (Rear) was established at Camp Moreell under the Commanding Officer of NMCB 7, Commander Honkomp, to run the Table of Allowance regeneration and reconstitution process and MPF unload.

When the MEF left the theater of operations in September, the MEG once again downsized and the staff was home by Labor Day. Honkonp became the MEG deputy and finished most of the R4 work in time to redeploy on schedule in October, with the remaining effort chopped to the newly arrived Air Det from NMCB 40. From September 2002 through October 2003, the MEG grew, peaked, and then downsized with remarkable agility, keeping the heartburn (and chaos) to a minimum. On November 14, 2003, I MEG and its subordinate units, along with the rest of I MEF, were collectively awarded the Presidential Unit Citation for their distinguished actions during Operation IRAQI FREEDOM I, from the beginning of major combat operations on March 21 through April 24, 2003. All Seabees and Marines who participated in the attack into Iraq were eligible to wear this coveted ribbon.[3]

Homecoming

The Seabees returned home to scenes of jubilant celebrations among their home front friends and family, who had followed their progress closely throughout the build-up in Kuwait and during the conflict itself, courtesy of the Defense Department's well thought-out media-embed program. Indeed, the program was one of the crowning successes of Operation IRAQI FREEDOM for the Seabees, who enjoyed widespread media coverage by CNN and the other news networks, and through non-traditional internet news sources.

Under the guidance of Lieutenant Commander Meg Reed, a 1st Naval Construction Division reservist from the Washington D.C. area, a total of sixteen media embeds were assigned to the MEG and evenly distributed among the three task forces and the command element. Consequently, during the conflict, Seabees were often guests on the television news shows and were also regularly featured in print news stories, reminiscent of the attention given to the exploits of their World War II forbearers by journalists such as William Bradford Huies. Rear Admiral Kubic occasionally spoke on the air with CNN's Kyra Phillips to update the country on the Seabees' status, while Lieutenant Harry Wong, appearing on Wolf Blitzer's show, even communicated with his family on Christmas Day.[4]

With the media taking such an avid interest in the Seabees in Iraq and forecasting their imminent return to the U.S., their families and loved ones had plenty of time to prepare for their homecoming. Needless to say, the Seabees were hardly ready for the reception that they received back home. In a stopover in Bangor, Maine (on his way back to Port Hueneme via Point Mugu Naval Air Station in California), Harry Wong encountered a pro-military group of retired folks that had arisen early that morning to meet him and his CBMU 303 crew. One of the group's women walked up to him, gave him a big hug, and thanked him profusely for what he and the Seabees had done in Iraq, leaving him slightly embarrassed. Lieutenant Wong was then pleasantly surprised at Point Mugu to find his sister Jean there waving a home-made "Welcome Home" banner. She had made a last-minute, overnight mad dash up from their hometown to greet him. Accompanying her were their sister Suzie and two nieces and a nephew. Not expecting to see Jean, he simply exclaimed "What are YOU doing here?"[5]

Equipment Operator 1st Class William Young from NMCB 133 also received the same treatment in Bangor, with the local VFW and other community groups showing up to greet the Seabees on his plane and give them cell phones with which to call their families. As Young later recollected, "they were all lined up and hugging us and it made you feel like a little hero—it was a real warm homecoming." Young's friend, Equipment Operator 3rd Class Adam Schneider reached Gulfport on a different flight. At the Air National Guard terminal there, he disembarked to a marching band, backed by a huge throng of cheering locals, along with the Chamber of Commerce and Gulfport's Mayor.[6]

Senior Chief Troy Kellerman, also from NMCB 133, landed on August 17 at the Gulfport airport and found her parents waiting to meet her. Kellerman had been deployed away from them many times before during her career, but had never had such an emotional reunion with her family until that day. As she later commented to Det 206 interviewers from the Naval Historical Center, "it was just great." All of the Seabees families had turned out, along with the local press, and "it was just like here we're having this huge party in this hangar when our plane landed; it was just already full of people there to greet us. And it was the best homecoming I had ever had."[7]

Chief Equipment Operator Rudolpho Santiago from Naval Construction Force Support Unit 2 had a particularly enjoyable flight home from Kuwait. His plane had been decorated with red, white, and blue trimmings and American flags on the inside, and adorned with drawings and letters from kids from all around the U.S. A big Statue of Liberty knitted flag hung right by the door as you entered the plane. "They treated us real nice," Santiago later commented. He hugged the flight attendant and told the grinning pilot that "It's good to be back on American soil."[8]

Seabees from all of the units that had built and fought in Iraq shared similar homecoming stories. One unit in particular, Reserve NMCB 21 from Lakehurst, New Jersey, stood out for special recognition after it returned home. These "Big Apple" Seabees had been called up for service with the New York State Militia after Al Qaeda's attacks on September 11, 2001 and had served with distinction throughout Operation IRAQI FREEDOM. The unit had largely been responsible for getting the port of Umm Qasr back into operation even before Baghdad fell, and played a key role in the early Phase IVB Civil Military Operations throughout southern Iraq. Consequently, Rear Admiral Kubic decided to honor five of its Seabees at a ceremony that took place in Times Square in October 2003.[9]

During the widely-publicized ceremony, Kubic awarded medals to Chief Construction Mechanic Patrick Sabatini, Equipment Operator 1st Class Daniel Quinn, Officer-in-Charge Commander Charles Shere, Builder 1st Class Ronald Cozz, and Utilitiesman 1st Class Daniel Hazley. In civilian life, Sabatini was a supervisor of mechanics for the New York Department of Sanitation. He was proud of his unit's accomplishments. He told reporters that "You have to give back to your country, that's why I'm a Reservist. It's the greatest country on the planet. It only became this way because of the people who sacrificed to go and do the things that needed to be done."

Quinn, a bus driver for the New York Department of Transportation," was equally effusive in his praise of the Seabees and their service in Iraq. "I'm a native New Yorker so I think it's great to be able to do it here. In fact, I drive my bus past here every day," he said. "Serving in Iraq was something I'm very proud of, especially after 9/11. That was the worst day since Pearl Harbor. I was proud to go, and I'd do it again in a heartbeat."

The Seabees weren't the only ones enjoying the accolades of a grateful American public. In October 2003, on the West Coast, in Oceanside, California, the U.S. Marine Corps held the largest military parade in the city's history. Led by Lieutenant General Conway, who had just returned from Iraq, the parade took on a new twist when Conway suddenly invited a contingent of on-looking Vietnam veterans to join the Marine formation near its front, and not at its tail end. It was a stunning gesture, and everyone who witnessed it applauded Conway for his magnanimity. One Vietnam veteran observer told staff writer J. Stryker Meyer of the *North County Times* that "I can't say enough about what that general did…When I saw them marching in the parade, it shook me up." "Don't get me wrong, the veteran insisted, "I don't want to take anything away from today's Marines and Sailors. They should feel real proud for what they did in Iraq. Please, I salute them, and I'm glad they had their parade…it was real nice for Vietnam veterans to get recognition too."[10]

Enduring Presence?

Parades and celebrations aside, by November, all R4 work was done and NMCB 40 was ready to redeploy. But, Kubic did not want to abandon Camp Moreell until he knew for sure what came next in the Global War on Terrorism. While he was wrestling with that decision, the 1st Naval Construction Division received an urgent Special Operations Force (SOF) tasking to deploy a fifty-man Det to Afghanistan to build a Special Forces camp for expanding operations. Kubic had Seabees and heavy equipment ready to go in forty-eight hours and launched from Ali Al Salem for a highly successful six-week mission. At that time it also became apparent that the MEF and Seabees were likely to return for a new phase of Operation IRAQI FREEDOM, called OIF II (numbered just like the Superbowls). Kubic decided to have a Det from NMCB 5 relieve NMCB 40's Det in mid-December and serve as a caretaker force until at least February.

With all the work that had been done in Camp Moreell, including the recent replacement of the galley and Morale, Welfare, and Recreation (MWR tents) with super seahuts, the admiral did not want to have to start from scratch again in some nasty section of Kuwaiti desert if Seabees should be ordered to return to Iraq. Once again he tried to get the MEF and MARCENT to partner with the Seabees on this caretaker effort, but they were not interested at that time in some unassigned future mission.

"Goin' home Seabees"

The story of Seabees and the newly created MEG in OIF I ended for all practical purposes in December 2003, about fifteen months after their adventure initially began. And what a historic and heroic adventure it was. How long the Seabees and Marines would remain in Iraq was uncertain in December 2003. But history would surely record that their highly successful efforts before, during, and after the 2003 Iraq War would make an enduring positive impact in the global struggle against Islamic terrorism at the beginning of the 21st century.

In his final analysis, Kubic believed that the war to liberate Iraq from Saddam's tyranny was "all about domestic tranquility and peace with freedom, not only for the troubled Middle East, but also for the U.S. and its Coalition allies and the rest of the global community." In December 2003, Seabees everywhere were proud of their accomplishments and happy to be "goin' home Seabees." Operation Iraqi Freedom I was over, but was the Marine/Seabee mission really completed? The unfortunate answer was no. Much more building and more fighting lay ahead for the Seabees, as the Iraq War entered a new, even more vicious phase in 2004. Continued fighting in Iraq not only challenged and stretched the U.S. military to its limit, but tested American resolve as the country was faced with the horror of continued armed conflict and the heavy price of freedom.

```
FM CG I MEF
TO 30TH NAVAL CONSTRUCTION REGIMENT//CO//
INFO   LTGEN HAILSTON
       RADM KUBIC
       MGEN AMOS
       MGEN MATTIS

BT
UNCLAS PERSONAL FOR WILLIAM L. RUDICH FROM LTGEN JAMES CONWAY//
N00000//
MSGID/GENADMIN/CG I MEF FWD//
SUBJ/ BRAVO ZULU TF M//
RMKS/ BILL, AS ELEMENTS OF TF M RETURN TO PARENT COMMANDS AND REINFORCE TF C, I WISH TO EXPRESS APPRECIATION ON BEHALF OF YOUR FELLOW AMERICAN AND BRITISH TROOPS WHO CONSTITUTE I MARINE EXPEDITIONARY FORCE.  THE DETERMINATION AND SKILL THAT YOUR SAILORS DISPLAYED WAS NOTHING SHORT OF MAGNIFICENT.  THE SPEED AND PRECISION YOUR TASK FORCE DEMONSTRATED DURING THE CONSTRUCTION OF THE HUGE CONCRETE PAD AT JABER, AND SIX MABEY-JOHNSON BRIDGES REFLECTS THE HIGHEST CALIBER OR TRAINING AND TECHNICAL PROFICIENCY. YOUR UNIT'S DEDICATION AND HARD WORK KEPT LINES OF COMMUNICATIONS GOING THROUGHOUT THE THEATER.  IN SUBSEQUENT ACTIONS, TASK FORCE MIKE'S WORK TO IMPROVE SECURITY POSITIONS AND ADD TO THE QUALITY OF LIFE FOR SERVICE MEMBERS AT LSA CHESTY, SALMAN PAK AND AD DIWANIYAH WAS EXEMPLARY AND CONTRIBUTED GREATLY TO THE STABILIZATION OF THE BATTLEFIELD.  AS MANY OF YOUR SAILORS DESERVEDLY RETURN TO HOME PORT AND LOVED ONES, WE WISH FAIR WINDS AND FOLLOWING SEAS TO ALL THE GREAT MEN AND WOMEN OF TASK FORCE MIKE.  SEMPER FIDELIS, BOLD EAGLE SIX//
```

I MEF Commanding General James Conway's official note of appreciation to Commodore Rudich, Task Force Mike, and the 30th Naval Construction Regiment, May 2003.

CHAPTER

14

Aftermath – OIF Continues

Operation IRAQI FREEDOM I was winding down by the early summer of 2003, with Saddam out of power but still on the lam, along with his sons and most of his Ba'ath Party henchmen and members of his Revolutionary Command Council. Their escape to the north and west of Baghdad was an indirect consequence of Turkey's refusal to allow the U.S. Army's 4th Infantry Division to stage and attack southward from its territory. Their faces appeared on a set of "personality identification playing cards" issued by CENTCOM to help U.S. and coalition troops identify the most-wanted members of President Saddam Hussein's government, mostly high-ranking Ba'ath Party members or members of his Revolutionary Command Council. Saddam was the Ace of Spades, the so-called "death card," while Qusay was the Ace of Clubs and Uday was the Ace of Hearts.[1]

Although major combat operations had ended with the fall of Baghdad and Saddam's flight, low-grade guerilla operations against the Coalition ensued. The Defense Department and CENTCOM thought that these were orchestrated by Saddam, his sons, and his vice-president and deputy chairman of the Revolutionary Command Council, Izzat Ibrahim ad-Douri, with funding from Syria, Saudi Arabia, and from the regional jihadist network. Iraqi dissatisfaction with the short-term performance of Bremer and the CPA obviously fueled the nascent resistance movement as well.

During Rear Admiral Kubic's first visit to the emerging Civil Military Operations Center (CMOC) at the Palestine Hotel in Baghdad on April 10, 2003, he experienced a preview of the difficulties which the Coalition would face in the months ahead. As

Kubic and his security team moved in a four Humvee convoy through the streets, Vehicle #3 (Kubic's vehicle) and Vehicle #4 came under small arms fire from a roof top on their left flank. The two lead vehicles accelerated, as did Kubic's to clear the zone. As the two lead vehicles moved quickly away from Kubic, he spotted Marines in a single Humvee that was apparently broken down. It too was coming under fire. Kubic ordered his driver to turn around and go help them. As his vehicle slowed to maneuver, Kubic saw two other Marine Humvees coming to aid their fellow Marines, and judged the situation to be well in hand. So he ordered his driver to turn around again and to catch up with the convoy's lead vehicles. Kubic later remembered that his entire Tactical Movement Team (TMT) performed superbly under fire with solid communications and rapid timely action.

As his convoy approached the Palestine Hotel, it encountered barriers restricting traffic flow. A large crowd had gathered and appeared to be demonstrating in support of a particular Iraqi leader in front of foreign TV cameras. The crowd became threatening as Kubic and his team moved slowly through it, and he finally had to dismount several Marines and Seabees, including a Corpsman, Doc Reed (who carried himself like a Marine), to keep the crowd at bay.

On the return trip from the hotel to Ah Rashid Military Academy where NMCB 4 was encamped, Kubic's convoy had to move back through the demonstrators, who were becoming angrier and more disorderly by this time. Throughout the entire war he had not chambered a round in his 9mm pistol until that day. But when he heard the AK-47 rounds firing in his direction on the way into the city, he decided that discretion was the better part of valor and jacked a round into his pistol's chamber, keeping it drawn and ready to fire for the rest of the movement that day. It appeared to him that the risks of moving around the city of Baghdad were very high as compared to the cities in the Shi'ite southern regions of Iraq. Looking back on this experience, the crowd's behavior and violent passion was an ill omen that portended the trouble that would occur later on when the Sunni insurgency exploded across Iraq.

Although Qusay and Uday were killed in a shootout with U.S. Army soldiers in Mosul on July 22, 2003, the level of violence against U.S. forces escalated, with numerous small arms and sniper engagements, mortar attacks, suicide vehicle bombs, and the employment of increasingly sophisticated road-side bombs, called "Improvised Explosive Devices" or IEDs for short.[2]

Following Baghdad's fall, the Coalition had wanted to rely on the United Nations to help stabilize Iraq and rebuild and legitimize its new provisional Governing Council. However, the U.N. mission to Iraq ended after a massive cement mixer truck bomb exploded outside its Canal Hotel headquarters in Baghdad on August 19, killing the U.N.'s top envoy in Iraq, Sergio Vieira de Mello, and at least twenty-one others. A hundred more were wounded. A second truck bomb on September 22 at the hotel killed the bomber and an Iraqi policeman and wounded nineteen others. A shadowy group led by terrorist chief Abu Musab al-Zarqawi claimed responsibility for both attacks, which led to the withdrawal of some six hundred U.N. staff members from Baghdad. Employees of other aid agencies followed. The Coalition Provisional Authority, the Iraqi Governing Council, and the U.S.-led Coalition had to go it alone from this point forth.[3]

That the situation in Iraq was taking an ominous new turn became apparent on August 29, when a car bomb at the Shi'ite Imam Ali Mosque in Najaf killed eighty-two Iraqis and wounded hundreds more. Among the dead was Ayatollah Mohammad Baqer Al-Hakim, the most prominent Shi'ite cleric to have supported the Iraqi Governing Council up to that time. No one claimed responsibility, but military intelligence suspected that Zarqawi's organization was behind it. The blast revealed that ordinary Iraqis were now terrorist targets. The massive Muslim-on-Muslim attack also signaled that Zarqawi's goal was to instigate a sectarian civil war between Shi'ites and Sunnis so that Al Qaeda could overthrow the Iraqi Governing Council, take over the country, and begin building a new pan-Islamic Caliphate, with Baghdad as its capital, based on the teachings and public statements of Osama bin Laden himself. This was a grim scenario indeed, one that caused U.S. commanders many sleepless nights.[4]

On December 13, 2003, U.S. Special Forces soldiers finally located and pulled a dirty, disheveled, and disoriented Saddam out of a "spider hole" at ad-Dawr during Operation Red Dawn. He was subsequently tried by the Iraqis, condemned, and then hanged on December 30, 2006. While Ambassador Bremer's announcement that "We got him!" electrified the world and bolstered hopes that the end of the Iraqi "resistance" was near, the violence in fact got worse, as operations by Saddam Loyalists gave way to those of newly allied Sunni insurgents and Zarqawi-backed jihadists, including foreign fighters from throughout the Middle East, South Asia, the Balkans, and Chechnya.[5]

The Defense Department's occupation strategy was to minimize the U.S. "footprint" in Iraq and keep the troops mostly inside fortified compounds, except when patrolling or responding to outbreaks of violence or bombing incidents. Secretary Rumsfeld's idea was that the Iraqis should come together and handle the growing terrorist problem themselves, making it easier for U.S. and Coalition Forces to leave Iraq when the time came. Several battalions of Iraqi soldiers intended for a new national army were beginning fast track training, but as events would later play out, the overall strategy proved to be fatally flawed.[6]

The ancient Babylonian city of Fallujah in Anbar Province, located about forty-three miles west of Baghdad on the Euphrates, became the flashpoint for the Sunni insurgency, backed by Zarqawi's terrorist network. The city had never really been pacified during Operation IRAQI FREEDOM I. Several terrorist attacks and high profile incidents there involving the 82nd Airborne and then the 101st Airborne's 3rd Armored Cavalry Regiment had resulted in numerous Iraqi deaths and had heightened tensions among the city's civilian leadership, U.S. forces, the Coalition Provisional Authority, and the Iraqi Governing Council. On February 12, 2004, a convoy carrying CENTCOM commander General John Abizaid, who had succeeded General Franks on July 7, 2003, and the 82nd Airborne's Major General Charles Swannack, came under intense rocket propelled grenade fire. Nobody was injured, but eleven days later, the insurgents staged a false emergency on the outskirts of the city to draw out the Iraqi police, and then simultaneously attacked three of their stations, the mayor's office, and a civil defense base, killing seventeen police officers and releasing eighty-seven prisoners.[7]

In March, I MEF, still under Lieutenant General Conway, took over responsibility for Fallujah, just in time for the city's insurgent explosion. On March 31, Iraqi insurgents ambushed a convoy (whose "movement through zone" had not been coordinated with I MEF) carrying Blackwater security contractors Scott Helvenston, Jerko Zovko, Wesley Batalona and Michael Teague, who were protecting a food shipment for Eurest Support Services (ESS). The insurgents fired rocket propelled grenades into the vehicles, killing the four Americans. An Iraqi mob dragged their bodies out into the street, and then beat and burned them, before stringing their charred, mutilated corpses up over a nearby Euphrates bridge.[8]

Horrific images of the incident were broadcast throughout the world. An outraged and indignant American public demanded that the U.S. government avenge the men's brutal deaths. On April 1, Brigadier General Mark Kimmitt, the Deputy Director for Operations and Chief Military Spokesman for Coalition Forces in Iraq, promised an "overwhelming" response and announced that "We will pacify that city."[9]

I MEF Commander Lieutenant General Conway opposed any general attack in favor of targeted operations against the various insurgent groups operating in Fallujah and continued engagement with municipal leaders. He later told the *Washington Post* in September (after his change of command ceremony) that "We felt like we had a method that we wanted to apply to Fallujah—that we ought to probably let the situation settle before we appeared to be attacking out of revenge. Would our system have been better? Would we have been able to bring over the people of Fallujah with our methods? You'll never know that for sure, but at the time we certainly thought so." Regardless of his personal opinion, Conway had no choice. As he said, "We follow our orders. We had our say, and we understood the rationale, and we saluted smartly, and we went about the attack."[10]

On April 4, I MEF launched Operation VIGILANT RESOLVE, the largest combat operation since Saddam's downfall nearly a year before. Under the immediate command of Major General James Mattis, still commanding the 1st Marine Division, some two thousand Marines and Seabees surrounded the city and attacked along its fringes. The attacking forces tried to minimize collateral damage and the number of casualties due to political considerations, but media images leaked out showing urban fighting at its ugliest, with plenty of civilian casualties and wide-spread property destruction.[11]

Pressure soon built on the Coalition Provisional Authority from local Iraqi leaders, the Governing Council, and the U.N. for an immediate ceasefire, and on April 9, a year to the day in which Baghdad fell, Ambassador Bremer abruptly announced that the Marines would stop their attacks. This order came just as I MEF was preparing for a pre-dawn attack on the last six hundred insurgents who were dug in near the bridge where the bodies of the Blackwater employees had been hung. This final assault was designed to complete the takedown of the insurgents and properly liberate Fallujah. Bremer's tactical pause rationale, as conveyed personally to the I MEF leadership in Fallujah by General Abizaid on Good Friday, 2004, was that the ceasefire would allow time for negotiations among the Iraqi Governing Council, insurgents, and city spokespersons. Bremer and Abizaid also recognized that a halt in operations would allow the delivery of supplies to the beleaguered residents of the city.[12]

Operation VIGILANT RESOLVE formally ended on April 28 with an agreement that Fallujah's population would keep the insurgents out of the city. The Coalition hastily organized and armed a so-called Fallujah Brigade of Iraqi (Sunni) national troops to take over patrol and security duties from the Marines. This Iraqi outfit proved to be a disaster, with its senior officers holding close ties to the former Ba'athist regime, and its troops actively sympathizing and abetting the enemy. After it imploded and was formally disbanded in September, its men surrendered their weapons, vehicles, and radios to the insurgents and in many cases joined their ranks against the Coalition.[13]

Despite his superb leadership throughout the harsh and chaotic First Battle of Fallujah, Conway was stunned by this all-around sorry episode. After his change of command, he bluntly told reporters that "When you order elements of a Marine division to attack a city, you really need to understand what the consequences of that are going to be and not perhaps vacillate in the middle of something like that. Once you commit, you got to stay committed."[14]

Noting that six Marines were killed and six wounded in the first three days of fighting in Fallujah, he added that "We were quite happy with the progress of the attack on the city. We thought we were sparing civilian lives everywhere and anywhere that availed itself to us. We thought we were going to be done in a few days. That's the Monday morning quarterbacking."

Although a stand off ensued, the end result was that the insurgents still controlled the city and the Marines and Seabees were justifiably upset (pissed off would be a better descriptor). Bremer's Coalition Provisional Authority and the Iraqi Governing Council looked weak, and Zarqawi and his Al Qaeda buddies had a sanctuary city from which to operate against U.S. and Coalition forces. Muslim passions were enflamed even further by the unfortunate Abu Ghraib scandal, which broke on April 28 just as Operation VIGILANT RESOLVE concluded. As a result of all of this, anti-Coalition terrorism spiraled out of control, and the "Sunni Triangle" came to be a deadly shooting gallery for American troops trying to hold the line against the Sunni-Al Qaeda alliance.

To add insult to injury, the Shi'ites in the south suddenly erupted into violence as well while the Marines were assaulting Fallujah, with the emergence of Muqtada al-Sadr and his Mahdi Army. This insurgent militia spearheaded Shi'ite attacks in An Najaf, Al Kufa, Al Kut, Karbala, and Sadr City in Baghdad throughout April and May. By early summer of 2004, Iraq looked like it was coming apart at its seams, even as the Coalition Provisional Authority formally transferred limited sovereignty to the Iraqi Interim Government on June 28. At that point, Bremer departed the country, leaving it in the hands of Prime Minister Iyad Allawi. Although the U.S. suggested that handing Iraq back over to the Iraqis might be the beginning of the end of the insurgency, in reality it was only the beginning of the violence that would consume the country in the coming years.[15]

The Seabees Return to Iraq

Just prior to the First Battle of Fallujah, the Seabees redeployed into the growing chaos of Iraq alongside I MEF as part of Operation IRAQI FREEDOM II. They would be encamped in the dangerous Anbar province this time, squarely in the thick of the action. The Operation IRAQI FREEDOM II deployments had begun in March 2004 with Seabees conducting Reception, Staging, Onward Movement, and Integration (RSO&I) from Camp Moreell in Kuwait and the Marines landing in a nasty piece of desert at rundown Camp Victory about fifteen minutes down the road from Camp Moreell. The MEG Advance Party had again returned to Kuwait, and the new deputy of I MEG, Commodore Mark Handley, and Rear Admiral Kubic had already made separate planning trips into Iraq. They learned that their previous MEG Task Force Endurance was appropriately named as they were now supporting the 82nd Airborne Division, in what was soon to be the MEF's new Area of Responsibility. The cycle started once again, and Seabees would now relieve their own former Task Force Endurance. The plan was for the Seabees to support Operation IRAQI FREEDOM II with two six-month deployments, followed by Operation IRAQI FREEDOM III, yet to be planned.[16]

Thus, a scaled down MEG once again assumed an active role in providing Engineer support for I MEF during its operations in and around Fallujah and throughout Al Anbar Province. Although, Seabees had emerged mostly unscathed from Operation IRAQI FREEDOM I, this time they would incur their first combat casualties due to hostile action since the Vietnam War during operations that took place in April and May, immediately following the First Battle of Fallujah.

The 1st Naval Construction Division had learned as early as the fall of 2003 that Seabees and the MEG would be needed again in Iraq. It soon became clear that I MEF would be deploying again to relieve the U.S. Army's 82nd Airborne Division with a mission to win over or snuff out the nascent insurgency in Al Anbar. As Kubic met with his planning staff, he told them that they needed to have a somewhat different focus in OIF II, based on what he had observed during his follow-up reconnaissance trips to Iraq. Although schools were important, it was clear to him that this time the Seabees did not need to target their CMO efforts on the children of Iraq, but rather on the youth, particularly the young men of high school and post-high school age who were being recruited into the insurgency.

Instead of having Seabees rehabilitating and building new facilities, like schools and clinics, Kubic believed that they needed to figure out how to get young Iraqis away from the troublemakers and into respectable trades so that they could build the schools and clinics in their own areas. The Seabees and Marines therefore established an Iraqi Construction Apprentice Program (ICAP) and lined up projects, with support from the Coalition Provisional Authority, valued at $17,000,000 to get ICAP and other CMO work underway. This program provided classroom and on-the-job training for young Iraqis, ages fourteen to nineteen, with the Seabees and Iraqi Engineer translators serving as instructors. The MEG provided the apprentices with a stipend of $5.00 per day while they learned a trade and earned new respect at home as they helped support their brothers and sisters, often with one or both parents missing from the household. The Iraqi Construction Apprentice Program was highly successful and was showcased in several CNN broadcasts highlighting the positive progress being made by Seabees and Marines in winning the hearts and minds of Iraqi youth and their families.[17]

I MEF was supposed to relieve the 82nd Airborne on or about April 6. But as previously described, the Marines ended up relieving the Army in March, ten to fourteen days earlier than planned. The MEG Seabees knew that work needed to be done in Fallujah to rid it of the insurgency. During the initial sixty days of their second deployment to Iraq, they had a deliberate plan to win the hearts and minds of the people in Fallujah through Marine Civil Affairs and Seabee construction, all of which had effectively stopped in the city by that point. But unfortunately the MEG did not get a chance to do that or even to assemble its full force structure before all hell broke loose. The killings of the Blackwater contractors upset the American public and effectively set aside I MEF's deliberate planning cycle which was designed to "prep the battlefield." Deliberate plans gave way quickly to immediate realities when CENTCOM ordered the Marines and Seabees to attack the city even though I MEF had not completed battlespace shaping, intelligence gathering, and CMO preparation. "No one was thinking about rebuilding at this point," Kubic recalled, "we were all going in now to wreck the place and destroy the bad guys."

As Operation IRAQI FREEDOM II kicked off, Marines and Seabees found that it was much more difficult to maneuver safely by vehicle given the increased insurgent threat. During the aftermath of Operation Iraqi Freedom I, they could easily move with three or four "soft" Humvees with two crew-served weapons. In Operation IRAQI FREEDOM II though, they needed at least six Humvees with at least four crew-served weapons for each movement. The insurgents were massing and ambushing in platoon size formations, and the Seabees could not afford to get overwhelmed. They also began to install their own armor plating (which the 1st Naval Construction Division had wisely ordered and shipped to Camp Moreell even before Seabees started to re-deploy) to harden their Humvees against IEDs. Also, the Division quickly ordered newly available "up-armor kits" to retrofit complete vehicles into hardened Humvees while stateside assembly lines were gearing up to build hardened Humvees from scratch to meet the ever growing IED threat. So, the 1st Naval Construction Division and the MEG quickly had to change and transform how Seabees were working and moving, how they were outfitting, and how they were training.

To meet the threat, the Seabees created larger, harder and more heavily armed Tactical Movement Teams (TMTs), which included at least six Humvees, four of which were crew-served "gun-trucks" (similar in concept to those previously employed with great success in Vietnam). Tactical Movement Teams were manned by twenty-four Seabees and could move both troops and convoys with greater fire power and more armor to counter the growing threat. The Tactical Movement Teams permitted a great deal of flexibility since the Seabees could inter-disperse long-haul trucks within them. As a result of this increased tactical capability, Seabees were able to continue to support their own logistics movements, and not place any additional force protection demands upon the already over taxed Marines whom they were there to support.

During this time, the Seabees also realized that they had to build more hardened facilities on their bases due to the increasing frequency of mortar attacks. So they developed what was ultimately called a Tactical Construction Team. The first such team was led by one of the Seabee Jedi from Operation IRAQI FREEDOM I, Senior Chief James P. Moran of NMCB 74. Moran and his Seabees actually went in alongside the attacking Marine force on the initial assault into Fallujah to establish hardened security strong points. Then, in a running day-long gun battle, this team established the initial cordon berm around the southeast corridor of Fallujah while the full assault was on-going.

I MEF had tasked the Seabees to work directly with the Marines to seal the southeast corner of Fallujah, which was a big stretch of open desert that needed to be enclosed with a three-kilometer berm. The Seabees were supposed to do half, and the Marine Engineers were supposed to do the other half. But as often happens in combat, the Marines were siphoned off into another area, so in the finest "We Build! We Fight!" tradition of the Seabees, Moran's Tactical Construction Team spent all day with their dozers building the berm, while their gun truck Humvees, armed with .50 caliber machine guns and MK-19 grenade launchers, engaged in a running battle with the insurgents, defending the job site without any tactical support from the Marines. A Seabee took a minor hit as the bullets started flying, but a corpsman sewed him up right there on the spot and he went back to work. This Seabee Tactical Construction Team ultimately completed the entire three-kilometer cordon itself, returning back to camp after dusk. Both Senior Chief Moran and Marine Staff Sergeant Plaster (Moran's tactical commander) won Bronze Stars with Combat "V"s for their leadership under fire that day.

Marines also came under heavy attacks in their combat outposts throughout Al Anbar Province. They needed hardened facilities just to eat and sleep safely, especially in a place like Hussaybah on the Syrian border, which was subjected to continuous rocket and mortar assault, including Chinese air burst rockets. Unfortunately, construction materials required to build proper hardened structures were in short supply, so the Seabees had to make do with what they had, much as NASA's engineers had to do during the Apollo 13 rescue. The MEG future ops team went through a couple of different designs, with reach back support from the Naval Facility Engineering Command's Atlantic Division (LANTDIV) to figure out how to build large hardened shelters using only HESCO (Hercules Engineering Solutions Consortium) barriers, sand bags, plywood, 2x4 and 4x4 lumber, and nails – lots of nails.

The ultimate solution revolved around constructing composite, built-up foundation plates, columns, beams and roof panels, all with available lumber and lots of nails. After the MEG finalized a rudimentary design, the Seabees started prefabrication work in Fallujah and then hauled the components to the Marine outposts where hardened facilities were needed the most. Until the MEG was able to get sufficient nail guns shipped into Iraq, every available Seabee was hammering day and night (some using both hands and two hammers) to get the necessary components fabricated so that the hardened shelters so desperately needed by the Marines could be constructed.

During the sudden Fallujah ceasefire imposed on April 9, 2004, a large number of terrorists and foreign fighters escaped from the city. The MEG quickly started seeing IED and mortar attacks all along the Euphrates River "rat line," running from Fallujah the whole way up to Hussaybah on the Syrian border. But the MEG still had to move troops and supplies through the danger zone so that it could continue contingency construction to improve force protection and the quality of life for the relatively isolated Marines.

Soon after the ceasefire, I MEF gave the Seabees a mission to build very heavily fortified positions right along the Syrian border to support the 3rd Battalion of the 7th Marines, commanded by Lieutenant Colonel Matt Lopez, which was based there right astride the border. The Seabees accordingly had to haul a great deal of Class IV material up to the new job sites. They also had a similar mission to support the Special Forces in Balad and in northern Iraq and in other remote places, all of whom were trying to stem the flow of foreign fighters into Iraq.

To undertake the new missions, Rear Admiral Kubic created two new MEG task forces. The first was Task Force Sierra, (for sustainment construction in Balad), and the second was Task Force Tango (for transition in Ramadi). Kubic's concept for Ramadi was that Task Force Tango would ultimately transition to contractor and Iraqi labor as Seabees and Marines gradually pulled out of a stabilized Al Anbar Province. Kubic also brought Task Force Charlie back, as the MEG's third task force, since the Seabees had started to do heavier construction, alongside a newly deployed U.S. Army battalion, a newly deployed U.S. Army engineer battalion from the

278th Armored Cavalry Regiment of the Tennessee National Guard (renamed the 278th Regimental Combat Team due to its task organized mission).

Hallowed Ground

Reserve NMCB 14, out of Jacksonville, Florida, comprised the main element of Task Force Tango and worked out of Base Junction City at Ramadi in the heart of the Sunni Triangle. Led by Commander John D. Prien, the battalion had been mobilized in March to work alongside NMCBs 5 and 74 on quality-of-life projects, such as building schools and clinics and teaching Iraqis the construction trade. Only two-weeks into its first combat call-up since World War II, NMCB 14 had undergone extra training in Gulfport and Kuwait to acquaint the unit's men and women with the new Seabee gun truck and convoy tactics. The Seabees did not yet have the necessary kits to upgrade the armor on their Humvees, but they did have a stock of plate steel and they used it to craft their own armor. They reinforced the turrets, doors, and floor panels as their first priority to get a number of up-armored Humvees ready for action.

On Friday, April 30, NMCB 14's Tactical Movement Team was returning from an important mission, having hauled a load of building materials up to its Det at Hussaybah Base where Marines were being pelted with indirect fire right on the Syrian border. It was a very urgent situation since heavy combat was ongoing at Hussaybah and the Marines were taking a lot of fire. Marines camped there had no safe place to sleep or eat, so the plan was to build hardened shelters for them. NMCB 14's logistics convoy mission to supply construction materials was very dangerous, and was protected with twelve Humvees, and numerous crew-served weapons. On its way back to Ramadi, the convoy had a serious incident along the highway in which an Iraqi vehicle made a hostile run at it as it entered a traffic circle. The Iraqi vehicle veered away at the last second and did not attack. But the encounter caused a delay as the convoy's officers and chiefs assessed the situation and regrouped.

Now traveling just after dusk because of the delay, the convoy reached the southeast side of the ancient Sumerian town of Hit. There, insurgents ambushed it with a very complex IED attack, employing new tactics, including what appeared to be vehicle mounted or otherwise elevated IEDs. Several Seabees were wounded, and sadly, two were killed in action, Hull Technician 2nd Class Jason B. Dwelley and Equipment Operator 3rd Class Christopher Dickerson, who were riding in the first two vehicles of the convoy. Equipment Operator 3rd Class Dickerson, although mortally wounded while driving vehicle #2, managed to maneuver his Humvee so that his .50 caliber machine gunner, Construction Mechanic 3rd Class Michael Rambo, could engage and take out the insurgent vehicle that appeared to have initiated the attack.

Farther down the road, another IED struck the convoy and wounded additional Seabees but without any further KIAs. The convoy finally made it back to Ramadi, but its loss of Dwelley and Dickerson was tragic and profoundly affected every Seabee deployed to Iraq and elsewhere around the world. "We had lost two Seabee brothers to a vicious and cunning enemy," Kubic lamented. In fact, those two Seabees were the first to be killed in action by a hostile force since the Vietnam War. "NMCB 14 was a very close knit unit, so the deaths were very traumatic for these Seabees," Kubic later noted.

Unfortunately, this was not the end of NMCB 14's trauma. Kubic had visited the base in Ramadi before, but had not been there since NMCB 14 had arrived in its entirety. As the double-hatted MEG/1st Naval Construction Division commander, he had been concerned that their tasking was being changed locally, and so he had preplanned a routine visit with them on May 2 to review their workload and make sure they were getting properly "snapped in" to this deployment. After the attack on April 30, 2004, the admiral felt that it was even more important for him to meet with NMCB 14's leadership and select members of the convoy to understand what exactly had happened, and what new tactics were being employed by the enemy to place and detonate what appeared to be elevated or vehicle mounted IEDs. So, on Saturday night, May 1, Kubic flew into the Marine Division headquarters at Blue Diamond directly across the Euphrates River from Base Junction City.

After some meetings on Sunday morning and a quick stop for Catholic Mass, he was to be picked up around noon by a NMCB 14 security convoy. This Tactical Movement Team had to drive out of its camp, cross a bridge, enter the Marine headquarters through another gate, and then come back to the Seabee camp. They had to make a short, fifteen to twenty minute combat patrol to reach Kubic's location, and then again to return to their camp across the river. As it turned out, these were the same Seabees who had been attacked on April 30th at Hit. Kubic's sense was they "felt this short patrol was the equivalent of getting back up on a horse that had just thrown them."

The convoy arrived about thirty to forty minutes late. Rather than just sending the normal five or six-vehicle Tactical Movement Team that would usually be required to move passengers this short distance, Kubic was surprised to see that NMCB 14 had assembled a double team with ten Humvees. Because of the April 30 IED attacks, they were all eager to go back out as a group. As they pulled into Blue Diamond, Kubic observed that they all appeared strong and confident. Concerned about the size of the convoy, but not wanting to dash the Seabees' renewed confidence, he quietly pulled aside the MEG security officer, Master Gunnery Sergeant Bill Higson, and told him that he felt that the convoy was too large. The admiral then asked Higson to work quietly with the team's leadership and to split the group into two movements for the return trip. That way, the Tactical Movement Team would present a lower profile to anyone who was watching.

The reduced Tactical Movement Team escorted Kubic safely to Base Junction City, following the first half of the now-split convoy at a safe distance. Once they were safely back in the NMCB 14 equipment yard, the Tactical Movement Team members all relaxed and conducted their normal post-convoy routine. They began cleaning their vehicles, turning in their crew served weapons, stowing their gear, and receiving instructions for the remainder of the day. There was relief in the air, and the team members congratulated themselves with a lot of good-natured "smokin' and jokin'" talk as they went about their routine "end of convoy" tasks. By all accounts, they were feeling pretty good about themselves because they had gone back "outside the wire," pulled together as a team, and successfully completed their mission.

Commander Prien met Rear Admiral Kubic near the NMCB 14 quarterdeck building. Kubic noted that Prien was not wearing his flak vest and Kevlar helmet, and asked him about it. Prien replied that Base Junction City had not received indirect fire in three weeks, and that its commander, an Army Colonel, had authorized all troops to "drop their load" so they could relax a bit while they were "inside the wire." Kubic later remembered that he had his doubts about the wisdom of shedding protective gear. But against his better judgment, he complied with base policy and dropped his load too.

Commander Prien wanted to brief Kubic immediately on what he and his staff knew about the IED attack. First though, Kubic wanted to inspect the vehicles which were damaged by the IEDs since they were sitting nearby in the yard. Kubic was particularly interested in seeing where the shrapnel had entered and where the targeted Seabees were sitting, particularly those who were killed and wounded, so he could begin to understand and visualize how the unusual attack materialized and what new enemy tactics may have been used. He had a lot of questions to answer because the MEG needed to provide intelligence back to the MEF so that the MEF G2 could warn the Marines and the Army about these new tactics, and the possibility of similar attacks elsewhere.

After Kubic inspected the first damaged vehicle, and while he was examining the second vehicle, disaster struck. Large 120mm mortar rounds suddenly started landing in and around the compound. The first mortar landed outside the berm that was around the Seabee Camp, but the second one was a direct hit, exploding near a group of convoy members. These Seabees were still finishing their post convoy tasks and their Chief had gathered them together a few minutes earlier simply to tell them, "Hey, you guys finish up what you're doing and then you're off until 1630." That was the designated time when Kubic was supposed to meet and speak with all the Seabees assigned to Ramadi at a secure in-door location.

Specifically, the second 120mm round landed about seven meters from the edge of the ongoing Seabee huddle (and about sixty to seventy meters from where Kubic was inspecting the blast-damaged Humvee), killing five and wounding twenty-eight others, with varying degrees of severity. Two more mortar rounds landed nearby a few seconds later with one sounding more like a dud, and the attack ended as suddenly as it had begun. The five Seabees who were killed that day in the Alfa yard were Equipment Operator 2nd Class Trace Dossett, Builder 2nd Class Michael Anderson, Steelworker 3rd Class Ronald Ginther, Builder 2nd Class Robert Jenkins, and Construction Mechanic 2nd Class Scott McHugh.

After the second mortar landed, Kubic yelled for a Corpsman, and several Seabees, including Lieutenant Matt Reithmiller and Master Gunnery Sergeant Higson, ran toward the impact point to offer assistance just as the third and fourth mortars hit. Kubic took cover for a few seconds, and then sprinted to the quarterdeck to notify the Battalion Command Operations Center and to ensure that ambulances were called. Then he returned outside to help tend to the wounded.

Corpsmen and medics converged on the scene. The lightly wounded Seabees helped their more severely wounded comrades, while others reacted quickly to provide combat life saver assistance and to move the casualties about two hundred meters to the I MEF medical company. Kubic and the NMCB 14 Seabees spent the rest of the day dealing with the casualties and the ramifications of the attacks. As Kubic later recalled, the Navy doctors, nurses, and corpsmen responded with professional valor as they dealt quickly with an overwhelming mass casualty situation, and Chaplain Devine (the Catholic priest who had just said Mass at Camp Blue Diamond earlier that morning) was there to comfort them all.

A major frustration was the lack of information on the medical status of the wounded evacuees once they left Ramadi. This was due to a recent Navy determination that medical information could not be released due to privacy considerations unless authorized by the wounded member. This created unnecessary trauma for family members who had to wait too long to learn about the status of the severely wounded Seabees who could not speak to provide such authorization. But, the joint medical system did provide superb care and swift medical action. The wounded survivors were quickly airlifted out of Ramadi and then out of Iraq, and after a brief stopover in Germany, they returned home for further treatment and a necessary rest and recovery period. They were all awarded Purple Hearts in a ceremony held at Naval Air Station Jacksonville on July 11, and most returned to duty.[18]

Altogether, seven Seabees died and over thirty were wounded on April 30 and May 2. Also, an Army Captain was KIA during the mortar attack and several other Soldiers were wounded. A follow-up analysis revealed that there were two dispersed 120 mm mortars firing from six-kilometer range, well beyond the then-focus of the Army's counter-battery radar which was set at about 1,500 meters based upon best available threat intelligence at that time. Clearly these were skilled Iraqi mortar men employing new tactics and aiming at the large Dining Facility. Range and the wind caused them to miss their target, with one stray round landing in the Alfa yard just as the Tactical Movement Team was called together to be dismissed. A direct hit on the Dining Facility would have caused even greater casualties. A couple of weeks later, Kubic heard that Navy SEALs ultimately settled the score with the two mortar men who had attacked the Seabees at Ramadi. He was also gratified to learn that the one attacker who survived his encounter with the SEALs was placed in a holding cell previously constructed by Seabees.

These attacks rank among the most devastating events in Seabee history. The last time Seabees had suffered mass casualties was at Phubai in Vietnam, where six Seabees were killed in a single day. NCB 133's disastrous landing on Iwo Jima in February 1945 though is perhaps most analogous to the May 2, 2004 Ramadi attack, in terms of total casualties and psychological impact. Like NCB 133 at Iwo Jima, the dual Iraqi attacks in the Sunni Triangle had bloodied and stunned NMCB 14, and left many Seabees questioning what went wrong.

On May 8, Seabees from NMCB 5 and 74 and the MEG command element gathered at Camp Fallujah to honor the fallen Seabees. Seven M-16 assault rifles were carefully placed, muzzle down, on the floor of the chapel, each accompanied by a pair of desert boots and topped with a Kevlar helmet. Tools commonly used by Seabees were laid by the boots. Commodore Mark Handley led the memorial service, telling the group that "These seven Seabees who lost their lives here in Iraq were directly contributing to improving the conditions for sustained peace. They served us proudly and with distinction, and they have built upon the Seabee legacy, which we all humbly enjoy." The solemn service ended when all the attending Seabees donned their covers and saluted their fallen comrades as Taps mournfully played in the chapel. Later in the day, NMCB 14 held a separate service at Base Junction City.[19]

Compounding the tragedy were a series of grossly misinformed news reports, originating from a *Miami Herald* reporter imbedded with the Marines, who wrote the first story about the mortar attack. She incorrectly reported that the Seabees had just "mustered in the yard of a Marine base for a visiting admiral." Her story was distributed on the wire service and other newspapers soon perpetuated the false information about what had happened. Due to a variety of media ground rule violations, this reporter subsequently had her credentials revoked and lost her imbed status with the Marines.[20]

The damage had been done though. Shortly thereafter, self-styled veterans' activist and muckraking columnist Colonel David H. Hackworth picked up on the story and published two incendiary articles on the popular websites *Military.com* and *DefenseWatch*. In his columns, Hackworth stretched and twisted the original incorrect story even farther, taking the allegations to the height of absurdity. He outlandishly claimed that just before the mortar attack Rear Admiral Kubic had ordered an assembly in the open area for a "pep talk," that Kubic had forced the Seabees to act as his personal "houseboys" during his "self-serving" trips, and that Kubic had awarded himself a bronze star for hunkering "down in the bunker with his staff" during a SCUD attack. Hackworth even accused Kubic of shipping a "fancy bar" back to the states from Fallujah as a "souvenir." None of the accusations were true, but that did not stop Hackworth from demanding a court-martial (and presumably a firing squad) for the admiral.[21]

Hackworth's sensationalism generated a fire storm, and the 1st Naval Construction Division had to answer a series of direct questions from the CNO concerning Hackworth's spurious allegations. Meanwhile, several NMCB 14 Seabees were appalled at Hackworth's columns. One of them, a Chief Yeoman (SCW/AW) who served as NMCB 14's acting administrative officer, posted a passionate defense to *Leatherneck*'s online forum that tried to set the record straight. She wrote:

> After reading Col. David Hackworth's column on the Seabee deaths, it is apparent to those of us who were there that Col. Hackworth has taken what is obviously scuttlebutt regarding the mortar attack on NMCB 14 and published it as gospel without reaching out to the command to verify before publishing. The truth is difficult enough for us to deal with, and we certainly do not need to continuously dispel myths.[22]

The Chief then demolished Hackworth's claims, one by one, citing a litany of facts about the mortar attack that were matter of public record and could not be disputed. Concerning the alleged "assembly" that Kubic supposedly called, she categorically stated that:

> At the time of the mortar attack, our convoy had just returned from a mission, and they were just plainly and simply in the wrong place at the wrong time. No members of the battalion were in the area unless they had a routine work-related reason to be there, and no one was ordered to report to the area, either by Adm. Kubic or anyone in the battalion for any reason at all…. Coincidentally, Adm. Kubic was in the same equipment yard inspecting vehicles that had been

damaged in an ambush two days earlier. He most likely didn't even acknowledge, let alone speak to, the troops who were out there.

She concluded her rebuttal to Hackworth with a plea:

> Inaccurate reporting and false accusations that the members were not properly trained or equipped or that the command or our superiors made poor or self-serving decisions does not contribute to anything good for us. We have enough to deal with for the rest of our lives. Please do not continue to cite us, and this most painful and horrific event in any agenda against Adm. Kubic.

Unfortunately, because of *Leatherneck.com*'s more limited audience, the Chief's frank and well informed open letter to Hackworth was not as widely read as his columns were, and it was soon buried deep under subsequent postings on the *Leatherneck* forum.

An "After Action Report on the Task Force Tango Indirect Fire Attack," filed by Investigative Officer Lieutenant Colonel T.J. Barrett (USMCR), had confirmed the Chief Yeoman's account of what happened. But the media chose not to follow-up and remained unaware of Barrett's investigation and his findings. In May 2005, Hackworth himself died of bladder cancer, leaving his allegations hanging out on the world-wide web. To spare NMCB 14 any further pain though, Rear Admiral Kubic chose not to defend himself publicly at the time, leaving behind an ugly perception in the minds of many that Hackworth was reporting the truth, the actual facts notwithstanding.[23]

Despite the twin attacks and mass casualties, and the ensuing Hackworth controversy, NMCB 14 rebounded and, along with all other Seabee battalions deployed to Iraq, quickly adapted to this new, more dangerous insurgency. NMCB 14 completed its deployment in November, and relinquished Seabee construction responsibilities to NMCB 23, headquartered at Fort Belvoir, Virginia. During the ceremony, Commander Prien told the subdued audience that "This is an historic day, as this is the first time in the annals of Seabee history that one Navy Reserve Seabee Battalion has relieved another Navy Reserve Seabee Battalion in a combat theater." Prien spoke of the seven NMCB 14 members killed earlier in their deployment and of how Seabees had turned tragedy into triumph by dedicating their sweat, ideas and project efforts to fallen

Seabee comrades. "This camp is hallowed ground, where Seabee blood has been spilled for the cause of freedom and the ongoing fight against terrorism," said Prien.[24]

The MEG learned many lessons from the attacks on NMCB 14. From that point forth, Seabees could not go out into the Iraqi communities without fear of drawing attacks, even to work with their apprentices and contractors. So the Seabees focused more on the contract work outside the gate, and executed a very significant external contracting program, superbly managed by the Naval Facilities Engineering Command's (NAVFAC's) Reserve Officer in Charge of Construction (OICC) Det. The Seabees continued to train people on the bases, worked to improve quality of life and force protection, and provided construction and convoys outside the wire as required, all the while continuously hardening existing vehicles and procuring the latest up-armored vehicles as they came off the assembly line.

Can Do — for the Long Haul

By late-2004, Seabees were clearly in Iraq for the long haul. And once again, it was time to plan offensive combat operations with I MEF. By November 2004, the Bush Administration finally decided that enough was enough in Fallujah, and it was now time to finish the job that was started and then aborted in April. Beginning on November 7, 2004 (three days after Bush won re-election to a second term), Operation PHANTOM FURY engulfed the city. Backed by the U.S.1st Cavalry and 1st Infantry Divisions, the British Black Watch Battalion, the Iraqi 36th Commando Battalion, and Special Forces units, I MEF attacked the thousands of insurgents and terrorists who had reinforced the remaining insurgents from the April battle and who had holed up in Fallujah in what was called the "heaviest urban combat since the Battle of Hue City in Vietnam." This time, the gloves were off, and led by the ruthlessly efficient Major General Mattis, the Marines slugged it out block by block, house by house. The worst was over in about two weeks, but fighting continued into December, with the Marines pulling back from the inner city in January 2005. After all was said and done, much of the city was leveled, but the insurgents were mostly wiped out. Seabee teams were soon in the city assessing the damage to its infrastructure and restoring critical services such as water and power.[25]

In January, after the fighting ended, the MEG participated in the construction of polling places in Anbar and the establishment of the I MEF Provisional Security Battalion, manned by more than three hundred MEG Seabees and Marines supporting the historic legislative elections that took place on January 30, 2005 with the Iraqi people choosing representatives for the newly-formed 275-member Iraqi National Assembly.[26]

Despite the election and formation of a new Iraqi government, violence throughout the country escalated even further, with operatives from the Al Quds Force of the Iranian Revolutionary Guards taking the field in support of Al-Sadr's Shi'ite Mahdi Army and adding to the general mayhem. U.S. casualties soared to over four thousand killed and 30,000 wounded over the next three years, as a vicious civil war gripped the country with at least five different competing parties (the U.S.-led Coalition and Iraqi National Government, the Sunni Insurgents, the Mahdi Army, the Iranian Revolutionary Guards, and Al Qaeda, among others) struggling for supremacy. After a wild rampage of kidnappings, torture, beheadings, car bombings, and assassinations, Zarqawi himself was finally tracked down and killed on June 7, 2006 by U.S. Special Forces, working in conjunction with Jordanian Intelligence and the U.S. Air Force.[27]

Still, the violence continued unabated until late 2006. Following the takeover of Congress by anti-war Democrats during mid-term elections, President Bush accepted Secretary Rumsfeld's resignation and changed the U.S. strategy in Iraq from one focused on maintaining a minimal American "footprint" to one based on a significant five brigade "surge" of U.S. troops into the country to restore security and to give the Iraqis enough breathing space to pull their country together. The "surge strategy" was based upon "clear, hold, and build" concepts first developed by U.S. Army Colonel Herbert R. McMaster, commanding the 3rd Armored Cavalry Regiment at Tal Afar in 2005, and then refined and adopted on a country-wide scale by Lieutenant General David Petraeus, who had commanded the 101st Airborne during Operation IRAQI FREEDOM I and had gone on to publish a cutting-edge counterinsurgency manual with Marine General James Amos in December 2006. The "Surge" depended upon the prior "awakening" and cooperation of formerly hostile Sunni tribes (which had become disgusted with Zarqawi's brutal methods and indiscriminate attacks on Muslims) and resulted in a flurry of captures and killings of large numbers of terrorists, insurgents, foreign fighters, and Iranian infiltrators.[28]

As of this writing (April 2009), General Petraeus' Surge is over and violence in Iraq has plummeted since 2007. The "end" of the

Global War on Terrorism, a term recently rejected by the Obama Administration in favor of the more ambiguous and politically correct 'Overseas Contingency Operation,' is still not in sight. And Soldiers, Marines and Seabees are still on the ground in Iraq and Afghanistan and elsewhere in the world, as they continue with steadfast resolve and 'Can Do!' spirit to build and to fight for peace with freedom.[29]

Postscript

Rear Admiral Chuck Kubic joined the retired list of the U.S. Navy as of February 1, 2005. On March 11, 2005, nearly two years after crossing the line of departure into Iraq, I MEG officially stood down as an active combat command element, and was relieved by the 30th Naval Construction Regiment in a transfer of authority ceremony in western Iraq. After retiring from the Navy, Kubic accepted a position as President of ECC International, where he was based in Virginia Beach but deployed to Iraq as a civilian construction contractor, working once again in Al Anbar as well as other parts of Iraq until May 2006.[30]

Later, Kubic reflected on the Seabees and their tremendous service during the Iraq War from 2002 through 2004. He wrote:

> I am especially proud of the Seabees who marched into harms way arm in arm with the Marine Corps during Operation Iraqi Freedom, as well as all the Seabees and civilians in the rear who supported them every step of the way. We are all indebted to the heroic service of the entire Seabee team, and we must never forget those who were severely wounded and those who paid the ultimate sacrifice so that others could live as free men and women.
>
> These OIF Seabees raised the bar set by their WW II Grandfathers and their Vietnam War Fathers. By their courageous work, they clearly honored those who have come before and set new standards for those who come after. As bridges to Baghdad were built physically across rivers and canals and inter-personally with Iraqi citizens, I never doubted they would meet my Commander's intent, stated simply: "Seabees will always succeed ... always!" Their Can Do legends are now a significant part of Seabee history, and their stories should be told with intense pride for decades to come.

Closing Thoughts

by
Rear Admiral Chuck Kubic, CEC, USN (Retired)

As I look back from the present day, the fast pace flow of interrelated events from 9/11 through the end of Operation IRAQI FREEDOM gives me pause for reflection. I am struck by the underlying complexity of the planning required to execute what was really a fairly simple strategic plan to strike back at terrorist sanctuaries, bring down the tyrannical regime of Saddam Hussein, and put Iraqis to work rebuilding their nation. I am also humbled by the dedication and sheer courage of the Seabees, Marines and Soldiers with whom I had the privilege to serve during these defining early years in the Global War on Terrorism. Their fathers and grandfathers from the World War II "greatest generation" should be justly proud of these equally great American warriors.

The Plan

Just to recap, the Operations Plan (OPLAN) for Operation IRAQI FREEDOM was truly innovative, and its success depended upon the full integration of superior intelligence (Information Operations), fast, lethal air/ground combat (Kinetic Operations), and large scale humanitarian construction (Civil Military Operations).
- Phase I of the Iraq OPLAN was focused on peacetime stabilization and containment of Iraq.
- Phase II addressed the buildup of forces and Information Operations (IO) prior to attack.
- Phase III was the quick and violent Kinetic Operations (KO) from the line of departure at the Kuwait-Iraq border to the Diyala River on the outskirts of Baghdad.
- Phase IVA was the take down of Baghdad.
- Finally, Phase IVB was the period of Civil Military Operations (CMO) throughout Iraq conducted by military forces in advance of full control by civilian leadership, i.e., American and then Iraqi leaders together with their staffs and contractors.

Phase IV B was initially planned to be a 120-day transition period subsequent to Kinetic Ops, with Civil Military Operations running from about G+30 to G+150. Throughout the phases of the war and the interplay of IO/KO/CMO, Engineers of all services played a key role. Despite the often-expressed attitude of some senior military leaders that "we are war fighters, not nation builders," nation building through CMO work is an essential and unavoidable part of the military's modern-day stabilization mission following a major conflict. In many respects, today's military should just accept this new reality, and train and equip for it just as thoroughly as it trains for kinetic warfare.

As stated earlier, Operation IRAQI FREEDOM was planned and fought based upon the innovative integration of Information Operations, Kinetic Operations, and Civil Military Operations. There was no desire by coalition forces to inflict unnecessary causalities or damage upon the Iraqi people during KO. Thus, commencing CMO even before we crossed the Tigris by employing U.S. troops, especially Engineers, was key to smooth and rapid transition to a secure environment in which a fledgling democracy and free enterprise could flourish.

Civil Military Operations

To complete the four-phase strategy for Operation IRAQI FREEDOM, U.S. Engineer troops were called upon to conduct a short period of Civil Military Operations that was intended to transition within four to six months into a civilian contractor effort. Our plan reflected the fact that our Nation could not afford to have its limited combat forces linked to long term nation building. A key lesson learned from Operation IRAQI FREEDOM was that civilian nation building plans must be integrated with military operational planning well before the war even starts.

Civilian contractors must be prepared to commence work very quickly upon the conclusion of major hostilities. They must also be prepared to take financial and security risks early in the recovery efforts to gain credibility and to build momentum. Major post-conflict reconstruction can be done effectively by Non-Governmental Organizations (NGOs) and the private sector, but such an effort must be well planned and requires the right kind of civilian political leadership and economic guidance.

America's military force has declined significantly in size over the past two decades, with much of its logistics and major construction capability contracted out to the private sector. Critics say "contracting out" diminishes our military force since military leaders genuinely focus on their mission and the welfare and protection of forces in the field, while the primary loyalty of private company leadership is to their shareholders. Where this attitude prevails, it could present an inherent conflict of interest in the battlefield outsourcing trend. But, in large measure, U.S. civilian contractors have shown themselves to be dedicated, dependable, and able to execute the specified tasks they have been assigned the past several years in Iraq and Afghanistan.

Clearly, we have now learned we need a proper blend of both troop and contractor construction and logistics capability. I saw both very good and very poor contractor support before, during, and after the war. In many cases, this support was quite expensive and was often quickly overwhelmed by spike loading of service/support requirements. Most significantly, on the opening day of the war when the seersucker cruise missile hit less than two hundred yards from my command tent, I saw panicked contractors bailing out as quickly as their legs and SUVs could get their backsides out of town. It was good we did not rely totally on their support.

Contractor Support

From a strategic viewpoint, I don't see an inherent conflict of interest in the proper employment of contracted construction and logistics support in contingency situations. In fact, it would be quite difficult and even more costly if we kept our troop construction and logistics forces sized during peacetime to meet full wartime requirements. But, all parties need to go into such contract arrangements with their eyes open. We need to establish doctrine for contingency contracting, embed it in our OPLANs, and exercise this essential capability continuously in peacetime.

Balanced employment and effective management of contract support is critical. We can not rely totally on contractors for any given service, and large contingency contracts can not be run by amateurs in the operating forces. A supply specialist who has been trained to make small purchases is simply not prepared to run contingency contracts that quickly surge into the multi-million dollar range. As we look to the future, we must train as we will fight, and it seems "contractors on the battlefield" are here to stay.

Unfortunately, civilian construction support for OIF I reconstruction got off to a slow start after the president declared the end of major combat operations on May 1, 2003. Major humanitarian construction by I MEF and the Seabees was also adversely constrained in the May-July 2003 period by our inability to receive any funding appropriated for this purpose, despite extensive project assessments and discussions with all the responsible agencies. Given the critical importance of Civil Military Operations during the recovery phase and the MEF's desire to minimize any additional Kinetic Operations and to maximize Iraqi jobs, we began to use funds seized from the former regime – packaged as bundles of $100 bills.

We used "Saddam's money" to buy construction materials in Iraq and Kuwait and to hire Iraqi workers (and ultimately Iraqi contractors) to get on with reconstruction, especially schools, hospitals and government buildings. MEG Civil Military Operations proceeded with a tightly constrained purse, while follow-on planning for the major U.S. contactor reconstruction effort moved forward at a seemingly snail's pace. But, there was a silver lining to this cloud. We quickly found very capable Iraqi small business contractors who were ready, willing, and able to submit fixed price bids for MEG projects, and to complete the work quickly and with good quality workmanship.

As the U.S. construction contracting effort began to engage in the south in late July, local Iraqi contractors were back in business and ready to serve as prime or sub contractors. Our plan was to ensure work would continue to flow after our departure to these hard working small businesses dispersed throughout the southern provinces. Our hope was we would not see a reversion to the former regime's patronage system where all work would be dispensed from Baghdad by those who survived "transition" as essential, useful and cooperative bureaucrats with allegiance only to those who were now in favor with the new government.

Lessons Learned

From an operational and tactical perspective, key lessons learned from the campaign throughout the IO, KO, and CMO phases will no doubt shape the way military Engineers are employed and work in the future. Clearly speed and communications were and will continue to be essential. The MEG Seabees were task organized to be light and fast — but we need to become even faster in the future. Engineers must retain organic long haul capability to move their own material, equipment, and gear to be fast and fully effective in a maneuver battle space. Engineers must also have top of the line voice/data communications, including sufficient bandwidth to support fast transmission of digital photos and engineering sketches/drawings. Finally, Engineers must be given adequate funding very early in the planning process for Class IV construction materials in support of Kinetic Operations, and for follow-on CMO projects. Seabees accomplished a lot with the money we were able to obtain for CMO work from May through August 2003 — but we could have done at least ten times more work if we had had proper and sufficient construction funding in place right as Baghdad fell.

The MEF's integrated IO/KO/CMO war plan was rooted in the belief that Iraqi forces would become pre-disposed to capitulate or desert with the right "info prep" of the battle space through leaflets, broadcasts, and covert operations. The MEF's leadership further believed that such behavior could be triggered when massive air/ground kinetic operations were initiated, reducing the number of enemy and especially civilian casualties, and significantly reducing the number of enemy prisoners of war the MEF would have to hold and care for. The war plan assumed soldiers from enemy formations who were defeated and demoralized could be bypassed. The plan further assumed these units could subsequently be re-integrated into a democratic, capitalist society by aggressive Civil Military Operations designed to rebuild damaged and neglected Iraqi infrastructure, thus creating new jobs for defeated soldiers.

Our plan was to commence Civil Military Operations quickly in the port of Umm Qasr shortly after the initial assault. We then planned to blend early CMO successes into the Information Operations being run in cities further to the north, including Baghdad. Our strategy projected that many Iraqis would choose not to fight when they heard and believed American forces where truly coming as liberators and rebuilders, rather than as conquerors and exploiters. Unfortunately our plan to put large numbers of former Iraqi soldiers to work was significantly constrained by lack of construction funding in the "golden months" after the fall of Baghdad.

An "Engineer's War"

Initially, there was some thought and deliberate planning around the concept that the invasion of Iraq could quickly become an "Engineer's War" with Engineers of all specialties playing an unusually large role staging the campaign and ensuring force mobility and survivability during the fast-moving attack.

Engineers, including the MEG Seabees, did play a major role before, during, and after major hostilities in Iraq. During the planning phase, we anticipated that most, if not all, bridges would be blown, that large open maneuver areas would be tactically inundated with water, that facilities for up to 40,000 Enemy Prisoners of War (EPWs) and an estimated 100,000 Displaced Civilians (DC) would have to be constructed, and that major battle damage would require quick repairs upon cessation of major hostilities. Had all this come to pass, I believe the term "Engineer's War" would have resonated across the battlefield.

However, as we all now know, the MEF captured all of the key southern bridges intact until we reached the Diyala River on the outskirts of Baghdad. Saddam's regime never executed its inundation strategy. Only about 8,000 EPWs materialized in the MEF Area of Responsibility, with virtually no Displaced Civilians, rather than the very large numbers originally envisioned. Battle damage was precise, including the bridge spans the MEF dropped, and lighter than expected, especially in and around Baghdad.

This is not to diminish the critical role that Engineers played. For the first time in recent history, Seabees joined the MEF order of battle in regimental formations, and maneuvered against a larger, well-entrenched enemy. Marine Corps Engineers were fearless as they placed assault and floating bridges, under fire, for the attacking 1st Marine Division. Combat Engineers located and neutralized large quantities of Captured Enemy Munitions and unexploded ordnance. Seabee Engineer Reconnaissance Teams (SERTs) maneuvered alongside the MEF assault elements and reconnoitered/planned Seabee work while receiving and returning fire.

Key to the assault was establishing and sustaining open roads capable of supporting high-speed logistics convoys. Initially, we had not planned to use Highway 1 as the Main Supply Route north — we thought logistics would flow up Highway 7 through and around Al Kut and on to Baghdad via Highway 6. When tactical plans changed, the Seabees quickly took on the job of completing the construction of over one hundred kilometers of Highway 1, including erecting bridging and filling major road and wet gaps.

Seabees also repaired and reopened an Iraqi asphalt plant to make a bituminous sealing material for improved road surfaces and dust control. Finally, the MEG Seabees moved quickly into the CMO phase of the campaign, starting in Umm Qasr, long before the coalition forces even crossed the Tigris. Ultimately, Seabees completed

158 major construction projects, including seventy-two schools, valued at over $7 million in less than four months. Many of these projects were completed with the help of Iraqi small business construction contractors, and were funded with U.S. dollars seized from the former regime. From this point of view, the CMO phase was truly an "Engineer's War." Seabees worked hand in hand with Marines to win the confidence of the Iraqi people and to gain their assistance in establishing the level of security necessary to restart local commerce and to begin the establishment of a democratic system of governance. In this respect, the "Engineer's War" continues, but the "troops" are now U.S. and foreign contractors, and a growing number of highly capable Iraqi contractors.

Iraq Reconstruction

In many respects, one would have to go back to World War II and Germany and Japan to find comparable situations in which the U.S. invaded a country, subdued its forces, replaced its government, and then undertook national reconstruction. It is hard to place the Iraq War and its aftermath exactly in this historical context. Considering this modern internet age, with its televised twenty-four hour news cycle, it is readily apparent that the U.S. government and its military forces had a much freer hand after World War II to do what they needed to do with less global visibility and certainly less daily media coverage of each and every minor setback on the road to recovery. Also, after the fall of Baghdad, the modern media never really pointed out that the former Nazi "werewolf brigade," comprised of Nazi SS fanatics, continued its guerilla operations in Germany against occupation forces well into 1947, and this type of lingering combat action certainly did not deter our post-war reconstruction efforts there.

Indeed, the major construction that put a USA stamp on the massive economic recovery of those countries after World War II didn't really get started until the early 1950's after new governments had been installed and official country to country agreements were signed to establish Army Corps of Engineers and Navy Civil Engineer Corps construction offices to build the new U.S. Bases in Germany, Spain, Japan, Thailand, Philippines, and elsewhere in the free world.

As Seabees departed for home in August 2003, it also seemed that a major difference between OIF I and World War II reconstruction was the expectation by some armchair generals and television pundits that this massive nation-building job could be done immediately with little or no outside money. However, it quickly became apparent that reconstruction in Iraq would be more about realigning and bedding down the new Iraqi military forces and police, providing better schools and clinics, and recovering from decades of neglect rather than battle damage repair. And as this effort continues, it should be equally apparent that this work now needs to be financed by the Iraqi people with oil revenues and by the international community with private and NGO investment.

Looking back, we certainly needed a lot more construction money in the "golden 120 days" after the fall of Baghdad, and we had no choice but to invest in the new Iraqi Armed Forces and basic infrastructure recovery. But, I don't believe the U.S. should continue to foot the bill for the continuing Iraq reconstruction effort. Looking ahead, the post-OIF recovery of Iraq is still on-going and needs to be the international equivalent, rather than an exact replica, of the WWII Marshall Plan.

Coalition Provisional Authority

I visited Baghdad in late August 2003 to meet with the Coalition Provisional Authority (CPA) staff and to transition our MEG Seabee reconstruction planning to CPA and Bechtel. I was confident the MEF and MEG had given a good accounting of themselves during the "120 day honeymoon" following the fall of Baghdad, and optimistic that civilian contractors could quickly build on our planning, subcontractor development, and initial execution successes. But, I was quickly distressed to see the growing "group think" within the ever-increasing staff inside the "Baghdad green zone."

As my briefing progressed with the CPA senior reconstruction staff, we began to discuss the political and economic issues I saw in southern Iraq that could impact the reconstruction efforts. I used that opportunity to press the previous MEF/MEG position advocating early elections of Mayors, followed by election of Governors concurrent with continued bottom up investing. We believed "bottom up" investing would grow and develop many local construction and supply businesses, and their owners and workers would quickly become leaders within a new Iraqi decentralize government with a free market, capitalistic economy.

To my surprise, my rather simple approach was met with skepticism and resistance by those who felt a more pragmatic approach would be to rely on Saddam's "de-Ba'ath'd" centralized bureaucracy and top-down investment to create a new and free Iraq. They soundly rejected early local elections for fear the "wrong people" would get elected (of course this happens in the USA all the time, only to be corrected in the next cycle), and because the Iraqis did not yet have a constitution and could not hold elections until they all endorsed a new constitution. I admitted I was not a political scientist but did point out our own independent Nation operated for thirteen years from 1776 to 1789 without a Constitution, and that an elected constitutional convention subsequent to local and provincial elections would give all Iraqi's a better sense of participation in a national unity government which could still protect their local and individual rights.

At this point, Ambassador Patrick Kennedy invited me to discuss my turnover brief and observations directly with Ambassador Bremer. We had a very cordial meeting that lasted nearly an hour. As I departed Bremer's office, I felt he and Kennedy understood what needed to be done, but I feared that their staff was inexperienced in contingency reconstruction and Civil Military Operations, and they were way too isolated in Baghdad. They simply did not understand that THEY were now responsible for building *"Bridges to Baghdad"* – in more ways than one. As I left Baghdad, I realized history would have to judge the success of their follow-on efforts. But it was clear by this point in time Seabees had built bridges and other critical facilities superbly throughout southern Iraq with the cooperation of Iraqi businesses and the Iraqi people. In September 2003, as OIF I was giving way to OIF II it was also clear these Seabees had raised the combat construction benchmarks set by their grandfathers and fathers in World War II and Vietnam to a new level, and could proudly say, "We Built. We Fought. (this) Mission Complete!"

Conclusion

When I started writing down my recollections and thoughts in the summer of 2003, I felt confident the story of Seabees in Iraq would wrap up with a neat and tidy conclusion by the fall of 2003. But today's world is simply not that neat and tidy. The events following 9/11 clearly shaped the Seabees, the MEG, and the Iraq War. The events and "lessons learned" chronicled in this narrative will similarly influence military and civilian actions into the future as successive stages of OIF/OEF and other battles against the forces of global terror unfold in the months and years ahead. Those actions will need to be the subject of yet other manuscripts by Seabees who live and build and fight in those campaigns yet to come.

But for now, it is time to put the events preceding, during and immediately after OIF I into their proper place in history and move on. For surely the next adventure will be just as difficult and possibly more dangerous and will require our full energy to be focused on the present and the future. After all is said and done, I suspect there will be nights in Iraq and elsewhere after the desert sun sets during which Seabees will gather together with nonalcoholic beer and good cigars and tell their sea stories about surmounted challenges, earned glories, and the personalities they confronted in the "good old days" when things were really tough in Kuwait and Iraq.

And do you know what? No matter how much they exaggerate, they will be right. Don't kid yourself by the speed of the attack, the resounding victory, and what you saw on TV. This was not an easy fight. But Seabees hung with the Marines and established a legacy of expeditionary combat construction that will be hard to top for decades to come. "With willing hearts and skillful hands, the difficult we do at once, the impossible takes a bit longer." Seabees Can Do!!!

RADM Charles R. Kubic

APPENDIX I

A History of the Civil Engineer Corps and the U.S. Navy Seabees, 1799 – 1991

Constructing the Civil Engineer Corps

The Navy's need for civil engineers and builders extends back to the 19th century when the service first began building its shipyards, docks, and other shore facilities to support its nascent fleet. These early civil engineering efforts were undertaken strictly by civilian professionals such as Benjamin Henry Latrobe and Loammi Baldwin, Jr. (known as the "Father of civil engineering in America") working under contract to the National government and only on American soil. Among the first of these projects was the Washington Navy Yard, authorized in 1799 by the first Secretary of the Navy, Benjamin Stoddert, and built on land set aside by George Washington for use by the Federal Government along the Anacostia River.[1]

However, during the War of 1812, Captain David Porter, commanding the 32-gun frigate *Essex*, demonstrated that Navy builders might occasionally find themselves in circumstances in which they would be forced to stop work and defend themselves. He had sailed the *Essex* around Cape Horn and into the Pacific Ocean in 1813, and had established what has been called the Navy's "first advanced base" at Nukahiva Island. During construction of the base's walled "village," which he named Madisonville, and a protective fort, his working sailors had to repeatedly lay down their tools and take up arms to fend off native attacks. The Royal Navy brought Porter's cruise to an abrupt halt in March 1814 at Valparaiso harbor in Chile. Madisonville was necessarily abandoned, and the building and fighting lesson was quickly forgotten as the U.S. government eschewed any further overseas naval ambitions until much later in the century. Although Porter and his sailors at Madison's Island were certainly no Seabees in the modern sense, as command historian of the Naval Facilities Engineering Command, Dr. Vincent A. Transano later argued, they essentially performed "the same functions that characterize today's Seabee builder-fighters."[2]

Afterward, the Navy slowly began developing its own dedicated corps of professional civil engineers to design and supervise construction of its expanding shore establishment. In August 1842, Congress abolished the Board of Navy Commissioners, which had been created in 1815 to advise the Secretary of the Navy on matters of design logistics, construction, and naval facilities management, in favor of a Bureau of Navy Yards and Docks. William P. S. Sanger became the new bureau's first official civil engineer. Under his supervision and that of the progressive-minded Bureau chief, Commodore Joseph Smith (serving in that position from 1846 to 1869), other civil engineers found employment with the Navy. In 1858, the Bureau drew up a series of rules for their regulation and guidance, thereby defining their duties and establishing their professional principles as civil servants.[3]

From the Bureau's establishment through the Civil War period, the Navy's civil engineers were strictly civilians. After the war though, Sanger and Smith lobbied hard for commissioning so that their engineers could exercise greater chain-of-command authority and work more efficiently while designing and building more modern shore facilities to service the fleet's newer steam-driven vessels. On March 2, 1867 Congress finally authorized President Andrew Johnson to appoint a formal Civil Engineer Corps (CEC) for the Navy, with its engineers permitted to hold staff officer rank. The very next day, Secretary of the Navy Gideon Welles commissioned Sanger and granted him the title of Senior Civil Engineer. He thus became the Navy's first uniformed civil engineer.[4]

In 1871, Congress authorized the President to grant CEC engineers relative rank and precedence with line officers, but limited their number to only ten. Despite the authorization, no administration acted on it until February 1881, when President Rutherford B. Hayes' Secretary of the Navy, Nathan Goff, Jr., bestowed the CEC with the relative ranks of lieutenant through captain and authorized the engineers to wear line officer uniforms.[5]

In the 1890s, Captain Alfred Thayer Mahan's theories on colonies, coaling stations, and global seapower projection, as outlined in his classic 1890 book, *The Influence of Seapower upon History*, began shaping U.S. naval thinking. Accordingly, the Navy ordered the CEC to supervise the construction of a new coaling station for the service's new steam-powered, all-steel warships at Pago Pago in American Samoa, which had previously been surveyed in 1879. The small station opened in 1892 and became the Navy's first advanced overseas base since Captain Porter's ill-starred Madisonville.[6]

The Spanish American War in 1898 allowed the Navy to implement and test Mahan's theories and had a significant impact on the development of the CEC. As the need for new bases became evident at the war's onset, President William McKinley invoked vested discretionary powers to increase the Navy's number of civil engineers from ten to eighteen to better support the fleet's operations against the Spanish Navy. Additionally, just two weeks before the war started in April, McKinley broke precedent by appointing Commodore Mordecai T. Endicott of the CEC as the new chief of the Bureau of Yards and Docks. This was the first time that a CEC officer, rather than a line officer, had ever served as Bureau chief. In fact, Endicott's elevation set an important new precedent in which, henceforth, all future chiefs of the Bureau of Yards and Docks would be chosen from the ranks of the CEC. Congress later placed this specific requirement for appointment to the post into law in June 1906.[7]

Spain signed a peace treaty with the U.S. in December 1898. Under the settlement, the U.S. bought the Philippines for $20,000,000 and assumed control of Puerto Rico and Guam, and while Spain ostensibly guaranteed Cuba's independence, the Cuban government became an American puppet. Consequently, the U.S. joined the ranks of the world's great colonial powers, with important strategic possessions in both the Atlantic and Pacific Oceans.[8]

Following the treaty, Endicott found that the bureau's eighteen civil engineers were wholly inadequate for further expanding the naval shore establishment, both in the U.S. and in the country's far-flung new territories. He urgently began lobbying for more commissioned engineers to help ease the Bureau's burgeoning postwar workload.[9]

On March 3, 1903, Congress authorized the Navy to increase the number of CEC officers from eighteen to forty (twenty-eight fully qualified civil engineers and twelve assistants). This number remained constant until the pressures of World War I forced Congress to increase the size of the Navy dramatically. In the Navy Appropriation Act of August 29, 1916, which launched an enormous new naval preparedness program, Congress linked the size of the CEC to the percentage of the service's line officers, which in turn was based upon the strength of the Navy's enlisted personnel. The act also established the Naval Reserve Force and allowed civilians to enroll in a Naval Reserve CEC. As a result, over the next two years, the CEC would ultimately grow to comprise seventy-four regular officers, twenty temporary officers, and one hundred ten reserve officers.[10]

The 12th Regiment (Public Works)

While the preparedness legislation bolstered the CEC, America's entry into World War I in April 1917 produced an instant shortage of shore facilities, particularly for the training of thousands of new sailors demanded by a modern wartime Navy. At the Great Lakes Naval Training Station in Illinois, then an obscure facility far removed from the coasts, only a few hundred enlisted men had passed through its gates over the years, and few officers ever visited it.[11]

War changed everything, and the Navy quickly directed the station to receive and train some 20,000 recruits through the summer. Tent cities soon surrounded the station, and its tiny Public Works Department struggled to construct sufficient facilities to house, feed, and care for the sudden influx of recruits, which would rise to over 50,000 by war's end. Because line officers were generally inexperienced with large-scale building projects, the chief of the Bureau of Yards and Docks, Rear Admiral Frederic Harris, appointed a CEC officer named Lieutenant Norman M. Smith in June 1917 to command the Great Lakes Public Works Department.[12]

With only a hundred men assigned to Public Works, Smith urgently needed large numbers of technical men, construction specialists, artisans, and accounting clerks to handle Great Lakes' expansion. But the number of available (and willing) civil service employees was prohibitive. After canvassing nearby communities, Smith found that the most suitable men did not want to work as civilians and desired to do their part for the Navy in uniform. He therefore determined that commissioning or enlisting them was the best solution to the staffing crisis.[13]

By December 1917, Smith had brought nearly a thousand professionals and skilled tradesmen into the service at Great Lakes. For administrative and discipline purposes, the Navy organized them into a military formation, the 12th Regiment (Public Works), on a basis similar to the station's other regiments. Since staff officers could not command military units under the Navy regulations of that time, the regiment fell under the immediate command of a line officer, Lieutenant William C. Davis, who was subordinated to the Public Works Officers. This military portion of Public Works became known as the "Regimental Division," and it maintained its own staff of officers and men who functioned purely on regimental matters.[14]

The officers and men of the 12th Regiment worked hard, usually ten to fourteen hours a day, with little liberty and few free Sundays. Most were older than ordinary recruits, and brought several years worth of trade experience with them into the ranks. While the 12th Regiment did not undergo the same basic training as the Navy's other recruits, its men did have to participate in two-hour military drills twice a week after supper, and in a short time, they learned how to march and to handle their rifles. On a voluntary basis, all Public Works officers attended a weapons course where they studied the fundamentals and mechanics of firing rifles, pistols, and machine guns, and later, larger guns and torpedoes.[15]

The 12th Regiment initially comprised three battalions with 1,500 men when it became fully operational on December 30, 1917. Its first semi-permanent regimental camp, called Camp Paul Jones, opened that same month, under Commander George A. McKay, who had replaced Smith as Public Works Officer several months before. McKay's tenure was equally short though, and another CEC officer, Commander Walter H. Allen, succeeded him on January 30, 1918. In April 1918, Allen reorganized both the Public Works Department and the 12th Regiment into five battalions with a total of 2,400 men.[16]

The 12th Regiment handled much of the station's construction and maintenance and supplemented civilian contractors. It also served as a training regiment from which the whole Navy could draw skilled tradesmen, such as "fire" men (for operating coal-based power plants), surveyors, draftsmen, electricians, carpenter's mates, and others. This was possible because virtually all of the station's recruits with prior trade experience had been sent directly to the Public Works Department, where each was examined and evaluated and assigned a rating based upon his respective skill level. Whenever the Navy called upon the station to furnish weekly or monthly drafts from the trade branches, the Public Works Department supplied the necessary skilled men.[17]

In March 1918, the Navy requested that Great Lakes supply two hundred men to build aviation stations on the French coast. Great Lakes not only complied but also offered to send a completely organized construction unit of four or five hundred skilled men from the 12th Regiment to do the work. Ultimately, three hundred and fifty Public Works men went to France specifically to build and operate the Poillac aviation station. The Navy likewise sent others "over there" to build new docks and wharves in French ports, and eight 820-foot steel towers for the Lafayette radio station at Croix d'Hins, which General John J. Pershing needed to communicate directly with the U.S. government. A special draft of 12th Regiment men actually served on the Western Front, but in a non-combatant capacity, in which they assembled and operated the trains for Rear Admiral Charles P. Plunkett's five long-range 14-inch railway guns.[18]

The regiment peaked in early November 1918 when it counted just over 6,200 men, organized into a final eleven battalions. However, after the Armistice, the 12th Regiment began declining rather quickly. Civilians replaced the enlisted men and officers as they demobilized, and after Germany signed the Versailles Peace Treaty on June 28, 1919, the regiment disbanded. Although it had been in existence for only two short years, and was an unofficial Navy unit organized and developed solely for the purposes of the Great Lakes training station, the 12th Regiment set a solid example for the service.[19]

In the March 1921 issue of the United States Naval Institute *Proceedings*, Commander Allen highlighted the 12th Regiment's successes and also demonstrated the necessity of military organization and management of men engaged in massive wartime construction, which the Navy had not appreciated when its numbers were small. He specifically pointed out that Great Lakes' use of a skilled enlisted workforce had circumvented all the inherent labor problems associated with contractors and civilian employees, and that his force had worked faster and more efficiently, without diminishment of quality, under war conditions. If enlisted workers, such as those in the 12th Regiment, could succeed at such a place as Great Lakes, then in his estimation, they could perform even better "in isolated localities or on a foreign shore."[20]

We Build! We Fight!

Beginning with the Washington Naval Arms Limitation Treaty of 1922, the Navy entered a long period of budget cuts and contraction, and two decades would pass before Allen's ideas about large formations of uniformed builders, working both at home and overseas in wartime, were put to the test. During the 1930s, Smith, McKay, Allen, and others formerly associated with the 12th Regiment, rose through the ranks of the CEC and the Bureau of Yards and Docks. They began developing contingency plans for "Navy Construction Battalions," based upon the model of the Great Lakes Public Works Department, which could support the fleet and the Marine Corps during a potential "war of movement" against Japan in the Pacific, as envisioned in the Navy's War Plan "Orange."[21]

Additionally, Bureau planners placed a heavy emphasis on the development of construction equipment designed especially for operations at advanced naval bases. They also anticipated that raw recruits earmarked for the battalions would be trained in naval trade schools, and then organized into units and commanded by line officers, who would have civil engineers on their staffs to direct construction operations in the field.[22]

While the bureau further shaped and refined its war plans in the late 1930s, naval construction remained on a peacetime footing, and was limited to bases owned or governed by the U.S., with most of the work permanent in nature. In 1940, the CEC and the bureau were involved in a number of large projects in the Pacific and the Caribbean as part of President Franklin D. Roosevelt's naval rearmament program. Roosevelt's Lend-Lease agreement with Great Britain significantly expanded the scope of the work, and in March 1941, the bureau began building four naval bases for the British, three in Northern Ireland and one in Scotland. A fueling depot in Iceland was shortly added to the construction list. The bureau planned for all of the work to be carried out under CEC supervision by American contractors, using technically skilled civilians from the U.S. in conjunction with local labor.[23]

However, in late October 1941, it became apparent that insufficient numbers of civilian employees were available to staff the naval offices at the new bases, so the Bureau of Navigation authorized the enlistment of ninety-nine men for a "Headquarters Construction Company" for the task. The bureau soon authorized four additional companies, and organized the first of these, on December 7, 1941, for duty in Iceland. Following the Japanese attack on Pearl Harbor, the bureau formed the 1st Construction Detachment around the nucleus of this new company. Its ninety-nine partly trained men, seven commissioned reservists, and one hundred forty fresh recruits soon began calling themselves "Bobcats" after Admiral Ernest J. King sent the detachment to Bora Bora (code-named "Bobcat") on January 27, 1942 to build a fueling station for supply ships bound for Australia and New Zealand. They represented the first official naval construction workers to enter the Pacific war zone.[24]

As the Japanese Empire swallowed up most of the U.S.' western Pacific territories and possessions in December 1941, the Bureau of Yards and Docks realized that civilian contractors and their employees could not effectively work in combat zones. Military law prevented civilians from resisting when Japanese forces attacked the bases they were constructing. If the Japanese caught them armed, then they could be summarily executed as guerillas. Moreover, the civilian workers already captured at Wake and Guam and in the Philippines had shown that they were not trained and disciplined enough to defend themselves.[25]

Despite the debacle, the bureau's officers thought that American construction workers, who were physically rugged and mentally toughened from their trades, could once again be quickly enlisted and organized into construction battalions. This time though the bureau decided that the new men's civilian skills would have to be supplemented with basic combat training. Unlike the training of U.S. Army and Marine combat engineers, who specialized in mine clearing, barrier breaching, combat demolitions, and assault bridging while in direct contact with the enemy, the proposed naval construction battalions' training would be for self-defense only. They would not be expected to charge into battle along side frontline engineers, but they would work behind the front lines on more enduring projects such as airfields, harbors, and docking facilities in military theaters all over the world. They would also evacuate the wounded, unload ships, and perform other general engineering functions as needed. But, under the Bureau's plan, they would be capable of fighting back effectively if attacked.[26]

On December 28, 1941, the Chief of the Bureau of Yards and Docks, Rear Admiral Benjamin C. Moreell asked the Bureau of

Navigation to authorize the creation of the first three naval construction battalions under military command. Each would be comprised of 1,073 men and 32 officers, and possess enough variety in trades and specialties so that it could be self-sufficient in carrying out its assigned construction work. The Bureau of Navigation granted Moreell's request on January 5, 1942, and the Bureau of Yards and Docks organized the first of the new battalions shortly thereafter.[27]

While organizing the first naval construction battalions in early months of 1942, Moreell realized that he needed to build a strong *esprit de corps* to boost their morale and weld them into a cohesive building and fighting force. Just as he began considering this issue, a solution to his problem presented itself. At the Quonsett Point, Rhode Island Naval Air Station, where some 250 construction battalion recruits had just arrived, their officer-in-charge heard about the cartooning skills of Carpenter's Mate 1st Class Frank J. Iafrate, who worked on the station as a plan files clerk. The Lieutenant approached Iafrate and described his men's future mission of following the Marines ashore and undertaking naval construction in combat zones. They would not be an offensive force but could defend themselves if they had to. He then asked Iafrate to design an insignia with a "Disney type" character that would graphically represent and identify the new unit.[28]

Iafrate agreed and began researching the character. A busy beaver was his first candidate for the logo but he quickly decided against it when he learned about its untoward tendency to run away when attacked. He then fell upon the idea of a bee, which was well known as a busy and benign worker unless provoked, at which point it returned with a sharp sting. After settling upon the bee as the representing character, Iafrate "animated" it, giving it a white "Dixie cup" hat to symbolize the Navy, a wrench and a hammer to highlight its construction skills, and a "Tommy" gun to emphasize its fighting ability. He then gave it a rank of Petty Officer 3rd Class, with appropriate rating insignia on each arm, along with CEC insignias on its wrist to associate it with the Civil Engineer Corps. For a name, Iafrate thought "Men of the Construction Battalions" was too awkward, but realized that he already had a bee character to represent the men, who happened to work at sea. Coincidentally, the Navy acronym for 'construction battalion' was 'CB,' and so he put it all together and came up with "Seabee" for a name.[29]

In 1942, the U.S. Navy launched an intense home front campaign to recruit skilled tradesmen into its newly authorized Construction Battalions to build the Navy's bases during World War II. (Library of Congress)

After nailing down the character concept and name, Iafrate drew the proposed insignia in about three hours on a Sunday afternoon, and presented it to the Lieutenant the following morning. The Lieutenant liked it, and forwarded it along with the 'Seabee' name up the chain of command. The fruits of Iafrate's labor soon landed on Moreell's desk, and the bureau chief immediately understood the intrinsic recruiting and public relations value of the insignia and name. Therefore, on March 1, he sought approval from the Bureau of Navigation to give his units the 'Seabee' designation and to enable them to display Iafrate's insignia on their equipment (but not on their uniforms). Four days later, on March 5, 1942, the Bureau of Navigation granted his request and authorized Moreell's construction battalions to become the U.S. Navy Seabees.[30]

To complement Iafrate's logo and name, Moreell also furnished the Seabees with a suitable motto, "Construimus, Batuimus," meaning (in Latin) "We Build! We Fight!" However, they soon earned another more popular slogan when Moreell's chief recruiting and training officer, Captain John R. Perry, visited Johnston Island early in the war. The air station's commanding officer met him at the airstrip, and after exchanging salutes, Perry asked how the Seabees were doing. The CO replied, "You mean those 'Can Do' boys? They can do anything you ask them to do. They're great!" From that moment forth, "Can Do!" entered Seabee lore as their most famous battle cry.[31]

As the Seabees' organization and collective identity emerged in 1942, Moreell struggled with a couple of key management and recruitment problems. First and foremost, the pre-war plan to place them under line officer command, with CEC officers serving as advisors, was both impractical and dangerous. The old 12th Regiment model at Great Lakes, situated inside the U.S. and far away from any fighting, had worked well because of the station's routine and operational stability. A war zone was far more fluid and unpredictable though, and Moreell and others in the bureau recognized that shifting administrative control back and forth among CEC and line officers in combat conditions would result in chaos, inefficiency, and increased costs in time, effort, and money.[32]

Further, most of the Seabees would be seasoned tradesmen, just like their 12th Regiment predecessors. It stood to reason that they would be more responsive to command by CEC officers, who "spoke their language" and understood their trades. Accordingly, Moreell secured a favorable opinion from the Navy's Judge Advocate Gen-

Carpenter's Mate 1st Class Frank Iafrate points to the Seabee cartoon that he designed. September 1, 1942.
(NARA-College Park, Still Picture Branch, RG 80-G 82535, Box 377)

eral office and persuaded Secretary of the Navy Frank Knox to sign an order giving CEC officers in charge of Seabee units command authority over all personnel attached to their units, including line officers. Knox's order effectively unified the Seabees' chain of command under the CEC and established its precedence in operational naval construction matters.[33]

Moreell also had to confront the same problem that Lieutenant Smith previously had to face at Great Lakes, but on a far larger scale, specifically that of recruiting sufficient numbers of skilled tradesmen and professional civil engineers to fill his new construction battalions. Many of these men were paid very well in their civilian occupations, and being older and more settled than recruits, they generally had wives and families to support. Moreover, most were exempt from the draft because of their ages or the nature of their occupations in critical war industries. Inducing them to leave civilian life to join the Seabees would not be easy.[34]

Fortunately, the Chief of the Bureau of Naval Personnel, Vice Admiral Randall Jacobs, recognized Moreell's need for a strong incentive to attract skilled workers to the Seabee ranks. He accordingly gave Moreell the authority to enlist them with ratings commensurate with their civilian construction experience and age. Most of these men, representing some sixty different trades, ultimately entered service rated Petty Officer 2nd Class, with starting pay and allowances set at $140 per month. Moreell procured competent civil engineering officers similarly, through naval reserve commissions, with their rank and pay set in accordance with age and experience.[35]

Moreell's recruitment program, which was boosted by Roosevelt's December 15, 1942 order giving Selective Service procurement control of qualified men, was a tremendous success. Within a year of the creation of the first naval construction battalion, Moreell reported to the Secretary of the Navy that the Seabees counted 210,000 officers and men within their ranks. By July 1945, the number of enlisted men swelled to over 247,000, and they were commanded by nearly 10,000 CEC officers, a far cry from the 247 officers who comprised the CEC in July 1940.[36]

As the numbers of Seabees quickly grew into the tens of thousands in early 1942, the Bureau of Yards and Docks had to provide sufficient training facilities for them. The first of these, named Camp Allen in memory of the 12th Regiment's last commanding officer, Commander Walter Allen, opened on March 21, 1942 at the Norfolk, Virginia training station. Camp Bradford, located on 1,600 acres of the Bradford Estate at nearby Little Creek, Virginia, opened soon afterward. To outfit and prepare freshly trained Seabees for their final transfer to their designated overseas destinations, the bureau also established advance base depots. The first of these opened on February 27, 1942 at Davisville, Rhode Island, and another opened at Port Hueneme, California in May. A third depot also opened at Gulfport, Mississippi on June 2.[37]

In mid-June 1942, the tens of thousands of Seabees began turning into hundreds of thousands of Seabees. The influx compelled Moreell to ask Navy Secretary Knox for the expansion of the Davisville, Rhode Island depot into a full Seabee training station. Knox agreed, and on 27 June, the bureau established Camp Endicott there. Another training facility, Camp Peary, was completed November 4, 1942. Named after the famed CEC officer and polar explorer Robert E. Peary, this enormous facility covered 11,000 acres and could comfortably accommodate 50,000 Seabee recruits. The bureau built Camp Peary to help centralize basic Seabee training and to replace the smaller, more confined Camps Allen and Bradford, both of which closed on March 17, 1943. Camp Peary operated until June 1944, when the bureau decided to abandon it and shift all future Seabee training to Camp Endicott. Two other installations, Camp Parks, established near Livermore, California in November 1942, and Camp Lee-Stephenson (named after the first two CEC officers killed in World War II), established at Quoddy Village, Maine in October 1943, also served as overflow training facilities during the war. [38]

The Seabees trained and deployed overseas in 151 regular naval construction battalions (NCBs). NCB 6 was the first to enter a combat zone, arriving on Guadalcanal in September 1942, where its men and officers soon found themselves working at one end of Henderson Field while entrenched Marines fought Japanese troops at the other. A number of other specialized units, including cargo-handling Special Battalions, the smaller Construction Battalion Maintenance Units (CBMUs), Underwater Demolition Teams (Navy "frogmen," the forerunners of the modern Navy SEALS), and reinforcing Construction Battalion Detachments, soon joined the Seabees abroad. At first each unit operated independently, with its commanding officer solely responsible for making all engineering and military decisions. However, the vast scale of the war required vast naval construction within the various military theaters.[39]

Out of necessity, Navy commanders began grouping various battalions and support units together to undertake larger, more complex construction projects. To coordinate their work, the bureau had to organize the battalions into naval construction regiments, the first of which was authorized by the Vice Chief of Naval Operations in December 1942 for the Alaskan sector. Fifty-three more would be formed over the next couple of years, and to manage them efficiently, the bureau organized them further into twelve brigades, three of which would be disbanded before V-J Day.[40]

As World War II entered its final phases, the bureau found that construction brigades too were insufficient for some of the Navy's more critical operating areas. Consequently, in August 1944, the bureau grouped the 2nd, 7th, and 8th Construction Brigades into a division level organization called the Hawaiian Area

That Seabees were expected to attack and fight like Marines was apparent at Camp Endicott, Davisville, Rhode Island, during combat training in "commando" tactics.

(NARA-College Park, Still Picture Branch, RG 80-G 40989, 40992, 40994, Box 184)

The direct ancestor of the Mabey & Johnson semi-permanent bridge was the British Bailey Bridge, used throughout World War II and later. (Top) Bremen, Germany, March 1947. (Bottom) A Bailey bridge under construction by men of the 10th Engineer Combat Battalion, 3rd U.S. Infantry Division, near Yonchon, Korea, March 7, 1952.

(NARA-College Park, RG 111-SC 282953, Box 545/ RG 111-SC 399538, Box 851)

Construction Brigade Command, under the command of Commodore John Perry, who had first encountered the "Can Do!" expression. This organization functioned until April 1945, when the Navy transferred the 2nd and 7th Brigades, along with Perry himself, to the Philippines to build Naval Operating Base Leyte-Samar. The two brigades joined the second section of the 3rd Brigade to form another division echelon command, again under Perry, called Construction Forces-Samar. This new command fell under the administrative control of the Commander in Chief, Pacific Ocean Area, Admiral Chester W. Nimitz, but was operationally subordinated to the Commander in Chief, Southwest Pacific Area, General Douglas MacArthur.[41]

Perry's job as the Samar area commander was to build the huge naval bases required there for the preparatory invasion of Okinawa, dubbed Operation ICEBERG, and the ultimate invasion of Japan, called Operation DOWNFALL. However, the sheer size and complexity of ICEBERG, called for an even higher command echelon to manage all of the engineering forces that would land on Okinawa to first support the Allied assault troops on the island and then turn it into a giant air and naval base for DOWNFALL.[42]

In early 1945, the commander of all Army and Navy construction units in the Pacific, Commodore Andrew G. Bisset, began assembling the combined joint Task Unit 99.3.5, which encompassed all construction forces slated for the Okinawa movement. These included 8th, 10th, and 11th Naval Construction Brigades, over 50,000 U.S. Army engineers, and some 15,000 British engineer troops, who had the mission of building B-29 bases at Kume Shima. Altogether, approximately 110,000 military engineers under Bisset's command were involved in the plan. This would be the largest concentration of military engineers for a single operation during the war.[43]

However, only part of Task Unit 99.3.5 arrived on Okinawa and started long-term construction before Emperor Hirohito broadcast his dramatic surrender message on August 14. An even larger engineering task force unit had been planned for DOWNFALL's first phase, called Operation OLYMPIC, which involved the invasion of Kyushu, the southern most of Japan's home islands. V-J Day mooted the task force though and it never left the preliminary planning stages. But its theoretical concept represented the pinnacle of organizational doctrine for combining large numbers of Seabees and Army engineers, as well as Allied engineering contingents, into a combined joint force to support large-scale assault forces over large operational areas. Five decades would pass before a similar organization of work would be explored and then implemented under war conditions.

Between their official birthday on March 5, 1942 and V-J Day, the Seabees built over 400 advanced bases throughout the world at a cost of $11 billion and participated in nearly every U.S. amphibious operation in every theater. In so doing, they earned lasting glory in such places as Normandy, where they helped demolish the fixed German defenses on Omaha and Utah beaches and then handled the "Mulberry" and "Gooseberry" artificial harbors, "Rhino" landing ferries and sea mule tugs, pontoon causeways, and fueling facilities for the Allied beach head.[44]

Moreell's foresight in insisting that the Seabees be combat-capable became readily apparent in a number of instances in which they had to take up arms and fight on their own account. For example, on Guam, Seabees from the NCB 48 stumbled upon camouflaged Japanese soldiers near one of the island's cliff areas. When the Japanese fled, the Seabees organized patrols and hunted them down, killing at least nine enemy soldiers in the so-called "Battle of the Cliff." In November 1943, during the Bougainville landing, Seabees from the NCB 25, which was supporting the 3rd Marine Division, manned anti-aircraft guns and engaged strafing Japanese fighters, shooting down one. At Leyte, in December 1944, NCB 61 became the first American unit ever to be attacked by Japanese paratroopers, who dropped near airstrips that the Seabees had been servicing. The Seabees quickly reacted and killed all two hundred of the enemy, but not before the Japanese succeeded in destroying a huge fuel dump nearby. In northern Bataan, Seabee rescue parties from the NCB 102 encountered Japanese ambushes while trying to reach downed Army airmen around Zigzag Pass on Telegraph Trail. Fierce fighting broke out, and four Seabees were killed and several more wounded in the unsuccessful effort to save the fliers.[45]

Iwo Jima was by far the Seabees' bloodiest battle in World War II. NCBs 31, 62, 70, and 133 landed with the Marines in the first assault phase and sustained very heavy casualties as they struggled to bring heavy equipment ashore and to repair the island's vital airfield. The Japanese defenders hit NCB 133 particularly hard, killing three of its officers and thirty-nine enlisted Seabees. Another two hundred and three (twelve officers and 191 enlisted) were wounded. Altogether, this amounted to a twenty-five percent ca-

Seabees pilot heavily-laden 'Rhino Ferries' (foreground) to the beaches of Normandy during D-Day as the Allies launch the long-awaited invasion of France on June 6, 1944. The Rhino ferry was a Seabee concept, a long self-propelled pontoon barge. (NARA-College Park, RG 80-G 47392, Box 216)

Navy and Coast Guard landing craft of all types crowd on to the assault beach on Iwo Jima during landing operations, as Marines and Seabees storm ashore into withering Japanese fire. (NARA-College Park, RG 80-G, 48302, Box 219)

sualty rate, which was higher than that of many Marine units that were in the thick of the fighting, and the highest of any Seabee unit in history.[46]

Although the Seabees have traditionally been depicted as building and fighting on the Pacific alongside the Marines, a number of Seabee units also drove deep into Europe as part of General Dwight D. Eisenhower's Allied Expeditionary Force. Three of these, CBMUs 627, 628, and 629, helped the American armies cross the Rhine River in March 1945, using pontoon barges and sea mule tugs, and special pontoon pile-driver rigs for bridge construction. They also supported the U.S. Army Corps of Engineers, which had the difficult task of spanning the Rhine with British-made prefabricated "Bailey" bridges, some forty-one of which, totaling 4812 feet, were built for Lieutenant General George S. Patton's Third Army alone during the assault crossing.[47]

While the three CBMUs occasionally had to work on the eastern Rhine riverbank, NCB 69 was the only construction battalion that the Allied high command posted inside Germany. Its first ele-

Armored dozers are not new to the modern battlespace. Here, some sixty years before the Israeli Defense Forces loaned their "Zionist Monsters" to the MEG, World War II Seabees have constructed an armored dozer cab and bullet shield from half-inch medium steel salvaged from shipyards.
(NARA-College Park, Still Picture Branch, RG 80-G, 48705, Box 221)

ments arrived at Vreden on April 24, and moved to Bremen three days later, after that city fell. There, NCB 69 went to work. Employing German civilians, the construction battalion re-roofed artillery-damaged buildings, installed and repaired plumbing, lighting, and power lines, and set up shops and offices, where necessary. Before NCB 69 began departing for England on June 22, its detachments also built or repaired officer and enlisted quarters and dock facilities at Bremerhaven, the designated port of entry for the Allied occupation army, and at Frankfurt-am-Main, which the U.S. Navy chose as its German headquarters.[48]

Much to "King Bee" Moreell's delight, the Navy Seabees captured the American public's imagination through a well-crafted public relations campaign. While the Seabees' name and insignia had been an early part of this effort, the debut of a 1944 John Wayne movie entitled *The Fighting Seabees* sealed their popularity on the home front. Although many of Moreell's gruff Seabees did not rate the film too highly because "It had too much love stuff in it," the film was a commercial success and contributed a new marching song, composed by Sam M. Lewis and Peter de Rose, to their institutional heritage. The lyrics proclaimed to an enthusiastic American audience:

> We're the Seabees of the Navy
> We can build and we can fight
> We'll pave the way to victory
> And guard it day and night.[49]

The publication of two classic books, *Can Do!* (1944) and *From Omaha to Okinawa* (1945), by *American Mercury* journalist and naval reservist William Bradford Huie, helped secure the Seabees' place in military history. Huie was an early version of a modern day "embedded" war correspondent, in the same tradition as his contemporary, Ernie Pyle, and recorded many of the Seabees' most cherished images and memories. While describing World War II as the largest "construction war in history," he outlined his famous "five roads to victory" theory, whereby the Seabees contributed significantly to the Allies' victory by extending, often under enemy fire, the country's ordnance and materiel supply infrastructure from the American mainland along three great, figurative Pacific "highways" to Japan, and over two more across the Atlantic to Germany. Over time, his "five roads" theory became another prominent pillar of the Seabees' growing institutional heritage.[50]

"King Bee" Vice Admiral Ben Moreell,
the "Father of the U.S. Navy Seabees," June 3, 1944.

(NARA-College Park, Still Picture Branch, RG 80-G 106015, Box 432)

On top of the public acclamation, the Seabees' contribution to the war effort also won high-level praise. In February 1944, from his headquarters in Brisbane, Australia, General MacArthur told Moreell that "the only trouble with your Seabees is that I do not have enough of them." After V-J Day, Secretary of the Navy James V. Forrestal announced that "The Seabees have carried the war in the Pacific on their backs...They paved the way for the success of every major amphibious invasion." Lieutenant General Holland M. "Howlin' Mad" Smith recalled that "The spirit of brotherhood existing between the Marines and the Seabees was forged in the holocaust of battle...The Seabees never let us down!|" Fleet Admiral Nimitz simply concluded that "Without them we could not have beaten the Japs."[51]

Demobilization, Reorganization, and Redeployment

After World War II ended, the Navy's rapid demobilization program sent hundreds of thousands of Seabees back to their professions and trades in the civilian world. Since most Seabees were reservists, the naval construction battalions disbanded so fast that only basic tasks across the Navy's enormous global shore establishment could be undertaken by the few who remained. In his annual report for 1946, Secretary of the Navy Forrestal lamented that untrained seamen had to be used to attempt to maintain the Seabees' authorized strength but admitted that this was a losing battle as their numbers also rapidly dwindled. He reported that from a strength of 8,000 officers and 238,000 enlisted men on V-J Day, organized into nine brigades, thirty-one regiments, and 338 battalions and smaller units, the numbers of Seabees had dropped to only 400 officers and 20,000 men, in two brigades, two regiments, and forty smaller units by 30 June 1946. It thus appeared that the Seabees were fading away like their old forerunners in the 12th Regiment.[52]

However, because of the Seabees' success and fame, the Navy resolved to make them a permanent part of the peacetime service so that the nuclei of their organization would be available for rapid expansion in future conflicts. Although most of their training facilities and depots closed across the country, the Navy opened the Construction Battalion Center at Port Hueneme in December 1945 to serve as the Seabees' home base. From here, the greatly diminished Seabees became involved a number of post-war projects that were important for the national defense as tensions with the Soviet Union began escalating toward a new "Cold" War. Among these was the construction of facilities on Bikini Atoll for Operation CROSSROADS in mid-1946, in which the Navy, in coordination with the U.S. Army Air Force, tested two atomic bombs against surplus American and captured Japanese ships.[53]

Also, in that same year, 173 Seabees accompanied Rear Admiral Richard E. Byrd to Antarctica as part of Task Force 68 for the U. S. Navy Antarctic Developments Project," codenamed Operation HIGH JUMP. This was a thirteen ship, 4,700 man, military exploration and mapping expedition aimed at consolidating and extending American sovereignty on the continent. Along with its surveying mission, Task Force 68 and its Seabee contingent also sought to train personnel and test equipment in a polar environment and to determine if bases could be built and maintained in the Antarctic and to identify possible base sites. Despite Rear Admiral Byrd's public protest that the expedition was not "primarily a lap in the race for uranium," Task Force 68's accompanying scientists also prospected for "Atomic Energy Source Materials" for new nuclear weapons, among other things.[54]

In 1949, the Navy reorganized the Seabees and grouped them into two new types of construction units – the Naval Mobile Construction Battalion (NMCB) and the Amphibious Construction Battalion (PHIBCB). The NMCBs took responsibility for land construction projects such as encampments, roads, bridges, depots, airstrips, and docking facilities. PHIBCBs, which descended from the Seabee Pontoon Operating Battalions of World War II, assumed the mission of planning causeways, constructing pontoon docks, and performing other work necessary for landing Marines and soldiers and heavy equipment as quickly as possible. Over the next four years, the Navy altogether organized thirteen of these new types of Seabee battalions, giving the U.S. naval construction force greater strategic mobility and specialization than it had ever had before.[55]

The new and improved Seabees proved their worth again after the Korean War erupted on June 25, 1950. In accordance with the post-World War II plan of building up its construction force around a small "nuclei" of career Seabees, the Navy called up over 10,000 mostly veteran reservists and quickly expanded the Seabees' ranks from 3,300 men to over 14,000. Just two months later, on September 15, the Seabees landed at Inchon as part of General MacArthur's amphibious assault far behind the North Korean lines. During the landing, they not only endured heavy enemy fire but also fought thirty-foot tides and swift currents while positioning pontoon causeways to supply and service the new beachhead.[56]

Over course of the next three years, the Seabees performed a number of important tasks for the Marines. Among these were the construction and maintenance of the "K-fields" for the various Marine Air Groups operating on the Korean peninsula, which the Navy expedited by breaking several Seabee units up into small detachments and assigning each a specific airfield of responsibility. The Seabees endeared themselves further to the Marines when nine of them, working around the clock in below zero weather, managed to keep twenty-one miles of rough road open between an isolated Marine intercept squadron and its supply depot.[57]

Perhaps the Seabees' most hair raising operation of the conflict began on June 6, 1952 when PHIBCB 1's Detachment "George" began building an emergency airstrip for damaged Marine and Navy aircraft on Yo Do island, located some four and a half miles off shore in Communist-held Wonsan Harbor. Called Operation CRIPPLED CHICK, the construction effort required Detachment George to build a 120-foot by 2,400-foot airfield, in 45 days, while working directly under the muzzles of North Korean and Chinese guns. Despite the island's rocky terrain and two enemy bombardments, the construction took only nineteen days. The elated Seabees of Detachment George dubbed the new airstrip "Briscoe Field," after 7th Fleet commander Vice Admiral Robert P. Briscoe, and opened it for business. The Marines first reaped the benefits of the detachment's courage and hard work on July 15 when seven returning F4U-4 Corsair pilots ran out of gas over Wonsan and landed on Briscoe field for refueling. This was the first of many such emergency landings that Marine and Navy aviators would make there in the future.[58]

Unlike World War II, the Seabees did very little direct defensive fighting. This was largely because the war's post-1951 front, which ran along the 38th Parallel, was static and resembled more of a World War I trench network than the more fluid combat environment experienced during World War II. Additionally, the North Koreans and Communist Chinese had no real airborne or amphibious capabilities, and the Korean peninsula's expansive geography gave the Seabees a relatively safe operating environment. Together, this allowed them to do their work well behind the lines without having to worry about sudden rearward enemy attacks on their camps. As a result, the Seabees did not have to fight in Korea as they had in World War II and suffered comparatively fewer casualties.

The U.S., North Korea, and China signed an armistice on July 27, 1953, which halted the fighting but failed to establish a permanent peace. Although the Korean War was effectively over, the Cold War between the U.S. and the Soviet Union began heating up. As a result, the Navy did not fully demobilize the Seabees as it had after World War II. Instead, it maintained an active duty force of approximately 10,000 Seabees in ten reduced strength NMCB and PHIBCB units and began a regular pattern of Seabee training and deployment to prepare for a possible third world war. Consequently, the Seabees found themselves more frequently rotating in and out of several forward naval operating bases, such as Guam, Okinawa, and a new naval station at Rota, Spain, which the Bureau of Yards and Docks had begun building in 1953 in cooperation with the Spanish Navy. To help Port Hueneme handle the increasing tempo of global construction operations, and to establish an Atlantic Coast Seabee base, the Navy also opened a second construction battalion center at Gulfport, Mississippi in 1952.

The Cold War kept the Seabees active through the 1950s and 1960s. In 1955, they returned to Antarctica during Operation DEEP FREEZE, and maintained a presence there as part of the Port Hueneme-based Naval Support Force-Antarctica (NSFA) until 1993, when they turned their duties over to civilian contractors. As the Soviet threat heightened, the Seabees became involved in operations of a more unconventional nature. For instance, in 1961, Seabee Mobile Recovery Teams began training for nuclear warfare at Port Hueneme, while in 1965, one hundred fifty-five Seabees deployed overseas to support the Department of State's anti-bugging and counterintelligence efforts at U.S. embassies.[59]

The onset of the Vietnam War in 1964 sent the Seabees' into a hot war zone once again. They had been operating peacefully in Vietnam since 1955, but rising tensions in 1963 led to the deployment of small Seabee "Teams" there to support South Vietnamese counterinsurgency operations and American internal development projects. A junior CEC officer, eleven enlisted men, and a corpsman comprised each of these teams.[60]

As fighting escalated and American forces began taking greater responsibility for military operations, the first full naval construction battalions began arriving in May 1965 and the Seabees immediately suffered their first combat casualties. Among these was their first ever Congressional Medal of Honor winner, Construction Mechanic 3rd Class Marvin G. Shields of Seabee Team 1104, which was posted with a U.S. Army Special Forces detachment at Dong Xoai. Shields earned his medal by showing "heroic initiative and great personal valor" during a ferocious Viet Cong (VC) attack on his detachment's compound on June 10, 1965. Wounded early in the battle, Shields not only rescued a more critically wounded man, but also continued carrying ammunition and supplies to the beleaguered compound, helped repel further enemy attacks, and silenced an enemy machine gun nest. The VC mortally wound him during this last action, which saved the lives of many of his Green Beret and Seabee comrades. President Lyndon B. Johnson awarded him the Medal of Honor posthumously on September 13, 1966, and the Navy later named a new fast frigate after him, the USS *Marvin Shields* (FF-1066), which entered service in 1971.[61]

Over the next three years, the number of Seabees "in-country" would swell to over 10,000 men, who were deployed in four headquarter staffs, fifteen Seabee Teams, twelve full battalions, and two maintenance units. The Navy ultimately organized these units into the 3rd Naval Construction Brigade, which oversaw all Seabee operations in Vietnam, under the direction of Commander of Naval Forces-Vietnam (COMNAVFORV). Additional Seabee units also rotated into Vietnam as the war reached its crescendo, including among others, the Atlantic Fleet NMCBs 1,6, and 7, and the re-commissioned NMCBs 40, 53, 58, 62, 71, 74, 121, 128, and 133.[62]

During their tours of the duty in Vietnam, the Seabees performed much of the same types of work that their World War II and Korean War forefathers had done. They built and maintained numerous roads, airfields, helicopter pads, bridges as well as fortifications, ammunition and fuel depots, port facilities, and other vital military and civilian structures. In the effort to win the hearts and minds of the Vietnamese people, the Seabees had also honed their skills as nation builders and humanitarian workers through the U.S. government's "Civic Action" program. Described by historian Richard Tregaskis as "one of their most important functions in the modern kind of war," Civic Action entailed the construction of countless roads, dams, bridges, schools, hospitals, and other basic infrastructure facilities throughout South Vietnam. The idea was, as President Johnson told reporters in February 1966, to help the Vietnamese people not only militarily but also in the "struggle against social injustice, against hunger, disease and ignorance, against political apathy and indifference."[63]

Unlike the Korean War, Vietnam was a guerilla war in a jungle environment, with close-quarter fighting conditions very similar to those experienced in the Philippines, Southwest Asia, and the South Pacific. As a result, the Seabees found that they had to be continually prepared to drop their tools and fight when attacked, as Seabee Team 1104 had done at Dong Xoai. Therefore, during the course of the war, they were forced to defend themselves in a number of notable actions.[64]

Perhaps the bloodiest of these occurred four months after Dong Xoai, on the night of October 1965, when a 200-strong VC raiding force attacked the unfinished Da Nang Naval Hospital. Following a mortar and machine gun barrage, the VC smashed through the Marines' security perimeter and assaulted NMCB 9's camp near the hospital. The battalion's commanding officer, Commander Richard E. Anderson, had been preparing for such an attack by clearing the underbrush around the area to establish clear fields of fire, and also by insisting on routine bunker drills. His Seabees were thus ready to fight back, and they did so successfully, with the help of Builder Arlen S. Jenks and Builder 3rd Class Ray A. Hansen, who kept the VC at bay but were both badly wounded. Constructionman Sydney L. Sutton manned another machine gun and also helped blunt the attack. The cost had been high though, with two killed and ninety-three wounded. The VC launched another attack again in January, this time with eighty one millimeter heavy mortars, but the Seabees' fierce return fire discouraged a direct assault on their camp.[65]

Seabee units operating out in the "boonies" were especially vulnerable to attack since the VC and North Vietnamese Army (NVA) recognized the political danger of Civic Action to their war aims. In one incident that took place in February 1966, fifteen to twenty VC guerillas ambushed a two-truck convoy driven by members of Seabee Team 0907 near the village of Ba Thap. Both trucks careened off the road, and the ensuing firefight degenerated into a fierce brawl in which the Seabees had to fight off the guerillas using not only their rifles and side arms but also their fists. The Seabees survived but were badly wounded during the attack. Other Seabee units working in remote areas shared similar experiences, which were made even more harrowing by the never ending threats of mines, booby-traps, sappers, and snipers, as well as sudden rocket and mortar attacks.[66]

As the numbers of Seabees peaked in 1968, so did the intensity of combat, particularly during the Tet Offensive, when they defended themselves against heavy VC and NVA attacks. The best example of Seabee fighting tenacity occurred on the first night of the offensive (January 31, 1968) at Tam Ky, forty miles south of Da Nang, when a combined force of VC and NVA troops attacked a U.S. Marine and Army of the Republic of Vietnam (ARVN) headquarters camp. A fifty-five man detachment from NMCB 6 under Lieutenant Gary Weisner joined the Marines and the ARVN troops to drive the VC/NVA troops back. Afterward, a body count revealed 581 dead guerillas and enemy soldiers, forty-six of which were attributed to Weisner's Seabees. Additionally, that same night, Seabees from NMCB 128 defended Camp Faulkner at Da Nang against enemy amphibious troops and sappers using their M-16 rifles, M-79 grenade launchers, and M-60 machine guns. Afterward, they spotted enemy rocket-launching positions and directed Marine artillery fire onto them. Finally, during the siege of Khe Sahn, which started ten days before Tet, detachments from NMCB 11 and 53 and CBMU 301 helped the Marines hold an estimated thirty to forty thousand NVA regulars at bay when they were not repairing the base's air strip. Three Seabees were subsequently killed and sixteen wounded at Khe Sahn before American reinforcements broke the seventy-seven day siege on April 8.[67]

Ultimately, heavy fighting associated with the Tet Offensive and Khe Sahn claimed fourteen Seabees lives with another fifty-seven wounded. By mid-1968, the Navy counted a total of fifty-seven Seabees killed and hundreds more wounded up to that point in the war. However, the Seabees' building and fighting in Vietnam was nearly finished from a military point of view, and their numbers began declining as part of a larger American movement toward disengagement. By the end of 1968, the numbers of Seabees in country had dropped from a high of 10,500 officers and men to 7,700. Their withdrawal continued steadily over the next three years, and the last full battalion in Vietnam, until NMCB 5, departed for Guam on November 7, 1971. CBMU 302 left for Subic Bay in February 1972, and the final four Seabee Teams, 0321, 7107, 7108, pulled out in the early spring of 1972.[68]

Into the Gulf

Following the Vietnam War, the Navy entered a difficult period of disarray and contraction, and the Seabees reverted to a peacetime strength of ten active duty battalions, with other construction support units maintained on a reserve basis. Despite the drawdown, the Seabees' duties and missions continued on a worldwide basis, particularly on the humanitarian and disaster relief fronts, which were modeled on their Civic Action programs in Vietnam. Unfortunately, a number of reorganizations within the Navy Department, beginning in 1966 with the abolition of the Bureau of Yards and Docks and its replacement with the Naval Facilities Engineering Command (NAVFAC), began diluting the Seabees' force strength by parceling them out within the Navy and Marine Corps logistics chains. The trend continued into the 1980s with additional reorganizations and realignments of the Reagan administration. But the growing organizational weakness of the Navy's overall construction establishment, which in many ways assumed the characteristics of a rear-echelon logistics organization rather than the large-scale building and fighting force of years past, did not become evident until the early 1990s.[69]

During the 1980s, the Middle East began supplanting the Communist bloc as the most serious challenge to American global interests. This region had been inflamed by a continuing conflict between Israel and the Palestinians and the sudden rise of virulent Islamic fundamentalism, beginning with the overthrow of the Shah of Iran in 1979 by the fanatical Shi'ite followers of Ayatollah Ruhollah Khomeini. Tensions became even more explosive when the self-made Sunni dictator of Iraq, Saddam Hussein, invaded Khomeini's new Islamic republic in September 1980, turning the Persian Gulf into a virtual shooting gallery.[70]

Over the next eight years, the two belligerents fought each other to a bloody stalemate along their shared border. The Iranian Army was much larger than Iraq's, and after evicting the Iraqis from their initial territorial conquests in 1982, had turned the tables on Saddam by launching their own offensives into Iraq. Saddam ultimately held them at bay though by modernizing his own army along Soviet lines and employing chemical weapons against them, killing and wounding thousands. Additionally, when the Iranian-backed Shi'ite Kurds in northern Iraq began stirring against his regime, Saddam responded by drenching forty of their villages with the same mustard and nerve agents that he had been using against the Iranians. The worst of these attacks occurred on March 16, 1988 against the Kurdish city of Halabja, where over 5,000 civilians were killed and 10,000 more injured.[71]

After slaughtering the Kurds, Saddam finally brought the Iranians to their knees later that summer through a series of hard-hitting, armored offensives combined with a large-scale, indiscriminate, aerial assault on Iranian cities using SCUD missiles, which the Iranians could hardly answer. When rumors circulated that Saddam had reconfigured his SCUDs to carry chemical warheads, mass panic ensued and the Iranian cities emptied. Faced with shattered morale on the home front and a hopeless military situation in the gulf, which had been kept open by the U.S. Navy, Khomeini's government sought a cease-fire through the United Nations (U.N.). After some wrangling, Saddam accepted, and on August 8, 1988 the U.N.'s Security Council passed Resolution 598, which essentially ended the war.[72]

Although neither side won any appreciable gains from the conflict, Saddam considered the outcome a "great victory." The relatively good performance of his army in the war's final stages encouraged him further, and by 1990, he was casting his eyes south to Kuwait, a small but extremely oil-rich nation that had supported Iraq during the war with generous loans. Burdened with a heavy war debt, Saddam had wanted the Kuwaitis to cancel their share of it, which amounted to an estimated $14 billion, but they had refused. Moreover, they were routinely exceeding their OPEC-established quotas for oil production, and thus driving down oil prices at Saddam's expense. He also suspected the Kuwaitis of illegally slant drilling across the border into Iraqi oil fields. They denied his allegations and rebuffed his demands for compensation. Stifled diplomatically, Saddam thus plotted a summer invasion to resolve his multiple problems with Kuwait once and for all.[73]

On August 2, 1990, Saddam's battle-hardened army rolled across the Kuwaiti border and seized the country. A week later, he formally declared Kuwait as Iraq's 19th province. American reaction to the Iraqi invasion was quick and forceful. On August 6, President George H. W. Bush announced that the U.S. was sending American forces to Saudi Arabia to defend that country against Iraq. This operation was named DESERT SHIELD and represented the largest American military build-up since the Vietnam War. DESERT SHIELD turned into DESERT STORM on January 16, 1991, when President Bush authorized Coalition forces to launch a massive campaign to liberate Kuwait from Saddam's control.[74]

During the conflict, the Navy Seabees accompanied the Marines to war for the first time since Vietnam, beginning with a 210-strong detachment from PHIBCB 1, which arrived in Saudi Arabia on August 13, 1990 and immediately went to work unloading ships from the Maritime Prepositioning Force. Elements from CBUs 411 and 415 arrived shortly afterward and began building Fleet Hospital 5 at Al Jubail. By September 14, Air Detachments from NMCBs 4, 5, 7, and 40, were also in theater, and their main bodies arrived by October 18. In December, NMCBs 24 (Reserve) and 74 relieved NMCBs 4 and 7, and joined NMCBs 5 and 40 in Bahrain. Altogether, some five thousand Seabees in regimental strength deployed to Saudi Arabia during this time. Placed under the command of Commodore Michael Johnson from the 3rd Naval Construction Regiment, they became a collective element of the Marine Air/Ground Task Force (MAGTF) for the impending war.[75]

This organizational arrangement was fully in accordance with the Navy and Marine Corps' Joint Doctrine for Civil Engineering Support that had been implemented on May 1, 1987 when the two services adopted specific Terms of Reference (TOR) to govern the Seabees' role as a general engineering support force to MAGTFs. This doctrine was the first time that the Navy and Marine Corps had attempted to capture the "informal and deeply rooted" relationship between the Seabees and the Marines on paper. Its intent was to "multiply" the engineering capabilities of MAGTFs by assigning the Seabees to the direct operational control of MAGTF commanders, with CEC liaison officers serving only in advisory capacities. The doctrine was "battalion centric" and made it clear that Seabee units could not be attached to any Marine organization, and they would complement rather than duplicate the capabilities of the Marine engineers. However, a MEF engineer officer, rather than a CEC officer, would advise a MAGTF commander on how best to employ all engineers under his command, including Seabees.[76]

While the theory looked good on paper, it somewhat resembled the old Bureau of Yards and Docks' pre-World War II plan for war against Japan and also depended upon a MAGTF's full understanding of the Seabees' capabilities in relation to Marine combat engineers. Unfortunately, most MAGTF commanders were Marine riflemen and not engineers, and they had only vague ideas of what Seabees did and how to manage them. Because the Seabees were not tactically mobile and did not have combat engineering skills (such as breaching and mine clearance) like Marine engineers, MARCENT made no attempt to organize them jointly into I MEF as an "organic" engineering force underneath a higher echelon CEC officer as in World War II. Instead, Commodore Johnson reported directly to the MARCENT and I MEF commander, Lieutenant General Walter E. Boomer, and the Seabees remained both homogenous and entangled within the I MEF logistics chain during Desert Shield and Desert Storm.[77]

Administered through the Marine Force Service Support Groups (FSSGs), which one Marine Reserve officer described as "lumbering dinosaurs" that "should have become extinct long ago," this engineer management scheme created a number of operational problems for both the Marines and the Seabees. First and foremost, without anyone with command authority to conduct resource analysis and set priorities, MARCENT found it impossible to mass Seabees and other engineer units for large projects. MARCENT found this especially frustrating since the senior Marine commanders felt that they had plenty of engineers in theater but just could not get their hands on them. The presence of U.S. Army and Coalition engineers compounded the Marines' engineer management dilemma further as MARCENT made no provision for handling a joint engineering force during its operations. Construction logistics likewise became problematic since Seabees required specialized construction materials that had to be tailored to specific jobs and ordered at the last minute. This required higher level planning, design, and procurement, which proved quite difficult under the doctrine's rigid MAGTF command scheme.[78]

Moreover, the flow of gear and equipment from their main body deployment sites in Guam and Roosevelt Roads and from their Gulfport and Port Hueneme warehouses was excruciatingly slow. NMCB 40, for instance, had packed up its equipment on Guam before flying into Saudi Arabia, but had sat waiting, unproductively, for the shipment, which arrived a couple of weeks later. In the meantime, the Seabees had to ship more equipment from Port Hueneme to Guam to support Reserve NMCB 23, which replaced NMCB 40. Thus, two shipments of gear and equipment had to be moved just to get one shipment into theater, and two Seabee units had to sit unemployed until everything they needed to start work had arrived. This type of inefficiency characterized the whole Marine support structure in which the Seabees were forced to operate, as revealed in the so-called "Aspin Report" of 1992, which assessed the lessons learned during the war.[79]

Despite the challenges, the Seabees performed well during DESERT SHIELD and DESERT STORM as they fell back into their traditional role as general engineers. Under threat of Saddam's so called "Weapons of Mass Destruction" (WMDs), as his chemical, biological, and radiological stockpiles became known, the Seabees widened taxi-ways and aircraft parking areas, and built numerous troop "bed down" facilities and supply depots, among many other things. They also built a headquarters complex for I MEF and base camps for the 3rd Marine Air Wing and Marine Aircraft Groups 11, 13, 16, and 26, and for the 1st and 2nd Marine Divisions (MARDIVs). Prior to DESERT STORM's ground phase, they developed and serviced the MARDIVs assembly areas, and also built and maintained a 200-mile, four land main supply route near the Kuwaiti border, which was critical to sustaining General Norman H. Schwarzkopf's "Hail Mary" ground attack plan.[80]

However, to support the planned Marine attack north into Kuwait, Boomer ordered Johnson in January to move the Seabees forward to the Kuwaiti border. It proved to be a difficult task because they simply had too much to carry. Just to get NMCB 74 into position, Johnson and his Chief of Staff, Commander William L. Rudich, had to order it to leave part of its equipment behind and then scavenge all line haul trucking from the other three battalions for two days at a time until the battalion was redeployed. The procedure had to be repeated with each battalion in turn. All in all, it took well over a week to move all the Seabees into their new positions.[81]

Johnson's Seabees moved just as slowly after Schwarzkopf's assault began on February 24, 1991 when they fell in behind the quickly advancing Marines. Once in Kuwait, and near the end of the ground war, they found their footing again and started work on a number of large facilities, including tent camps for 42,000 Marines and soldiers, three galleys, ten aircraft parking aprons, five ammunition supply points, two expeditionary airfields, and two hangars. The Seabees also constructed several Enemy Prisoner of War camps to help house the tens of thousands of Iraqi soldiers who chose to surrender to Coalition forces rather than fight for Saddam.[82]

During DESERT STORM's six-week air campaign, the U.S. led Coalition devastated both Iraq's civilian and military infrastructure, leaving Saddam's forces reeling. Saddam retaliated by indiscriminately attacking cities in Saudi Arabia, Bahrain, and Israel with conventionally armed SCUD missiles, by releasing an enormous oil slick into the Persian Gulf on January 25, and by setting afire hundreds of Kuwaiti oil wells. He also attempted to emulate his successful armor tactics from the Iranian war by seizing the town of Khafji in Saudi Arabia on January 29. Early in that battle, a few Seabees and Marine forward observers were all that stood between the Iraqis and the northeastern Saudi oil fields since Schwarzkopf had moved most of his ground forces west in preparation for his "Hail Mary" attack. Marine and Saudi-Qatari reinforcements soon arrived, and backed by overwhelming Coalition airpower, counterattacked and routed the Iraqis.[83]

By the time that Schwarzkopf finally launched his ground campaign, Saddam's army was in no shape to resist, and on February 27, the last battered Iraqi unit fled Kuwait. With his political and military objectives fulfilled, President Bush ordered a cease-fire, beginning at 8:00 a.m. local time on February 28, exactly 100 hours into the campaign. The war formally ended on April 11, when the U.N. Security Council formally declared a cease-fire after Iraq's rubber-stamp National Assembly voted to accept Resolution 687, which spelled out the Coalition's conditions for a permanent cease-fire. Along with most other U.S. and Coalition units, the Seabees quickly departed the Middle East and returned in triumph to their home bases, with America seemingly at peace for the foreseeable future.[84]

APPENDIX II

Acronyms

AAOE	Arrival Assembly Operations Element
APOD	Air Port of Departure
AM	Aluminum Matting
AOR	Area of Responsibility
ARVN	Army of the Republic of Vietnam
ASP	Ammunition Supply Point
ASR	Alternate Supply Route
ATO	Air Tasking Order
AVLB	Armored Vehicle Launched Bridges
BEEP	Battalion Equipment Evaluation Program
BPT	"Be Prepared To"
BUG	Battle Unit Global
C^2	Command and Control
CAG	Civil Affairs Group
CBO	Congressional Budget Office
CBC	Construction Battalion Center
CBMU	Construction Battalion Maintenance Unit
CBR	Chemical/Biological/Radiological
CBU	Construction Battalion Unit
CCRF	Continental U.S. Contingency Response Force
CEC	Civil Engineer Corps
CENTCOM	United States Central Command
CESE	Civil Engineering Support Equipment
CFLCC	Combined Forces Land Component Commander
CG	Commanding General

ACRONYMS

CJTF-CM	Combined Joint Task Force Consequence Management
CM	Core Module
CMO	Civil Military Operation
CMOC	Civil-Military Operations Center
CNO	Chief of Naval Operations
CO	Commanding Officer
COA	Course of Action
COC	Command Operations Center
COMNAVFORV	Commander of Naval Forces-Vietnam
COMPACFLT	Pacific Fleet Command
CONCAP	Construction Capability
CONUS	Continental United States
CPA	Coalition Provisional Authority
CSH	Combat Surgical Hospital
CSSB	Combat Service Support Battalion
DACOWITS	Defense Committee for Women in the Service
DC	Displaced Civilian
DED	Detailed Equipment Decontamination
DERF	Defense Emergency Relief Fund
DET	Detachment
DFT	Deployment for Training
DLA	Defense Logistics Agency
DOD	Department of Defense
DRR	Deliberate Runway Repair
EPW	Enemy Prisoner of War
ERDC	Engineer, Research and Development Center
ESB	Engineer Support Battalion
EOC	Engineer Operations Center
EUCOM	U.S. European Command
EWL	Engineering Work Line
FARP	Forward Air Refueling Point
FOB	Forward Operating Base
FRAGO	Fragmentary Order
FSSG	Force Service Support Group
GOPLATS	Gas and Oil Platforms
GOSP	Gas-Oil Separation Plant
GPR	Ground Penetrating Radar
GWOT	Global War on Terrorism
HA	Humanitarian Assistance/Holding Area

HESCO	Hercules Engineering Solutions Consortium
HET	Heavy Equipment Transporter
HF	High Frequency
HMMWV	High-Mobility Multipurpose Wheeled Vehicle (Humvee)
HQ	Headquarters
HUMINT	Human Intelligence
IAEA	International Atomic Energy Agency
ICAP	Iraqi Construction Apprentice Program
IDF	Israeli Defense Force
IED	Improvised Explosive Device
ILO	Integrated Logistics Overhaul
IO	Information Operation
JCS	Joint Chiefs of Staff
JFCOM	Joint Forces Command
JTAM	Jump Through Ass Mission
KBR	Kellogg Brown & Root
KIA	Killed in Action
KO	Kinetic Operation
LANTDIV	Atlantic Division
LAR	Light Armored Reconnaissance
LCAC	Landing Craft Air Cushion
L/D	Line of Departure
LNO	Liaison Officer
LOC	Line of Communication
LSA	Logistics Support Area
MAGTF	Marine Air/Ground Task Force
MARCENT	U.S. Marine Corps Forces Central Command
MARDIV	Marine Division
MARFORPAC	U.S. Marine Forces-Pacific
MAW	Marine Air Wing
MEF	Marine Expeditionary Force
MEFEX	MEF Command Element Exercise
MEG	Marine Expeditionary Force Engineer Group
MEU	Marine Expeditionary Unit
MGB	Medium Girder Bridge
MHG	MEF Headquarters Group
MILCON	Military Construction
MJB	Mabey & Johnson Bridge

ACRONYMS

MLC	Military Logistics Command/MEF Logistics Command
MLO	Materials Liaison Officer
MOASS	Mother of All Sand Storms
MOPP	Military Operational Protective Posture
MOUT	Military Operations on Urban Terrain
MP	Military Police
MPCOA	Most Probable Course of Action
MPF	Maritime Pre-positioning Force
MPF (E)	Maritime Prepositioned Force (Enhanced)
MPSRON	Maritime Pre-positioning Ship Squadron
MRBC	Multi Role Bridge Company
MRE	Meal-Ready-to-Eat
MSA	Munitions Storage Area
MSC	Major Subordinate Command
MSR	Main Supply Route
MSTP	MAGTF Staff Training Program
MTVR	Medium Tactical Vehicle Replacement
MV	Merchant Vessel
MWR	Morale, Welfare, and Recreation
NAB	Naval Amphibious Base
NATO	North Atlantic Treaty Organization
NAVCENT	U.S. Naval Forces Central Command
NAVFAC	Naval Facilities Engineering Command
NBC	Nuclear, Biological, and Chemical
NCA	National Command Authority
NCD	Naval Construction Division
NCF	Naval Construction Force
NCFSU	Naval Construction Force Support Unit
NCB	Naval Construction Battalion (World War II)
NCB	Naval Construction Brigade (Modern)
NCR	Naval Construction Regiment
NHC	Naval Historical Center
NGO	Non-government Organization
NIPRnet	Non-classified Internet Protocol Router Network
NMCB	Naval Mobile Construction Battalion
NSFA	Naval Support Force-Antarctica
NVA	North Vietnamese Army
NVG	Night Vision Goggles
O&M	Operations and Maintenance
OEF	Operation ENDURING FREEDOM
OIC	Officer in Charge
OICC	Office in Charge of Construction

OIF	Operation IRAQI FREEDOM
OMB	Office of Management and Budget
OPLAN	Operations Plan
OPNAV	Office of the Chief of Naval Operations
OPNAVINST	Chief of Naval Operations Instruction
OPT	Operational Planning Team
ORHA	Office of Reconstruction and Humanitarian Assistance
ORCON	Originator Controlled
ORM	Operational Risk Management
PACDIV	Pacific Division
PACFLT	U.S. Pacific Fleet
PACOM	Pacific Command
PHIBCB	Amphibious Construction Battalion
PHIBLEX	Amphibious Landing Exercise
PSYOPS	Psychological Operations
PWRMS	Prepositioned War Reserve Material System
R4	Retrograde, Regeneration, Reconstitution, and Redeployment
RCT	Regimental Combat Team
RF	Radio Frequency
RFF	Request for Forces
RIP	Relief-in-Place
ROC	Rehearsal of Concept
ROK	Republic of Korea
ROTC	Reserve Officer Training Corps
ROWPU	Reverse Osmosis Water Purification Unit
RPG	Rocket Propelled Grenade
RRR	Rapid Runway Repair
RSO&I	Reception, Staging, Onward Movement, and Integration
RTCH	Rough Terrain Container Handler
SATCOM	Satellite Communication
SCIF	Sensitive Compartmented Information Facility
SCUD	NATO Codename for Soviet-built SS-1 Intermediate Range Ballistic Missile
SWC	Seabee Warfare Combat
SEAL	U.S. Navy Sea/Air/Land Commando
SECDEF	Secretary of Defense
SIPRnet	Secret Internet Protocol Router Network
SITREP	Situation Report
SOP	Standard Operating Procedure
SPOD	Sea Port of Departure
SRG	Seabee Readiness Group

ACRONYMS

TAA	Tactical Assembly Area
TACON	Tactical Control
TEOC	Tele-Engineering Operations Center
TOA	Table of Allowance
TOR	Terms of Reference
TOW	Tube-launched, Optically tracked, Wire-guided missile
TPFDD	Time-Phased Force and Deployment Data
TTPs	Tactics, Techniques, and Procedures
UAV	Unmanned Aerial Vehicle
UCT	Underwater Construction Team
U.K.	United Kingdom
UMCC	Unit Movement Control Center
U.N.	United Nations
UNMOVIC	United Nations Monitoring, Verification and Inspection Commission
USA	U.S. Army
USAF	U.S. Air Force
USAID	U.S. Agency for International Development
USMC	U.S. Martine Corps
USN	U.S. Navy
USNR	U.S. Naval Reserve
UXO	Unexploded Ordnance
VC	Viet Cong
VTC	Video Teleconference
WIA	Wounded in Action
WMD	Weapon of Mass Destruction

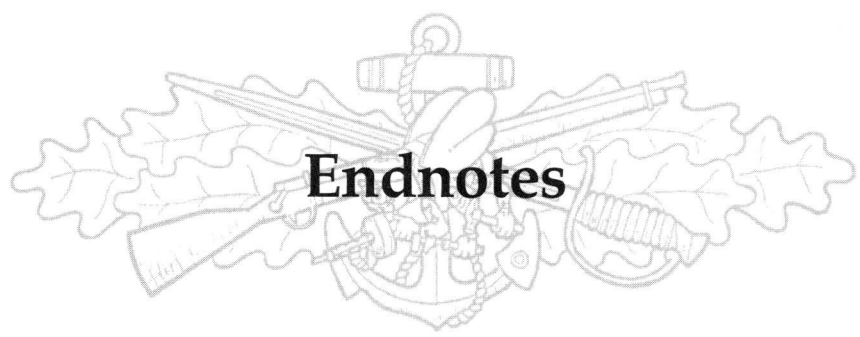

Endnotes

Foreword

1. Dani Dodge, "Returning Seabees Find Role Different," *Ventura County Star*, April 7, 2003; Journalist 2nd Class Chad V. Pritt, "Seabees Awarded Bronze Stars for OIF," Story Number NNS031230-01, *Navy News Service*, December 30, 2003.

Chap 1 — Can Do!

1. The proper shorthand name for Saddam Hussein is 'Saddam.' As Kenneth M. Pollack notes in *The Threatening Storm: The Case for Invading Iraq*, (New York, New York: Random House, 2002), footnote 2, 429, most Iraqis at birth are traditionally given their own first name followed by their father's name. Since 'Hussein' is his father's name, it is most appropriate to simply call the Iraqi dictator 'Saddam'; For the development of OPLAN 1003V, see General Tommy Franks, with Malcolm McConnell, *American Soldier*, (New York, New York: Regan Books, 2004), pp. 382-431.

2. In January 2008, FBI agent George Piro told *60 Minutes* correspondent Scott Pelley that Saddam admitted to him during interrogation that the U.S.-led invasion of Iraq in March and April 2003 had come as a surprise. Saddam apparently expected only a four-day aerial attack like Operation DESERT FOX in 1998, and never expected an all-out invasion by the U.S.-led Coalition. According to Piro, Saddam maintained the façade that his regime possessed Weapons of Mass Destruction to prevent an Iranian invasion, which he believed more likely; CBSNews.com, "Interrogator: Invasion Surprised Saddam," January 24, 2008.

3. See Franks, *American Soldier*, pp. 331, 418-419, and Lieutenant General Michael DeLong, Lieutenant General (USMC), with Noah Lukeman, *Inside CENTCOM: The Unvarnished Truth About the Wars in Afghanistan and Iraq*, (Washington, DC: Regnery Publishing, 2004), pp. 79, 84; Edward J. Marolda and Robert J. Schneller, Jr., *Shield and Sword: The United States Navy and the Persian Gulf War*, (Annapolis, Maryland.: Naval Institute Press, 2001), pp. 226-227, 314, 337-339.

4. DeLong, *Inside CENTCOM*, 85-86; For a detailed description of the Iraqi state and its society on the eve of Operation IRAQI FREEDOM, see Pollack, *The Threatening Storm*, pp. 110-147; For Saddam's methods and strategic goals, see Charles Duelfer, "Comprehensive Report of the Special Adviser to the Director of Central Intelligence on Iraq's WMD Weapons of Mass Destruction," Volume I of

III, Washington, DC: Central Intelligence Agency, 2004, pp. 1-24, 48-49. For Saddam's subversion of the United Nations Oil-For-Food Program, see Paul A. Volcker, Richard J. Goldstone, and Mark Pieth, "Interim Report of the Independent Inquiry Committee into the United Nations Oil-For-Food Programme," February 3, 2005; Franks, *American Soldier*, p. 337.

Chap 2 — New Doctrines

1. Joint doctrine has been an intensely divisive topic within the armed services since before World War II. The 1980 DESERT EAGLE debacle in Iran and the troubled 1982 invasion of Granada demonstrated much of the folly associated with their rigid pursuit of prior parochial interests to the detriment of America's warfighting capabilities. Edward N. Luttwak's *The Pentagon and the Art of War: The Question of Military Reform* (New York: Simon and Schuster, 1985) highlighted some of the absurdities within the defense establishment arising from the services' doctrinal and operational rivalry with one another. His book influenced a number of powerful Republican and Democratic lawmakers, including Senators Barry Goldwater, Samuel Nunn, William S. Cohen, and Representatives William Nichols and Les Aspin, among others, and directly led to the passage of the Goldwater-Nichols Act. For the best and most thorough history of the Goldwater-Nichols Act, see James R. Locher III, *Victory on the Potomac: The Goldwater-Nichols Act Unifies the Pentagon* (College Station, Tex.: Texas A&M University Press, 2002); For problems and service resistance to joint doctrine, see Christopher M. Bourne, Unintended Consequences of the Goldwater-Nichols Act, *Joint Force Quarterly*, Spring 1998, 99-108, and Douglas Macgregor, The Joint Force: A Decade, No Progress, *Joint Force Quarterly*, Winter 2000-01, pp. 18-23.

2. United States Marine Corps Headquarters, Marine Corps Doctrine Publication 1, *Warfighting*, 1997 revision of Fleet Marine Force Manual 1, 1989, by General Alfred M. Gray, (Washington, DC: Department of the Navy, 1997), 72-75; See also United States Marine Corps, "Expeditionary Maneuver Warfare," in *Marine Corps Gazette*, February 2002, pp. A-1 through A-10.

3. Gray, *Warfighting*, pp. 72-75.

4. Ibid.

5. Michael C., Howard, Colonel, USMC, and Major James D. Gonsalves, USMC, Major Larry F. X. Henigan, USMC, Captain Joseph C. Swanson, USMC, and Lieutenant (JG) Mark V. Rossi, CEC, USN, I MEG War Diary, *"MEG My Day": A History of the First Marine Expeditionary Force Engineer Group "The MEG" in Operation IRAQI FREEDOM*, (Norfolk, Virginia: 1st Naval Construction Division, 4 July 2003), Chapter 2, pp. 1-4, (Hereafter Cited as *MEG History*); Larry W. Berquist, Major, USMC, "Combat Engineer Battalion: A Time for Change," Quantico, Virginia: Marine Corps Command and Staff College, 1990), pp. 7-9.

6. Ibid.; The short-lived Marine Engineer Regiments had a lasting impact on the Marines' organization structure. To this day, the 16th, 17th, 18th, 19th, and 20th are not assigned to regimental units in the modern Marine Corps, whose sequence runs from 1st to 29th Marines. See Berquist, "Combat Engineer Battalion," p. 8.

7. *MEG History*, Chapter 2, pp. 1-4.

8. Ibid.

9. Ibid.; U.S. Marine Corps and U.S. Navy, Fleet Marine Force Manual 13-4/Naval Warfare Publication 22-9, *Naval Construction Force Support of MAGTF Operations*, August 1991, (Washington, D.C.: Department of the Navy, 1991), 5005-5007 (5-4 through 5-7); Bisset's command included 8th, 10th, and 11th Naval Construction Brigades, over 50,000 U.S. Army engineers, and some 15,000 British engineer troops, who had the mission of building B-29 bases at Kume Shima. Altogether, he was responsible for approximately 110,000 military engineers in preparation for the Okinawa Campaign. See Appendix 1.

10. Message from CG I MEF and COMMARFORPAC, "Subject: FLEET OPERATIONAL NEEDS STATEMENT (FONS)/MARINE ENGINEER GROUP," November 1, 1997, Center for Naval Analysis; MCCDC, "Total Force Structure Division and a Capability Assessment Council, "Subject: FLEET OPERATIONAL NEED STATEMENT FOR MEF ENGINEER GROUP (MEG) HEADQUARTERS (HQ) FOR CONTINGENCY OPERATIONS, (undated but late 1997 or early 1998), Center for Naval Analysis.

11. Ibid.

12. Office of the Chief of Naval Operations and Headquarters U.S. Marine Corps, Naval Warfare Publication 4-04.1 and Marine Corps Warfare Publication 4-11.5, *Seabee Operations in the MAGTF*, (Washington, DC: Department of the Navy, 1997); Navy Warfare Development Command, Naval Warfare Publication 4-04.2, *Navy Civil Engineer Operations for Component Commanders*, (Washington, DC: Department of the Navy, 1998); Chief of Naval Operations, OPNAV INSTRUCTION 5450.46K, Subject: Naval Construction Force (NCF) Policy, May 25, 1999.

13. *MEG History*, Chapter 2, pp. 1-4.

14. Rick Kohout (I MEF CNA Field Representative), "Assessing the MEF Engineer Group Concept," December 2001.

15. Ibid; I MEF, "MEG Decision Brief," Camp Pendleton, California, January 24, 2001, (Power Point presentation), Center for Naval Analysis; I MEF Decision Paper, Re: MEF Engineer Group, February 12, 2001, Center for Naval Analysis.

16. For a comprehensive background to the 9/11 attacks and discussions of the complex history of terrorism, the rise of militant Islam, and the struggle to combat Al Qaeda, see Simon Reeve, *The New Jackals: Ramzi Yousef, Osama Bin Laden, and the Future of Terrorism* (Boston, Massachusetts: Northeastern University Press, 1999); Bernard Lewis, *The Crisis of Islam: Holy War and Unholy Terror* (New York: Random House, 2004); Daniel Pipes, *Militant Islam Reaches America* (New York: W.W. Norton & Company, Inc., 2002); Ahmed Rashid, *Taliban: Militant Islam, Oil, and Fundamentalism in Central Asia* (New Haven, Connecticut: Yale University Press, 2000), Ahmed Rashid, *Jihad: The Rise of Militant Islam in Central Asia* (New Haven, Connecticut: Yale University Press, 2002); For the U.S. government's institutional failure to sufficiently understand and confront the Al Qaeda threat before 9/11, see *9/11 Commission Report: Final Report of the National Commission on Terrorist Attacks Upon the United States*, (New York, New York: W.W. Norton & Company, 2004), pp. 108-143, 145-214, 339-360.

17. Bob Woodward, *Bush at War*, (New York, New York: Simon & Schuster, 2002), pp. 1-3, 31-33, 74-78.

18. Fred Peck, "Still Doing the Impossible: A New Operational Construct for "The Marine Corps After Next," in *Navy League of the United States*, November 2002.
19. Peck, "Still Doing the Impossible"; Sergeant Joseph R. Chenelly, USMC, "Operation Swift Freedom: From a Cloud of Dust to a New Base," in *Defend AMERICA: U.S. Department of Defense News about the War on Terrorism*, December 3, 2001; *History of the 15th Marine Expeditionary Unit*, 2003; Captain James Ostrich Interview with Commander Robyn Eastman, January 12, 2005, 4-6, hereafter cited as Ostrich/Eastman Interview.
20. James P. Rife Interview with Chief Equipment Operator Charles Hair, January 12, 2005, 7-8, hereafter cited as Rife/Hair Interview; James P. Rife Interview with Captain William C. McKerall, January 13, 2005, 3, 27, hereafter cited as Rife/McKerall Interview.
21. Ostrich/Eastman Interview, p. 5.
22. For more on Brigadier General Donald C. Wurster, see his official U.S. Air Force biography at http://www.af.mil/bios/bio.asp?bioID=7672.
23. Command Histories for NMCBs 1 and 4, 2001-2002, Operational Archives Branch, U.S. Naval History and Heritage Command.

Chap 3 — War Plans

1. General Tommy Franks, with Malcolm McConnell, *American Soldier*, (New York, New York: Regan Books, 2004), 315; Bob Woodward, *Plan of Attack*, (New York, New York: Simon & Schuster, 2004), 1-5; Volcker, "Interim Report."
2. United States Department of State, Office for the Coordinator for Counterterrorism, *Patterns of Global Terrorism 2001*, May 2002. For specifics on Iraq as a state sponsor of terrorism, see "Overview of State-Sponsored Terrorism," in United States Department of State, Office for the Coordinator for Counterterrorism, *Patterns of Global Terrorism 2001*, April 2003, 79; United States Department of State, Counterterrorism Office, *Patterns of Global Terrorism 2002*, Appendix G, "Iraq and Terrorism," Secretary of State Colin L. Powell, Excerpt from Remarks to the United Nations Security Council, 5 February 2003.
3. Ibid.
4. Powell, Excerpt from Remarks to the United Nations Security Council, 5 February 2003.
5. The "Secret" Downing Street Memo concerning IRAQ: PRIME MINISTER'S MEETING, 23 JULY, From: Matthew Rycroft, Date: 23 July 2002, S 195 /02,

    cc: Defence Secretary, Foreign Secretary, Attorney-General, Sir Richard Wilson, John Scarlett, Francis Richards, CDS, C, Jonathan Powell, Sally Morgan, Alastair Campbell, published in *The Sunday Times*, May 1, 2005; Jeffrey Goldberg, "A Little Learning: What Douglas Feith Knew, and When He Knew it," in *The New Yorker*, May 9, 2005 Issue.
6. Woodward, *Plan of Attack*, 1-2, 119-120; Franks, *American Soldier*, pp. 315, 329.
7. James P. Rife Interview with Lieutenant Commander David H. McAlister, January 26, 2005, pp. 7-8, hereafter cited as Rife/McAlister Interview; Rife/McKerall, Interview, pp. 5-6, 11-12.
8. James P. Rife Interview with Command Master Chief Jim Fairbanks, January 12, 2005, pp. 17-18, hereafter cited as Rife/Fairbanks Interview.

9. Rife/McKerall Interview, p.12.
10. Ibid.
11. Daryl C. Smith, "1st Naval Construction Division Established: Realignment Unifies Seabee Command to Better Serve Fleet," in *The Flagship*, August 29, 2002; For detailed description of the *Sea Power 21* strategy, see Vern Clark, Admiral, USN. "Sea Power 21 Series-Part I: Projecting Decisive Joint Capabilities," in *U.S. Naval Institute Proceedings*, October 2002; Cutler Dawson, Vice Admiral, and Vice Admiral John Nathman, USN, "Sea Power 21 Series-Part III: Sea Strike: Projecting Persistent, Responsive, and Precise Power," in *U.S. Naval Institute Proceedings*, December 2002; Charles W. Moore, Vice Admiral, and Lieutenant General Edward Hanlon, Jr., USMC, "Sea Power 21 Series-Part IV: Sea Basing: Operational Independence for a New Century," in *U.S. Naval Institute Proceedings*, January 2003; Richard W. Mayo, Vice Admiral, and Vice Admiral John Nathman, USN, "Sea Power 21 Series-Part V: ForceNet: Turning Information into Power," in *U.S. Naval Institute Proceedings*, February 2003; Michael Mullen, Vice Admiral, USN, "Sea Power 21 Series-Part VI: Global Concept of Operations," in *U.S. Naval Institute Proceedings*, April 2003; Alfred G. Harms, Jr., Vice Admiral, Vice Admiral Gerald L. Hoewing, and Vice Admiral John B. Totushek, USN, "Sea Power 21 Series-Part VII: Sea Warrior: Maximizing Human Capital," in *U.S. Naval Institute Proceedings*, June 2003; Robert J. Natter, Admiral, USN, "Sea Power 21 Series-Part VIII: Sea Trial: Enabler for a Transformed Fleet," in *U.S. Naval Institute Proceedings*, November 2003; Michael G. Mullen, Admiral, USN, "Sea Power 21 Series-Part IX: Sea Enterprise: Resourcing Tomorrow's Fleet," in *U.S. Naval Institute Proceedings*, January 2004.
12. Smith, "1st Naval Construction Division Established," August 29, 2002; *MEG History*, Chapter 1, p. 3.

Chapter 4 — The Road to War

1. President George W. Bush's "Preemptive Doctrine" Speech given at West Point on June 1, 2002. Bush specifically stated that "Our security will require all Americans to be forward-looking and resolute, to be ready for preemptive action when necessary to defend our liberty and to defend our lives... There can be no neutrality between justice and cruelty, between the innocent and the guilty. We are in a conflict between good and evil, and America will call evil by its name. By confronting evil and lawless regimes, we do not create a problem, we reveal a problem. And we will lead the world in opposing it."
2. President George W. Bush's Remarks at the United Nations General Assembly, September 12, 2002.
3. *The National Security Strategy of the United States*, September 17, 2002.
4. Franks, *American Soldier*, (New York, New York: Regan Books, 2004), pp. 342-343; Woodward, *Plan of Attack*, (New York, New York: Simon & Schuster, 2004), pp. 58, 61.
5. *MEG History*, Chapter 3, pp. 1-3; 1st Naval Construction Division, 30th Naval Construction Regiment/Task Force Charlie/Task Force Mike *Unit History*, pp. 1-4, hereafter cited as *30th NCR History*.
6. Woodward, *Plan of Attack*, p. 23.
7. Ibid.

ENDNOTES

8. *30th NCR History*, 1.
9. *30th NCR History*, pp. 1-2; Naval Mobile Construction Battalion 74, "After Action Report: Operation Enduring Freedom and Operation Iraqi Freedom, 2002-2003," Gulfport, Mississippi, pp. 1, 5-6.
10. NMCB 74, "After Action Report," p. 6; Secretary of Defense William S Cohen's harsh treatment of the commander of the Dhahran-based 4404th Wing (Provisional), Brigadier General Terryl J. Schwalier, in the aftermath of the Khobar Towers bombing resulted in greatly intensified security measures for all Air Force facilities worldwide. See Richard J. Newman, "From Khobar to Cole," in *Air Force Magazine: Journal of the Air Force Association*, Volume 84, Number 3, March 2001, pp. 48-51.
11. *30th NCR History*, pp. 1-2; NMCB 74, "After Action Report," p. 6.
12. Chief Builder (SCW) Wayne Jensen, NMCB 74, quoted in "Weapons of Mass Construction" by Journalist 1 Stan Travioli and Journalist 2 Traci Feibel, in *Seabee Magazine*, 2003 Special Commemorative Double Issue, pp. 31-32.
13. Ibid.; James P. Rife Interview with Commander Cliff Maurer, February 1, 2005, pp. 5- 8, (Hereafter cited as Rife/Maurer Interview); NMCB 74, "After Action Report," pp. 6-7, 11.
14. Ibid.
15. NMCB 74, "After Action Report," pp. 1, 5-6, 9, 11; Rife/Maurer Interview, pp. 5- 8.
16. Ibid.
17. *30th NCR History*, p. 2.
18. Woodward, *Plan of Attack*, pp. 192-204; Dilip Hiro, *Secrets and Lies: Operation Iraqi Freedom and After*, (New York, New York: Nation Books, 2004), pp. 97-110; "President George W. Bush Signs Iraq Resolution," October 16, 2002; Public Law 107-243, October 16, 2002; United Nations Security Council Press Release SC/7564, November 8, 2002; Secretary of State Colin Powell, televised news conference, December 19, 2002.
19. Ibid.
20. Franks, *American Soldier*, pp. 409-410.
21. Ibid; Woodward, *Plan of Attack*, pp. 236-237.
22. *30th NCR History*, p. 2-3; Commander Andrew Storch and Captain James Ostrich interview with Chief Equipment Operator Rudolfo Santiago, February 5, 2005, pp. 17-18, hereafter cited as Storch-Ostrich/Santiago Interview; JO1 Stan Travioli, "Let's Roll: Seabee Camp in Kuwait Named for Flight 93 Heroes," in *Seabee Magazine*, 2003 Special Commemorative Double Issue, p. 46.
23. Ibid; James P. Rife Interview with Navy Counselor 1 Michael Hill, January 13, 2005, pp. 5, 31-32, hereafter cited as Rife/Hill Interview.
24. *30th NCR History*, p. 3.
25. Rife/Hair Interview, pp. 3-4.

Chap 5 — Bridging Issues

1. *MEG History*, Chapter 9, p. 12.
2. *MEG History*, Chapter 5, pp. 1-6.

3. Colonel Michael C. Howard (USMC Reserve), "'Basra to Baghdad': The 1914-18 British Campaign for Mesopotamia," *Marine Corps Gazette*. Vol. 87, Issue 9, (Quantico, Virginia: September 2003).
4. Ibid.
5. *MEG History*, Chapter 5, pp.1-6.
6. Rife/Seignious Interview, 3-4; Rife/McAlister Interview, pp.12-13.
7. *MEG History*, Chapter 5, pp. 6-7.
8. Ibid; Rife/McAlister Interview, pp.12-13.
9. Ibid; *MEG History*, Chapter 5, pp.1-6.
10. *MEG History*, Chapter 3, pp.10-13.
11. 1st Naval Construction Division, Execution Order #001, January 26, 2003.

Chap 6 — Learning Curves

1. Press briefing by Hans Blix, Executive Chairman of UNMOVIC, and Mohamed ElBaradei, Director General of IAEA (unofficial transcript), 9 January 2003, United Nations, New York.
2. Hans Blix, "An Update on Inspection to the United Nations Security Council," January 27, 2003.
3. President George W. Bush, State of the Union Address, January 28, 2003.
4. U.S. Secretary of State Colin Powell Addresses the U.N. Security Council, February 5, 2003.
5. Bill Gertz, "Iraq Strengthens Air Force with French Parts," *Washington Times*, March 7, 2003.
6. *MEG History*, Chapter 3, pp. 20-22, Chapter 4, pp. 9-10; Captain James Ostrich Interview with Lieutenant Harry Wong, February 2, 2005, pp. 5-8; James P. Rife Interview with Senior Chief Troy Kellerman, January 11, 2005, pp. 3-4, hereafter cited as Rife/Kellerman Interview; Captain James Ostrich Interview with Lieutenant Ron Birnbaum, February 7, 2005, pp. 4-5, hereafter cited as Ostrich/Birnbaum Interview; Captain James Ostrich Interview with Chief Builder Chad Eagle, February 7, 2005, pp. 18-19, hereafter cited as Ostrich/Eagle Interview; Commander Andrew Storch Interview with Lieutenant (Junior Grade) Jerome Arabe, February 5, 2005, pp. 6-8, hereafter cited as Storch/Arabe Interview; James P. Rife Interview with Captain Christopher J. Honkomp, February 1, 2005, pp. 5-7, hereafter cited as Rife/Honkomp Interview; Lieutenant John Garofolo, USCGR with Commander Scott Jerabek, USNR, June 5, 2003, for Naval Coastal Warfare Group One, Task Group 51.9, Task Force History: Operation Iraqi Freedom; "Constructing Camp Patriot," and "Concept to Completion: The PhibCBs Make Freedom's Footprint," in *Seabee Magazine*, Special Commemorative Double Issue 2003, Volume 2, Numbers 1 & 2, 42-45; Senior Chief Journalist Scott D. Williams, "Navy Amphibious Command Deploys to Kuwait," Story Number NNS030127-17, January 27, 2003.
7. Journalist 1st Class Joseph Krypel, "The ELCAS Modular Solution," *Seabee Magazine*, Volume 2, Number 1 and 2, Summer 2003, pp.35-39, also in *Navy Civil Engineer*, Volume 40, Number 2, 2003, pp.16-21.

ENDNOTES

8. Kirk Ross, "Marine Engineer Group-A Force for the Future," in Naval Institute *Proceedings*, Volume 129, July 2003, pp. 84-86; Rife/McAlister Interview, pp. 7-8; Captain James Ostrich Interview with Lieutenant Julio Palacio, February 5, 2005, pp. 28-29, hereafter cited as Ostrich/Palacio Interview; Captain James Ostrich and Commander Andrew Storch Interview with Chief Builder Joe Franz, February 5, 2005, 7, hereafter cited as Ostrich-Storch/Franz Interview.

9. Commander Andrew Storch Interview with EO1 Frederick Kyriss, February 5, 2005, pp. 6-9, hereafter cited as Storch/Kyriss Interview; Storch-Ostrich/Santiago Interview, p. 14.

10. Commander Andrew Storch Interview with Lieutenant (Junior Grade) Jerome Arabe, February 5, 2005, pp. 8-14, hereafter cited as Storch/Arabe Interview; Rife/Hill Interview, pp. 4-5.

11. Rife/Honkomp Interview, pp.10, 24-25.

12. Rife/Kellerman Interview, 17; Captain James Ostrich Interview with Chief Equipment Operator James Mellow, February 6, 2005, 5, hereafter cited as Ostrich/Mellow Interview; Captain James Ostrich Interview with Senior Chief Equipment Operator Charles Cox, February 5, 2005, pp. 8-9, hereafter cited as Ostrich/Cox Interview; Storch-Ostrich/Santiago Interview, pp. 8-9.

13. Nicholas E. Reynolds, Colonel, USMC (Retired), *Basrah, Baghdad, and Beyond: The U.S. Marine Corps in the Second Iraq War*, (Annapolis, Maryland: Naval Institute Press, 2005), 37-38. Reynolds' work, based heavily upon primary sources material from I MEF and oral history interviews from key MEF officers and written for the USMC History and Museums Division, is the official history of the Marines during the first phase of Operation IRAQI FREEDOM. Although necessarily subjective and "unfinished," as the division's director notes in his foreword, it is the best account to date of I MEF's planning and operations during the conflict from a command point of view; *MEG History*, Chapter 3, pp. 9-10.

14. United States Marine Corps Headquarters, Marine Corps Doctrine Publication 1, *Warfighting*, 1997 revision of Fleet Marine Force Manual 1, 1989, by General Alfred M. Gray, (Washington, DC: Department of the Navy, 1997); United States Marine Corps, "Expeditionary Maneuver Warfare," in *Marine Corps Gazette*, February 2002, pp. A-1 through A-10; Chief of Naval Operations, OPNAV Instruction 5450.46K, Subject: Naval Construction Force Policy, May 25, 1999, Operational Archives Branch, U.S. Naval History and Heritage Command; Office of the Chief of Naval Operations and Headquarters U.S. Marine Corps, Naval Warfare Publication 4.04.1 and Marine Corps Warfare Publication 4-11.5, *Seabee Operations in the MAGTF*, (Washington, DC: Department of the Navy, 1997); Navy Warfare Development Command, Naval Warfare Publication 4-04.2, *Navy Civil Engineer Operations for Component Commanders*, (Washington, DC: Department of the Navy, 1998).

15. Reynolds, *Basrah, Baghdad, and Beyond*, 35; *MEG History*, Chapter 3, p.1.

16. Naval Education and Training Program Development Center, NAVEDTRA 10479-A. *Seabee Combat Handbook*,1976 Edition; NAVEDTRA 10479-C2, *Seabee Combat Handbook*, 1985 Edition; NAVEDTRA 14234, *Seabee Combat Handbook*, Volume I, 1993.

17. Office of the Chief of Naval Operations, OPNAVINST 1410.1B, December 18, 1998, Operational Archives, U.S. Naval History and Heritage Command; James P. Rife Interview with Lieutenant Commander Russell B. Seignious, p. 4, January 13, 2005, hereafter cited as Rife/Seignious Interview.
18. The Seabee Combat Warfare Specialist designation if one of four that the Navy authorizes. The others are Enlisted Surface Warfare Specialist (ESWS), Enlisted Aviation Warfare Specialist (EAWS), and Enlisted Submarine Specialist (ESS); CDR Ross S. Selvidge, CEC, USNR, of NMCB 16 (Reserve), designed the Seabee Combat Warfare Specialist insignia device in 1991, and the Navy formally approved it in 1993. See Larry G. DeVries, Captain, CEC, USNR, "The Design of the Seabee Combat Warfare Device," available online at http://home.earthlink.net/~larrydev/SCWSdesignpage.html; OPNAVINST 1410.1B.
19. Command Master Chief (SCW) Kevin J. Eichman, "SCW@War," in *Seabee Magazine*, Special Commemorative Double Issue 2003, Volume 2, Numbers 1 & 2, p. 47; Lieutenant Mike Chucran, CEC, USN, "ACBs Create New Range for Camp Patriot," in *Seabee Magazine*, Special Commemorative Double Issue 2003, Volume 2, Numbers 1 & 2, p. 44.
20. Rife/Kellerman Interview, pp. 12-14.
21. Ibid., 5-8; Reynolds, *Basrah, Baghdad, and Beyond*, pp. 27-28.
22. Rife/Hill Interview, pp.10-14.
23. Ibid.
24. For U.S. and U.N. suspicions that Saddam had maintained Weapons of Mass Destruction after DESERT STORM, see Kenneth M. Pollack, *The Threatening Storm: The Case for Invading Iraq* (New York, New York: Random House, 2002), pp. 170-180, 371-376; Richard Butler, *The Greatest Threat: Iraq, Weapons of Mass Destruction, and the Growing Crisis of Global Security*, (New York, New York: Public Affairs, 2000); General Tommy Franks, with Malcolm McConnell, *American Soldier*, (New York, New York: Regan Books, 2004), pp. 416-419; Bob Woodward, *Plan of Attack*, (New York, New York: Simon & Schuster, 2004), pp. 244-250, 404; Reynolds, *Basrah, Baghdad, and Beyond*, 43-44; Chief Warrant Officer William Hudson and Major Ted McKeldon Interview with Lieutenant General James T. Conway, March 2003, p. 5, Marine Corps History and Museums Division, USMC Historical Center; For "sliming," see Reynolds, *Basrah, Baghdad, and Beyond*, p. 57.
25. Rife/Kellerman Interview, pp. 8-9.
26. *MEG History*, Chapter 3, pp-16-17.
27. Reynolds, *Basrah, Baghdad, and Beyond*, pp. 57, 68, 91.

Chap 7 — Concept of Operations

1. For detailed treatment of OPLAN 1003V and the operations of both the U.S. Army and Marine Corps, excluding I MEG, during OIF I, see Gregory Fontenot, E.J. Degen,and David Tohn, *On Point: The United States Army in Operation Iraqi Freedom*, (Annapolis, Maryland: Naval Institute Press, 2005) and Colonel Nicholas E. Reynolds, USMC (Retired), *Basrah, Baghdad, and Beyond: The U.S. Marine Corps in the Second Iraq War*, (Annapolis, Maryland: Naval Institute Press, 2005). See also General Tommy Franks, with Malcolm McConnell, *American Soldier*,

(New York, New York: Regan Books, 2004) for details concerning the development of OPLAN 1003V.
2. Reynolds, *Basrah, Baghdad, and Beyond*, pp. 17-22, 29-43.
3. Ibid.
4. Fontenot, *On Point*, pp. 46-48.
5. Ibid, pp. 77-79.
6. *MEG History*, Chapter 4, pp.5-6.
7. For I MEF's complete order of battle during Operation IRAQI FREEDOM, see Appendix C in Reynolds, *Basrah, Baghdad, and Beyond*.
8. Reynolds, *Basrah, Baghdad, and Beyond*, pp. 41-42.
9. *MEG History*, Chapter 4, pp.5-7.
10. Ibid, pp. 1-2.
11. Ibid, pp. 2-4.
12. Ibid, pp. 7-11.
13. Ibid, pp. 11-14.
14. Ibid., pp. 15-17.
15. Captain James Ostrich Interview with Chief Equipment Operator Richard Zylla February 7, 2005, pp. 17-19.
16. Ibid, pp. 20-21, 29-30.
17. Reynolds, *Basrah, Baghdad, and Beyond*, pp. 101-102.
18. *MEG History*, Chapter 3, pp.13-14.

Chap 8 — "Hitting Pads"

1. On March 5, 1942, the old Bureau of Navigation had formally authorized Rear Admiral Ben Moreell to organize and deploy his new naval construction battalions to help win World War II.
2. U.S. Secretary of State Colin L. Powell, "Remarks to the United Nations Security Council," February 14, 2003, available online at http://www.globalsecurity.org/wmd/library/news/iraq/2003/iraq-030214-17763pf.htm.
3. Woodward, *Plan of Attack*, 357-372; President George W. Bush, "Remarks by the President in Address to the Nation," March 17, 2008, available online at http://www.whitehouse.gov/news/releases/2003/03/20030317-7.html.
4. *MEG History*, Chapter 6, pp. 1-2.
5. Ibid, pp. 2-4.
6. Ibid.
7. Ibid.
8. Ibid, pp. 3-6.
9. Reynolds, *Basrah, Baghdad, and Beyond*, pp. 59-62.
10. Ibid, pp. 100-106; Fontenot, *On Point*, pp. 52-54, 70-71, 80, 88.
11. Reynolds, *Basrah, Baghdad, and Beyond*, pp. 24-29, 66-72.
12. Woodward, *Plan of Attack*, pp. 374-375, 380-392, 396-399.
13. *MEG History*, Chapter 6, pp. 4-5.

14. Telephone Interview with Lieutenant Commander Bill Sloan by James P. Rife, February 9, 2005.
15. *MEG History*, Chapter 6, pp. 5-6.

Chap 9 — Into Iraq

1. *MEG History*, Chapter 6, pp. 5-7.
2. Ibid; TAA Stethem was named after Steel Worker 2nd (Diver) Class Robert Stethem of Underwater Construction Team 1, who had been killed by Hezbollah terrorists aboard the hijacked TWA Flight 847 on June 15, 1985. He was posthumously awarded the Purple Heart and Bronze Star, and is buried in Arlington National Cemetery. In 1994, the US Navy named the USS *Stethem* (DDG-63) in his honor.
3. Ibid, pp. 5-7.
4. *MEG History*, pp. 14-15; 1st Naval Construction Division, 22nd Naval Construction Regiment/Task Force Charlie Unit History, June 2003, p. 3-4, hereafter cited as *22nd NCR History*; Rife/McKerall Interview, pp. 6-7.
5. James P. Rife Interview with Lieutenant Phil Lavallee, January 13, 2005, pp. 4-6, hereafter cited as Rife/Lavallee Interview.
6. Unfortunately, the MEG staff was never able to convince the V Corps Army MPs to fall in on the Seabee-built Holding Area and upgrade it rather than building a separate EPW Facility for themselves. They wanted to go it alone.
7. Rife/McKerall Interview, p. 26.
8. James P. Rife Interview with Senior Chief Jeffrey Weigel, January 11, 2005, pp. 11-12, hereafter cited as Rife/Weigel Interview; Rife/Hill Interview, pp. 18-19.
9. Captain James Ostrich Interview with Construction Electrician 1st Class Alexander Semmler, February 7, 2005, pp. 12-13, hereafter cited as Ostrich/Semmler Interview.
10. Rife/Kellerman Interview, pp. 18-20.
11. *MEG History*, Chapter 6, p. 14.
12. *22nd NCR History*, pp. 3-4.
13. *MEG History*, Chapter 6, pp. 13-14.
14. Ibid, pp. 7-12, 16-18; For a comprehensive account of the Battle of An Nasiriyah from I MEF's perspective, see Reynolds, *Basrah, Baghdad, and Beyond*, pp. 73-86.
15. *MEG History*, Chapter 6, pp. 7-12, 16-18; Colonel Greg Plush, "Up Close and Personal: Marine Report from An Nasiriyah," undated but early April 2003.
16. *MEG History*, Chapter 6, pp. 8-9.
17. 1st Naval Construction Division, I MEF Purple Heart Nomination for Lieutenant Commander Bill Sloan.
18. *MEG History*, Chapter 6, pp. 9-13.
19. Ibid, pp. 13-14, 18-22.
20. Ibid, p.10.
21. Ibid, pp. 13-14.
22. Ibid, p. 18.

23. Reynolds, *Basrah, Baghdad, and Beyond*, pp. 90, 92-94.
24. Harlan Ullman, "'Shock and Awe' Lite", *Baltimore Sun*, April 1, 2003.

Chap 10 — Across the Tigris

1. *MEG History*, Chapter 6, pp. 23-25.
2. Ibid; As a historical note, the MEG Seabees contingency support of Task Force Tarawa (the 2nd Marine Division) at An Nasiriyah is reminiscent of the World War II role of Naval Construction Battalion 74 in November of 1943 when it (then serving as 3rd Battalion, 18th Marine Engineer Regiment) landed on Betio Island, Tarawa Atoll, and built and fought alongside the 2nd Marine Division in the face of savage Japanese resistance.
3. Ibid.
4. Ibid, pp. 29-30.
5. Ibid, pp. 15-18.
6. Ibid, pp. 20-23; *22nd NCR History*, pp. 3-6.
7. *22nd NCR History*, p. 6.
8. Ibid, pp. 4-5.
9. *MEG History*, Chapter 6, pp. 27-29.
10. Ibid.
11. Ibid, p. 25.
12. Matt Zeigler, *Three Block War: U.S. Marines in Iraq*, (iUniverse, 2004), pp. 33-34; Michael Wilson, "Lost Tank leaves 4 Dead, Many Questions," *New York Times*, April 1, 2003; Elliot Blair Smith, "Crossing the Euphrates," Part Three of a Four Part Series in *USA Today*, March 30, 2003; Ostrich/Semmler Interview, pp. 12-13.
13. The four Marine crew members who drowned in the Hermes were Staff Sergeant Donald May Jr., Corporal Robert Marcus Rodriguez, Lance Corporal Patrick O'Day, and Private 1st Class Francisco Martinez Flores; Department of Defense New Release No. 179-03, "DOD Identifies Marine Casualties," March 31, 2003; Patrice O'Shaughnessy, "Lost in Iraq: Seven New York Heroes," *New York Daily News*, February 14, 2004.
14. Rife/Honkomp Interview, pp. 13-22.
15. Ibid.
16. *MEG History*, Chapter 6, pp. 30-31.
17. Ibid, pp. 31-32.
18. Ibid, pp. 32-33.
19. Ibid, pp. 34-35.

Chap 11 — Babylon Falls

1. *MEG History*, Chapter 6, pp. 36-38.
2. For a more comprehensive account of the overall Marine assault into Baghdad, see Reynolds, *Basrah, Baghdad, and Beyond*, pp 98-113.
3. *MEG History*, Chapter 6, p. 37.

4. Interview with Colonel David Perkins, Commander of the 2nd Brigade, 3rd Infantry Division, "Iraqis Underestimating U.S. Ability in Urban Warfare," *Frontline*, February 26, 2004; For a detailed account and discussion of the U.S. Army "Thunder Runs," see Fontenot, *On Point*, pp. 340-374.
5. Reynolds, *Basrah, Baghdad, and Beyond*, pp. 109, 158; "Marine: Flag a Symbol of Liberation, Not Occupation," CNN.com, April 10, 2003; Andy Newman, "A Nation at War: Symbols; Atop Statue, Marine Thrills Army of Fans Back Home," *New York Times*, April 11, 2003; James Meek and Suzanne Goldenberg, "The Day the Statue Fell," *The Guardian*, March 19, 2004.
6. *MEG History*, Chapter 6, pp. 38-40.
7. Ibid, pp. 44-45.
8. Ibid; Reynolds, *Basrah, Baghdad, and Beyond*, pp. 115-120.
9. Captain James Ostrich Interview with Lieutenant Harry R. Wong, February 2, 2005, pp. 4-13, hereafter cited as Ostrich/Wong Interview.
10. Ibid, pp. 24-27.
11. Ibid, pp. 30-34.
12. Ibid, pp. 37-40.
13. *MEG History*, Chapter 7, p. 27.
14. Ibid, 3.
15. Woodward, *Plan of Attack*, pp. 412-413; President George W. Bush, "Remarks by the President from the USS Abraham Lincoln At Sea Off the Coast of San Diego, California," May 1, 2003.
16. *MEG History*, Chapter 7, pp. 15-20.
17. Ibid, 15-17.

Chap 12 — Stabilization and Civil Military Operations

1. *MEG History*, Chapter 7, pp. 1-5.
2. Ibid, Chapter 6, p. 1.
3. Ibid; "Rumsfeld Blames Iraq Problems on 'Pockets of Dead-Enders,'" *USA Today*, June 18, 2003.
4. *MEG History*, pp. 4-5.
5. Ibid, pp. 5-10.
6. Bob Woodward, *State of Denial*, (New York, New York, Simon & Schuster, 2006), pp. 105-107, 113, 116-119, 123-134.
7. *MEG History*, Chapter 7, p. 1.
8. Woodward, *State of Denial*, pp. 193-202, 206-208, 219-220; David Leigh, "General Sacked by Bush Says He Wanted Early Elections," *The Guardian*, March 18, 2004; L. Paul Bremer & Malcolm McConnell, *My Year In Iraq: The Struggle to Build a Future of Hope*, 1st edition, (Canada: Simon & Schuster, January 2006).
9. *MEG History*, Chapter 7, pp. 5-10.
10. Ibid.
11. Ibid, pp. 9-10.

12. Ibid, pp. 11-13.
13. Ibid, pp. 20-22.
14. Ibid, pp. 28-29.
15. Jim Forbes, "West Virginia National Guard Soldier Recalls Iran Capture," *The State Journal*, April 5, 2007.
16. *MEG History*, Chapter 7, pp. 22-23.
17. Ibid.
18. For a discussion of the intelligence failures regarding Saddam's WMDs and supporting programs, see U.S. Department of Defense, Inspector General, Deputy Inspector General for Intelligence, "Review of Pre-Iraqi War Activities of the Office of the Under Secretary of Defense for Policy," Report Number 07-INTEL-04, Project Number. D2006-DIYT01-0077.000, February 9, 2007; See also Charles Duelfer, *Comprehensive Report of the Special Adviser to the Director of Central Intelligence on Iraq's WMD Weapons of Mass Destruction*, (Washington, DC: Central Intelligence Agency, 2004).
19. Lieutenant Eric Breitenbach and Keely West, "In Memoriam: Builder 3rd Class Doyle W. Bolinger, 1982-2003," *Seabee Magazine*, Volume 2, Numbers 1 and 2, Summer 2003, pp. 12-13.

Chapter 13 — Homeward Bound

1. *MEG History*, Chapter 7, pp. 29-32.
2. Craig Gima, "Pearl Harbor-based Seabees Return to a Warm Welcome," *Honolulu Star-Bulletin*, May 26, 2003; Journalist 2nd Class (SW) Chad V. Pritt, "Seabees Awarded Bronze Stars for OIF," Story Number NNS031230-01, *Navy News Service*, December 30, 2003; Journalist 2nd Class (SW) Chad V. Pritt, "Change of Command for 30th Naval Construction Regiment, Story Number NNS040422-11, *Navy News Service*, April 22, 2004.
3. 1st Naval Construction Division, MARADMIN Message 507/03, "Announcement of Approved Presidential Unit Citation," November 14, 2003; Daryl C. Smith, "Seabees Earn Presidential Unit Citation," Story Number NNS031121-13, *Navy News Service*, November 21, 2003.
4. Ostrich/Wong Interview, p. 13.
5. Ibid, pp. 46-47; Asian Chamber of Commerce, "Mad Dash to Welcome Navy Lt. Home," *Asian Sunews*, Phoenix, Arizona, 2003.
6. Commander Andrew Storch Interview with Equipment Operator 1st Class William Young and Equipment Operator 3rd Class Adam Schneider, January 12, 2005, pp. 19-24.
7. Rife/Kellerman Interview, p. 32.
8. Commander Andrew Storch and Captain James Ostrich Interview with Chief Equipment Operator Rudolpho Santiago, February 5, 2005, pp. 57-58.
9. Chief Journalist John Harrington, "Big Apple Seabees Awarded in Times Square," Story Number: NNS031009-06, *Navy News Service*, October 9, 2003.
10. J. Stryker Meyer, quoted in *North County Times*, October 26, 2003.

Chapter 14 — Aftermath – OIF Continues

1. Since 2003, a veritable cottage industry of Iraq war literature, much of it politicized, has emerged, with a large number of works analyzing the outbreak of the Iraqi insurgency and the U.S. and Coalition response. For more detailed discussions about post-2003 operations in Iraq through 2008, see (among many others) Donald P. Wright, and Colonel Timothy R. Reese, *On Point II: Transition to the New Campaign: The United States Army in Operation Iraqi Freedom, May 2003-January 2005*, (Fort Leavenworth, Kansas: U.S. Army Combined Arms Center, Combat Studies Institute, 2008); Bob Woodward, *State of Denial*, (New York, New York: Simon & Schuster, 2006); Colonel Garland H. Williams, *Engineering Peace: The Military Role in Post-conflict Reconstruction*, (Washington, D.C.: Institute of Peace Press, 2004); Dilip Hiro, *Secrets and Lies: Operation "Iraqi Freedom" and After: A Prelude to the Fall of U.S. Power in the Middle East?*, (New York, New York: Nation Books, 2004); Ricardo S. Sanchez and Donald T. Phillips, *Wiser in Battle: A Soldier's Story*, (New York, New York: HarperCollins, 2008).
2. CNN.com, "Pentagon: Saddam's Sons Killed in Raid," July 22, 2003; Romesh Ratnesar, "Hot on Saddam's Trail," *Time*, August 3, 2003.
3. Dexter Filkins, "After the War: The Attack; Inquiry in U.N. Bombing Focuses On Possible Ties to Iraqi Guards," *New York Times*, August 22, 2003; Alex Berenson, "The Struggle for Iraq: Casualties; Car Bombing Outside U.N. Mission in Baghdad Kills at Least One and Injures Others," *New York Times*, September 22, 2003.
4. Neil Macfarquhar and Richard A. Oppel, Jr., "After the War: Attack at Shrine; Car Bomb in Iraq Kills 95 at Shiite Mosque," *New York Times*, August 30, 2003.
5. CNN.com, "Saddam 'Caught Like a Rat' in a Hole," December 13, 2003.
6. Wright, *On Point II*, pp. 25-45, 87-129; Fred Barnes, "How Bush Decided on the Surge," *Weekly Standard*, Volume 13, Issue 20, February 4, 2008.
7. Donna Miles, "Abizaid, Swannack Escape Injury in Fallujah Attack," *Armed Forces Press Service*, February 12, 2004; Robert Hodierne and Rob Curtis, "Insurgents Attack Five Sites, Kill 17 Iraqi Policemen," *Army Times*, February 14, 2004.
8. Laura Parker, "What Exactly Happened That Day in Fallujah?" *USA Today*, June 11, 2007.
9. U.S. Department of Defense, Coalition Provisional Authority Briefing with Brigadier General Mark Kimmitt, Deputy Director for Coalition Operations; and Dan Senor, Senior Advisor, CPA, Baghdad, Iraq, April 1, 2004.
10. Rajiv Chandrasekaran, "Key General Criticizes April Attack in Fallujah," *Washington Post*, September 13, 2004.
11. Associated Press, "U.S. Launches 'Vigilant Resolve'," April 5, 2004; Rory McCarthy, "Uneasy Truce in the City of Ghosts," *The Guardian*, April 24, 2004.
12. U.S. Department of Defense, Coalition Provisional Authority Briefing with Brigadier General Mark Kimmitt, Deputy Director for Coalition Operations; and Dan Senor, Senior Advisor, CPA, Baghdad, Iraq, April 17, 2004.
13. Glenn Kessler, "Weapons Given to Iraq Are Missing," *Washington Post*, August 6, 2007; Shaun Waterman, "Analysis: U.S. Lost Fallujah's Info War," *United Press International*, January 2, 2008.

14. Chandrasekaran, "Key General Criticizes April Attack."
15. Gary C. Gambill, "Iran, Sadr, and the Shiite Uprising in Iraq," *Middle East Intelligence Bulletin*, Volume 6, Number 4, April 2004; Fareed Zakaria, "A 'Shiite Strategy' in Iraq?," *Washington Post*, September 14, 2004.
16. University of California-Berkley College of Engineering, "Alumnus Maurer heads Seabees in Iraq conflict," *Forefront*, Winter 2005.
17. Elaine Eliah, "Apprentice Program Teaches Construction Skills to Young Iraqis," *Armed Forces Press Service*, December 29, 2005.
18. Journalist 2nd Class Jennifer Valdivia, "NMCB 14 Seabees Receive Purple Heart," Story Number NNS040714-15, *Navy News Service*, June 14, 2004.
19. Chief Journalist Siegfried Bruner, Ensign Tony Hollobraugh, and Journalist 2nd Class Mike England, "Seabees Gather to Honor Their Fallen Comrades," *Seabee Magazine*, Volume 3, Numbers 1 and 2, 2004, pp. 8-9.
20. 1st Naval Construction Division, "Response to CNO Questions Concerning the "Hackworth Article," March 2005.
21. Colonel David H. Hackworth, "Another Shameful Navy Cover-Up," Military.com, March 15, 2005; Colonel David H. Hackworth, "Ahoy to the Navy's Top Brass," April 5, 2005; Hackworth was involved in other sensational stories throughout his career, including his 1996 investigation into CNO Admiral Jeremy M. Boorda's wearing of potentially unauthorized V (for valor) devices on his Navy Achievement and Commendation medals. Boorda committed suicide rather than challenge Hackworth's report.
22. Chief Yeoman (SCW/AW) Josephine D'*****o, "No Seabee Cover-up at Base Junction City," posted on *Leatherneck.com*, March 21, 2005 (Surname partially redacted under the forum's privacy guidelines).
23. Joe Holley, "David Hackworth Dies; Esteemed Army Colonel Defied Military Brass," *Washington Post*, May 6, 2005; "After Action Report, Task Force Tango Indirect Fire Attack: 021432DMAY2004," Lieutenant Colonel T.J. Barrett (USMCR) to Captain Mark Handley, CEC, USN, Deputy Commander, I MEG, June 6, 2004, 1st Naval Construction Division.
24. Chief Journalist (AW) Suzanne Speight and Photographer's Mate 2nd Class (AW) Michael D. Heckman, "Historic Wartime Turnover By Navy Reserve Seabee Battalions In Iraq," Story Number NNS041116-04, *Navy News Service*, November 16, 2004.
25. For the best account of the 2nd Battle of Fallujah from the Marines' perspective, see Bing West, *No True Glory: A Frontline Account of the Battle for Fallujah*, (New York, New York: Bantam, 2005); Steven Komarow, "Fallujans Reluctant to Go Home, Despite Aid," January 5, 2005, *USA Today*.
26. Photographer 3rd Class Todd Frantom, "Building Democracy in Iraq," *All Hands*, May 2005, pp. 22-31.
27. Jason Burke, Peter Beaumont, and Mohammed al-Ubeidy, "How Jordanians Hunted Down Their Hated Son," *The Guardian*, June 11, 2006; World Tribune.com, "U.S. Praises Jordan Special Forces for April Al Qaida WMD Bust," August 31, 2004; Bill Powell and Scott MacLeod, "Zarqawi's Last Dinner Party," *Time*, June 11, 2006; Dexter Filkins, Mark Mazzetti, and Richard A. Oppel, Jr., "How Surveillance and Betrayal Led to a Hunt's End," *New York Times*, June 9, 2006.

28. Barnes, "How Bush Decided on the Surge"; Fred Kaplan, "Challenging the Generals," *New York Times*, August 26, 2007; George Packer, "Letter from Iraq: The Lesson of Tal Afar," *The New Yorker*, April 10, 2006; Lieutenant General David H. Petraeus (USA) and Lieutenant General James F. Amos (USMC), "Counterinsurgency," U.S. Army Field Manual 3-24, USMC Warfighting Publication 3-33.5, (Washington, DC: Departments of the Army and Navy, December 2006).
29. Scott Wilson and Al Kamen, "'Global War on Terror' is Given New Name," *Washington Post*, March 25, 2009.
30. Daryl C. Smith, "Phillips Assumes Command of 1st Naval Construction Division Story Number: NNS041119-21, *Navy News Service*, November 19, 2004; Chief Journalist (AW) Suzanne Speight, "I MEG Relinquishes Authority to 30NCR, and the Work to Aid Iraqi Citizens Goes On," *Seabee Magazine*, Volume 4, Issue Number 1, 2005.

Appendix 1 — History

1. United States Navy, Bureau of Yards and Docks, *Activities of the Bureau of Yards and Docks: World War, 1917-1918*, (Washington, D.C.: Government Printing Office. 1921), 33-34; United States Navy, *100th Anniversary, Navy Civil Engineer Corps, 1867-1967: Men Methods-Materials*, (Washington, D.C.: Government Printing Office, 1967), 4-5; Eugene J. Peltier, Rear Admiral, C.E.C, U.S.N, *The Bureau of Yards and Docks of the Navy and the Civil Engineer Corps*, (New York, New York: Newcomen Society in North America, 1961), 8-11; Kenneth J. Hagan, *This People's Navy: The Making of American Sea Power*, (New York, New York: The Free Press, 1991), 37-53.
2. Vincent A. Transano, *History of the Seabees*, Prepared for the Naval Historical Center, 1997, pp. 1-3, available online at http://www.history.navy.mil/faqs/faq67-1.htm; Hagan, *This People's Navy*, 89; A complete account of Porter's cruise in the *Essex* can be found in David Foster Long, *Nothing Too Daring: A Biography of Commodore David Porter, 1780-1843*; (Annapolis, MD: United States Naval Institute, 1970), pp. 71-141; For Porter's first hand accounts of his construction activities on Madison's Island, see David Porter, Captain, USN, *Journal of a Cruise*, Edited by R. D. Madison and Karen Hamon, (Annapolis, MD: Naval Institute Press, 1986), 357-367, 374-379 and a revised second edition, *A Voyage in the South Seas in the Years 1812, 1813, and 1814: with Particular Details of the Gallipagos and Washington Islands*, (London, England: R. Phillips, 1823), 97-100; For Madisonville as the Navy's first "advanced base," see United States Navy. Bureau of Yards and Docks, *Building the Navy's Bases in World War II: History of the Bureau of Yards and Docks and the Civil Engineer Corps, 1940-1946*, Volume II of II, (Washington, D.C.: Government Printing Office, 1947), introductory account with illustration, hereafter cited as *Building the Navy's Bases*, Vol. II
3. U. S. Navy, *100th Anniversary, Navy Civil Engineer Corps*, 2, 4-5; Peltier, *The Bureau of Yards and Docks of the Navy and the Civil Engineer Corps*, 8-11; Bureau of Yards and Docks. *Activities*, 34-35.
4. Ibid.
5. Peltier, *The Bureau of Yards and Docks of the Navy and the Civil Engineer Corps*, 12-13; U. S. Navy, *100th Anniversary, Navy Civil Engineer Corps*, 2, 4-5; U.S. Navy,

Annual Report of the Secretary of the Navy, Fiscal Year 1886, (Washington, D.C.: Government Printing Office), 102, 104-105.

6. Alfred Thayer Mahan, *The Influence of Sea Power upon History, 1660-1783*, (Gretna, Louisiana: Pelican Publishing Company, Inc., 2003); William Bradford Huie, *Can Do!: The Story of the Seabees*, New York, New York: E. P. Dutton & Company, Inc., 1944), 62.

7. Peltier, *The Bureau of Yards and Docks of the Navy and the Civil Engineer Corps*, 12-13; U. S. Navy, *100th Anniversary, Navy Civil Engineer Corps*, 5-7; Bureau of Yards and Docks. *Activities*, 35.

8. Ibid.

9. Ibid.; Huie, *Can Do!*, 62-63; U.S. Navy, *Annual Report of the Secretary of the Navy*, Fiscal Year 1898, (Washington, D.C.: Government Printing Office), 177-204, 237-239; *Annual Report of the Secretary of the Navy*, Fiscal Year 1899, 234-236; *Annual Report of the Secretary of the Navy*, Fiscal Year 1900, 207-209, 291-297; *Annual Report of the Secretary of the Navy*, Fiscal Year 1901, 202.

10. Bureau of Yards and Docks. *Activities*, 35.

11. Ibid.

12. Transano, *History of the Seabees*, 3; Commander Walter H. Allen, Civil Engineer Corps, USN, "The Twelfth Regiment (Public Works) at Great Lakes," in United States Naval Institute *Proceedings*, Volume 47, No. 3, March 1921, pp. 367-376, hereafter cited as "12th Regiment."

13. "12th Regiment," 369.

14. Ibid., 370-371; Admiral Ben Moreell, Civil Engineer Corps, USN, "The Seabees in World War II," in United States Naval Institute *Proceedings*, March 1962, pp. 84-101, hereafter cited as "Seabees."

15. "12th Regiment," 370-371, 373.

16. Transano, *History of the Seabees*, 5-6; "12th Regiment," 371.

17. Ibid., 370-371, 373.

18. Ibid., 372; Bureau of Yards and Docks. *Activities*, 365-379.

19. Ibid.

20. Transano, *History of the Seabees*, 7; "12th Regiment," 374-376.

21. "Seabees," pp. 84-101.

22. Ibid.

23. "Seabees," 87-88; United States Navy. Bureau of Yards and Docks, *Building the Navy's Bases in World War II: History of the Bureau of Yards and Docks and the Civil Engineer Corps, 1940-1946*, Volume I of II, (Washington, D.C.: Government Printing Office. 1947), 133-149, hereafter cited as *Building the Navy's Bases*, Vol. I.

24. "Seabees," 87-88; *Building the Navy's Bases*, Vol. I, 133-135; Edmund L. Castillo, *The Seabees of World War II*, (New York, New York: Random House, 1963), 13-29.

25. "Seabees," 87-88; *Building the Navy's Bases*, Vol. I, 133-135.

26. Ibid.

27. Ibid.

28. *Building the Navy's Bases*, Vol. I, 134-135; "Seabees," 95, 97; Frank J. Iafrate, "The Origin of the Seabees Insignia & Name," undated public relations flyer, available online at http://www.missico.com/personal/seabees/seabee_origin.htm.
29. Ibid.
30. Ibid.; March 5 has since been celebrated as the Seabees' official anniversary.
31. Transano, *History of the Seabees*, 7; "Seabees," 91, 97.
32. "Seabees," 88, 93; *Building the Navy's Bases*, Vol. I, 134-135.
33. Ibid.
34. "Seabees," 88; *Building the Navy's Bases*, Vol. I, 135; Moreell later wrote that the average Seabee age was about 33 throughout the war.
35. "Seabees," 89; *Building the Navy's Bases*, Vol. I, 135.
36. *Building the Navy's Bases*, Vol. I, 135.
37. Ibid., 138-143.
38. Ibid., 143-144.
39. Ibid., 136-137; *Building the Navy's Bases*, Vol. II, 243-244.
40. Ibid., 136-137.
41. Ibid., 137; U. S. Navy, *100th Anniversary, Navy Civil Engineer Corps*, 16; "Seabees," 94 (See photograph caption).
42. Ibid.
43. Ibid.; United States Navy, *Senior Commander Biographies*, "Vice Admiral Andrew G. Bisset," and "Rear Admiral John R. Perry," Washington, D.C.: Navy Department Library; Edmund L. Castillo, *The Seabees of World War II*, (New York, New York: Random House, Inc., 1963), 153; For the enormous magnitude of the Okinawa Campaign, see Roy E. Appleman, James M. Burns, Russell A. Gugeler, and John Stevens, *The United States Army in World War II: The War in the Pacific, Okinawa: The Last Battle*, (Washington, D.C.: Government Printing Office, 1948); For details of Operation DOWNFALL, see Thomas B. Allen and Norman Polmar, *Code-Name Downfall*, (New York, New York: Simon & Schuster, 1995), and Richard B. Frank, *Downfall: The End of the Imperial Japanese Empire*, (New York: Random House, 1999), 117-130.
44. "Seabees," 94; Transano, *History of the Seabees*, 13; Castillo, *The Seabees of World War II*, 101; *Building the Navy's Bases*, Volume II, 95-120; Alfred B. Stanford, *Force Mulberry: The Planning and Installation of the Artificial Harbor of U.S. Normandy Beaches in World War II*, New York, New York: William Morrow and Company, 1951; The complete works and deeds of the U.S. Navy Seabees during World War II are too numerous to recount here. For a more detailed treatment of the Seabees during this period, see both Huie's *Can Do!* and his follow-up work, *From Omaha to Okinawa: The Story of the Seabees*, (E. P. Dutton & Company, Inc., 1945). See also Hugh B. Cave's, *We Build, We Fight*, (New York, New York: Harper and Brothers, 1944). For the U.S. Army's perspective, see Karl C. Dod, *United States Army in World War II: The Technical Services: The Corps of Engineers: The War Against Japan*, (Washington, D.C. U.S. Army, Office of the Chief of Military History, 1966); For the Marines' perspective, see Lieutenant Colonel Frank O. Hough, Major Verle E. Ludwig, and Hnery I. Shaw, Jr., *History of U.S. Marine Corps Operations in World War II: Pearl Harbor to Guadalcanal*, Volume I, (Washington, D.C.: Historical Branch, G-3 Division,

Headquarters, U.S. Marine Corps, 1958); Henry Shaw, Jr., and Major Douglas T. Kane, *History of U.S. Marine Corps Operations in World War II: Isolation of Rabaul*, Volume II, (Washington, D.C.: Historical Branch, G-3 Division, Headquarters, U.S. Marine Corps, 1963); Henry I. Shaw, Jr., Bernard C. Nalty, and Edwin T. Turnbladh, *History of U.S. Marine Corps Operations in World War II: Central Pacific Drive*, Volume III, (Washington, D.C.: Historical Branch, G-3 Division, Headquarters, U.S. Marine Corps, 1966); George W. Garand and Truman R. Strobridge, *History of U.S. Marine Corps Operations in World War II: Western Pacific Operations*, Volume IV, (Washington, D.C.: Historical Branch, G-3 Division, Headquarters, U.S. Marine Corps, 1971); Benis M. Frank and Henry I. Shaw, Jr., *History of U.S. Marine Corps Operations in World War II: Victory and Occupation*, Volume 5, (Washington, D.C.: Historical Branch, G-3 Division, Headquarters, U.S. Marine Corps, 1968).

45. Huie, *From Omaha to Okinawa*, 141-142, 153-154, 193-194, 207-208

46. Huie subsequently dedicated *From Omaha to Okinawa* to the forty-two Seabees of Construction Battalion 133 who were killed at Iwo Jima. He included a complete list of casualties from the battalion during the battle on pp. 63-68.

47. *Building the Navy's Bases*, Volume II, 119-120; Alfred M. Beck, Abe Bortz, Charles W. Lynch, Lida Mayo, and Ralph F. Weld, *United States Army in World War II: The Technical Services: The Corps of Engineers: The War Against Germany*, (Washington, D.C.: Government Printing Office, 1985), 513-514.

48. Ibid.

49. "Seabees," 92-93.

50. Huie, *Can Do!*, 65; Huie's Atlantic "highways" were the Argentia-Iceland-Londonderry road in the north and the Miami-Trinidad-Natal-Ascension-Freetown road in the south. His Pacific "highways" ran through Sitka-Kodiak-Dutch Harbor-Adak-Attu in the far northern latitudes, Pearl Harbor-Midway-Wake-Guam-Cavite along the central axis, and through the Pearl Harbor-Palmyra-Canton-Samoa-Fiji-Espiritu Santo-Noumea axis to Australia, the Solomons, and the Indies in the south.

51. Castillo, *The Seabees of World War II*, 158; "Seabees," 97-98; Lieutenant General Holland M. Smith, quoted in U.S. Navy, Chief of Naval Operations, Publication NWP4-04.1, "Seabee Operations in the MAGTF," (Washington, D.C.: Department of the Navy, 1997), 1-1.

52. U.S. Navy, *Annual Report of the Secretary of the Navy*, Fiscal Year 1946, (Washington, D.C.: Government Printing Office) 43-44.

53. *Building the Navy's Bases*, Vol. I, 149; "Seabees to Remain as a Potent Postwar Unit." *Our Navy*, 41 (First of December 1946), 36-37.

54. Ibid.; Transano, "History of the Seabees," 18-20; U.S. Naval Historical Center, "Seabees Remember Korea," in *Seabee Magazine*, Volume 2, Numbers 1 and 2, 2003, 64-67; Larry G. DeVries, CEC, USNR (Ret.), "Seabees in Korea, 1950-1953, in *Seabee Magazine*, Volume 2, Numbers 1 and 2, 2003, 68-70; Lisle A. Rose, *Assault on Eternity: Richard E. Byrd and the Exploration of Antarctica, 1946-47*, (Annapolis, Maryland: Naval Institute Press, 1980), 35-41, 46-47, 49, 55; United States Navy, Task Force 68, "Army Observer's Report on Operation Highjump/Task Force 68, U.S. Navy," (Washington, D.C.: Department of War, 1947), 1-5, 326-328; Reports and reference files for Operation HIGH JUMP are

located in Record Group 313 (records of the U.S. Naval Support Force, Antarctica, 1939-1980) at the National Archives and Record Administration facility in College Park, Maryland.

55. Transano, *History of the Seabees*, 21-23; U.S. Naval Historical Center, "Seabees Remember Korea," in *Seabee Magazine*, Volume 2, Numbers 1 and 2, 2003, 64-67; Larry G. DeVries, CEC, USNR (Ret.), "Seabees in Korea, 1950-1953, in *Seabee Magazine*, Volume 2, Numbers 1 and 2, 2003, 68-70.

56. Ibid; Joseph F. Jelley, "Engineers at War: Seabees Engineer Amphibious Landing at Inchon, Korea," *Civil Engineering*, Volume 21, (June 1951), 323-5.

57. U.S. Naval Historical Center, "Seabees Remember Korea," in *Seabee Magazine*, Volume 2, Numbers 1 and 2, 2003, 64-67; Larry G. DeVries, CEC, USNR (Ret.), "Seabees in Korea, 1950-1953, in *Seabee Magazine*, Volume 2, Numbers 1 and 2, 2003, 68-70.

58. Steve Karoly, "Operation Crippled Chick: ACB 1 Builds Emergency Airstrip Behind Enemy Lines," *Seabee Log*, No. 5 (Winter 1999).

59. "Seabees Tame Snow Cats and Weasels on the Job in Antarctica." *All Hands*, Number 513, (October 1959), 55; "South Pole Gets Atomic Power." *All Hands*, Number 547, (August 1962), 2-5; U.S. Navy records pertaining to its involvement in the United States Antarctic Program can be found in Records of the Chief of Naval Operations, Oceanographer of the Navy on Operation DEEP FREEZE, Operational Archives Branch, Naval Historical Center, Washington, D.C. For historical background and records description, see http://www.history.navy.mil/ar/oscar/oceanographer.htm; A.G. Gardner "Seabee Mobile Recovery Teams," *All Hands*, Number, 528 (January 1961), 14-16; Andrew J. Glass, "Spies Open New Worlds for Seabees," United States Naval Institute *Proceedings*, Number 750, (August 1965), 148, Report from the *New York Herald Tribune*, May 24, 1965.

60. Transano, *History of the Seabees*, 24-31; See also Edward J. Marolda, *By Sea, Air, and Land: An Illustrated History of the U.S. Navy and the War in Southeast Asia*, 242-250, (Washington, D.C.: Government Printing Office, 1994). For a more in depth treatment, see Richard Tregaskis, *Southeast Asia: Building the Bases, The Construction History in Southeast Asia*, (Washington, D.C.: Government Printing Office, 1975).

61. Officer in Charge, Seabee Team 1104, LTJG F. A. Peterlin to Commander Naval Construction Battalions, Pacific, Subject: Dong Xoai Incident; report on, June 19, 1965, Naval Historical Center, Operational Archives, "Post-1946 Reports," Box: 390, Folder: CB Team 1104; Commander Naval Construction Battalions, Pacific, to Distribution List, Subject: Dong Xoai Incident; information concerning, August 6, 1965, Naval Historical Center, Operational Archives, "Post-1946 Reports," Box: 369, Folder: Naval Construction Battalions, Pacific; Congressional Medal of Honor Citation to Construction Mechanic Third Class Marvin G. Shields, Naval Historical Center, Operational Archives, "Vietnam C.F.," Box: 199, Folder: IND. Pers.-Shields, M.G., CMA3; LTJG Frank A. Peterlin, CEC, USNR, "The Battle of Dong Xoai," in *The Navy Civil Engineer*, Volume 6, Number 6, November-December 1965, 28-30; The story of CM3 Marvin Shields and Seabee Team 1104 at Dong Xoai is also told in Tregaskis, *Southeast Asia: Building the Bases*, 117-133; William D. Middleton, "Seabees in Viet Nam," Naval Insti-

tute *Proceedings*, Number 774, (August 1967), 54-64; and William D. Middleton, "Seabees at Dong Xoai '... a New Kind of Fighting Man,'" United States Naval Institute *Proceedings*, Number 827 (January 1972), 30-36.

62. Marolda, *By Sea, Air, and Land*, 242-250; Charles J. Merdinger, "Civil Engineers, Seabees, and Bases-Viet Nam," United States Naval Institute *Proceedings*, Number 807, (May 1970), 254.

63. Tregaskis, , *Southeast Asia: Building the Bases*, 49, 295, 307, 309-310, 313, 356.

64. Ibid., 157, 164-168

65. Ibid.

66. Ibid., 174-176, 314.

67. Ibid., 358, 380-381, 385.

68. Ibid., 398, 436; Marolda, *By Sea, Air, and Land*, 242-250; Charles J. Merdinger, "Civil Engineers, Seabees, and Bases-Viet Nam," United States Naval Institute *Proceedings*, Number 807, (May 1970), 254.

69. James P. Rife Interview with RADM Charles R. Kubic, 3 December 2004, 4-5, (Hereafter cited as Rife/Kubic Interview).

70. See Dilip Hiro, *The Longest War: The Iran-Iraq Military Conflict*, (New York, New York: Routledge, 1991), and Kenneth M. Pollack, *Arabs at War: Military Effectiveness, 1948-1991*, (Lincoln, Nebraska: University of Nebraska Press, 2002) 182-235, for the best analyses of the Iran-Iraq War.

71. Hiro, 200-201; Pollack, 228-229; For Saddam's use of chemical weapons against the Kurds in 1987-88, see "Saddam's Chemical Weapons Campaign: Halabja, March 16, 1988," United States Department of State, Bureau of Public Affairs, Washington, D.C., March 14, 2003, available online at http://www.state.gov/r/pa/ei/rls/18714.htm. According to Pollack, Saddam launched over 200 specially modified, extended range "al-Husayn" SCUD missiles at Iranian cities, primarily Tehran and Qom, between February and August 1988.

72. Hiro, 248-249.

73. Ibid., 254-266.

74. Ibid.

75. United States Department of Defense, *Conduct of the Persian Gulf War: Final Report to Congress*, (Washington, D.C.: Government Printing Office, 1992), 442-44; Command Histories for Naval Mobile Construction Battalions 5, 7, and 40, 1990-1991, Post 1 January 1990 Command Files, Operational Archives Branch, Naval Historical Center, Washington, D.C; Marolda and Schneller, *Shield and Sword*, 107-108, 129, 254, 279, 285, 339-340; Transano, *History of the Seabees*, 41-42; U.S. Navy, Chief of Naval Operations, Publication NWP4-04.1, "Seabee Operations in the MAGTF," (Washington, D.C.: Department of the Navy, 1997), 1-2; Rife/Kubic Interview, 3-5.

76. Rife/Kubic Interview, 3-5; U.S. Navy, Publication NWP4-04.1, "Seabee Operations in the MAGTF," 1-2, 3-2 through 3-5.

77. Ibid.

78. Ibid.; Captain Carlton W. Meyer, USMCR, "The FSSG Dinosaurs," in *Marine Corps Gazette*, Volume 75, Number 10, (October 1991), 32-36; Marolda and Schneller, *Shield and Sword*, 107-108, 129, 254, 279, 285,

79. U.S. Congress, House of Representatives, Committee on Armed Services, "Interim Report of the Committee on Armed Services, House of Representatives, on the Persian Gulf War, March 30, 1992, (Washington, D.C.: Government Printing office, 1992), 65-68.
80. U.S. Navy, Publication NWP4-04.1, "Seabee Operations in the MAGTF," 1-10; Command Histories for NMCBs 5,7, and 40, 1990-91, Post 1 January 1990 Command Files, Operational Archives Branch, Naval Historical Center.
81. Ibid.
82. "Seabee Operations in the MAGTF," 1-10; Command Histories for NMCBs 5,7, and 40, 1990-91.
83. Marolda and Schneller, *Shield and Sword*, 277-306, 310-312.
84. Ibid.; Rife/Kubic Interview, 3-5.

Bibliography of Selected Works

Primary Sources

Bremer, L. Paul, & Malcolm McConnell. *My Year In Iraq: The Struggle to Build a Future of Hope*, 1st edition. Canada: Simon & Schuster, January 2006.

Combs, Lewis B. "An Account of the Navy's Civilian Engineer Corps," *Military Engineer*, 12 (March 1943), 103.

_____. "Functions of the Civil Engineer Corps in the Naval Establishment," *Civil Engineering*, 12 (June 1942), 320-3.

DeLong, Michael, Lieutenant General. *Inside CENTCOM: The Unvarnished Truth About the Wars in Afghanistan and Iraq*. Washington, D.C.: Regnery Publishing, 2004.

Department of Defense. *Joint Vision 2010: America's Military: Preparing for Tomorrow*, Washington, D.C.: Government Printing Office: July 1996.

Department of Defense. *Joint Vision 2020*, Washington, D.C.: Government Printing Office, June 2000.

Duelfer, Charles. *Comprehensive Report of the Special Adviser to the Director of Central Intelligence on Iraq's WMD Weapons of Mass Destruction*. Washington, D.C.: Central Intelligence Agency, 2004.

Franks, Tommy, General, with Malcolm McConnell. *American Soldier*. New York, New York: Regan Books, 2004.

Johnson, Thomas A. COMCBPAC Reports: Seabee Teams. Pearl Harbor, Hawaii: Commander, Construction Battalions, U. S. Pacific Fleet, 1969.

National Commission On Terrorist Attacks Upon the United States. *The 9/11 Commission Report: Final Report of the National Commission on Terrorist Attacks Upon the United States.* New York, New York: W.W. Norton & Company, July 22, 2004.

Petraeus, Lieutenant General David H. (USA) and Lieutenant General James F. Amos (USMC). U.S. Army Field Manual 3-24 and Marine Corps Warfighting Publication 3-33.5, *Counterinsurgency.* Washington, D.C.: Headquarters, Department of the Army, December 2006.

Porter, Captain David. *Journal of a Cruise.* Edited by R. D. Madison and Karen Hamon. Annapolis, MD: Naval Institute Press, 1986.

_____. *A Voyage in the South Seas in the Years 1812, 1813, and 1814: with Particular Details of the Gallipagos and Washington Islands.* London, England: R. Phillips, 1823.

Sanchez, Ricardo S., and Donald T. Phillips. *Wiser in Battle: A Soldier's Story.* New York, New York: HarperCollins, 2008.

U.S. Department of Defense, Inspector General, Deputy Inspector General for Intelligence. "Review of Pre-Iraqi War Activities of the Office of the Under Secretary of Defense for Policy." Report Number 07-INTEL-04, Project Number. D2006-DIYT01-0077.000. February 9, 2007.

United States Navy. *100th Anniversary, Navy Civil Engineer Corps, 1867-1967: Men Methods-Materials.* Washington, D.C.: Government Printing Office, 1967.

Secondary Sources

Allard, Dean C. "Interservice Differences in the United States, 1945-1950: A Naval Perspective," in *Airpower Journal*, Winter 1989 Issue.

Allen, Walter H. "The Twelfth Regiment (Public Works) at Great Lakes." United States Naval Institute *Proceedings*, March 1921.

Anonymous. *Imperial Hubris: Why the West is Losing the War on Terror.* Washington, D.C.: Brassey's, Inc., 2004.

Barker, A.J. *The Bastard War: The Mesopotamian Campaign of 1914-18.* New York, New York: Dial, 1967.

BIBLIOGRAPHY

Barnett, Roger W. *Asymmetrical Warfare: Today's Challenge to US Military Power*. Washington, D.C.: Brassey's, Inc., 2003.

Biddescombe, Perry. *Werwolf!: The History of the National Socialist Guerrilla Movement, 1944-1946*. Toronto, Canada: University of Toronto Press, 1998.

Bodansky, Yossef. *The Secret History of the Iraq War*. New York, New York: Regan Books, 2004.

Bourne, Christopher M. "Unintended Consequences of the Goldwater-Nichols Act," *Joint Force Quarterly*, Spring 1998, 99-108.

Braddon, Russell. *The Siege*. New York, NY: The Viking Press, 1970.

Castillo, Edmund L. *The Seabees of World War II*. New York, New York: Random House, 1963.

Cave, Hough B. *We Build, We Fight*. New York: Harper and Brothers, 1944.

Clancy, Tom, with General Tony Zinni, and Tony Koltz. *Battle Ready*. New York, New York: G.P. Putnam's Sons, 2004.

Cogan, Charles G. "Desert One and Its Disorders," *The Journal of Military History*, Vol. 67, No. 1, January 2003.

Coletta, Paolo E., ed. *United States Navy and Marine Corps Bases, Domestic*. Westport, CN: Greenwood Press, 1985.

_____, ed. *United States Navy and Marine Corps Bases, Overseas*. Westport, CN: Greenwood Press, 1985.

Cooper, Philip C. Pete. *The Engineer in War and Peace: From Guadalcanal to Main Street*. Baltimore, Maryland: Gateway Press, 1996.

Cordesman, Anthony H. *The Iraq War: Strategy, Tactics, and Military Lessons*. Washington, D.C.: The Center for Strategic and International Studies Press, 2003.

_____. *The Lessons of Afghanistan: War Fighting, Intelligence, and Force Transformation*. Washington, D.C.: The Center for Strategic and International Studies Press, 2002.

_____. *The War after the War: Strategic Lessons of Iraq and Afghanistan*. Washington, D.C.: The Center for Strategic and International Studies Press, 2004.

DeVries, Larry G. "Seabees on Guadalcanal," *WWII Naval Journal*, July/August 1994, 3-6.

Dod, Karl C. *The Corps of Engineers: The War Against Japan*. Washington, D.C.: Office of the Chief of Military History, 1966.

Feith, Douglas J. *War and Decision: Inside the Pentagon at the Dawn of the War on Terrorism*. New York, New York: HarperCollins Publishers, 2008.

Fontenot, Gregory, Colonel, Lieutenant Colonel E. J. Degen, and Lieutenant Colonel David Tohn. *On Point: The United States Army in Operation Iraqi Freedom*. Annapolis, Maryland: U.S. Naval Institute Press, 2005.

Frank, Benis M., and Henry I. Shaw, Jr. *History of U.S. Marine Corps Operations in World War II: Victory and Occupation*. Vol. V. Washington, D.C.: Historical Branch, G-3 Division, Headquarters, U.S. Marine Corps, 1968.

Friedman, Norman. *Seapower and Space: From the Dawn of the Missile Age to Net-Centric Warfare*. London: Chatham Publishing, 2000.

_____. *Terrorism, Afghanistan, and America's New Way of War*. Annapolis, Maryland: Naval Institute Press, 2003.

Garand, George W. and Truman R. Strobridge. *History of U.S. Marine Corps Operations n World War II: Western Pacific Operations*. Vol. IV. Washington, D.C.: Historical Branch, G-3 Division, Headquarters, U.S. Marine Corps, 1971.

Gardner, A. G. "Seabee Mobile Recovery Teams," *All Hands*, No. 528 (January 1961), 14-6.

Glass, Andrew J. "Spies Open New Worlds for Seabees." United States Naval Institute *Proceedings*, No. 750 (August 1965), 148. Report from the *New York Herald Tribune*, May 24, 1965.

Hiro, Dilip. *Secrets and Lies: Operation "Iraqi Freedom" and After: A Prelude to the Fall of U.S. Power in the Middle East?*. New York, New York: Nation Books, 2004.

Hough, Frank O., Lieutenant Colonel, Major Verle E. Ludwig, and Henry I. Shaw, Jr. *History of U.S. Marine Corps Operations in World War II: Pearl Harbor to Guadalcanal*. Vol. I. Washington, D.C.: Historical Branch, G-3 Division, Headquarters, U.S. Marine Corps, 1958.

Howard, Michael C., Colonel (USMC Reserve). "'Basra to Baghdad': The 1914-18 British Campaign for Mesopotamia," *Marine Corps Gazette*. Vol. 87, Issue 9. Quantico, Virginia: September 2003.

Howard Michael C, Colonel (USMC Reserve), and Stephen J Flynn. "'MEG' My Day," *Marine Corps Gazette*. Vol. 88, Issue 3. Quantico, Virginia: March 2004, 23-27.

Huie, William Bradford. *Can Do!: The Story of the Seabees*. New York, New York: E. P. Dutton, 1944.

_____. *From Omaha to Okinawa: The Story of the Seabees*. New York: E. P. Dutton, 1945. 257p. Enser: p. 314. Smith: 9892. Ziegler: 2613.

Jelley, Joseph F. "Engineers at War: Seabees Engineer Amphibious Landing at Inchon, Korea," *Civil Engineering*, 21 (June 1951), 323-5.

Keegan, John. *The Iraq War*. New York, New York: Alfred A. Knopf, 2004.

Kimmel, Jay. *U. S. Navy Seabees Since Pearl Harbor*. Portland: Curey/Stevens Publishing Inc. 1995.

Lewis, Bernard. *The Crisis of Islam: Holy War and Unholy Terror*. New York: Random House, 2003.

Locher, James R., III. "Taking Stock of Goldwater-Nichols," *Joint Force Quarterly*, Autumn 1996, 10-17.

_____. *Victory on the Potomac: The Goldwater-Nichols Act Unifies the Pentagon*. College Station, Texas: Texas A&M University Press, 2002.

Long, David F. *Nothing Too Daring: A Biography of Commodore David Porter, 1780-1843*. Annapolis, MD: United States Naval Institute, 1970.

Luttwak, Edward N. *The Pentagon and the Art of War: The Question of Military Reform*. New York: Simon and Schuster, 1984.

Macgregor, Douglas A. "The Joint Force: A Decade, No Progress," *Joint Force Quarterly*. Winter 2000-01.

Marolda, Edward J. and Robert J. Schneller, Jr. *Shield and Sword: The United States Navy and the Persian Gulf War*. Annapolis, Md.: Naval Institute Press, 2001.

Merdinger, Charles J. "Civil Engineers, Seabees, and Bases-Viet Nam," United States Naval Institute *Proceedings*, No. 807 (May 1970), 254.

Middleton, William D. "Seabees at Dong Xoai '... a New Kind of Fighting Man,'" United States Naval Institute *Proceedings*, No. 827 (January 1972), 30-6.

―――――. "Seabees in Viet Nam," Naval Institute *Proceedings*, No. 774 (August 1967), 54-64.

Millar, Ronald W. *Death of an Army: The Siege of Kut, 1915-16*. Boston: Houghton, Mifflin, 1970.

Miniter, Richard. *Shadow War: The Untold Story of How Bush is Winning the War on Terror*. Washington, D.C.: Regnery Publishing, 2004.

Moberly, F.J. *The Campaign in Mesopotamia, 1914-18*, in *History of the Great War, Based on Official Documents*. 4 Vols. London: His Majesty's Stationery Office, 1927.

Moreell, Benjamin. "The Seabees in World War II." United States Naval Institute *Proceedings*, No. 709 (March 1962), 85-101.

Marolda, Edward J. and G. Wesley Pryce, III. *A Select Bibliography of the United States Navy and the Vietnam Conflict*. Washington: Naval Historical Center, Department of the Navy, 1983.

Murray, Williamson, and Major General Robert H. Scales, Jr. *The Iraq War: A Military History*. Cambridge, Massachusetts: The Belknap Press of Harvard University Press, 2003.

Nasse, Jean-Yves. "US Navy Seabees, 1941-1945: Part One-1941-1944: USN Construction Battalions in Europe," *Militaria Magazine*, No. 1 (February 1994), 18-26.

―――――. "United States Navy Seabees, 1941-1945: Part 2-1941-1945: Naval Construction Battalions in the Pacific," *Militaria Magazine*, No. 21 (November 1995), 11-16.

Peltier, Eugene J., Rear Admiral, C.E.C, U.S.N. *The Bureau of Yards and Docks of the Navy and the Civil Engineer Corps*. New York: Newcomen Society in North America, 1961.

Pipes, Daniel. *Militant Islam Reaches America*. New York, New York: W. W. Norton & Company, 2002).

Pollack, Kenneth M. *Arabs at War: Military Effectiveness, 1948-1991.* Lincoln, Nebraska: University of Nebraska Press, 2002.

_____. *The Threatening Storm: The Case for Invading Iraq.* New York, New York: Random House, 2002.

Rashid, Ahmed. *Jihad: The Rise of Militant Islam in Central Asia.* New Haven, Connecticut: Yale University Press, 2002.

_____. *Taliban: Militant Islam, Oil, and Fundamentalism in Central Asia,* New Haven, Connecticut: Yale University Press, 2000.

Record, Jeffrey. *Dark Victory: America's Second War Against Iraq.* Annapolis, Maryland: Naval Institute Press, 2004.

Scarborough, Rowan. *Rumsfeld's War: The Untold Story of America's Anti-Terrorist Commander.* Lanham, Maryland: Regnery Publishing, 2004.

"Seabees to Remain as a Potent Postwar Unit." *Our Navy,* 41 (First of December 1946), 36-37.

"Seabees Tame Snow Cats and Weasels on the Job in Antarctica." *All Hands,* No. 513 (October 1959), 55.

Shaw, Henry I., Jr., Bernard C. Nalty, and Edwin T. Turnbladh. *History of U.S. Marine Corps Operations in World War II: Central Pacific Drive.* Vol. III. Washington, D.C.: Historical Branch, G-3 Division, Headquarters, U.S. Marine Corps, 1966.

Shaw, Henry I., Jr., and Major Douglas T. Kane, *History of U.S. Marine Corps Operations in World War II: Isolation of Rabaul.* Vol. II. Washington, D.C.: Historical Branch, G-3 Division, Headquarters, U.S. Marine Corps, 1963.

Skordiles, Kimon. *The Seabees in War and Peace: A Comprehensive Account of the Activities of the U.S. Navy Men Who Helped Build a Better World and Fought to Preserve It.* Vols. I and II. Pasadena, California: Argus, 1972.

"South Pole Gets Atomic Power." *All Hands,* No. 547 (August 1962), 2-5.

Stanford, Alfred B. Force *Mulberry: The Planning and Installation of the Artificial Harbor of U.S. Normandy Beaches in World War II.* New York, New York: William Morrow and Company, 1951.

Transano, Vincent A., ed. *History of the Seabees*. Port Hueneme: Command Historian, Naval Facilities Engineering Command, 1994.

Tregaskis, Richard. *Southeast Asia: Building the Bases, The Construction History in Southeast Asia*. Washington, D.C.: Government Printing Office, 1975.

United States Navy. Bureau of Yards and Docks. *Building the Navy's Bases in World War II: History of the Bureau of Yards and Docks and the Civil Engineer Corps, 1940-1946*. Vols. I and II. Washington, D.C.: Government Printing Office. 1947.

United States Navy. Bureau of Yards and Docks. *The Civil Engineer Corps of the United States Naval Reserve*. Washington, D.C.: Government Printing Office, 1942.

United States Navy. Naval Civil Engineering Laboratory, Port Hueneme, CA. *Men, Methods, Materials, 1867-1967: 100th Anniversary Navy Civil Engineer Corps*. Washington, D.C.: Naval Facilities Engineering Command, 1967.

West, Bing, and Major General Ray L. Smith. *The March Up: Taking Baghdad with the 1st Marine Division*. New York, New York: Bantam, 2003.

West, Bing. *No True Glory: A Frontline Account of the Battle for Fallujah*. New York, New York: Bantam, 2005.

Williams, Garland H., Colonel. *Engineering Peace: The Military Role in Postconflict Reconstruction*. Washington, D.C.: Institute of Peace Press, 2004.

Woodward, Bob. *Bush at War*. New York, New York: Simon & Schuster, 2002.

_____. *Plan of Attack*. New York, New York: Simon & Schuster, 2004.

_____. *State of Denial*. New York, New York, Simon & Schuster, 2006.

Wright, Donald P., and Colonel Timothy R. Reese. *On Point II: Transition to the New Campaign: The United States Army in Operation Iraqi Freedom, May 2003-January 2005*. Fort Leavenworth, Kansas: U.S. Army Combined Arms Center, Combat Studies Institute, 2008.

Wright, Evan. *Generation Kill: Devil Dogs, Iceman, Captain America, and the New Face of American War*. New York, New York, New York: G.P. Putnam's Sons, 2004.

Zeigler, Matt. *Three Block War: U.S. Marines in Iraq*. iUniverse, 2004.

Oral Histories

All Released by the Naval Expeditionary Combat Command on June 12, 2008, via FOIA Request

SKCS Richard M. Alvarado	NCFSU 2 (PRI 2)	February 5, 2005
LTJG Jerome Arabe	I MEF HQ Recon Unit	February 5, 2005
LCDR Joel Baldwin	NMCB 4	January 4, 2005
LT Ron Birnbaum	NMCB 5	February 7, 2005
EOCS Charles Cox	NCFSU 2	February 5, 2005
BUC Chad Eagle	UCT 2	February 7, 2005
CDR Robyn Eastman	22nd NCR	January 12, 2005
CMDCM Jim Fairbanks	22nd NCR	January 12, 2005
BUC Joe Franz	30th NCR	February 5, 2005
EOC Charles Hair	NMCB 74	January 12, 2005
NC1 Michael Hill	NMCB 74	January 13, 2005
CM Paul Hoffman	22nd NCR	January 12, 2005
CAPT Christopher Honkomp	NMCB 7	February 1, 2005
CDR Scott Hurst	22nd NCR	January 12, 2005
BUC Dan Jolin	30th NCR	February 4, 2005
BUCS Troy Kellerman	NMCB 133	January 11, 2005
EO1 Frederick Kyriss	NCFSU 2	February 5, 2005
LT Phil Lavallee	NMCB 133	January 13, 2005
CDR Mark Libonate	NMCB 74	January 11, 2005
CDR Cliff Maurer	NMCB 74	February 1, 2005
LT David McAlister	1st NCD	January 26, 2005
CAPT Will McKerall	22nd NCR	January 13, 2005
EOC James Mellow	NCFSU 2	February 6, 2005
SW2 Jacob Pagan	NMCB 4	February 5, 2005
LT Julio Palacio	30th NCR	February 5, 2005
CAPT Bill Rudich	30th NCR	March 2, 2005
EOC Rudolfo Santiago	NCFSU 2	February 5, 2005

EO3 Adam Schneider	NMCB 133	January 12, 2005
LCDR Russ Seignious	20th SRG	January 13, 2005
CE1 Alexander Semmler	UCT 2	February 7, 2005
LCDR Bill Sloan	22nd NCR	January 13, 2005
EA1 Oliver Taylor	NMCB 74	January 11, 2005
SWC Howard Tomme	NMCB 133	January 13, 2005
CUCM Jeffrey Weigel	NMCB 74	January 11, 2005
LT Harry Wong	CBMU 303	February 2, 2005
EO1 William Young	NMCB 133	January 12, 2005
EOC Richard Zylla	NMCB 4	February 7, 2005

Index

A

Abizaid, John, 300, 301
Abu Ghraib scandal, 302
Abu Nidal organization (ANO), 29
Abu Sayyaf terrorist group, 27–28
Ad Diwaniyah and Al Amarkeziyah Secondary School, 253, 272
ad-Douri, Izzat Ibrahim, 297
Afghanistan, 23–26
Ahmed Al Jaber Air Base, 49–53, 56
Ah Rashid Military Academy, 298
Air Detachments (Air Dets), 17, 48
Air Det Table of Allowance (MCA), 57
airfields and Rhino Snot, 276
Air Port of Departure (APOD), 18, 101
Air Tasking Orders (ATOs), 151
Al Amarkeziyah Secondary School, 253, 272
Al Anbar Province, 303–304
Al Basrah, 261
Al Firdus (Paradise) Square, 226–227
Al-Hakim, Ayatollah Mohammad Baqer, 299
Al Hillah, 255, 283–284
Ali Al Salem Air Base, 45, 47
    AM-2 matting for helicopter pads, 49
    bridge OPT, 67
    Camp Moreell, 105
    camp site for Seabees, 55
    logistics cell, 137
    Munitions Storage Area, 53
    Munitions Supply Point, 88
Ali Mosque, 299
al-Islam, Ansar, 30
Al Jaber Air Base, 45–47, 86–87
Al Kut, 240–243, 286–287
Allawi, Iyad, 303
Allen, Walter H., 333–335, 341
Allied Expeditionary Force, 348
Al Nida Division, 124
Al Qaeda, 20–21, 30, 43, 299
al-Sahaf, Mohammed Saeed, 226
Alternate Supply Route Hueneme, 202–203
al-Zarqawi, Abu Mus'ab, 30, 299
Ambush Alley, 150, 168, 183, 190, 193
Ammunition Supply Point (ASP), 147
Amos, James, 85, 245, 317
Amphibious Construction Battalion (PHIBCB), 1, 84, 352–353, 359
Amphibious Landing Exercise (PHIBLEX), 17
Anbar province, polling places construction, 316
Anderson, Doug, 203
Anderson, Michael C., 311, v
Anderson, Richard E., 356
An Nasiriyah, 123, 212–216, 252
    battle for, 183–187
    Iraqi Zone Commander, 184
    Israeli D-9 dozer, 185
    power plants, 270–271
    Saddam Fedayeen, 199
    SERT 74, 188
    USMC combat engineers, 185
    water works, 270–271
An Nasiriyah Bridges, 168, 188, 193
An Numaniyah Airfield, 216–218, 224, 248, 252
An Numaniyah Bridge, 217, 219
Arabe, Jerome, 108
Arab Liberation Front (ALF), 29
Area of Operations (AOs), 169
armed forces reevaluating missions and doctrines, 11–28
armored dozers, 185, 348
Armored Vehicle Launched Bridges (AVLBs), 35, 63
Army
    assuming responsibility for Baghdad, 233
    competition for equipment, 102
    joint warfare, 11–12
Army and Marine Multi-Roll Bridge Companies, 36
Army Engineers
    battalions, 39
    combat support missions, 130
    supplementing Seabees and Marine Engineers, 102
Army Mechanized Engineer Battalion, 36
Army Multi Role Bridge Companies (MRBCs), 148
Army Wheeled Engineer Battalion, 36

Arraf, Jane, 280
Arrival Assembly Operations Element (AAOE), 137
asphalt plant, 275–276, 324
Aspin Report, 361
As Samawah and mass gravesites, 283–284
assault bridges, 64, 324
Assault Float Bridges, 63
Atta, Mohammed, 31
Azzi, Mechanic 3rd Class, 268

B

Ba'ath Party, 184, 230
Babylon, restored city of, 237–238
Babylon Palace, 236–238
Baghdad
    air strikes, 223
    Al Firdus (Paradise) Square, 226–227
    assault, 223–226
    block-by-block urban conflict, 226
    Diyala River, 222
    final battle for, 180
    Iraqis defending bridges, 222
    moving around in, 298
    Office of Reconstruction and Humanitarian Assistance, 230
    Saddam's palace, 230
    taking down, 223
    toppling Saddam's statue, 227
    twin Diyala Bridges, 227–230
    U.S. air strike, 153
"Baghdad Bob," 226
Baghdad Division, 123–124
Bailey, Donald, 68
Bailey bridges, 70
Baldwin, Joel E., v
Baldwin, Loammi, Jr., 329
banks, U.S. currency hidden in, 269
Barrett, T.J., 315
Base Junction City, 308, 310–314
Basilan Island-Philippines, 23, 27–28
Basrah, Baghdad, and Beyond (Reynolds), 121, x
Basrah and Beating Retreat, 285–286
Basrah International Airport, 285–286
Batalona, Wesley, 300
Battalion Equipment Evaluation Program (BEEP), 138–139
Battle for An Nasiriyah, 183–187

Battle of the Cliff, 346
Beamer, Todd, 56
Beating Retreat in Basrah, 285–286
Bechtel, 265
beds and butts, 103–106
Bin Laden, Osama, 20–21, 30, 83, 299
Bisset, Andrew G., 15, 345
Black Hawk Down, 126
Blair Airfield, 240–243
Blitzer, Wolf, 292
Blix, Hans, 53, 81–82, 144
Blount, Buford "Buff" C., 140, 148
Board of Navy Commissioners, 330
Bollinger, Doyle, 287, v
Boomer, Walter E., 360, 362
Bottorff, Dave, 7
Brabham, James A., 34
breach lanes, 167
breach plan, 141
Breitenbach, 207
Bremer, L. Paul, 266, 299, 301, 303, 327
bridge Operational Planning Team (OPT), 66–67
Bridgepark Davisville, 56, 198–199, 218
bridges
    An Nasiriyah, 193
    Assault Float Bridges, 63
    AVLBs (armored vehicle launched bridge), 63
    Bailey bridges, 70
    building, 193–195
    bureaucratic errors, 75–78
    Class-70 "Compact 200 Super Logistics Support Bridges," 68
    culvert-based river crossing design, 64–65
    damages to, 277–278
    earth moles, 72
    erector set style bridging, 66
    floating bridges, 77
    funding, 66
    Mabey & Johnson bridges, 70–71
    making rivers fit, 65–70
    Medium Girder Bridges (MGBs), 63
    minimizing components, 72
    mole piers, 66
    pipe culverts, 65
    procurement, 76
    repairing, 277–280
    Ribbon Bridges, 63

INDEX

semi-permanent, 62–65
unique in components and assembly, 66
bridging companies command and control issues, 41–42
Brims, Robin, 140, 243, 245, 261, 285
Briscoe, Robert P., 353
Briscoe Field, 353
British Bailey Bridge, 344
British 'Basrah to Baghdad' campaign disaster, 63
British Black Watch Battalion, 316
British military, 63
Brown, Chris, 126
Brown, Larry, 39–41, 149
Brown & Root, 252, 268
"Budweiser," 23
bunker drills, 117–118
Bureau of Navigation, 335–337, 339
Bureau of Navy Yards and Docks, 330–331, 336–337, 357
Bush, George H. W., 359
Bush, George W., 21
    House Joint Resolution 114, 53
    "Mission Accomplished!", 239–240
    National Security Strategy of the United States of America, 44
    Saddam serious threat, 31
    tightening screws on U.N. and Iraq, 53
    tying Saddam to terrorist threat, 82
    ultimatum, 144–149
    USS *Abraham Lincoln*, 239
    violations and internal atrocities of Saddam's regime, 82
Bush Administration
    Causus belli, 82
    doctrine of preemption, 43–44
    escalation of rhetoric, 43–44
    Global War on Terrorism, 29
    groundwork for new war, 44
    nexus between Iraq and Al Qaeda, 30–31
    OPLAN 1003, 31–32
    President's domestic policy initiatives, 9
    underestimating Al Qaeda threat, 21
    war plan, 31–32
business leaders, 273
Byrd, Richard E., 351–352
Byrne, Shawn, 138

C

Camp 93, 56, 95, 101, 106
Camp Allen, 341
Camp Babylon, 237
Campbell, Lieutenant (Junior Grade), 192, 193
Camp Bradford, 341
Camp Castle, 105–106
Camp Commando, 45–46, 88, 100, 165
    AT&T phone strongback tents, 235
    bunker drills, 117
    Camp Maintenance headquarters, 235
    CBMU 303, 235
    drills and false alarms, 154–155
    impact of Iraqi Seersucker missile, 100
    Iraqi counterstrike, 153–157
    making more functional, 46
    Marines commended for, 106
    MEG Command Bunker, 154
    MEG headquarters, 46
    MEG (Main), 292
    missiles shot at, 156
    rainy winter season, 46
    SCUD bunkers, 235
    SCUD launches, 156
    SERT 5, 218
    spaces available, 106
Camp Endicott, 341–343
Camp Fox, 96, 288
Camp Lee-Stephenson, 342
Camp Matilda, 142
Camp Moreell, 55–56, 147
    building up, 105
    Reception, Staging, Onward Movement, and Integration (RSO&I), 303
    spaces available, 106
Camp Parks, 342
Camp Patriot, 84
Camp Paul Jones, 333
Camp Peary, 341–342
Camp Rhino, 24–25
camps
    ad hoc planning, 105
    construction, 55–56
Camp X-Ray terrorist detention facility, 25
Can Do!, 7, 339, x
Can Do! (Huie), 349
capitalism, 273
car bombings, 299

cargo-handling Special Battalions, 342
Catto, William D., 77
cemetery at Al Kut, 240–243
Charlie Task Force, 42, 78
chemical weapons, 223
chemical weapons sites, 282–284
Chetelat, Aaron, 154–155
Chief of Naval Operations, 16, 42, 57
Chin, Edward, 227
CH-46 Sea Knight helicopter, 212
Chulyab mission, 26
CIA Human Intelligence (HUMINT), 158
Civic Action, 355, 356
Civil Engineer Corps (CEC), 4
   appointing, 330
   constructing, 329–331
   "crossed bananas" uniform, 6
   increasing number of, 332
   officers, 340
civil engineers, 329–330, 340–341
Civil Military Operations Centers (CMOCs), 264, 297
Civil Military Operations (CMO), 320–323, ix
Clark, Regina, v
Clark, Vernon, 42, 224
Clarke, Senior Chief, 118
Class-70 "Compact 200 Super Logistics Support Bridges," 68, 72
Class IV material procurement, 62–65
clear, hold, and build concepts, 317
Clinton Administration and Al Qaeda threat, 21
Clyde, Andrew, 137
CNN, 280
Coalition, 153, 167, 297–298, 299
Coalition forces, 231, 244, 261
Coalition Forces Land Component Commander (CFLCC), 261
"Coalition of the Willing," 144
Coalition Provisional Authority (CPA), 299, 326–327
Coast Guard and Iwo Jima, 347
Cold War and Seabees, 353–354
Coleman, John, 40, 264
Combat Service Support Battalions (CSSBs) 12 and 18, 137
Combat Service Support Group 11, 193–194
Combined Forces Land Component Commander (CFLCC), 67, 147–149

Combined Joint Task Force (CJTF) 7, 266–267
Combined Joint Task Force Consequence Management (CJTF-CM), 23
Command Group Meeting, 182
Commando Camp, 103
command staff and special band of pirates, 134–135
Concept of Operations (CONOPS), 35, 123–124, 188–189
Congressional notification, 50
Construction Battalion Center (CBC), 351
Construction Battalion Maintenance Unit (CBMU) 301, 342, 357
Construction Battalion Maintenance Unit (CBMU) 303, 54, 84, 293
   Babylon Palace, 236–237
   Baghdad, 236
   branding, 234
   Camp Commando, 235
   Camp Patriot tent city, 235
   command center for Franks in Qatar, 234
   command post close to Baghdad, 235–236
   confidence in, 233
   grading beaches, 235
   high praise for, 234
   Kuwait, 84, 234–235
   MPSRON debarkation, 78
   older than active Seabees, 233
   rescuing failing maintenance contractor, 106
Construction Battalion Maintenance Unit (CBMU) 627, 348
Construction Battalion Maintenance Unit (CBMU) 628, 348
Construction Battalion Maintenance Unit (CBMU) 629, 348
construction battalions recruiting skilled tradesmen, 338
Construction Battalion Unit (CBU) 411, 359
Construction Battalion Unit (CBU) 415, 359
Construction Capability (CONCAP) Contractor, 268
construction equipment, 334
Construction Forces-Samar, 345
construction materials, shopping for, 273–274
Continental United States (CONUS), 32
Contingency Engineer Unit, Pacific, 23

INDEX

Contingency Response Force (CCRF), 32
contractors
    food service, 104
    killings, 305
    reconstruction efforts, 262
    support, 321–322
convoys
    leading battalion to nowhere, 113–115
    plans, 141–142
    training, 112
Conway, James T., 40, 85, 104, 146, 181, 201, 225, 243, 245, 261
    approving Mabey & Johnson bridges, 74
    attacking Baghdad, 223
    bare bones holding area, 161
    Blair Field project, 242
    Camp Commando, 46
    chaos over reconstruction, 266
    coordinated 1st Marine Division's attack, 159
    flexibility in moving forces, 133
    forcing bridge command and control issue to, 41
    I MEF commander, 38
    insistence on MEG, 41
    insurgent groups, 301
    intent for I MEF, 122
    local civilian contractors, 159
    Marine Corps Planning System, 39
    MEG giving options on Baghdad, 224
    military parade, 294–295
    NBC threat, 115
    striking back, 157
Cook, Andrew, 204
Cooke, Len, 24
Core Modules (CMs), 57
Cox, Charles, 109, 207
Cozz, Ronald, 294
Crafts, Michael, 154–155
Crawford, Master Chief, 5
crossed bananas uniform, 6
Cross of Sacrifice, 242, 250
culvert-based river crossing design, 64–65
culvert bridges, 68, ix

D-Day, 147–148
dead enders, 261
de-Ba'athification policy, 266–267
decapitation strike, 153
decentralized democracy, 273
decontamination gear, 116
Defense Advisory Committee for Women in the Service (DACOWITS), 152
Defense Emergency Relief Fund (DERF) authorization, 50
Defense Logistics Agency (DLA), 74, 76, 137
DefenseWatch, 313
de Mello, Sergio Vieira, 299
demobilization, 351–357
demobilizing reserves, 239
Department of Defense (DOD), 11–28
Department of Environmental Protection Police Precinct building, 25
de Rose, Peter, 349
DESERT SHIELD, 359–361
DESERT SHIELD/DESERT STORM, 57
DESERT SPEAR exercise, 38
DESERT STORM, 11–13, 359
    construction battalion commanders, 37
    1st Force Service Support Group, 34
    ground campaign, 9
    Seabees, 360–361
Detachment (Det) 133, 162, 181
Detatchment (Det) 21, 209–210
developmental projects, 263
Devine, Chaplain, 312
de Weldon, Felix, iii
DeWitt, Operator 3rd Class, 152
Dhi Qahr (An Nasiriyah), 261
Dickerson, Christopher M., 308–309, v
Displaced Civilians (DC), 324
Division engineers, 19
Diyala Bridges, 229
Diyala River, 222, 247
Dossett, Trace W., 311, v
double BEEP, 138–139
Dwelley, Jason B., 308
Dwelley, Trace W., v
D-9 "Zionist Monster" Armored Dozers, 99

D

Dailey, Al, 282, 283
Da Nang Naval Hospital, 355–356
Davis, William C., 333

E

earthen moles, 72, 74
Eastman, Robyn, 118, 154–155
Echo (Endurance) task force, 42

Edelson, Mark, 165
Eichman, Kevin J., 112
8th Construction Brigade, 342
8th Engineer Support Battalion (ESB), 36, 39, 160, 190, 217, 219, 225, 241
8th Naval Construction Brigade (NCB), 345
18th Air Assault Brigade, 140
18th Marines, 13
82nd Airborne Division, 300, 303
Eisenhower, Dwight D., 348
El Baradei, Mohammed, 81
11th Marine Expeditionary Unit, 161
11th Naval Construction Brigade (NCB), 345
embarkation masters, 118–119
Endicott, Mordecai T., 331–332
Enemy Prisoner of War (EPW) Holding Area Thomas, 161–164, 181
Enemy Prisoners of War (EPWs), 161, 324
Engineer, Research, and Development Center (ERDC) Tele-Engineering Operations Center (TEOC), 67
Engineer Concept of Operations, 189
engineer groups, 13–14
Engineering Work Lines (EWLs), 135–136
Engineer Operations Center (EOC), 22
engineers, 303, 322–324
Engineer Support Battalions (ESBs), 141
Engineer's War, 323–325
Engle, Gary, 135
Environmental Products & Applications, Inc., 24
equipment
    offloading, 59
    redundancy, 73
erector set style nonstandard steel bridging, 66
Espinoza, A.J., 136
Essex, 329
Euphrates River, 182–183, 278
Eurest Support Services (ESS), 300

F

Fallujah, 259
    engineer support, 303
    fallen Seabees, 313
    hardened security strong points, 306–307
    insurgents, 302, 304–305, 316
    Marines stopping attacks, 301–302
    ordering Marines and Seabees to attack, 305
    prefabrication work in, 307
    sealing southeast corner, 306
    sudden ceasefire, 307
    Sunni insurgency, 300
    targeted operations, 301
    Zarqawi and Al Qaeda sanctuary, 300, 302
Fallujah Brigade, 302
Feith, Douglas J., 31
15 May Organization, 29
51st Mechanized Division, 158
15th Marine Expeditionary Unit (MEU), 24, 122–123
5th Marine Amphibious Corps, 14
The Fighting Seabees, 7, 349, ix
1st Construction Detachment, 336
1st Force Service Support Group (FSSG), 38, 41, 123, 141
1st Infantry Division, 316
First Marine Expeditionary Force (I MEF) Engineer Group, ix
1st Marine Division (MARDIV), 122, 149, 222
    An Nasiriyah (Iraq), 123
    Baghdad, 226
    direct support to, 36
    Diyala River, 225
    Hantush Airfield, 201
    Highways 1 and 7, 201
    Jalibah Airfield, 123
    Line of Departure, 158–159
    priority sustaining, 202
    Relief in Place (RIP), 262
    southern oilfields, 123
    urban combat, 145
1st Marine Division's Reconnaissance Battalion, 201
1st Marine Expeditionary Force Engineer Group (I MEG), 34
1st Marine Expeditionary Force (I MEF), 13
1st Naval Construction Division (NCD), 23–24, 42–43, 47, 56–60, 61, 84, 295, 304, x
1st Naval Construction Division (NCD) Command Operations Center, 118
1st United Kingdom Armoured Division, 123, 140–141, 207, 244, 285–286
five roads theory, 349

Fleisch, David L., 53, 129, 147
Flexi-Float Corporation, 77
floating bridges, 77, 324
Flood, Lance, 208
Fly-In Echelon, 57
food service, 104–105
Force Service Support Groups (FSSGs), 20
foreign fighters, 200, 307
Forrestal, James V., 350
Forward...from the Sea strategy, 12–13
4th Civil Affairs Group, 178, 214
4th Force Service Support Group (FSSG), 38–39
4th Infantry Division, 140
478th Combat Engineer Battalion, 129–130
478th Corps Mechanized Battalion, 102
Franks, Thomas R. "Tommy," 25, 31, 54, 120
   command center in Qatar, 234
   ordering 4th Infantry Division to Kuwait, 122
   tactical pause, 199
From Omaha to Ikinawa (Huie), 349
From the Sea strategy, 12

G

Gabriel, Terri, 105
Gallo, Geoff, 154
Garcia, Al, 238, 239, 252, 255, 277, 288, 291
Garin, Patrick, 66
Garner, Jay, 266
Gas and Oil Platforms (GOPLATS), 151, 158
gas masks, 115–116
gas-oil separation plant (GOSP), 158
G-Day (Ground Attack Day), 157, 160
Gephardt, Bridgepark Officer-in-Charge Lieutenant (Junior Grade), 198–199
Gerken, Lieutenant, 255
Germany and Oil-for-Food scandal, 83
Gfrerer, James P., 181
Ginther, Ronald A., 311, v
Global War on Terrorism (GWOT), 1, 21, 23, 318
G-4 Logistics section, 136–138
Goff, Nathan, Jr., 331
Goldwater-Nichols Defense Reorganization Act, 12
Gonsalves, James D., 154, xi
Gorilla Snot, 25
governates, 244, 264

Gray, Alfred M., 12–13, 109
Great Lakes Naval Training Station, 332
Great Lakes Public Works Department, 332–333
Grey, Gary, 67
Gross, Jimmy, 182
Ground Penetrating Radar (GPR) Team, 283
Gulfport Construction Battalion Center, 76

H

Habes, Sarah, 253, 272
Hackworth, David H., 313–314
Hagee, Michael W., 16–17, 19, 31–32, 34, 39
"Hail Mary" ground attack plan, 361–362
Hailston, Earl B., 31, 33, 85
   Central Command's (CENTCOM) plan for Iraq, 1–2
   go early, go ugly strategy, 3, 121
   meeting Kubic in Bahrain, 10
   request for forces, 47–48
Hair, Charles "Chuck," 59
Halloway, Mess Specialist Seaman (MSSN), 232
hallowed ground, 308
Hammurabi, 238
Hammurabi Division, 226
Handley, Mark, 303, 313
Hanging Gardens, 238
Hansen, Ray A., 356
Harbison, James, 14
Harris, Frederic, 332
Hawaiian Area Construction Brigade Command, 342, 345
Hazley, Daniel, 294
heavy construction equipment, 59
Heavy Equipment Transporters (HETs), 102
Heine, Bob, 162
Helvenston, Scott, 300
Hendricks, Kent, 93
Henigan, Larry F. X., xi
High-Mobility Multipurpose Wheeled Vehicle (HMMWV or Humvee), 19, 256–257, 305
Highway 1
   asphalt plant, 275–276
   best route for movement, 274
   bridge and SERT 74, 192
   at the Euphrates, 182–183
   I MEF's responsibility, 149

imperative to improve, 193–195
maintenance, 274
repair of, 193
War on Dust, 274–276
Highway 7
alternate route, 193–195
at the Euphrates, 182–183
potential ambush areas, 203
reducing significance, 149
Higson, Bill, 310, 311
Hill, Michael, 108, 113, 163
Hit (Iraq), 308–309
Hoeppner, Douglas, 159
homecoming
reserve demobilization, 289–290
Seabees, 292–295
stories, 293–295
Hong, Kirby, 67
Honkomp, Christopher J., 108, 212, 214–215, 292
Horn, Dusty, 113
hospitals, 271–273
Republic of [South] Korea (ROK) Engineers, 284–285
Houser, Vicki, 136, 137
Howard, Michael C., 14, 63, 142, 145, 165, 242, xi
Hueneme-based Naval Support Force-Antarctica (NSFA), 354
Huie, William Bradford, 292, 349
Hussaybah Base, 308
Hussein, Qusay, 298
Hussein, Saddam, 2, 230, 358, ix
atrocities against people, 283–284
Babylon Palace, 233, 236–237
capture of, 299
chemical weapons and biological weapons, 280–282
devastation in Middle East, 362
flight, 297
gassing Kurds and Iranian soldiers, 2
Global War on Terrorism, 43–44
hanging, 299
invasion in Kuwait, 359
last chance to disarm, 53
mustard and nerve agents, 358
nuclear, biological, and chemical (NBC) weapons, 115
Oil-for-Food Program, 3
paying suicide bombers' families, 30
private deals with key U.N. leaders, 29
regime falls, 3, 226–227
SCUD missiles, 358
sneaking out of Baghdad, 226
three-pronged strategy, 125
toppling, 120
U.N. resolutions, 29
weapons inspectors, 53, 81
Weapons of Mass Destruction (WMDs), 361
Hussein, Uday, 275, 298

I

Iafrate, Frank J., 111, 337, 339, 340
I Marine Expeditionary Force Engineer Group (MEG), 122
command element, 134–135
CONOPs, 130–131
constructing connector route, 202
"fog of war" situation, 195–196
matching skills to jobs, 107–109
model for managing, 14
officially stood down, 318
operational control of Seabees to, 79
potential river crossing wet gaps, 62–63
replacing assault bridges, 64
I Marine Expeditionary Force (MEF)
An Numaniyah, 216–217
Area of Operations (AOs), 169
Area of Responsibility, 124
Armored Vehicle Launched Bridges (AVLBs), 35
assault bridges, 35
Civil Military Operations (CMO), 249
Concept of Operations, 123–124
hazardous mission, 122
Marine Corps staff, 38
not formally recognized MEG, 58
operational battle space, 124–125
operational boundary, 149–150
organization for battle, 122–123
planning effort, 33
post-hostility operations, 124
preparations for redeployment, 124
Seabees and, 32, 106
stabilization mode, 231
street battles, 126
supporting Army's flanking attack, 123
supporting Army's V Corps' attack, 124

INDEX

sustaining 1st Marine Division, 202
tactical and rear command posts, 58
I Marine Expeditionary Force (MEF) Engineer, 20
I Marine Expeditionary Force (MEF) Provisional Security Battalion, 316–317
I MEF Exercise (MEFEX), 71
Improvised Explosive Devices (IEDs), 257, 298
insurgents, 305
Internal Look war game, 14, 54
Iran, 3, 358
Iranian Revolutionary Guards, 317
Iraq, 82
    Al Nida Division, 249
    Al Qaeda, 83
    Al Qaeda safe haven, 30
    Ba'ath Party, 184
    blowing bridges and culverts, 193–194
    blue on blue (friendly fire) casualties, 184
    car bombings, 299
    chemicals and, 30
    chemical weapons, 2, 223
    civil war, 317
    cultural bridges, 254
    de-Ba'athification policy, 266–267
    decentralized democracy, 273
    demobilizing troops, 289
    Desert Storm, 2
    destroying oil fields, 158
    domestic and international political tensions, 54
    dust problems, 250
    fate of missing, 283
    feigning surrender, 184
    fierce fighting by, 200
    fighting Iran, 358
    Gas and Oil Platforms (GOPLATS), 151
    governates, 244
    handling terrorist problem, 300
    heavier casualties on, 200
    hiding in hospitals, schools, and apartments, 184
    Kuwaiti Bedouins, 184
    Marine snipers, 185
    material breach of U.N. resolutions, 53
    materials and equipment, 81–82
    minimizing U.S. footprint in, 300
    mole piers, 68
    moving against, 31
    not wearing uniforms, 184
    Palestinian *intifadah,* 30
    Phase IV Civil Military Operations, 40
    planning for invasion, 33–34
    poor marksmen, 204
    producing MC-70, 275
    reconstruction, 265–267, 325–326
    regrouping and organizing counterattack, 200
    Republican Guard units, 3
    roadblocks, 184
    road signs, 184
    Rocket Propelled Grenade Launcher (RPG), 185
    Saddam Fedayeen, 184–185
    Seabees returning, 303–308
    Shi'ite Kurds, 358
    Special Operations Forces, 122
    state sponsor of terrorism, 29–30
    surge of U.S. troops, 317
    tactical pause, 199
    terrorist targets, 299
    36th Commando Battalion, 316
    United Nations (U.N.) sanctions and weapons inspections, 2
    U.S. casualties, 317
    U.S. strategy in, 317
    violence, 317
    WMD capability, 31, 81
Iraqi Ababil 100s, 100
Iraqi armor unit, 158
Iraqi attack, 120–122
Iraqi Construction Apprentice Program (ICAP), 304
Iraqi counterstrike, 153–157
Iraqi flag, 272
Iraqi forces, 323
Iraqi Governing Council, 299
Iraqi Intelligence Services, 30
Iraqi military, 125–127
Iraqi National Assembly, 317
Islam and Wahhabism, 20–21
Islamic fundamentalism, 358
Islamic terrorists, 3
Israel Defense Force (IDF) D-9R Armored Bulldozers, 145, 185
Iwo Jima, 346, 348

J

Jacobs, Randall, 341
Jaenke, Jamie S., v
Jalibah as MEG objective 53, 194
James, Evans, 210
Jenkins, Robert B., 311, v
Jenks, Arlen S., 356
Jensen, Wayne, 51
Jiffy Clean truck concept, 117
Jiffy Teams, 117
Johnson, Andrew, 330
Johnson, Bill, 19
Johnson, Lyndon B., 354, 355
Johnson, Michael, 15, 22, 359–360, 362
Johnson, Ron, 184
Joint Forced Command (JFCOM), 23
Joint Task Force 58, 24
joint warfare, 11–12
Jolin, Daniel, 137
Jones, Dennis, 144
jump Command Post, 232

K

Kayashi, Keith, 67
Kedge Hammer training exercise, 35–38
Kellerman, Troy, 109, 112, 164, 293
Kelley, John F., 230
Kellogg, Brown and Root (KBR), 268
Kelso, Frank B., 12
Kennedy, Craig, 188, 192
Kennedy, Patrick, 327
Khan, Charlie, 21–22
Khomeini, Ayatollah Ruhollah, 358
Kimmitt, Mark, 301
King, Ernest J., 336
Kissinger, Henry, 266–267
Knott, Eric L., v
Knox, Frank, 340
Knox, Navy Secretary, 341
Kole, Pete, 35, 39–40, 79, 102–103, 129, 206
Komppa, Charles V., v
Korean Engineer Battalion, 138. 216
Korean War, 13, 352
Korea Operations Plan (OPLANs), 14
Korea's 1100th Engineer Battalion (ROK), 130
Korthaus, Bradley S., 210
Krats, Lance Corporal, 268

Kubic, Andy, 6
Kubic, Bill, 5
Kubic, Charles Brian (C.B.), 6, 26
Kubic, Charles R. "Chuck," 25, 85, 165, 180, 245, 250, 252, xi
   Air Force Reserve Officer Training Corps (ROTC) cadet, 5
   bridge Operational Planning Team (OPT), 66
   "Budweiser," 23
   bunker built for, 117–118
   Chief of Naval Operations (CNO) Scholar, 7
   children, 6
   0930C MEG "Battle Brief" meeting, 153
   command and control of I MEF Engineer Group (I MEG), 23
   command and control of new Seabee Division, 23
   command bunker at Camp Commando, 182
   communications with Seabees, 22
   convoy and demonstration, 298
   Director of the Strategic Programs Office, 8
   education, 4–7, 9
   entry into U.S. Navy, 5
   Euphrates River, 175
   Fragmentary Order, 190
   improving tempo of operations, 17–20
   MEG Operations Battle Brief, 182
   MEG Situation Report (Sitrep), 182
   MEG task forces, 307
   MEG War Council, 88
   mole pier approach, 69
   Naval Facilities Engineering Command (NAVFAC), 8
   Naval Mobile Construction Battalion (NMCB) 4, 7
   Navy's construction battalion operations, 1
   operations summaries, 182
   overturning Operational Planning Team's recommendations, 40–41
   planning Iraqi invasion, 33–34
   planning Seabee draw down in Iraq, 238
   planning trips into Iraq, 303
   President of ECC International, 318
   providing bridging funds, 66
   raising MEG up, 79–80

Ramadi, 309–310
Rear Admiral (Lower Half), 10
Rear Admiral (Upper Half), 42
reflections, 319–328
resolidifying MEG concept, 41–42
retirement, 318
scrambling to command bunker, 155–156
Seabees base and headquarters camp, 45–46
2nd Naval Construction Regiment (NCR), 10
Senior Policy Analyst for President Reagan's Domestic Policy Council, 8
September 11th terrorist attacks, 22
specialized gas mask, 118
1st Naval Construction Division, 61, 79, 118
successfully completing MEG's mission, 127–128
tending to wounded, 311
3-tier assessment of requirements, 262–265
3rd Naval Construction Brigade (NCB), 1, 10, 17
"Two Way Flexure of Steel Deck Reinforced Slabs" thesis, 7
victory message to NMCB 74, 245
"Wagon Master," 23
water treatment plant, 213
wet gap crossing Courses of Action, 68
White House Fellow, 8
White House Office of Policy Development, 8
White House Senior Staff Member, 9
Kubic, Charlie, 6
Kubic, Katie, 6
Kubic, Louis, 5
Kubic, Roberta Mologne, 5
Kurdistan Workers' Party (PKK), 29
Kuwait
  Ali Al Salem Air Base, 45, 47
  CBMU 303 going to, 234–235
  closing open pit quarries, 50
  C-130 parking apron, 49
  demobilizing troops, 289
  early Seabee projects, 49–53
  funding for projects in, 50
  government impeding Seabees' work, 50
  invaded by Iraq, 359
  Kubic visiting, 45
  Maritime Pre-positioning Ship Squadrons, 59
  materials shortage, 51
  MEG Advance Party, 303
  munitions storage area (MSA), 49
  Rudich arrival in, 61
  Seabee camp and base, 45–46
  Seabees sneaking into, 47–49
  as staging base, 44
  weather and construction schedule, 51
Kuwaiti Air Force, 45
Kuwaiti Bedouins, 184
Kuwaiti prisoners of war, 283–284
Kuwait/Iraq Theater of Operations, 48
Kuwaitis
  Al Jaber Air Base, 45–47
  breach of obstacles erected by, 141
  compliance without enthusiasm, 44
  impounding HESCO (Hercules Engineering Solutions Consortium) blast protection barriers, 50
  opened berms for I MEF, 159
  permanent air basing facilities, 45
Kuwaiti Theater of Operations (KTO), 15, 84
Kyriss, Frederick, 107, 109

L

Lacey, Olin, 215
Latrobe, Benjamin Henry, 329
Lavallee, Phil, 162, 282, 283
Leatherneck's online forum, 314–315
Lehnert, Mike, 85, 245
Lend-Lease agreement, 334
Lengkeek, Jeff, 26, 118, 155–156
Lewis, Sam M., 349
Libonate, Mark, 196, 290
logistics
  planning and organization, 136–138
  support, 119
Logistics Support Area Chesty, 218–219
Logistics Support Area Daly, 220
Long, Brandon, 281
Lopez, Matt, 307
Lucky Sentinel exercise, 14
Lussier, John "Skip," 239

M

Maabot oil platform, 281
Mabey & Johnson Bridge Qualified (MJBQ'd), 115
Mabey & Johnson Bridges (MJB), 70–71, 94, 175, 248, 251, ix
   best product choice for Iraq, 74
   building new, 229
   components for floating bridges, 77
   equipment rather than material, 76
   making "river fit bridge," 94
   NMCB 4, 247
   NMCB 133, 278
   ordering, 77
Mabey & Johnson Company, 68, 74, 77
Mabey & Johnson over-bridge, 180, 228–229
Mabey & Johnson training, 115
MacArthur, Douglas, 345, 350, 352
machine guns, 185
Mac Moles, 73–75
Madisonville, 330
MAGTF Staff Training Program (MSTP) mentor, 34
Mahan, Alfred Thayer, 331
Mahdi Army, 303
Main Supply Route (MSR) Dallas, 181
Main Supply Route (MSR) Tampa, 181, 186–187
major construction projects, 325
maneuver battlespace, 19
maneuver warfare, 12–13, 16
Manipon, Manuel, x
marching song, 349
Marine Air/Ground Task Force (MAGTF), 359–360
Marine AV-8B Harrier attack jets, 49
Marine Combat Engineer Battalion, 13
Marine Corps
   criticized MEG concept, 15
   From the Sea strategy, 12
Marine Corps Gazette, 63
Marine Corps Systems Command, 76–77
Marine Expeditionary Force Engineer Group (MEG), 14
   battle space, 124–125
   Class IV construction material and bridge components, 197–198
   command element, 16–17
   compromise command system, 20
   Concept of Operations (CONOPS), 15, 35
   conceptual changes, 14
   delaying closure of Army units in, 102
   doctrine, ix
   Easter Sunday (2003), 232
   event-driven mission, 133
   Fedayeen fighters, 196
   feeding and beding down engineer units, 103–106
   first battle-related casualties, 186–187
   first enemy contact, 183
   formalizing concept, 16–17
   forward elements, 130–131
   G-4 Logistics section, 136–138
   identifying objectives, 131
   Karbala, An Najaf, Al Hillah, Ad Diwaniyah and As Samawah, 233
   logistics planning and organization, 136–138
   Mabey & Johnson bridges, 76, 94
   Mabey & Johnson training, 115
   maneuver plan, 109–110
   Marine resistance to, 38–42
   matching skills, personnel, and equipment, 37
   maximizing flexibility, 37
   media embeds, 292
   mission, 127–128
   need for, 32–35
   not formally existing, 79
   Nuclear/Biological/Chemical plan, 117
   on-the-job accidents, 286–287
   operational part of MEF for deliberate OPLANs, 20
   Operations Battle Brief, 182
   opposition to, 34
   organization and operational hurdles, xi
   original Order of Battle, 92
   planners, 63
   planning, 35–37
   positioning assets, 261
   primary mission, 71
   projected casualties, 152
   purchasing supplies from local vendors, 252
   questioning costs, 20
   satellite communication (SATCOM) capabilities, 224
   shifting stance, 136

Situation Report (Sitrep), 182
splitting assets among task forces, 37
standing up, 78–80
tactical communications, 224–225
task forces, 42
task forces in Iraq, 217–219
22nd Naval Construction Regiment, 36
265th Army Engineer Group, 35
Marine Expeditionary Force Engineer Group (MEG) Advance Party, 303
Marine Expeditionary Force Engineer Group (MEG) Command Bunker, 100, 154
Marine Expeditionary Force Engineer Group (MEG) Command Element, 103, 156–157, 291–292
Marine Expeditionary Force Engineer Group (MEG) Command Operations Center (COC), 71, 181–182
Marine Expeditionary Force Engineer Group (MEG) staff, 61, 154–155, 156, 160
Marine Expeditionary Force Engineer Group (MEG) Validation Conference, 16–17
Marine Expeditionary Force (MEF), 154
    amphibious assault, 16
    backload, 290
    competition for equipment, 102
    downsizing, 288
    facilities services contracts, 104
    Fusion Board, 264–265
    resource distribution, 15
    roles and responsibilities, 15
    southern governates, 244
    tent-leasing strategy, 104
Marine Expeditionary Force (MEF) Engineer, 34–35, 62, 74
Marine Expeditionary Force (MEF) G-3 staff, 189
Marine Forces-Pacific (MARFORPAC), 1
Marine Logistics Command (MLC), 137, 288
Marine Pioneer (shore party) Battalion, 13–14
Marines
    attacking inland, 122
    bypassing enemy's defenses, 13
    combat engineers, 336
    command ownership, 38
    contingency construction, 27
    difficulties supporting, 36
    engineers badly positioned, 16
    maneuvering with other services, 13
    maneuver warfare, 12–13, 16
    9th Engineer Support Battalion, 27
    operations for revised OPLAN 1003, 31–32
    refining tactical doctrine, 12
    resistance to MEG, 38–42
    2nd Tank Battalion, 205
    snipers and Iraqis, 185
    temporal advantage, 13
    traditional spatial maneuver, 12
Maritime Prepositioning Force (MPF), 18, 57, 84, 290
Maritime Pre-positioning Ship Squadron (MPSRON), 18, 59
Maritime Propositioned Force (Enhanced) - MPF (E), 58
Marsh, Clyde W., 84
mass graves, 280–284
M1A1 Tanks, 185
Material Liaison Office (MLO), 137
Mattis, James N., 24–25, 38-39, 85, 123, 142, 185, 205, 245, 266, 301, 316
    chaos over reconstruction, 266
    1st Marine Division, 38
    1st Marine Expeditionary Force, 38
    Joint Task Force 58 mission, 38
    Marine Corps Planning System, 39
Mattox, Doug, 165
Maurer, Clifford M., 48, 66–69, 71, 108, 232
Mazur, Alec, v
McAlister, Dave, 22, 71, 73–74, 93, 118, 165
McCarty, Robert, 137, 268, 269
McGibbon, Steelworker 2nd Class, 191, 203
McHugh, Scott R., 311, v
McKay, George A., 333, 335
McKerall, William C., 36, 78–79, 163, 238–239, 252
McKiernan, David D., 103, 148–150, 261
McKinley, William, 331
McMaster, Herbert R., 317
McNelis, Sean, 48
MC-70 road oil, 274–275
media interest in Seabees, 292–293
Medium Girder Bridges (MGBs), 63
Medium Tactical Vehicle Replacement (MTVR), 186
MEF Command Element Exercises (MEFEX's), 14, 33, 38

415

MEF Headquarters Group (MHG), 154
Mellow, James, 109
Meyer, J. Stryker, 295
Miami Herald, 313
MI-6 intelligence service, 31
Mike (Mobility) task force, 42
military
    construction supporting invasion of Iraq, 3
    joint characteristics, 12
Military.com, 313
Military Operational Protective Posture (MOPP) suits, 116
Military Operations in Urban Terrain (MOUT), 145, 185
Mina el-Bakr, 281
Mobile Recovery Teams, 354
Modular Table of Allowance, 58, 60
mole area, backfilling, 74
Mole-Bridge COA, 70–71
mole piers, 66, 69
Moran, James P., 71, 93, 306
Moreell, Benjamin C., 55, 336–337, 339–341, 350
Moreno, Fabricio, v
mortars, 185
Morton, Douglas G., 25, 161, 279
Mother of All Sand Storms (MOASS), 163–164, 171, 194
MOVAC vibratory hammer, 72–73
Mujahedin-e-Khalq (MEK), 29
Mundy, Carl E., Jr., 12
Muqtada al-Sadr, 303
Muslim-on-Muslim attack, 299

N

National Command Authority (NCA), 101
National Security Strategy of the United States of America, 44
Natonski, Richard E., 85, 145, 185, 200–201, 205–206, 243, 245
Naval Construction Battalion (NCB) 6, 342
Naval Construction Battalion (NCB) 14, 308
Naval Construction Battalion (NCB) 25, 346
Naval Construction Battalion (NCB) 31, 346, 348
Naval Construction Battalion (NCB) 48, 346
Naval Construction Battalion (NCB) 61, 346
Naval Construction Battalion (NCB) 62, 346, 348
Naval Construction Battalion (NCB) 69, 348–349
Naval Construction Battalion (NCB) 70, 346, 348
Naval Construction Battalion (NCB) 102, 346
Naval Construction Battalion (NCB) 133, 346, 348
naval construction battalions (NCBs), 336–337, 342, 351
Naval Construction Force (NCF), 14, 57
Naval Construction Force (NCF) Policy, 16
Naval Construction Force Support of MAGTF Operations, 14–15
Naval Construction Force Support Unit (NCFSU) 2
    improving road surface, 178
    MPSRON debarkation, 78
Naval Facilities Engineering Command (NAVFAC), 57, 357
    Reserve Officer in Charge of Construction (OICC) Det, 316
Naval Facilities Engineering Command (NAVFAC) engineers, 19
Naval Facility Engineering Command's Atlantic Division (LANTDIV), 306
Naval Mobile Construction Battalion (NMCB), 18–19, 352, x
Naval Mobile Construction Battalion (NMCB) 1, 27–28, 289–290
Naval Mobile Construction Battalion (NMCB) 3, 9, 17
Naval Mobile Construction Battalion (NMCB) 4, 359
    Air Detachment and Walter Well Team, 27
    Alternate Supply Route Hueneme, 202–203
    assault and bridging plan, 146
    Diyala River bridge, 220
    Highway 1, 201
    holding turf while building bridges, 229–230
    Kuwait, 84
    Mabey & Johnson bridges, 175, 179, 180, 228–229, 247
    NMCB 1, 27–28
    Salman Pak, 223
    SPCM (Sand Pile Culvert Module) and Mabey & Johnson bridging parts, 202

INDEX

Task Force Charlie, 290–291
Task Force Mike, 146
Naval Mobile Construction Battalion (NMCB) 5, 146, 359
  Ahmed Al Jaber, 53
  Air Detachments (Dets), 48
  Ali Al Salem, 55
  Camp Moreell, 56
  Kuwait, 84
  Munitions Storage Area, 53
  Munitions Supply Point, 88
  relieving, 138–139
  returning home, 146–147
Naval Mobile Construction Battalion (NMCB) 6, 356
Naval Mobile Construction Battalion (NMCB) 7, 212, 359
  Alternate Supply Route Dallas, 207
  Civil Engineering Support Equipment (CESE), 130
  contracting with local builders, 215
  hospitals, schools, and water plants, 213
  Jiffy Decon team, 220
  Kuwait, 84
  Logistics Support Area Viper, 218
  Mabey & Johnson bridges, 220
  Main Supply Route maintenance, 218
Naval Mobile Construction Battalion (NMCB) 9, 355–356
Naval Mobile Construction Battalion (NMCB) 11, 357
Naval Mobile Construction Battalion (NMCB) 14, 308–310, 314–316
Naval Mobile Construction Battalion (NMCB) 15, 84
  Camp Babylon, 237
Naval Mobile Construction Battalion (NMCB) 21, 84, 208–209
Naval Mobile Construction Battalion (NMCB) 23, 260, 315
Naval Mobile Construction Battalion (NMCB) 25, 84
Naval Mobile Construction Battalion (NMCB) 40, 48, 260, 359
Naval Mobile Construction Battalion (NMCB) 53, 357
Naval Mobile Construction Battalion (NMCB) 74, 36, 86, 359
  Ahmed Al Jaber aircraft apron, 53
  HESCO barriers, 259
  Kuwait, 84
  leaving equipment behind, 15
  Logistics Supply Area Chesty, 218
  Mabey & Johnson bridges, 173, 175, 201, 219
  Main Supply Route Tampa, 218
  MPSRON debarkation, 78
  replacing assault floating bridge, 217
  returning home, 290
  working conditions, 52
Naval Mobile Construction Battalion (NMCB) 128, 356
Naval Mobile Construction Battalion (NMCB) 133, 24, 241, 250, 287
  Bridge Park Davisville, 206
  camp improvement projects, 25
  Fedayeen's movement, 200–201
  helicopter insertion of troops, 24
  improving road surface, 178, 206
  Mabey & Johnson bridges, 278
  MEG Command Bunker, 154
  moving quickly and deeply, 25–26
  MPSRON debarkation, 78
  Task Force Charlie, 78
  working on north taxiway, 241
Naval Mobile Construction Battalion (NMCB) 21 (Reserve), 294
Naval Mobile Construction Battalion (NMCB) 24 (Reserve), 359
Naval Operating Base Leyte-Samar, 345
naval rearmament program, 334
Naval Reserve Civil Engineer Corps (CEC), 332
Naval Reserve Force, 332
Navy
  civil engineers and builders, 329
  civil engineers civilians, 330
  Iwo Jima, 347
  joint warfare, 11–12
  professional civil engineers, 330
  Public Works Department, 332
  From the Sea strategy, 12
Navy Appropriation Act, 332
Navy Civil Engineer Operations for Component Commanders, 16
Navy Construction Battalions, 334
Navy Explosive Ordinance Disposal (EOD) Team, 208
Navy Explosive Ordnance Disposal (EOD) Detachment, 207

417

Navy frogmen, 342
Navy SEALS, 158, 342
Neal, Leonard, 137
Nebuchadnezzar Division, 226
New Diyala Bridge (Bridge #3), 227–228
Night of 1,000 Iraqis, 173, 195–197
night vision goggles (NVGs), 113–114
Nimitz, Chester W., 345, 350
19th Marines, 13
9th Engineer Support Battalion (ESB), 27
NORAD, 154
North Atlantic Treaty Organization (NATO), 11
nuclear, biological, and/or radiological attack threat, 115–119
Nuclear/Biological/Chemical (NBC), 117–118
Nukahiva Island, 330

O

O'Bannon, Presley, 122, 230
Objective Rhino, 24
Odierno, Raymond T., 122
Office of Reconstruction and Humanitarian Assistance (ORHA), 230, 262, 265–267
Office of the Coalition Provisional Authority (CPA), 266–267
oil wells, 158
Old Diyala Bridge, 229
Oliver Taylor, 177
Olsen, Rick, 67, 68
O&M funding, 213
1092nd Combat Engineer Battalion, 102
   civilian teams traveling in Persian Gulf, 281
   delay in receiving equipment, 130
   extending tour of duty, 291
   Rumaylah oilfield security, 280–281
1092nd Engineer Battalion (Corps Wheeled), 220
1092nd Engineer Battalion of the West Virginia National Guard, 102, 220
101st Airborne Division, 54, 300
130th Corps Wheeled Battalion, 102
1003 Victor (1003V), 63
on-the-job accidents, 286–287
Operational Planning Team (OPT), 39–40, 62, 69
Operational Risk Management (ORM), 286

Operation ATLAS RAIL, 64
Operation CRIPPLED CHUCK, 353
Operation CROSSROADS, 351
Operation DEEP FREEZE, 354
Operation DESERT STORM, 159
Operation DOWNFALL, 345
Operation ENDURING FREEDOM (OEF), 23, 27–28, 48
Operation HIGH JUMP, 351
Operation ICEBERG, 345
Operation IRAQI FREEDOM (OIF)
   Civil Military Operations, 320–321
   enemy threat, 185
   lessons learned, 322–323
   Operations Plan (OPLAN), 319–320
   phases, 165
   Seabee involvement in, 4
Operation IRAQI FREEDOM (OIF) I, xi
   regimental-sized, task-oriented formation, ix
   Seabees, 176, ix
   Stabilization Phase, 169
   winding down, 297
Operation IRAQI FREEDOM (OIF) II, 256, 257, 295, 303, 305
Operation OLYMPIC, 345
Operation PHANTOM FURY, 316
Operations Plan (OPLAN) 1003, 31–33, 35, 120
Operations Plan (OPLAN) 5027, 32–33
Operations Plan (OPLAN) 1003V, 2, 121–122, 124–125, 127–128
Operation SWIFT FREEDOM, 24
Operation VIGILANT RESOLVE, 259, 301, 302
OPNAV INSTRUCTION 5450.46K, 16
Originator Controlled (ORCON) information, 32–33
Ostrich, Jim, x
Overaker, Patrick, 252, 268

P

Pacific Division (PACDIV), 22
Pacific Fleet (PACFLT), 1
Pacific Fleet Command (COMPACFLT), 59
Pacific Fleet Commander, 20
Pacific Fleet Seabees, 42
Palestine Islamic Jihad, 30
Palestine Liberation Front (PLF), 29

INDEX

Palestinian *intifadah*, 30
Patriot Missiles, 100
Patterns of Global Terrorism 2001, 29
Patton, George S., 348
Peary, Robert E., 342
Perone, Master Chief, 108
Perry, John R., 339, 345
Pershing, John J., 334
Petraeus, David, 317
PHIBCBs 1 and 2, 84
Philippines and Abu Sayyaf terrorist group, 27–28
Phillips, Dave, 129
Phillips, Kyra, 292
pipe culvert Course of Action (COA), 65, 69, 71
pipe culverts, 65–67, 73
planning for beds and butts, 106
Plunkett, Charles P., 334
Plush, Greg, 184
Poillac aviation station, 334
pontoon bridges, 279
Pontoon Operating Battalions of World War II, 352
pontoon or medium girder assault bridges, 35
Popular Front for the Liberation of Palestine-General Command, 30
Porter, David, 329–330
Port Hueneme, 351, 354
Powell, Colin, 30, 53, 82–83, 143, 144
power plants, 270–271
Pre-N-Day force, 54
Prepositioned War Reserve Material System (PWRMS) warehouses, 57
Prien, John D., 308, 310–311, 315–316
Proceedings, 334
projected casualties, 152
projects
    deliberate basis, 263–265
    developmental, 263
    expeditionary basis, 262–265
    hospitals, 271–273
    identification and selection, 267–270
    money for, 263–264
    Paying Agents, 264
    power plants, 270–271
    purchasing construction materials, 269
    reviewing, 264
    Rumaylah oilfield security, 280–281

Sarabadi Bridge, 276–277
schools, 271–273
seized cash, 268, 269–270
shopping for construction materials, 273–274
Tigris River, 277–280
water works, 270–271
WMDs and mass graves, 280–284
psychological operations (PSYOPS) vehicles, 185
Public Works, 333
Pulaski, Corporal, 268
Puller, Lewis Burwell "Chesty," 218

Q

Qatar, 234
Quinn, Daniel, 294

R

Ramadi, 307, 309
Rambo, Michael, 309
Ramey, Peter, 39, 41, 142, 145
Rashid Military Academy, 231
"reach-back" engineering support, 19
Reception, Staging, Onward Movement, and Integration (RSO&I), 14
reception, staging, onward movement, and integration (RSO&I) process, 129–130
reconnaissance, 19
reconstruction, 262, 265–270
redeploy, constitute, surge plan, 239
redeployment, 351–357
Reed, "Doc," 156, 298
Reed, Meg, 292
"Regime Death Squads," 184
Regimental Combat Team (RCT) 1, 216, 225
Regimental Combat Team (RCT) 2, 200
Regimental Combat Team (RCT) 5, 217
    Ad Diwaniyah, 205
    attacks, 216
    Line of Departure, 158
    Relief in Place, 262
    Rumaylah Oil Fields, 158
Regimental Combat Team (RCT) 7, 205, 216, 217, 225
Regimental Combat Teams (RCT), 146, 201
Regular Army, 125
Rehearsal of Concept (ROC) drills, 142
Reithmiller, Matt, 311

419

Relief in Place (RIP), 138–139, 262
Republican Guards, 125–125
  Al Nida Division, 217
  lacking ability to engage in sustained, high intensity combat, 125
  morale and discipline, 125
  most competent, 125
  units, 3
Republic of [South] Korea (ROK) Engineers, 284–285
reserve demobilization, 289–290
Reserve Marines, 16–17
Reserve Officer Candidate Program, 6
reserves
  demobilizing, 239
  mobilization, 119
  resources, 107–109
Retrograde, Regeneration, Reconstitution, and Redeployment (R4), 288–289
Reverse Osmosis Water Purification Unit (ROWPU), 209
Reynolds, Nicholas E., 121, x
Rhino Ferries, 347
Rhino Snot, 25, 276
Ribbon Bridges, 63
rivers, making fit bridges, 65–70
roads
  Baghdad, 63
  Highway 1 to Saddam Canal, 202
  keeping open, 324
Robbins, Chief Steelworker, 207
Roberson, Gunnery Sergeant, 194
Roberts, Ray, 51
Romero, Command Master Chief, 180
Roosevelt, Franklin D., 334
Rossi, Mark V., xi
Rough Terrain Container Handlers (RTCHs), 102
Route 1, 207
Rovinski, Gary T., v
Royal Marines' 3rd Commando Brigade, 140
Royal Navy, 330
Rudich, William L., 14, 33, 36, 48, 160, 173, 180, 225, 362, x
  arrival in Kuwait, 61
  Bronze Star, 290
  command post, 224
  Davisville Bridge Park, 201
  disastrous session for MEG, 39
  matching skills to specific jobs, 108
  MEG's Concept of Operations, 40
  multiple jobs of, 61–62
  Reserve Naval Construction Support Force Unit (NCFSU) 2, 58
  retirement, 290
  returning home, 290
  Task Force Charlie, 78
  Task Force Mike, 78–79
Rumaylah Oil Fields, 158, 280–281
Rumsfeld, Donald H., 21, 26, 31, 54, 101, 120, 261, 266, 317
Russia and Oil-for-Food scandal, 83
Russ Seignious, 71

S

Sabatini, Patrick, 294
Saddam Canal, 182–183, 202–203, 205
Saddam Fedayeen, 126, 184–185, 199–200
Salaman Pak Air Base, 220
Samarra, 230
Sanchez, Rick, 266–267
Sand Pile Culvert Modules (SPCMs), 73–75, 95
Sanger, William P.S., 330
Santiago, Rudolpho, 107, 293–294
Sarabadi Bridge, 251, 276–277
Saudis and fueling political troubles, 44
Schneider, Adam, 293
schools
  renovation, 271–273
  Republic of [South] Korea (ROK) Engineers, 284–285
Schwarzkopf, Norman H. and "Hail Mary" ground attack plan, 361–362
SCIF (Sensitive Compartmented Information Facility), 67
SCUD missiles, 358
Seabee battalions, 14–15
Seabee Bridge, 23
Seabee BUG, 23, 118
Seabee Bunker, 22–23
Seabee Camp 93, 105
Seabee Combat Handbook, 111
Seabee Combat Warfare Specialist (SCW) program, 111–112
Seabee Engineer Reconnaissance Team (SERT) 4
  Bridge Reconnaissance mission, 179
  under fire, 203–204

INDEX

Jump Command Post, 224
Qalat Sikar airfield, 203
reconnoitering damaged bridges, 227
reestablishing contact with, 225
Relief-in-Place, 203, 204
tactical communications, 224–225
Seabee Engineer Reconnaissance Team (SERT) 5
  Ambush Alley, 190, 203
  An Nasiriyah, 188
  Army and Marine maneuver forces, 187
  Camp Commando, 218
  combat action, 189–190
  command and control, 150
  Crossing Area Engineers, 188
  firefight locations, 168
  first direct combat action, 190
  under heavy attack, 191
  Qalat Sikar, 203
  reconnoitering bridges, 191
  Regimental Combat Team 1 and, 187
  returning home, 203
  route and bridge reconnaissance, 203
  Task Force Mike's operational control, 188
  3rd Infantry Division and, 188
Seabee Engineer Reconnaissance Team (SERT) 7, 203
Seabee Engineer Reconnaissance Team (SERT) 74
  An Nasiriyah, 188, 195
  behind Army and Marine forces, 187
  bridge over Saddam Canal, 205, 218, 219
  command and control, 150
  communications with, 192
  connector route, 192
  Crossing Area Engineers, 188
  Highway 1, 193
  Highway 1 bridge, 192
  mineral products staging area, 195
  on move, 170
  Task Force Mike's operational control, 188
  Task Force Tarawa and, 187
  3rd Infantry Division, 146, 188
Seabee Engineer Reconnaissance Team (SERT) 133
  Alternate Supply Route Dallas, 187
  Enemy Prisoner of War holding area, 163
  Logistics Support Area Chesty, 218

Task Force Charlie and, 187
Task Force Mike and, 204
Task Force Tarawa and, 146
Seabee Engineer Reconnaissance Teams (SERTs), 17, 18–20, 128, 324
  Camp 93, 92
  command and control, 160, 190
  drawing enemy fire, 189
  effectiveness example, 205
  expertise and engineering assessments, 205
  under fire, 187–193
  heavy communications capability, 204–205
  humanitarian service projects, 205
  on the move, 203–205
  operational control, 189
  providing valuable information, 204
  Recon element, 19
  regimental command elements, 19
  Security element, 19
  tactics, techniques, and procedures, 19
  training curriculum, 187–188
  vulnerability, 187
Seabee gunners, 256
Seabee Jedi, 71–73, 93
Seabee Light Regiment, 18
Seabee/Marine expeditionary engineering operations, ix
Seabee Materials Liaison Officer (MLO), 76
Seabee Operations in the MAGTF, 16
Seabees, 25
  advance bases, 341
  advanced bases, 346
  Air Detachment (Air Det), 17
  Al Jaber Air Port, 46–47
  Allied Expeditionary Force, 348
  Al Qaeda, 24
  Amphibious Construction Battalion (PHIBCB), 352
  Anbar province, 303
  Babylon Palace, 237–238
  battalion centric, 17
  berm-reduction operations, 93
  Bikini Atoll, 351
  Bush's ultimatum, 144
  Camp Rhino, 24–25
  celebrating birthday, 143
  chain of command, 340
  Civic Action, 11, 355, 356

421

Cold War, 353–354
combat-capable, 346
combat casualties, 354
combat training, 343
command by CEC officers, 339
command chains, 37
construction projects, 342
contribution to war effort, 350
convoy training, 112
culvert-based river crossing design, 64–65
D-Day, 347
defensive units, 16
demobilization, 351–357
DESERT SHIELD, 360–361
DESERT STORM, 360–361
Dets or NMCBs, 17–18
discreetly moving, 4
down, set, hike plan, 239
employment flexibility, 18
enemy action, 196
Enemy Prisoner of War camps, 362
equipment, 25
expeditionary engineering and job site defense missions, 89
five roads theory, 349
flow of gear and equipment, 361
force strength, 357
founding, 4
general engineering support force to MAGTFs, 360
general engineers and contingency builders, 16
global realignment of forces, 42
hardened facilities, 306
headquarters, 55
heavier combat construction detachment, 17
highly skilled specialists, 16
high threat areas
holding turf while building bridges, 229–230
home base, 351
humanitarian and disaster relief, 4, 11, 357
Inchon, 352–353
infantry combat skills, 111–112
initial beddown projects, 49–53
insignia, 337, 339
Iraq, 303–308, 316–318

Iwo Jima, 346, 348
K-fields, 352
killed, v
Korean War, 352
Kuwait, 1, 33, 45–53, 90–91
leadership of food service operations, 104–105
lighter, faster and more agile, 28, 322
limited usefulness, 16
management and recruitment problems, 339
manning defenses, 208
marching song, 349
Marine maneuver warfare doctrine, 15
Marines and, 109
material procurement, 76
MEG command and staff, 19–20
Middle East, 357–363
Mobile Recovery Teams, 354
modular packing and loading concept, 57
moving to Kuwaiti border, 362
naval construction battalions (NCBs), 342
naval construction regiments, 342
Naval Mobile Construction Battalion (NMCB), 352
Nuclear-Biological-Chemical drills and false alarms, 96–97
Nuclear/Biological/Chemical (NBC) weapons, 115–116
Operation Iraqi Freedom, 4
ordering bridging sets, 76
origin of name, 337
peacetime service, 351
people and resources, 37
Pontoon Operating Battalions of World War II, 352
post-war projects, 351
primary joint mission, 35
public relations campaign, 349
rear echelon engineering forces, 109
Reception, Staging, Onward Movement, and Integration (RSO&I), 303
reconnaissance, 18, 19
redeploy, constitute, surge plan, 239
redeployment, 351–357
regiments, 17–18
reorganization, 351–357, ix
required proficiencies, 109–111

INDEX

responding on the fly, 46
SCW designation insignia, 111
security, 195
semi-permanent bridging problem, 64
skilled workers, 340–341
special aluminum matting (AM-2) parking areas, 49
specialized construction materials, 361
special place in hearts and minds, 7
successes, 4, 28
supporting I MEF forces, 32
supporting Marines' critical supply lines, ix
Syrian border, 307
Tables of Allowance, 16, 18, 290
Tactical Movement Teams (TMTs), 305
Task Force 68, 351–352
task units, 14–15
tempo of operations, 17–20
training facilities, 341–342
training regimen, 109–110
Vietnam War, 354–357
war footing, 20–21
"We Build! We Fight!" battle cry, 7
worldwide duties and missions, 357
Seabee Team 1104, 354
Seabee warfare qualified, 111
Sea Port of Departure (SPOD), 18, 101
Sea Power 21, 42
2nd Battalion of the 8th Marines, 200
2nd Construction Brigade, 342
2nd Force Service Support Group (FSSG) 8th Engineer Support Battalion, 63
2nd Light Armored Reconnaissance Battalion, 205
2nd Marine Aircraft Wing, 241
2nd Marine Expeditionary Brigade, 122
22nd Marine Expeditionary Unit (MEU), 17
2nd Marines, 159
2nd Naval Construction Brigade, 23, 28, 42
Secretary of the Navy, 330
Secret Internet Protocol Network (SIPRnet), 118
Seersucker counterstrike, 153–157
Seignious, Russ, 93
seized cash, 269–270
semi-permanent bridging, 62–65
Semmler, Alexander, 164, 211
September 11th terrorist attacks, 20–22
17th Marines, 13

7th Armoured Brigade, 140
7th Brigade, 345
7th Construction Brigade, 342
Shear, Greg, 33
Shelton, Mike, 42
Shere, Charles, 294
Sheroda, Anne Renee, 6
Shields, Marvin G., 354
Shi'ite Kurds, 358
Shi'ites, 284, 302–303
Shock and Awe, 150–152
Shock and Awe: Achieving Rapid Dominance (Ullman and Wade), 121
shopping and capitalism, 273
single Engineer battlespace manager concept, 20
SIPRnet for secure voice-only conference calls, 181–182
16th Air Assault Royal Irish Brigade, 282–283
16th Marines, 13
skilled tradesmen, recruiting, 340–341
Sloan, Billy, 154, 155, 186–187
Smith, Holland M. "Howlin' Mad," 14, 350
Smith, Joseph, 330
Smith, Norman M., 332–333, 335
soccer, 254
Society of American Military Engineers Regional Conference tournament, 21
soldiers, level of violence against, 298
Sorenson, Bill, 137
Soviet Union, 11
Spanish American War, 331
Spanish Marines, 17
special band of pirates, 134–135
Special Forces, 54, 316
Special Operations Forces (SOFs), 151
An Nasiriyah Bridges, 188
infiltrating Iraq, 122
Special Republican Guard, 126
Stalder, Keith, 190, 245
steel military bridges, ix
Stinso, Jerry, 255
Stockdale, James, 8
Stoddert, Benjamin, 329
Storch, Andrew, x
Streiter, Lieutenant (Junior Grade), 207
Structural Journal, 7
Sullivan, Allen, 203
Sunni Triangle, 302

Sutton, Sydney L., 356
Swannack, Charles, 300
Swanson, Joseph C., xi

T

Table of Allowance, 16, 18, 57, 108–109
Tactical Assembly Area (TAA), 101
Tactical Assembly Area (TAA) Coyote, 101, 136–137
Tactical Assembly Area (TAA) Fox, 105, 136
Tactical Assembly Area (TAA) Stethem, 159
Tactical Construction Team, 306
Tactical Movement Teams (TMTs), 298, 305, 308, 310
tactical pause, 199
Tajikistan, 23, 26–27
Taliban, 43
Tanner, Robert, 25
Task Force 68, 351–352
Task Force 99.3.5, 345
Task Force Charlie, 49, 78, 132–134, 255, 307
    Al Amarah, 282–283
    Blair Airfield, 249
    Camp 93, 56
    Change of Command, 252
    communications difficulties, 204
    construction on Natonski's command post, 206
    Davisville Bridge Park, 218
    deliberate runway repairs (DRR) at Blair Airfield, 241
    Enemy Prisoner of War (EPW) holding area, 132, 161
    enemy prisoner of war/humanitarian assistance (EPW/HA) facility, 128
    equipment decontamination, 116–117
    floating pontoon bridge, 249
    force protection operations, 261
    getting into fight, 205–207
    Iraqi counterattacks, 196–197
    "Jiffy Clean" Nuclear-Biological-Chemical Decontamination Team, 96
    Jiffy Teams, 117
    Line of Departure, 160
    Mabey & Johnson bridges, 132
    Main Supply Routes, 261
    maintenance and dust control efforts, 206
    maintenance and road improvements, 181
    Marines and, 200, 206
    MEG Command Element, 291
    NMCB 4 assigned to, 291
    open runways, 241
    resources, 107
    road improvements, 128
    road maintenance, 134
    Sarabadi Bridge, 251
    Seabee units, 288
    second-echelon construction projects, 79
    Task Force Mike and, 132, 134
    Weapons of Mass Destruction site, 261
task force convoys, 113
Task Force Echo, 132–134, 206, 208
    Al Jaber or Ali Al Salem, 132
    Alternate Supply Route Dallas, 207
    An Nasiriyah, 261
    Camp Castle, 106
    Camp Fox, 96
    disestablishing, 288
    Engineering Work Line (EWL), 136
    478th Engineer Battalion, 220–221
    getting into fight, 205–207
    helping Iraqi people rebuild, 208
    Highway 1 and alternate Supply Route Dallas, 220
    Jiffy decontamination teams, 133
    Korean Engineer Battalion, 138
    limited availability of equipment, 130
    long-term contingency construction, 79
    Marine Aircraft Wing, 128–129
    multi-service component representation, 129
    newly arriving MEG units, 129
    1092nd Engineer Battalion (Corps Wheeled), 220
    potential bridging operations, 132
    public utilities in An Nasiriyah, 220
    rear area security, 210
    resources, 107
    Rumaylah oilfield security, 280–281
    2nd Force Service Support Group (MEF Logistics Command), 129
    securing bridge, 206
    south of Euphrates River, 220
    Task Forces Mike and Charlie, 128, 132
    3rd Marine Aircraft Wing and MEF Logistics Command, 128
    training and preparing for additional missions, 220

INDEX

Umm Qasr, 132, 207–210, 261
USAF Civil Engineer Squadron, 128
Task Force Endurance
   82nd Airborne Division, 303
   ROK engineers, 284
Task Force Mike, 78, 99, 131, 133–134, 190, 248, x
   active missions for, 195
   An Nasiriyah, 131, 194
   An Numaniyah, 217
   Baghdad, 174
   border obstacles, 144–145
   bridge-crossing sites, 131
   bridging operations, 133
   building throughout night, 196–197
   bulldozers, 144
   command and control, 225
   communications difficulties, 204
   Diyala River, 245
   engineering support, 231
   Engineering Work Line (EWL), 136
   1st Marine Division, 261
   Highway 1, 275
   Iraqi counterattacks, 196–197
   line haul operations, 218
   Line of Departure, 170
   linking Highways 1 and 7, 133
   logistics support, 79
   Logistics Support Area Daly, 220
   Mabey & Johnson bridges, 173–174, 194, 227
   Main Supply Route Maintenance, 131, 218
   Marine invasion force, 79
   MEG Bridge Park Davisville, 131
   MEG's Main Effort unit, 128
   Night of 1,000 Iraqis, 197
   Non-Standard Bridges, 128, 131
   pre-attack positions, 105
   quality of life projects, 218
   reconnaissance of connector route, 192
   resources, 107
   route maintenance, 128
   runway repairs, 218
   special dive teams, 130
   support priority, 131
   tactical communications, 224–225
   Task Force Tarawa, 160
   temporary bridge replaced, 217
   training phase, 79

twin Diyala bridges, 261
Underwater Construction Team (UCT) 2, 210–212
vulnerability, 185
War on Dust, 274–276
West Euphrates Bridge, 194
Task Force Romeo, 38–39
task forces
   deployed in northern Kuwait, 144
   formal relief-in-place (RIP) between, 136
   funding for reconstruction, 268
   Jiffy Teams, 117
   Tactical Assembly Area Coyote, 144
Task Force Sierra, 307
Task Force Tango, 139–140, 307–308
Task Force Tarawa, 122, 159, 205–206
   Al Amarah, 282–283
   An Nasiriyah, 150, 183, 200–201
   Area of Operations (AOs), 169
   border security operations, 262
   captured RPGs and ammunition, 185
   central governates, 244
   force protection operations, 261
   Israeli D-9 dozer, 185
   MOASS, 194
   moving north, 123
   repelled assault, 200
   SERT 133, 146
   torture chambers, 184
Task Force Tripoli
   American Prisoners of War, 230–231
   Relief in Place, 262
   Samarra, 230
   Tikrit, 230–232
Taylor, Oliver, 177
Teague, Michael, 300
10th Engineer Combat Battalion, 344
10th Naval Construction Brigade (NCB), 345
terrorist attacks, 300–301
terrorists, escaped from Fallujah, 307
Tet Offensive, 356
Tharp, Jerry A., v
3rd Combat Support Battalion, 211
3rd Infantry Division (U.S. Army), 140–141, 149, 159, 183, 188, 344
3rd Marine Aircraft Wing (MAW), 26, 122, 226
3rd Naval Construction Brigade (NCB), 1, 14, 22, 23, 28, 42, 355

Kedge Hammer training exercise, 35–37
operational engineering planning in Pacific and Asia, 32
sneaking Seabees into Kuwait, 33
3rd Naval Construction Brigade/Pacific Division Engineer Operations Center, 22–23
358th Civil Affair Brigade, 264
31st Seabee Readiness Group, 49
30th Naval Construction Regiment (NCR), 35–36, 38–49, 40, 61–62, 65, 78, 105, 318, x
30th Naval Construction Regiment (NCR) Command Element, 290
30th Naval Construction Regiment/31st Seabee Readiness Group, 49
Thomas, Mark, 136
Thompson, Gary, 32
Tigris River, 249, 277–280
Tikrit, 230–232, 244
Tillotson, Commodore, 209
Time Phased Force Deployment Document (TPFDD), 84, 101
Time Phased Force Deployment Document (TPFDD) by Request for Forces (RFF), 101–103, 118–119
Timmons, Kevin, 155, 156, 180
Toner, Francis L., IV, v
tower of Babel, 237–238
training, 304
Transano, Vincent A., 330
transitional government, 265–267
Tregaskis, Richard, 355
trucking shortage, 141–142
truck stop from hell, 197–199
Tsutahara, Melvin, 67
Turkish Parliament, 122
Turpin, Emory J., v
twenty-first century warfighting, 12
12th Regiment, 332–335
22nd Naval Construction Regiment (NCR), 10, 36, 78
20th Marines, 13
twin Diyala Bridges, 227–230, 261
278th Armored Cavalry Regiment of the Tennessee National Guard, 308
265th Army Engineer Group, 34–36, 39–40, 79, 102–103, 129–130, 291
"Two Way Flexure of Steel Deck Reinforced Slabs" thesis, 7

U

ULCHI Focus Lens exercise, 14, 16–17
Ullman, Harlan K., 121, 199
Ulmen, Eric, 71, 93, 137
Umm Qasr
  Civil Military Operations, 323
  humanitarian support operations, 261
  power plants, 270–271
  reconstruction and Civil Military Operations, 207
  relief ship, 209
  Task Force Echo, 207–210
  water system, 263
  water works, 270–271
Underwater Construction Team (UCT) 2, 210–212
Underwater Demolition Team (UCT) 2, 342
unexploded ordnance (UXO), 228
United Airlines Flight 93, 56
United Nations Monitoring, Verification and Inspection Commission (UNMOVIC), 53
United Nations (U.N.)
  authorizing military force against Iraq, 144
  inspectors report, 81
  mission ending in Iraq, 299
  Oil-for-Food Program, 3
  stabilizing Iraq, 299
  withdrawal of staff members, 299
United Nations (U.N.) Security Council Resolution 1441, 53
Unit Movement Control Center (UMCC), 138
U.S. Agency for International Development (USAID), 265
U.S. Agency for International Development (USAID)/Bechtel contract, 212
U.S. Air Force (USAF)
  Ahmed Al Jaber, 51
  Special Operations Force, 27
U.S. Army Corps of Engineers, 348
U.S. Army National Guard and Reserve engineers, 17
U.S. Army's 82nd Airborne Division, 262, 304
U.S. Army's 3rd Infantry Division, 159
U.S. Army's 4th Civil Affairs Group (CAG), 213

Index

U.S. Army's 4th Infantry Division, 122, 206
U.S. Army's 507th Maintenance Company, 211, 231
U.S. Army's V Corps, 121–122
U.S. Army (USA)
  Baghdad, 244
  combat engineers, 336
  Kuwait, 2
  Tikrit, 244
U.S. Army V Corps' 3rd Infantry Division, 146
U.S. bridges, 77
U.S. Central Command (CENTCOM), 1–2
U.S. currency hidden in banks, 269
U.S. European Command (EUCOM), 9
U.S. law, 152
U.S. Marine Corps Forces Central Command (MARCENT), 1, 44–45
U.S. Marine Corps (USMC), 185, 294–295
U.S. Maritime Corps (USMC), 185
U.S. Maritime (USMC), 185
U.S. Navy Antarctic Developments Project, 351
U.S. Navy's Civil Engineering Corps, 6
U.S. Navy's Military Sealift Command, 18, 59
U.S. State Department, 29–30
U.S. 1st Calvalry Division, 316
The U.S. Marine Corps in the Second Iraq War (Reynolds), 121
US Army HET (Heavy Equipment Transport) trucks, 145
Usher, Edward G., 38, 39–41, 245
U.S./Korea Combined Forces Command, 14
USNS *Bellatrix* (T-AK-288), 59
U.S.S. *Peleliu* (LHA-5), 24
USS *Abraham Lincoln*, 239
USS *Marvin Shields*, 354

V

Valezquez, Geraldo, 67
V Corps, 149–150
vehicles, 116–117
VFW, 293
Video Teleconference (VTC) phones, 181
Vietnam War, 6, 354–357
V-J Day, 345

W

Wade, James P., 121
"Wagon Master," 23
Wahhabism, 20–21
Waldhauser, Tom, 85
warfighting in twenty-first century, 12
Warfighting manual, 12–13
War on Dust, 274–276
war plan, 31–32
Washington, George, 329
Washington Naval Arms Limitation Treaty, 335
Washington Navy Yard, 329
Washington Times, 83
Wasit (Al Kut), 261
water works, 270–271
weapons inspections, 82
Weapons of Mass Destruction (WMDs), 3, 280–284, 361
Weigel, Jeffrey, 112, 163
Weisner, Gary, 356
Welles, Gideon, 330
Wheeler, Gerald, x
White, Timothy, 137
Williamson, Lieutenant Commander, 146
Wilmore, Charlie, 200, 279
Wolfe, Duane G., v
women and schools, 272
Wong, Harry, 233–238, 248, 292–293
Worcester, Jim, 79, 80, 103, 128–129, 208
Woodward, Bob, 317
Wurster, Donald C., 27
WWI British cemetery, 242

Y

Young, William, 293

Z

Zarqawi, Abu Musab, 83, 299, 317
Zeda, Lieutenant, 146
Zimmerman, Charles, 72
Zinni, Anthony C., 13–14, ix, xi
Zionist Monsters, 145, 348
Zovko, Jerko, 300
Zylla, Richard, 139

About the Authors

Rear Admiral Charles R. "Chuck" Kubic, CEC, USN (Retired) is the former Commander of the 1st Naval Construction Division (1st NCD) and the I Marine Expeditionary Force Engineer Group (I MEG). During Operation Iraqi Freedom, he led the U.S. Navy Seabees as they built and fought in Iraq alongside the U.S. Marines during the march to Baghdad in 2003. He is currently the President of ECC International, LLC a global expeditionary engineering, design-build construction, and munitions response company headquartered in Burlingame, CA. He resides in Virginia Beach, Virginia, with his wife Anne.

James P. Rife is a Senior Historian with History Associates Incorporated, a historical research and analysis firm based in Rockville, Maryland. He is the author of *The Sound of Freedom: U.S. Naval Weapons Technology at Dahlgren, Virginia, 1918-2005*, published in 2007, and *Caring & Curing: A History of the U.S. Indian Health Service*, published in 2009. He resides in Gettysburg, Pennsylvania, with his wife Samantha and son Joshua.